W9-CRJ-172

Human Trafficking

This book examines all forms of human trafficking globally, revealing the operations of the trafficking business and the nature of the traffickers themselves. Using a historical and comparative perspective, it demonstrates that there is more than one business model of human trafficking and that there are enormous variations in human trafficking in different regions of the world. Drawing on a wide body of academic research – actual prosecuted cases, diverse reports, and fieldwork and interviews conducted by the author over the last sixteen years in Asia, Latin America, Africa, Europe, and the former socialist countries – Louise Shelley concludes that human trafficking will grow in the twenty-first century as a result of economic and demographic inequalities in the world, the rise of conflicts, and possibly global climate change. Coordinated efforts of government, civil society, the business community, multilateral organizations, and the media are needed to stem its growth.

Louise Shelley is a Professor in the School of Public Policy and the founder and Director of the Terrorism, Transnational Crime and Corruption Center (TraCCC) at George Mason University. She is a leading U.S. expert on transnational crime and terrorism, with a particular focus on the former Soviet Union. Dr. Shelley is the author of *Policing Soviet Society* (1996), *Lawyers in Soviet Work Life* (1984), and *Crime and Modernization* (1981), as well as numerous articles and book chapters on all aspects of transnational crime, corruption, and the crime-terror nexus.

More praise for *Human Trafficking*

"Using her unique global network and unparalleled access to informants and data, Louise Shelley has written the single most important volume on human trafficking to date. It provides the most comprehensive and convincing explanation of the causes and consequences of human trafficking that I have read, examines the financial side of human trafficking, and explains how the phenomenon has developed in very different ways across the world's main regions. Her conclusion that human trafficking will continue to grow in the twenty-first century poses an enormous challenge for policymakers to rethink their current approaches."

– Khalid Koser, Geneva Centre for Security Policy

"Louise Shelley has drawn on her scholarly skills and practical experience to produce an invaluable contribution to our understanding of human trafficking, particularly the trafficking of women and children. Her book not only provides us with a sense of the root causes and motivations of those trafficked as well as the means and methods of the traffickers and their clients, but also offers sound analysis and policy recommendations for governments, international organizations, and private institutions to combat this growing global problem."

– Ambassador (Retired) Melvyn Levitsky,
Gerald R. Ford School, University of Michigan

Human Trafficking

A Global Perspective

LOUISE SHELLEY
George Mason University

CAMBRIDGE
UNIVERSITY PRESS

CAMBRIDGE UNIVERSITY PRESS
Cambridge, New York, Melbourne, Madrid, Cape Town, Singapore,
São Paulo, Delhi, Dubai, Tokyo, Mexico City

Cambridge University Press
32 Avenue of the Americas, New York, NY 10013-2473, USA

www.cambridge.org
Information on this title: www.cambridge.org/9780521130875

© Louise Shelley 2010

This publication is in copyright. Subject to statutory exception
and to the provisions of relevant collective licensing agreements,
no reproduction of any part may take place without the written
permission of Cambridge University Press.

First published 2010
Reprinted with Corrections 2010

Printed in the United States of America

A catalog record for this publication is available from the British Library.

Library of Congress Cataloging in Publication Data
Shelley, Louise I.
Human trafficking : a global perspective / Louise Shelley.
p. cm.
Includes index.
ISBN 978-0-521-11381-6 (hardback) – ISBN 978-0-521-13087-5 (pbk.)
1. Human trafficking. I. Title.
HQ281.S63 2010
306.3'62–dc22 2010021484

ISBN 978-0-521-11381-6 Hardback
ISBN 978-0-521-13087-5 Paperback

Cambridge University Press has no responsibility for the persistence or
accuracy of URLs for external or third-party Internet Web sites referred to in
this publication and does not guarantee that any content on such Web sites is,
or will remain, accurate or appropriate.

To Richard A. Isaacson for all his support

Contents

Acknowledgments

This book is the culmination of sixteen years of study and meeting with people who work on a regular basis to understand and confront the problem of human trafficking. Travels to almost every continent and collaboration with scholars, nongovernmental organizations (NGOs), and practitioners from many parts of the world have broadened my understanding of the subject matter. International conferences, particularly the rare ones that have addressed the financial side of human trafficking, have been particularly valuable. I am especially grateful to TraCCC (Terrorism, Transnational Crime and Corruption Center), which over the last decade has been such a center of stimulating thought, scholarship, meetings, and seminars on human trafficking around the world owing to the participation of wonderful scholars, staff, visitors, and graduate students.

I have benefited from colleagues around the world who have helped me understand the dynamics of crime in their region. The first person to open my eyes to the pervasiveness of the trafficking problem, particularly in Asia, was Dr. Sobha Spielmann of Mahidol University, Thailand, who invited me twice during the 1990s to work with her in Thailand. These visits in 1992 and 1995, sponsored by two grants from the United States Information Agency (USIA) through their Academic Specialist grants, helped me to understand the complexity of the problem in Thailand and in neighboring countries in Southeast Asia. I subsequently learned much more on the problem in other parts of Asia through my work with Ruchira Gupta, the prizewinning filmmaker and Indian activist, on a USAID project concerning Asia. My understanding of problems in North Asia grew through my work with Shiro Okubo of Ritsumeikan University, Kyoto, Japan, and attendance at conferences he sponsored in Kyoto.

The focus of my work on human trafficking for many years was that emanating from the former Soviet Union. Through the work at TraCCC I have had the opportunity to work with many colleagues and visiting scholars and to support research on this topic in Russia, Ukraine, and Georgia. My Russian colleagues, from whom I have learned the most on human trafficking and to whom I owe so much, include Liudmila Erokhina, Elena Tiuriukanova, and Anna Repetskaya, with whom I produced a book called *Torgovliia Liud'mi* (*The Trade in People*). Subsequent work with Tania Pinkevich and Natalia Lopashenko have helped me understand the complexities of getting policy implemented once legislation has been passed. The Department of Justice representative to Embassy Moscow, Terry Kinney, who prosecuted one of the first major transnational trafficking cases in the United States, also helped me understand the problems affecting international cooperation in fighting the problem.

Contributing to my understanding of the diversity of the problem in the former USSR were visiting scholars and practitioners that TraCCC hosted from Kyrgyzstan, Moldova, Russia, Ukraine, and Uzbekistan. The most notable of them was Ambassador Larisa Miculet, who was a visiting scholar twice from Moldova before she became ambassador to Israel. In addition, I was able to interview specialists in Tajikistan through a U.S. State Department Specialists' grant in 2006. Arzu Kilercioglu, who worked with us at TraCCC, introduced me to the problem in Turkey.

Colleagues from other parts of the world helped me understand the unique aspects of trafficking in their region. In the early 1990s, Cyrille Fijnaut made me aware of the seriousness of trafficking from Eastern Europe and the former USSR in the Netherlands and Belgium. Other Europeans on visits to Europe as well as civil society and practitioner visits to TraCCC in Washington, DC, helped me understand other aspects of the problem in that region.

I spent my sabbatical in the early 1990s with Ernesto Savona at what later became Transcrime, a European center for policy research on human trafficking. In the late 1990s, Paul Holmes of the London police force and Liz Kelly of London Metropolitan University introduced me to the British dimensions of the problem. In August 2006, I spent time at the University of Uppsala as a guest of Ana Jonsson and learned more of the Swedish efforts to combat trafficking.

The SOCA (Serious Organised Crime Agency) office at the British embassy in Washington arranged for fine and highly knowledgeable anonymous readers on the European chapter. I am very grateful to Andy Cooke-Welling of SOCA, who arranged this. Recently, my work with Cornelius Friesendorf, then of DCAF, the Geneva Centre for the Democratic Control of Armed Forces, gave me more insights into the diverse European experience as well as that of human trafficking in conflict regions.

In 2001–2002, I made two separate trips to South Africa, where I had the chance to meet practitioners and specialists on human trafficking from much of sub-Saharan Africa. At the 2nd World Conference on Criminal Investigation, Organized Crime and Human Rights in Durban in December 2001, I was hosted and helped by Anthony Minnaar. In 2002, I visited the Institute for Security Studies, both in Pretoria and Capetown, and was introduced to more aspects of organized crime by Charles Goredema and Peter Gastrow. More recently, Richard Danziger of the International Organization for Migration (IOM) has brought important research on Africa to my attention.

Many trips to Latin America have helped me understand trafficking in the region. These include my Fulbright fellowship in Oaxaca and Mexico City in 1992–1993. In the late 1990s, I was also in Bolivia and Honduras. In 2001, I met women activists from Argentina and elsewhere when I attended the conference "Foro De Mujeres contra Corrupción." Several years later I attended a meeting on organized crime at the Núcleo de Estudos da Violência at the University of São Paulo, Brazil, directed by Sergio Adorno that gave me more insights into the relationship of organized crime and human trafficking.

Understanding the complexity of human trafficking in my own country has been a challenge. Robert Trent, now retired from the Immigration and Naturalization Service, opened my eyes to the distinct forms of human trafficking and how Chinese organized crime operates in the United States. Meetings with law enforcement and NGOs from Southern Florida, Los Angeles, the mid-Atlantic region, and the Midwest have made me understand the geography of human trafficking and its distinct features.

I have learned so much from my colleagues and students with whom I worked at TraCCC when it was located at the American University. They include Sally Stoecker, John Picarelli, Karen Saunders, Saltanat Sulaimanova Liebert, and Ruth Pojman. These individuals are now well known as scholars and practitioners in the field.

A few trafficking conferences I have attended stand out, and their presentations are cited in this book. The most important academic meetings were "Criminal Trafficking and Slavery" held in February 2006 at the

University of Illinois in Champaign-Urbana and "The Commodification of Illicit Flows: Labour Migration, Trafficking and Business" sponsored by the Center for Diaspora and Transnational Studies of the University of Toronto, October 9–10, 2009. Other conferences whose insights contributed to this book include "Pathbreaking Strategies in the Global Fight against Sex Trafficking," sponsored by the U.S. government in Washington, DC, in February 2003 and the Organization for Security and Co-operation in Europe (OSCE)–sponsored conference the same month in Ioannina, Greece, that examined the impact of trafficking in human beings on the international economy and the national economies of the OSCE states. More recently, I attended the joint UN-OSCE meeting to intensify the fight against money laundering and human trafficking in the Mediterranean region in Larnaca, Cyprus, in September 2008.

Since coming to George Mason University in August 2007, I have received wonderful support from the School of Public Policy, which has enabled me to complete this book. Dean Kingsley Haynes and James Finkelstein have given me course release and summer support that were invaluable to my research and writing. I have also learned much from teaching my first course on human trafficking and smuggling and benefited much from the insights of my students from the United States and abroad, many of whom had worked with and observed the problem firsthand. They also gave me advice on what was working and not working in the book as I gave them drafts to read. Several of my students read sections of the book in which they have expertise. I would particularly like to thank Beatriz Cuartas, Banu Demiralp, Andy Guth, and Nelly Mobula for their assistance. I also thank John Tuohy, who worked as a research intern at TraCCC and read through earlier drafts and gave me expert advice.

I want to thank two anonymous reviewers of the book for their helpful suggestions. I also thank Eric Crahan, my editor at Cambridge University Press, and Jason Przybylski, Senior Editorial Assistant there. Thanks also to Jayashree Prabhu, who oversaw the copyediting process.

I want to thank Alison Rea and Miles Benson, who read parts of the book and have used their insights as journalists to help me understand how to make the material more accessible. I am enormously grateful to Sally Stoecker, who read through the book and used her great understanding of trafficking to fine-tune the arguments. Joyce Horn has been a fine professional editor, formatting my 1,001 footnotes and ensuring that all made sense. As she has worked with me for a decade, editing both colleagues' and my own work on trafficking, she has acquired her own expertise that was invaluable beyond the professional editing. Richard Isaacson has supported me through the whole process and has read multiple versions of the manuscript, always helping me to improve the quality of my thinking. He has kept me moving toward the completion of this work, always providing great encouragement and moral support.

Introduction

In June 2006, the BBC reported that auctions of Eastern European women had been held at Stansted, Gatwick, and other London airports. According to the Crown Prosecution Service, the women were sold for £8,000 each (then approximately U.S. $15,000). The auctions of young women destined for sexual slavery in Britain occurred in open, highly policed locales. One auction even took place in front of a cafe at Gatwick Airport.[1] Such appalling news reveals that slave markets are no longer history. Once immortalized in historical lithographs and paintings, slave auctions occurred right outside the city that is the global headquarters for human rights organizations such as Amnesty International and Anti-Slavery.

If the auctioneers had been selling illicit drugs in such a public place, there would have been immediate arrests. Yet there was no such intervention to protect the young women. Ostensibly, the British police are not corrupt and had not been paid off. Why would such auctions be tolerated in a society that was an early advocate of the abolition of slavery? How can this occur in a country that values its contribution to the rule of law?

Part of the answer is that Great Britain, like most other countries, did not view human trafficking as serious a threat as the international drug

[1] "Slaves Are Auctioned by Traffickers," June 4, 2006, news.bbc.co.uk/2/hi/uk_news/5046170.stm (accessed August 27, 2008); "Women for Sale in Gatwick Slave Auctions," *Evening Standard*, www.thisislondon.co.uk/news/article-23388098-details/women+for+sale+in+Gatwick+Slave+Auctions/article.do (accessed August 27, 2008).

trade. Yet these auctions in the United Kingdom as well as deaths of large numbers of smuggled Chinese migrants in two separate cases at the beginning of the century served as a wake-up call.[2] Combating organized immigration crime became a high priority of a new state agency that was created in the United Kingdom to combat serious organized crime.[3] So far, few other countries have yet to allocate the resources needed to fight human trafficking, even though it has become one of the fastest growing forms of transnational crime worldwide.

Auctions of sexual trafficking victims may be the most visibly egregious part of the problem, but they are the tip of an iceberg of a massive international problem of human trafficking that encompasses many diverse forms of exploitation. Humans are also trafficked for labor exploitation, for marriage, for begging, for service as child soldiers, and for their organs.[4] Every continent of the world is now involved, and even a country as small and isolated as Iceland, with a population of 250,000, has had human trafficking cases.[5]

Transnational criminals have been major beneficiaries of globalization. Human smuggling and trafficking have been among the fastest growing forms of transnational crime because current world conditions have created increased demand and supply. Migration flows are enormous, and this illicit trade is hidden within the massive movement of people.[6] The supply exists because globalization has caused increasing economic and demographic disparities between the developing and developed world,

[2] "Britain's Straw Says Truck Deaths a Warning," Reuters, June 19, 2000; Warren Hoge, "Trucker Found Guilty in Death of Immigrants," *New York Times*, April 5, 2001, A6. "Smugglers jailed over Chinese deaths," May 11, 2001, http://news.bbc.co.uk/2/hi / europe/1325826.stm (accessed July 23, 2009); Patrick E. Tyles, "19 Die as Tide Traps Chinese Shellfish Diggers in England," *New York Times*, February 7, 2004, http://www.nytimes.com/2004/02/07/world/19-die-as-tide-traps-chinese-shellfish-diggers-in-england.html?scp=1&sq=%20Chinese%20Shellfish%20Diggers&st=cse (accessed July 23, 2009).

[3] www.soca.gov.uk/orgCrime/immigration.html (accessed July 21, 2009).

[4] Daan Everts, "Human Trafficking: The Ruthless Trade in Human Misery," *Brown Journal of World Affairs* 10, no. 1 (Summer/Fall 2003), 149–58; Alexis A. Aronowitz, *Human Trafficking, Human Misery: The Global Trade in Human Beings* (Westport, CT: Praeger, 2009), 110–121. Marriage brokers can be facilitators of victimization as they obtain wives for men with known histories of violent spousal abuse. See Suzanne H. Jackson, "Marriages of Convenience: International Marriage Brokers, 'Mail-Order Brides', and Domestic Servitude," *University of Toledo Law Review* 38 (2007): 895–922.

[5] www.protectionproject.org/human_right_reports/report_documents/iceland.doc (accessed August 27, 2008).

[6] Moisés Naím, *Illicit: How Smugglers, Traffickers and Copycats Are Hijacking the Global Economy* (New York: Anchor Books, 2006), 88–91.

along with the feminization of poverty and the marginalization of many rural communities. Globalization has also resulted in the tremendous growth of tourism that has enabled pedophiles to travel and many to engage in sex tourism. Trafficking has expanded because the transportation infrastructure is there and transportation costs have declined. The end of the Cold War resulted in the rise of regional conflicts and the decline of borders, leading to an increased number of economic and political refugees. Furthermore, many rebel groups turned to illicit activity, including human trafficking, to fund their military actions and obtain soldiers. Demand has also increased as producers depend more on trafficked and exploited labor to stay competitive in a global economy in which consumers seek cheap goods and services, including easily available and accessible sexual services.

Supply and demand have created a flourishing business for traffickers. Traffickers choose to trade in humans, as Chapters 3 and 4 discuss more fully, because there are low start-up costs, minimal risks, high profits, and large demand. For organized crime groups, human beings have one added advantage over drugs: they can be sold repeatedly. In drug trafficking organizations, profits flow to the top of the organization. With the small-scale entrepreneurship that characterizes much of human trafficking, however, more profits go to individual criminals – making this trade more attractive for all involved.

Human smugglers and traffickers are not always motivated exclusively by profit. Some consciously engage in this activity to fund a terrorist group, a guerilla movement, or an insurgency. Others trade in people to provide suicide bombers.[7]

Everywhere in the world, the consequences of trafficking are devastating for its victims and the larger community. Those victimized in this open slave market were not only the young women destined for sexual slavery. All of society suffers from such victimization. Other casualties include the principles of a democratic society, the rule of law, and respect for human rights. The degradation of the women in full view of the public deals a direct blow to the rights of women and to gender equality.

[7] Sara A. Carter, "Taliban Buying Children for Suicide Bombers," July 2, 2009, www.washingtontimes.com/new/2009/jul/02/taliban-buying-children-to-serve-as-suicide-bomber/ (accessed July 21, 2009); information on the Hezbollah was obtained from an observer at the Hezbollah in Austria; U.S. State Department. Human Rights on Nepal, 2005, http://www.state.gov/g/drl/rls/hrrpt/2005/61709.htm (accessed June 22, 2007); "Stolen Kids Turn into Terrifying Mascots," http://www.cnn.com/2007/WORLD/ africa/2906193.stm (accessed April 30, 2007).

The full costs of human trafficking, however, will become evident only in coming decades as the harm compounds and the worldwide recession that began in 2007 reveals its full costs.

Defining the Scale of the Problem

The scale of human trafficking is now significant.[8] Crafting even inexact estimates of the number of people trafficked annually is difficult, at best, because of the covert nature of the problem. Compounding the difficulties in estimation, trafficking is often perpetrated by distinct ethnic groups that are hard for outsiders to penetrate.[9] According to the Government Accountability Office (GAO), many U.S. government estimates of the numbers of trafficked individuals are dubious.[10] Yet almost every expert on human trafficking and smuggling, whether practitioner or scholar, agrees that the problem is significant and increasing as both demand and supply for people are rising. The growth of human trafficking and smuggling has been most apparent in the past two decades.

Europe is facing increasing illicit migration from Africa, the Middle East, and Asia, with an estimated 400,000 people entering Europe illegally each year.[11] It is estimated that as many as 850,000 illegal immigrants have been entering the United States annually since 2000, although the number has declined since the onset of the recession in 2007.[12] Many of these illicit immigrants have paid human smugglers and cannot be considered victims of trafficking. But all too often those who pay smugglers become victims of trafficking along the way or on arrival.

[8] Aronowitz, *Human Trafficking, Human Misery.*

[9] See Andrea di Nicola, "Researching into Human Trafficking: Issues and Problems," in *Human Trafficking*, Maggy Lee, ed. (Cullompton and Portland, OR: Willan Publishing, 2007), 39–72; Frank Laczko and Marco Gramegna, "Developing Better Indicators of Human Trafficking," *Brown Journal of World Affairs* 10, no. 1 (Summer/Fall 2003), 179–94.

[10] "Human Trafficking: Better Data, Strategy, and Reporting Needed to Enhance U.S. Antitrafficking Efforts Abroad," GAO-06–825, July 18, 2006, http://www.gao.gov/docsearch/abstract.php?rptno=GAO-06–825 (accessed August 27, 2008).

[11] Ben Hall, "Immigration in the European Union: Problem or Solution?" http://www.oecdobserver.org/news/fullstory.php/aid/337/Immigration_in_the_European_Union:_problem_or_solution_.html (accessed August 27, 2008).

[12] Fact Sheet No, 3 "Illegal Immigration to the United States: Causes and Policy Solutions," http://udallcenter.arizona.edu/programs/immigration/publications/fact_sheet_no_3_illegal_immigration.pdf (accessed August 27, 2008); Julia Preston, "Mexican Data Show Migration to U.S. in Decline," *New York Times*, May 15, 2009, A1.

In 2004, the U.S. government provided an approximation of the size of the international trafficking problem, suggesting some 600,000 to 800,000 people were victims of trafficking worldwide, of which 80 percent were female, 50 percent were minors, and 70 percent were trafficked for sexual exploitation.[13] As previously mentioned, the GAO criticized these estimates. In 2006, the Trafficking in Persons Report (TIP) attempted to provide alternative statistics, citing data from the International Labour Organization (ILO) that includes trafficking both across borders and within individual countries. According to their data, 12.3 million people worldwide are in forced bonded labor, child labor, and sexual servitude.[14] Their report, "A Global Alliance Against Forced Labor," states "9.8 million are exploited by private agents and 2.5 million are forced to work by the state or by military groups."[15] The most numerous victims are in the Asian region, estimated by the ILO to number 9.5 million. ILO estimated that 2.5 million are victims of human trafficking, of which about two-thirds are women and children trafficked into commercial sexual exploitation. But at least one-third are also trafficked for other forms of economic exploitation. These victims are more often men and boys.[16] UNICEF has estimated that 300,000 children younger than age 18 are trafficked to serve in armed conflicts worldwide.[17]

Transnational crime was once synonymous with the drug trade. Yet trafficking in persons is now perpetrated on such a large scale that it is a prime activity of many transnational crime groups. Like the drug trade, the trade in people is driven, in part, by demand in the developed world. Some transnational crime groups such as the Chinese Triads, Thai, Indian, Pakistani, Nigerian, Mexican, Russian-speaking, Albanian, and Balkan specialize in trading humans.[18] Particularly active in trafficking women for the sex trade are Russian-speaking, Thai, Japanese *yakuza*,

[13] www.ojp.usdoj.gov/ovc/ncvrw/2005/pg51.html (accessed July 21, 2009).

[14] U.S. Department of State, *Trafficking in Persons Report* (Washington, DC: U.S. Department of State, 2006), 6.

[15] ILO, Report of the Director General, *A Global Alliance Against Forced Labor* 2005, 10–12, http://www.ilo.org/wcmsp5/groups/public/–dgreports/–com/documents/publication/kd00012.pdf (accessed August 27, 2008).

[16] ILO, "A Global Alliance Against Forced Labor," Global Report on the follow-up to the ILO Declaration on Fundamental Principles and Rights at Work (Geneva: ILO, 2005).

[17] U.S. Department of State, *Trafficking in Persons Report* (Washington, DC: U.S. Department of State, 2007), 26.

[18] Testimony of Roger Plant, "Human Trafficking in China: ILO Activities and Lessons for International Policy Coordination," hearing on Combating Human Trafficking in China: Domestic and International Efforts, US Congressional-Executive

and Indian groups.[19] Yet many other lesser-known groups also traffic women for sex, labor, and marriages such as Dominican, Filipino, and Turkish crime groups, as well as small-scale entrepreneurs around the world.[20]

None of this activity can function without the complicity of law enforcement and the corruption of officials in source, transit, and destination countries. In all regions, the crime groups are able to function effectively because they cultivate close links to law enforcement, embassy personnel, and other officials such as border guards who can assist their trade.[21] In fact, in societies as diverse as Thailand, Nigeria, and Russia,

Commission on China, Washington, DC, 6 March 2006, http://www.cecc.gov/pages/hearings/2006/20060306/RogerPlant.php (accessed August 27, 2008); Amy O'Neill, *International Trafficking in Women to the United States: A Contemporary Manifestation of Slavery* (Washington, DC: Center for the Study of Intelligence, 1999), 55–62; M. R. J. Soudijn, *Chinese Human Smuggling in Transit* (Den Haag: Boom Jurisdische Uitgevers, 2006); K. Farr, *Sex Trafficking: The Global Market in Women and Children* (New York: Worth Publishers, 2005); Obi N. I. Ebbe and Dilip K. Das, *Global Trafficking in Women and Children* (Boca Raton: CRC Press, 2008); A. A. Aronowitz, "Smuggling and Trafficking in Human Beings: The Phenomenon, the Markets that Drive It and the Organizations that Promote It," *European Journal on Criminal Policy and Research* 9 (2001), 163–65; D. Hughes and T. Denisova "The Transnational Political Criminal Nexus of Trafficking in Women from Ukraine," *Trends in Organized Crime* 6, nos. 3/4(2001), 43–67; D. M. Hughes, "The Natasha Trade – The Transnational Shadow Market of Trafficking in Women," *Journal of International Affairs* 25 (2000), 18–28.

19 Ebbe and Das, *Global Trafficking in Women and Children*; Pasuk Phongpaichit, Sangsit Phiriyarangsan, and Nualnoi Treerat, *Guns, Girls, Gambling, Ganja: Thailand's Illegal Economy and Public Policy* (Chiang Mai: Silkworm, 1998); James O. Finckenauer, "Russian Transnational Organized Crime and Human Trafficking," in *Global Human Smuggling: Comparative Perspectives*, David Kyle and Rey Koslowski, eds. (Baltimore and London: Johns Hopkins University Press, 2001), 166–86; Vidyamali Samarsinghe, *Female Sex Trafficking in Asia: The Resilience of Patriarchy in a Changing World* (New York: Routledge, 2008); S. M. Tumbahamphe and B. Bhattarai, "Trafficking of Women in South Asia," http://www.ecouncil.ac.cr/about/contrib/women/youth/ english/traffic1.htm (accessed November 10, 2003); Siddhart Kara, *Sex Trafficking: Inside the Business of Modern Slavery* (New York: Columbia University Press, 2009).

20 Dina Siegel and Yucel Yesilgoz, "Natashas and Turkish Men: New Trends in Women Trafficking and Prostitution," in *Global Organized Crime: Trends and Developments*, Dina Siegel, Henk van de Bunt, and Damian Zaitch (Dordrecht, Boston, London: Kluwer Academic Publishers, 2003), 73–83; IOM Migration Information Programme, "Trafficking in Women from the Dominican Republic for Sexual Exploitation," excerpted in *Trends in Organized Crime* 3, no. 4 (1998), 26–29 "Trafficking in Women from the Dominican Republic for Sexual Exploitation," http://www.oas.org/atip/country%20specific/TIP%20DR%20IOM%20REPORT.pdf (accessed September 15, 2008).

21 Leslie Holmes, "Corruption and Trafficking: Triple Victimisation?" in *Strategies Against Human Trafficking: The Role of the Security Sector*, Cornelius Friesendorf, ed. (Vienna: National Defence Academy and Austrian Ministry of Defence and Sport, 2009), 89–121.

law enforcement officials often facilitate human trafficking.[22] In other cases, a significant proportion of police income is derived as a result of their tolerance of trafficking.[23] The following telling quote from the noted antislavery advocate, Kevin Bales, also applies outside the Thai context: "To be sure, a brothel owner may have some ties to organized crime, but in Thailand organized crime includes the police and much of the government. Indeed, the work of the modern slaveholder is best seen not as aberrant criminality but as a perfect example of disinterested capitalism."[24]

The profits from such activities are significant and rising. Current estimates by the United Nations Office of Drugs and Crime place human trafficking as the second most profitable form of transnational crime after the sale of drugs and rank it more profitable than the sale of arms. One analysis suggests that the profits of current day slavery are much greater than in the old world.[25] The International Organization for Migration estimates that profits of $7 billion were made from trafficking in persons in 1997.[26] These profits have grown since then as the scale of human trafficking and smuggling has increased.[27] A recent study, based on previously cited ILO data, estimates the profits of commercial sex trafficking and forced labor are much higher. According to this study, the annual profits from commercial sexual exploitation were $33.9 billion, based on approximately 1.4 million trafficked people engaged in commercial sexual exploitation.[28] These calculations were based on trafficking victims serving a smaller number of clients than is usually the case in most parts of the world. Almost half of these profits came from

[22] Phongpaichit, Phiriyarangsan, and Treerat, *Guns, Girls, Gambling, Ganja*; Osita Agbu "Corruption and Human Trafficking: The Nigerian Case," *West African Review* 4, no. 1 (2003), 1–13; *Trafficking in Persons Report 2004* (Washington, DC: U.S. Department of State, 2004), 168.

[23] Phongpaichit, Piriyarangsan', and Treerat, *Guns, Girls, Gambling, Ganja*, pp.157, 179, 182, 18, 263.

[24] Kevin Bales, *Disposable People: New Slavery in the Global Economy* (Berkeley and Los Angeles: University of California Press, 1999).

[25] UN World Drug Report 2007, http://www.unodc.org/pdf/research/wdr07/WDR_2007.pdf (accessed September 14, 2008), 170; Kara, *Sex Trafficking*, 24.

[26] David Kyle and Rey Koslowski, "Introduction," in *Global Human Smuggling*, Kyle and Koslowski, eds., 4.

[27] Testimony of Roger Plant, "Human Trafficking in China."

[28] Peter Belser, "Forced Labor and Human Trafficking, Estimating the Profits," Cornell University, ILR School, http://digitalcommons.ilr.cornell.edu/cgi/viewcontent.cgi?article=1016&context=forcedlabor (accessed September 6, 2008), 5, 14.

industrialized nations. In second place were the countries of Asia with $11.2 billion, followed by transitional countries with $3.5 billion, Latin America with approximately $2 billion, Middle East and North Africa with approximately $1 billion, and half that from sub-Saharan Africa, where wages are low.[29] The estimates are $10.4 billion for those in all situations of forced labor exploitation, $3.8 of which derives from trafficked laborers.[30] The greatest profits are generated from those exploited in industrial societies where wage scales are higher.

Legislative Framework that Defines Human Smuggling and Trafficking

Illegal movement of persons generally encompasses two related activities: migrant smuggling and the trafficking of persons for the purpose of exploitation. In short, both activities involve the recruitment, movement, and delivery of migrants from a host to a destination state. What separates the two activities, however, is that the traffickers enslave and exploit trafficked persons, while smuggled migrants have a consensual relationship at the onset with their smugglers. Moreover, many smuggled individuals are free at the end of their journey or after a period of indentured servitude.

The growth in these two forms of illegal movement of people has been significant and consistent, driving the international community to define the problem and initiate collective action to curtail these pervasive phenomena. In 2000, the United Nations adopted protocols to address human smuggling and trafficking along with the United Nations Convention on Transnational Crime.[31] Their adoption in tandem reflects the international understanding that human smuggling and trafficking are part of the organized crime problem.[32] The Trafficking Protocol, which came into force on Christmas Day in 2003, had 117 signatories as of September 2008.[33] The Protocol Against Smuggling of Migrants by Land,

[29] Ibid., 14.

[30] Ibid., 11.

[31] Kara Abramson, "Beyond Consent, Toward Safeguarding Human Rights: Implementing the United Nations Trafficking Protocol," *Harvard International Law Journal* 44, no. 2 (Summer 2003), 473–502; Janice G. Raymond, "The New UN Trafficking Protocol," *Women's Studies International Forum* 25, no. 5 (2002), 491–502.

[32] Phil Williams and Ernesto Savona, eds., *The United Nations and Transnational Organized Crime* (London and Portland, OR: Cass, 1996).

[33] http://www.unodc.org/unodc/en/treaties/CTOC/countrylist-traffickingprotocol.html (accessed January 27, 2009).

Sea and Air was adopted shortly after in January 2004 once it had the requisite 40 signatories. By September 2008, it had 112 signatories.[34]

The protocols on human smuggling and trafficking supplement the United Nations Convention on Transnational Organized Crime, which sought to provide a unified definition for identifying transnational criminal organizations:

> "Organized criminal group" shall mean a structured group of three or more persons, existing for a period of time and acting in concert with the aim of committing one or more serious crimes or offences established in accordance with this Convention, in order to obtain, directly or indirectly, a financial or other material benefit. "Serious crime" shall mean conduct constituting an offence punishable by a maximum deprivation of liberty of at least four years or a more serious penalty. "Structured group" shall mean a group that is not randomly formed for the immediate commission of an offence and that does not need to have formally defined roles for its members, continuity of its membership or a developed structure.... [A]n offence is transnational in nature if: (a) It is committed in more than one state; (b) It is committed in one state but a substantial part of its preparation, planning, direction or control takes place in another state; (c) It is committed in one state but involves an organized criminal group that engages in criminal activities in more than one state; or (d) It is committed in one state but has substantial effects in another state.[35]

The United Nations' transnational crime definition provides the overarching framework for the protocols. It addresses the size, duration, and the multijurisdictional aspects of the acts of these crime groups. Furthermore, it provides the flexibility to examine transnational organized crime outside of such traditional ethnic groups as Russian-speaking organized crime groups, Chinese Triads, Japanese Yakuza, and Italian Mafia families.

The Convention and its protocols set the problem of trafficking and smuggling within a criminal context. Throughout the negotiations over the UN Protocol to Prevent, Suppress and PunishTrafficking in Persons, there were two competing feminist responses to the way to define the phenomenon. There was extensive debate "whether prostitution *per se* is slavery and therefore equivalent to trafficking in persons."[36] With the

[34] http://www.unodc.org/unodc/en/treaties/CTOC/countrylist-migrantsmugglingprotocol.html (accessed January 27, 2009).

[35] UN General Assembly, "Convention against Transnational Organized Crime," November 2, 2001 (New York: United Nations Publications), 25–26.

[36] Melissa Ditmore and Marjan Wijers, "The Negotiations on the UN Protocol on Trafficking in Persons," *Nemesis* 4 (2003), 80; for further discussion of this see Jo Dozema, "Who Gets to Choose? Coercion, Consent and the UN Trafficking Protocol," *Gender and Development* 10, no. 1 (March 2002), 20–42.

adopted definition, there is no consideration of voluntary sex work. The gender discussions of prostitution that have been featured in the collections of Kamala Kempadoo and others scholars who suggest that women who work as prostitutes have rights that should be recognized.[37] Instead the approach taken by the United Nations addresses the criminals who enslave women and children. It takes a law enforcement perspective.

The convention was adopted in November 2000 by the UN General Assembly. "It opened for signature by Member States at a High-level Political Conference convened for that purpose in Palermo, Italy, on 12–15 December 2000 and entered into force on 29 September 2003."[38] This Convention was a necessary prerequisite to the adoption of the Protocol to Prevent, Suppress and Punish Trafficking in Persons, Especially Women and Children and the Protocol Against Smuggling of Migrants by Land, Sea and Air. The definition of trafficking developed within UN Protocols has served as a basis for developing policies to prevent trafficking, protect victims, and prosecute offenders.[39]

The definition of trafficking developed by the United Nations is a consensual document that was agreed on by member states. It, therefore, represents the interests of governments rather than individuals. Its focus is on border security, illegal migrants, and organized crime. It does not address the needs of trafficking victims as do some national and regional legislation on human trafficking that were developed subsequently.[40]

The definition of trafficking in article 3a of the anti-trafficking protocol attached to the Convention of Transnational Organized Crime defines the problem in the following way:

> The recruitment, transportation, transfer, harbouring or receipt of persons, by means of the threat or use of force or other forms of coercion, of abduction, or

[37] For example, see Kamala Kempadoo, ed. (with Jyothi Sanghera and Bandana Pattanaik), *Trafficking and Prostitution Reconsidered: New Perspectives on Migration, Sex Work and Human Rights* (Boulder, CO: Paradigm, 2005); Kamala Kempadoo and Jo Dozema, *Global Sex Workers: Rights, Resistance and Redefinition* (New York and London: Routledge, 1998); Thanh-Dam Truong, Saskia Wieringa, and Amrita Chhachhi, *Engendering Human Security Feminist Perspectives* (London and New York: Zed Books, 2006); Anne Gallagher, "Human Rights and the New UN Protocols on Trafficking and Migrant Smuggling: A Preliminary Analysis," *Human Rights Quarterly* 23 (2001), 975–1004.

[38] http://www.unodc.org/unodc/en/treaties/CTOC/index.html (accessed July 21, 2009).

[39] http://www.uncjin.org/Documents/Conventions/dcatoc/final_documents_2/convention_%20traff_eng.pdf (accessed September 7, 2008).

[40] Council of Europe Convention on Action against Trafficking in Human Beings and the Trafficking Victims Protection Act in the United States both pay attention to victims.

fraud, of deception, of the abuse of power or of a position of vulnerability or the giving or receiving of payments or benefits to achieve the consent of a person having control over another person, for the purpose of exploitation. Exploitation shall include, at a minimum, the exploitation or the prostitution of others or other forms of sexual exploitation, forced labour or services, slavery or practices similar to slavery, servitude or the removal of organs.[41]

This broad definition of trafficking includes sex trafficking as well as trafficking into exploitative work situations such as domestic help, agricultural workers, and workers in dangerous industries as well as those trafficked as child soldiers. It also includes trafficking for adoptions, into begging, and the less well-known and analyzed problem of organ trafficking.

The Protocol Against the Smuggling of Migrants by Land, Sea and Air defines the problem in the following way:

"Smuggling of Migrants" shall mean the procurement, in order to obtain directly or indirectly, a financial or other material benefit, of the illegal entry of a person into a State Party of which the person is not a national or a permanent resident.[42]

Although the phenomena of human smuggling and trafficking are clearly delineated legally, in reality the situation is often not as clear.[43] Because trafficking often occurs within the context of large-scale migration, there are numerous possibilities for abuse. Individuals may start off as paying clients of human smugglers but some of the migrants, especially women and children, become trafficking victims.[44]

Apart from the United Nations Conventions, other supranational bodies have adopted anti-trafficking laws. In July 2002, the EU Council adopted the Framework Decision on Combating Trafficking in Human Beings. Shortly after, the Council of Europe Convention on Action against Trafficking in Human Beings was adopted in May 2005 and came into force in February 2008 after obtaining the requisite signatures from

41 http://www.unodc.org/unodc/en/treaties/CTOC/index.html (accessed July 21, 2009).

42 http://www.uncjin.org/Documents/Conventions/dcatoc/final_documents_2/convention_smug_eng.pdf (accessed July 21, 2009).

43 For a discussion of this see, e.g., Bridget Anderson and Julia O'Connell Davidson, "Is Trafficking in Human Beings Demand Driven?" A Multi-Country Pilot Study 9 (IOM December 2003), http://www.compas.ox.ac.uk/about/publications/Bridget/Anderson04.pdf? event=detail&id=2932 (accessed September 14, 2008).

44 Benjamin S. Buckland, "Smuggling and Trafficking: Crossover and Overlap," in Friesendorf, *Strategies Against Human Trafficking*, 146, 151.

member states.[45] It was "intended to supplement the limited or non-existent protection scheme of the UN Trafficking Protocol."[46]

The adoption of these legal documents by multinational bodies has been followed by the adoption of trafficking laws in many countries in accordance with the framework provided by the United Nations. Passage of laws does not ensure compliance with the provisions by individual states. Between 2003 and 2007, there were an average of 6,509 prosecutions annually with 3,361 convictions. With an estimated half-million to 4 million victims of trafficking annually, these judicial statistics reflect a massive impunity for traffickers.[47] Moreover, most trafficking cases involve only a small number of defendants who usually receive either short terms of imprisonment or small fines with no confiscation of profits. This is the only category of serious crime to be treated with such leniency by the courts worldwide. It reflects the absence of political will, inadequate protection for victims, and the limited allocation of resources by individual governments to enforce the trafficking laws. It also reflects long-held biases against women who are blamed for "getting themselves into these situations" or "deserving of their fate." Therefore, trafficking and smuggling continue on a massive scale, exploiting the limitations of enforcement in a globalized world where there is little harmonization of laws among countries, numerous porous borders that can be crossed, an economic motivation to migrate, and employers willing to exploit workers.

Global Reach of Smuggling and Trafficking

Trafficking, as opposed to slavery, was often confined to countries and regions. Trafficking within countries and continents still exists on a large scale in Asia and Africa.[48] Yet increasingly, victims often travel long distances to their point of exploitation where there is a demand for cheap labor and sexual service, recalling the long voyages of the global slave trade of earlier centuries.[49]

[45] http://www.coe.int/t/dg2/trafficking/campaign/Source/PDF_Conv_197_Trafficking_E.pdf (accessed July 21, 2009).

[46] Allison Jernow, "Human Trafficking, Prosecutors and Judges," in Friesendorf, *Strategies Against Human Trafficking*, 346.

[47] Richard Danziger, Jonathan Martens, and Mariela Guajardo, "Human Trafficking and Migration Management," in Friesendorf, *Strategies Against Human Trafficking*, 294; *Trafficking in Persons Report 2008* (Washington, DC: U.S. Department if State, 2008), 37.

[48] Aronowitz, *Human Trafficking, Human Misery*, 7–9.

[49] Karen E. Bravo, "Exploring the Analogy Between Modern Trafficking in Humans and the Trans-Atlantic Slave Trade," *Boston International Law Journal* 25, no. 2 (Fall 2002), 207–95.

Many countries are simultaneously source, host, and transit countries for victims of human trafficking. For example, Russia is a major source of sexual trafficking victims and a host country for both victims of sexual and labor trafficking. Furthermore, it is a transit country for many Asian smuggling victims whose destination is Western Europe. The richer states of the former Soviet Union receive women from Moldova and Ukraine, and many trafficked laborers from the Caucasus and Central Asia.[50]

The problem of sexual trafficking is pronounced in Asia but also more recently in the developed world and some countries in the Middle East where men have disposable incomes. Women forced to provide sexual services in Asia are most often native born or from other Asian countries, but, as Chapter 5 discusses, women more recently are also imported from other regions to work in the Asian sex industry. In Europe the preponderance of prostitutes are women trafficked from outside the older member states of the European Union. Women are imported from Eurasia, Asia, Latin America, and Africa. But many newly rich countries in the developing world are also magnets for traffickers. Traffickers in the Middle East, particularly the Gulf States, Israel, and Egypt, import women from the former USSR and Eastern Europe as well as Asia.[51] The problem of labor trafficking is often less recognized but no less acute in affluent countries. In the United States, millions migrate illegally, primarily from Mexico and Latin America; an unknown but not insignificant percentage become victims of labor trafficking as they are subject to coercion and deception on arrival. Hundreds of thousands more are smuggled into Europe from North Africa or through Turkey and Eastern Europe to the prosperous countries of Western Europe, which need laborers because of their low birth rates. The Middle East imports laborers from the Philippines, Bangladesh, Pakistan, Thailand, and other poor Asian countries. In the Dubai airport, the author observed a long row of middle-aged Thai women being escorted through the airport while their hands were tied to a rope. Some of the women laborers in Middle Eastern households

[50] See Saltanat Sulaimanova, "Trafficking in Women from the Former Soviet Union for the Purposes of Sexual Exploitation," in *Trafficking and the Global Sex Industry*, Karen Beeks and Delila Amir, eds. (Lanham, MD: Lexington Books, 2006), 61–75; Liz Kelly, "A Conducive Context: Trafficking of Persons in Central Asia," in *Human Trafficking*, Maggy Lee, ed. (Cullompton and Portland, OR: Willan Publishing, 2007), 73–91.

[51] U.S. Department of State, *Trafficking in Persons Report 2008* (Washington, DC: U.S. Department of State, 2008); report on Azerbaijan; protectionproject.org/human_rights_reports/report_documents/kazakhstan.doc (accessed September 16, 2008); Elena Tiuriukanova, *Prinuditel'nye trud v sovremennoi Rossii* (Moscow: ILO, 2004).

and the men engaged in hard physical labor become trafficking victims.[52] Children have been trafficked to become camel jockeys.[53]

Australia, a vast and lightly populated continent, has tried to limit entry of migrants into their country with a high standard of living. Therefore, traffickers and smugglers have exploited the demand for entry into Australia. The extent to which there has been coercion and therefore trafficking rather than just smuggling has not been clearly determined and the number of detected and prosecuted trafficking cases remains small. Most victims originate from Southeast Asia drawn by Australia's economic strength in the region.[54]

Significant victimization occurs in conflict regions. Internally displaced peoples and refugees are especially vulnerable to exploitation. Women and children often become commodities that finance the armed conflicts, sold like drugs and arms. Children are also trafficked to provide soldiers or scout for land mines. This problem is particularly pronounced in Africa but is not confined to that continent. Trafficked child soldiers have been used in the conflicts in Sudan, Sierra Leone, and Liberia.[55] They have also been observed in East Timor, Myanmar, and in Colombia.[56] Women are trafficked, as discussed in Chapter 1, to service peacekeepers in the Balkans, Africa, and in other conflict regions.[57]

Children are trafficked for adoptions from the developing world, primarily Latin America, the former USSR, and Asia, to parents in North

52 For analyses of trafficking in the Middle East see works and speeches of Mohammed Mattar of the Protection Project, Johns Hopkins University, for example, http://www.wilsoncenter.org/index.cfm?fuseaction=events.event_summary&event_id=17638 (accessed September 5, 2008) as well as discussions with Dr. Mattar by the author.

53 Steven Nettleton, "The Hard Road Home for Young Camel Jockeys from Bangladesh," http://www.unicef.org/infobycountry/bangladesh_35935.html (accessed August 18, 2008). Since 2005, UAE has forbidden camel jockeys younger than 16.

54 Judy Putt, "Human Trafficking to Australia: A Research Challenge," *Trends and Issues in Crime and Criminal Justice* 338, http://www.aic.gov.au/publications/tandi2/tandi338.html (accessed September 5, 2008); Australian Institute of Criminology, 2009, http://www.aic.gov.au/publications.current series/mr/1–20/06.aspx (accessed November 29, 2009).

55 "Child Soldier Use 2003," A briefing for the 4th UN Security Council Open Debate on Children and Armed Conflict, Coalition to Stop the Use of Child Soldiers, www.child-soldiers.org; Global Report on Child Soldiers 2008, http://www.childsoldiersglobalreport.org/overview-and-benchmarks (accessed September 13, 2008); Interact – Children in Armed Conflict Review and Evaluation Workshop, June 22, 2004, Pretoria, South Africa, Institute for Security Studies, http://www.iss.co.za/pubs/CReports/2004/interactjun.pdf (accessed September 13, 2008).

56 Ibid. and http://www.child-soldiers.org/childsoldiers/questions-and-answers (accessed September 13, 2008).

57 "Trafficking, Slavery and Peacekeeping: The Need for a Comprehensive Training Program," Conference Report, Turin, Italy, May 9–10, 2002. Organized by TraCCC and

America and Western Europe who pay high fees to secure desired babies.[58] In Southeast Asia and within the Roma community in France, Greece, and Bulgaria pregnant women have been trafficked to secure their babies after birth.[59]

Tour organizers in wealthy countries organize travel to many regions of the world to enable men to exploit trafficked women and children locally. Often arrangements are made over the Internet to enhance anonymity for the customer.[60] The customers travel from Western Europe, the United States, and Japan to Asia, Africa, and Latin America as well as to the former Soviet states in order to obtain the sexual services of minors that they cannot legally obtain at home. Currently 32 countries have extraterritorial laws that allow the prosecution of their nationals for participating in sex tourism abroad, regardless of whether sex tourism or sex with a minor is punishable in the country where it occurred.[61] As countries such as the United States and France criminalize sex tourism, men have been returned home from Costa Rica, Russia, and Cambodia to face prosecution.[62]

Organ trafficking assumes various forms. Organs extracted from prisoners in China after their execution have been shipped to the United States for use in medical procedures.[63] Often the true nature of the commodity is

United National Interregional Crime and Justice Research Institute (UNICRI), http://www.unicri.it/TraCCC%20docs/TIP&PKO_EWG_Report_Final.pdf (accessed July 20, 2007).

58 Ethan B. Kapstein, "The Baby Trade," *Foreign Affairs* 82 (Nov/Dec 2003), 115–25; David M. Smolin, "Child Laundering: How the Intercountry Adoption System Legitimizes and Incentivizes the Practices of Buying, Trafficking, Kidnapping, and Stealing Children" *Wayne Law Review* 52 (2006), 113–200.

59 "Pregnant Women Being Trafficked for Their Babies," May 22, 2009, www.radioaustralia.net.au/asiapac/stories/200905/s2578788.htm; L'esclavage, en France, aujourd'hui, no. 3459, 2001, Tome II, Auditions, Vol. 1; Niki Kitsantonis and Matthew Brunwasser, "Baby Trafficking Is thriving in Greece," December 18, 2006, http://www.childtrafficking.org/cgi-bin/ct/main.sql?file=view_document.sql&TITLE=-1-&AUTHOR=-1&THESAURO=-1&ORGANIZATION=-1&TOPIC=-1&GEOG=-1-&YEAR=-1&LISTA=No&COUNTRY=-1&FULL_DETAIL=Yes&ID=2816 (accessed July 23, 2009); Ane-Marie Green, "Bulgaria: Baby Trafficking," July 2006, http://www.rte.ie/news/features/bulgaria/essay.html (accessed July 23, 2009).

60 http://www.usdoj.gov/criminal/ceos/sextour.html (accessed September 16, 2008).

61 http://crime.about.com/od/sbex/a/cst1.htm (accessed September 16, 2008).

62 Protection Project, *International Child Sex Tourism: Scope of the Problem and Comparative Case Studies* (Washington, DC: Protection Project, Johns Hopkins University, 2007), 50–60; P. W. "Sept Ans de Prison Pour Tourisme Sexuel," *France* 12 (March 2009), 10.

63 Michael E. Parmly, Principal Deputy Assistant Secretary of State, Bureau of Democracy, Human Rights, and Labor, "Sale of Human Organs in China," hearing before the

disguised. In many societies, individuals are prohibited from selling their body parts for profit. These procedures, therefore, often fall under the control of the criminal world, which extracts significant sums for their services. In this illicit trade, a criminal who is part of a larger network may pair a poor individual from a developing country with an affluent buyer of his organ. They meet in a country with a loosely regulated hospital system where there is little control over hospital procedures.[64]

A Gender Perspective

Human trafficking is the only area of transnational crime in which women are significantly represented – as victims, perpetrators, and as activists seeking to combat this crime. As the previously cited ILO data indicate, women are disproportionately the victims of human trafficking, particularly trafficking for sexual exploitation, domestic servitude, and marriage. Unfortunately, women are all too often perpetrators and facilitators of human trafficking, as Chapter 3 discusses. Yet at the same time, women are increasingly mobilizing on the regional, national, and international levels to combat human trafficking. Their activism occurs through nongovernmental organizations that develop prevention programs and provide support to victims. Women in many regions of the world also use the political process to push for international assistance programs for counter-trafficking, the development of anti-trafficking legislation at the national and multinational levels and an effective response by the state to the perpetrators and the victims of trafficking.[65]

Women and girls are victimized in all regions of the world. Yet the greatest likelihood of trafficking occurs where women and girls are denied property rights, access to education, economic rights, and participation in the political process. Women and female children are particularly vulnerable to trafficking because of their low social status and the lack of investment in girls. The view in some societies that females can be used to advance a family's economic position results in girls in many societies

Subcommittee on International Operations and Human Rights, House International Relations, June 7, 2001, http://www.state.gov/g/drl/rls/rm/2001/3792.htm (accessed September 16, 2008).

64 Nancy Scheper-Hughes and Loïc Wacquant, eds., *Commodifying Bodies* (London: Sage, 2002); Aronowitz, *Human Trafficking, Human Misery*.

65 Hilary Rodham Clinton, "Partnering Against Trafficking," *Washington Post*, June 17, 2009, http://www.washingtonpost.com/wpdyn/content/article/2009/06/16/AR2009061602628.html (accessed July 23, 2009).

being sold off to repay a family's debt, provide cash for a medical emergency, or compensate for an absence of revenue when crops have failed. Often women are expected to go abroad to send remittances home to their families. Without the support of their families, some become victims of labor and sexual trafficking. Discrimination against women is a major causal factor of trafficking not only in Asia, where ILO data suggest the problem is most pronounced, but also in Latin America, Africa, and the Middle East.

Research suggests that women and children have been among the largest losers of globalization.[66] The global financial crisis that began in 2008 has also hit females particularly hard. The crisis has resulted in many girls being pulled out of school, given less to eat, and forced to work at young ages to support their families.[67] Without the skills to survive in the world, these girls will be especially vulnerable to traffickers in the future because they have no skills to protect themselves from the ploys of the traffickers.

Women, as much as they are victims, are also facilitators of this human trade. Women exploit other women and young girls in domestic servitude. Women in couples often facilitate the trafficking activities of their husbands and lovers. Yet women can often act independently. In many regions of the world, women who have aged as prostitutes recruit the next generation of trafficking victims, often through networks of friends and family. Yet their involvement does not always end with recruitment. Women often train the trafficking victims, run the brothels, and maintain control of their victims through violent means. The largest smugglers and traffickers can sometimes profit significantly from this trade, as has been seen in China, where women have headed large smuggling operations. Their success in this area has been explained by women's superior network skills and the limited violence in Chinese smuggling.[68] Their significant roles in human trafficking differ from women's role in the drug trade, where women rarely have positions of authority.[69]

[66] Women and the Economy, Globalization and Migration, www.unpac.ca/economy/g_migration.html (accessed July 21, 2009).

[67] Discussion with Save the Children official on field reports from the countries in which they work, April 2009, Washington, DC.

[68] Sheldon X. Zhang, Ko-lin Chin, and Jody Miller, "Women's Participation in Chinese Transnational Human Smuggling: A Gendered Market Perspective," *Criminology* 45, no. 3 (August 2007), 699.

[69] There are exceptions. For example, women can be high-level money launderers for Mexican drug trafficking families such as the Tijuana cartel.

Just as women were key figures in the antislavery movement of the past, the exploitation of fellow human beings, particularly of females of all ages galvanizes women to action. Many women have understood the global reach and threat of organized crime through their attempts to combat human trafficking.

Gaining Awareness of the Problem – Developing a Global Vision

This book draws on almost two decades of research and observation around the world. I first became aware of the problem of trafficking in the waning days of the Soviet Union. Every hotel I stayed at and every restaurant I ate in throughout Russia and Ukraine was filled with prostitutes. But this was not the familiar sight of poorly educated prostitutes soliciting men on the streets. Often the women were multilingual and educated. Never alone, they were always accompanied by highly visible thugs, the most typical gangster element of organized crime.

The rise of trafficking in the Soviet Union, which had banned and suppressed prostitution for most of the Soviet period, was very surprising. This prostitution, tightly controlled by organized crime, did not prove to be a transitory phenomenon that accompanied the collapse of the Soviet Union. Within a few years, the images I saw in Russia and Ukraine were replicated throughout the world. An international trade in "Natashas," as the Slavic women were called,[70] arose as post-Soviet criminals became major beneficiaries of globalization.

Not only were these women highly visible in Western Europe and the United States, but trips to such diverse places as Japan, Argentina, and South Africa revealed the presence of trafficked Slavic women in newspaper ads. Photos of Slavic women were posted at the entrances of nightclubs in the Roppongi entertainment district of Tokyo.

In the early 1990s, I traveled to Thailand to help develop a graduate curriculum in criminology and criminal justice. Invited by a scholar at Mahidol University, the leading medical school in Thailand operating under royal patronage, this curriculum was being introduced by my host, Sobha Spielmann, a high-ranking Thai woman. She insisted that the program include human trafficking even though some courses would be taught to senior police officials, a group profiting significantly from the pervasive trafficking. In the early 1990s, little had been written on the topic even though hundreds of thousands of young girls were forced into

[70] Hughes, "The Natasha Trade."

prostitution in Bangkok and beach resorts. The introduction of the topic into the academic program, according to the university rector, was an act of courage because Thailand's economy was highly dependent on the sex industry and its related tourism. But as the leading medical school, they had the responsibility to address the spread of AIDS. Trafficking in women was leading to the spread of the disease and as many of 20 percent of the military recruits from the northern region of the country, the source of most of the trafficked women, were testing positive for the disease. The related deaths were apparent as I traveled through the communities of the Northern Hills Tribes, as funeral corteges for young girls filled the roads in these important source regions for the traffickers. Clearly, trafficking was becoming both a health and a security threat for the country.

The difficulty of combating trafficking is not only its profitability. The sex industry is organized by powerful crime groups with ties to the police and the politicians.[71] The criminals are not only local. The Yakuza established links with their Thai counterparts to provide women for Japanese sex tours to Thailand.[72]

In 1993, I spent my sabbatical year teaching in Mexico and Italy. There I was introduced to other aspects of the human trafficking problem. In Northern Italy, I was in language classes with refugees from Kosovo displaced by the war. Those in class with me had a place to live and asylum status; others were less fortunate and became victims of the large sex trafficking industry in Italy.[73]

In Oaxaca, where I taught in 1993 on a Fulbright at the Institute of Sociology, I learned much of the hardship of labor migrants to the United States. Oaxaca, one of the poorest states in Mexico with a large indigenous population, is a major source of illegal migrants.[74] At that time, the term "human trafficking" was not yet widely used. But the conditions described to me of difficulties of traversing the border, the payments to

[71] Phongpaichit, Piriyarangsan, and Treerat, *Guns, Girls, Gambling, Ganga*.

[72] David Kaplan and Alec Dubro, *Yakuza: Japan's Criminal Underworld* (Berkeley: University of California Press, 2003); Shared Hope International, *Demand: A Comparative Examination of Sex Tourism and Trafficking in Jamaica, Japan, the Netherlands, and the United States* (Washington, DC: Shared Hope International, 2007), 131.

[73] IOM, "Victims of Trafficking in the Balkans," http://www.iom.hu/PDFs/VoT%20in%20the%20Balkans.pdf (accessed September 16, 2008); H. Richard Friman and Simon Reich, eds., *Human Trafficking, Human Security and the Balkans* (Pittsburgh: University of Pittsburgh Press, 2007).

[74] David Bacon, *Illegal People How Globalization Creates Immigration and Criminalizes Immigrants* (Boston: Beacon Press, 2008), 23–33.

cross-border facilitators, and of labor exploitation of relatives and community members in the United States raised my consciousness of the scale and the severity of the exploitation of Mexicans within the United States.

Therefore, by the early 1990s, I had gained personal insight into the diversity of human trafficking in the former USSR, Western Europe, Asia, and Latin America. At that time, all seemed to be distinct examples of human exploitation rather than a symptom of a larger global phenomenon of human trafficking, a rising form of transnational crime.

In 1993, my Russian colleagues urged me to start a Russian-American project to help them study organized crime in their country. Many of the Russian criminologists were females with no experience in studying organized crime. But seemingly like so many women in the world, their concern for studying transnational crime resulted from their awareness of the increasingly visible trafficking of women.[75] By 1995, TraCCC, the Terrorism, Transnational Crime and Corruption Research Center that I founded and directed, had established organized crime study centers with Russian colleagues in St. Petersburg, Moscow, Ekaterinburg, and Irkutsk. The networks of the criminals stretched from the borders of Western Europe to the borders of Lake Baikal in distant Siberia and subsequently to the Far East, a region adjoining China, and close to Japan and Korea. All of the centers' locales were major sources of trafficked women.

Researching the trafficking and organized crime phenomena was not easy. There were no specific laws and hence no cases. Many law enforcement officials refused to recognize that the problem of trafficking existed, insisting instead that the women willingly became prostitutes, a stance that was maintained as a result of constant pay-offs to the police by the criminals. My Russian colleagues took several years of intense work to develop analytical methods that would allow them to study trafficking.[76]

[75] A. L. Repetskaya, *Transnatsional'naia organizovannaia prestupnost'* (Irkutsk: Irkutsk Academy of Economics and Law, 2001). Dr. Repetskaya was one of the original researchers of the TraCCC center in Russia.

[76] A rich body of literature has since been developed but, unfortunately, not much of it has been translated. See, in Russian, www.crime.vlad.ru, Vladivostok Web site, and http://sartraccc.sgap.ru, Saratov Web site. In English see *Human Traffic and Transnational Crime: Eurasian and American Perspectives*, Sally Stoecker and Louise Shelley, eds. (Lanham, MD: Rowman and Littlefield, 2005) and Robert Orttung and Anthony Latta, *Russia's Battle with Crime, Corruption and Terrorism* (New York and London: Routledge, 2008).

TraCCC received delegations throughout the late 1990s from Southeast Asia, the Indian Subcontinent, and from Europe.[77] As we prepared training materials to combat human trafficking from the former Soviet Union, we learned much from visiting law enforcement officials from Great Britain, Belgium, Netherlands, France, Italy, and Germany trying to arrest the growth of human trafficking.[78] Their limited success showed the challenges of fighting trafficking even in countries with well-resourced law enforcement, limited corruption, and the political will to address these problems. The experiences of a senior Belgian police officer illustrated how corruption and criminalization of police in the source country undermined Western capacity to fight trafficking. The Belgian police chief hosted an Albanian law enforcement delegation to promote a joint investigation of Albanian traffickers. One of the Albanian police officers, on arriving in Belgium, immediately took off with a known Albanian criminal. After the Albanian delegation returned home, the senior Belgian police officer received death threats by telephone at his home; the voice was recognizable as the Albanian police officer who had gone off with the Albanian criminal in Belgium. The criminal-law enforcement nexus in Albania undermined Belgian capacity to combat trafficking at home.

In the late 1990s and before September 11th, I visited several different countries in Central and South America. The trafficking victims were not only Latin Americans; clearly the region was a destination and transit region for human smugglers and traffickers. On arrival in landlocked Bolivia, I spotted Chinese restaurants. Local officials explained that a minister was recently ousted for his protection of Chinese smugglers. In Argentina, I met representatives of an anti-trafficking NGO, the Raquel Liberman group, named in honor of a 1930s victim of the white slave trade who denounced her traffickers and the corrupt officials who were their accomplices.[79] Human trafficking was a resurgent problem in Argentina with women trafficked from within the country, other parts of South America, and even as far as from Russia and Ukraine. Central America was a conduit for human trafficking and smuggling to the United States from South America and China. Gangs were emerging as potent

[77] Vidyali Samarsinghe helped lead a panel discussion on South Asian human trafficking.

[78] This work was done with John Picarelli and Sally Stoecker, and my research has been informed by these discussions.

[79] Nora Glickman, *The Jewish White Slave Trade and the Untold Story of Raquel Liberman* (New York: Garland, 2000); Isabel Vincent, *Bodies and Souls: The Tragic Plight of Three Jewish Women Forced into Prostitution in the Americas* (New York: HarperCollins, 2005).

organized groups and many feared their involvement in diverse forms of cross-border crime including human smuggling.

Two trips to South Africa in 2001 and 2002 introduced me to the rising problems of illegal migration, human smuggling, and trafficking in sub-Saharan Africa. AIDS followed the truck routes of Southern Africa, where many prostitutes, some of them trafficked women, contributed to the spread of the disease along these highly traveled paths. South Africa, with its large economy, superb transportation, and communications links, was a magnet for transnational crime groups. Therefore, trafficking and other forms of organized crime were not only a local problem but also had transnational dimensions.[80]

More recently, I have worked in Turkey, a crossroads between the Middle East, the former Soviet Union, and Western Europe. Turkey has large numbers of trafficked women from the former Soviet Union, their presence in Turkey explained by alliances and business relationships of Turkish criminals with their counterparts from the former Soviet Union. But human trafficking and smuggling is a much broader problem as men are smuggled from India, Pakistan, and Afghanistan to Europe traversing Turkish territory. Kurds eager to leave Iraq are moved through Turkey by their Turkish Kurdish compatriots.[81] But what starts out as smuggling often ends as trafficking.

Work with the U.S. border patrol and with some local police departments has helped me understand the significant dimensions of human smuggling and trafficking in the United States. These issues were not high-priority law enforcement problems in the United States until the passage of the Trafficking Victims Protection Act (TVPA) in 2000. Even now, they receive less priority than the drug trade. In doing this research, I was increasingly struck by the disproportionate attention I and others have paid to trafficking from abroad without understanding the depths and the diversity of the problem domestically.

Sources for the Book

My travel and academic work had provided extensive personal exposure to the problem of trafficking at two of its epicenters, the former USSR and

[80] Unesco, *Human Trafficking in South Africa: Root Causes and Recommendations* Unesco, 2007, http://unesdoc.unesco.org/images/0015/001528/152823e.pdf (accessed September 16, 2008).

[81] A. Içduygu and S. Toktas "How Do Smuggling and Trafficking Operate via Irregular Border Crossings in the Middle East? Evidence from Fieldwork in Turkey," *International Migration* 40, no. 6 (2002), 25–54.

Thailand; however, I lacked the materials necessary to write a scholarly analysis at that time. As the 1990s continued, there began to be many more sources of solid information about human trafficking. Fine investigative journalism began documenting the problem in magazine articles and films.[82] Stories on trafficking continue to fill the news media. Many serious documentary films have been produced as well as fictionalized accounts of human trafficking that have been shown on television and in the movies, including the Canadian documentary *Sex Slaves*, *Born into Brothels*, *Trading Women*; the Swedish *Lilya 4-Ever*; and the Indian *Selling of Innocents*.

In the 1990s, several Western European countries, including France, Belgium, and the Netherlands, held parliamentary hearings on the problem of sex trafficking, and much attention was paid to this problem by the European Community.[83] The Russian Duma held parliamentary hearings in 1997.[84] The British government commissioned a national report on the status of the problem.[85] The United States, following the passage of TVPA, produces an annual report on the status of trafficking worldwide. The United States government devotes tremendous resources in its embassies throughout the world and in its TIP (Trafficking in Persons) office in Washington to produce this report. Although the rankings of individual countries' willingness and capacity to combat trafficking into different tiers have proven highly controversial, the reports have provided valuable information of national, regional, and global trafficking.[86]

Many international and multilateral organizations documented the trafficking phenomenon in various areas of the world.[87] The International

[82] For an example, see Gillian Caldwell, Steven Galster, and Nadia Steinzor, "Crime & Servitude: An Exposé of the Traffic in Women for Prostitution from the Newly Independent States," Global Survival Network, Washington, DC, 1997, 9.

[83] "L'esclavage, en France, aujourd'hui," Assemblée Nationale no. 3459, 2001; Conny Rijken, *Trafficking in Persons Prosecution from a European Perspective* (The Hague: T.M.C. Asser Press, 2003); on November 26, 1992 the Belgian parliament held hearings on human trafficking, http://en.wikipedia.org/wiki/Parliamentary_inquiries_by_the_Belgian_Federal_Parliament (accessed May 19, 2009).

[84] These hearings were sponsored with TraCCC, which was then called the Transnational Crime and Corruption Center. For a discussion of these see "Professionals Providing Solutions Employee Profile: Ruth Pojman," REACT, GAIN_Insight_07_to_08–2009.pdf (accessed August 31, 2009).

[85] Liz Kelly and Linda Regan, "Stopping Traffic: Exploring the Extent of, and Responses to, Trafficking in Women for Sexual Exploitation in the UK," London, Home Office, Police Research Series, Paper 125, 2000.

[86] http://www.advocacynet.org/resource/1020 (accessed July 23, 2009).

[87] Obi N. I. Ebbe, "Introduction: An Overview of Trafficking in Women and Children," in *Global Trafficking in Women and Children*, Obi N. I. Ebbe and Dilip K. Das (Boca Raton, FL: CRC Press, 2008), 6.

Organization for Migration, which for many years followed migration flows, has developed specialists in many regions to document the problems of human trafficking, producing numerous publications worldwide.[88] Different units of the United Nations have also begun to focus on this issue including UNICEF and the United Nations Office on Crime and Drugs (UNODC) in Vienna. UNICEF, with World Vision, focused on trafficking in the Mekong Delta Region of Southeast Asia.[89] The UNODC's major report, *Trafficking in Persons: Global Patterns*, helped lay out the global problem of trafficking.[90] The Organization for Security and Co-operation in Europe (OSCE), the International Labour Organization (ILO), the Asian Development Bank, and more recently the Organization of American States (OAS), have also analyzed the trafficking issue and attempted to mobilize resources to combat the problem.[91]

Many human rights organizations such as Amnesty International,[92] Human Rights Watch,[93] and Oxfam[94] focused in the past on abuses committed by the state. Disproportionate attention, therefore, was paid to the police, soldiers, and peacekeepers who violated rights rather than to the human rights violations committed by nonstate actors such as criminals, insurgents, and guerillas. Their focus has now shifted. Considerable

[88] See, for example, IOM, *Trafficking in Women and Children from the Kyrgyz Republic*, 2000, iom.ramdisk.net/.../Kyrgyzstan_Report%20on%20Trafficking_2000_En_1071070736.pdf (accessed July 31, 2009) as well as numerous reports on their Web site concerning human trafficking, http://www.iom.int/jahia/page748.html (accessed July 31, 2009).

[89] Economic and Social Commission for Asia and the Pacific, "Sexually Abused and Sexually Exploited Children and Youth in the Greater Mekong Subregion: A Qualitative Assessment of Their Health Needs and Available Services," St/ESCAP/2045, New York, United Nations, 2000; http://www.worldvision.com.au/learn/policyandreports/files/human-trafficking.pdf (accessed September 16, 2008).

[90] http://www.unodc.org/unodc/en/human-trafficking/publications.html(accessed September 6, 2008), 36.

[91] The OSCE, which unites the United States, Europe and the countries of the former Soviet Union, developed a specialized office to combat trafficking that is based in Vienna. Its Human Rights Office in Warsaw produced numerous reports. The ILO commissioned a study on forced labor in Russia. See Tiuriukanova, *Prinuditel'nye trud v sovremennoi Rossii;* Laura Langberg, "A Review of Recent OAS Research on Human Trafficking in the Latin American and Caribbean Region," *International Migration* 43, nos. 1–2, 129–39.

[92] Amnesty International Press Release, "Afghanistan: No Justice and Security for Women," October 6, 2003, http://web.amnesty.org/library/Index/ENGASA110252003?open&of=-ENG-AFG (accessed January 19, 2004).

[93] Human Rights Watch, "Hopes Betrayed: Trafficking of Women and Girls to Post-Conflict Bosnia and Hercegovina for Forced Prostitution," www.protectionproject.org/.../see_bosnia_humanrights.htm (accessed July 22, 2009).

[94] Susanne Louis B. Mikhail, "Child Marriage and Child Prostitution: Two Forms of Sexual Exploitation," in *Gender, Trafficking and Slavery*, Rachel Masika, ed. (Oxford: Oxfam, 2002), 48.

human and financial resources are spent on documenting labor and sexual trafficking, particularly in the developing world and in conflict regions. Specialized NGOs have also developed serious and focused activities and analyses of trafficking that are international and regional in scope. This human rights activism, like its nineteenth century predecessors, often has a strong religious component. International groups focus on slavery and trafficking such as Anti-Slavery and Free the Slaves.[95] Examples of this include La Strada, an NGO that combats trafficking in Eastern Europe, the Suzanne Mabarak Women's International Peace Movement,[96] which has developed a significant research report to engage the business community, Visayan Forum in the Philippines, and Apne Aap in India.[97]

In the last decade, growing academic scholarship from diverse perspectives has developed on the issue of trafficking. Fine research and case studies have focused on Europe, North America, Asia, and Australia but much less has been done by foreign or domestic specialists to study trafficking in Latin America or North or sub-Saharan Africa.[98] Absence of research or reports is most acute in the Gulf States and other countries in the Middle East where there are large numbers of poor laborers from Asia who, all too often, are subject to labor and sexual exploitation.

Human trafficking and smuggling research has been studied in the context of the illicit global economy, rising illegal migration, and as a regional and international policy issue. Feminist and gender perspectives have been applied to human trafficking analyses.[99] Most published books on trafficking are collections from specialists on particular regions or

[95] http://www.freetheslaves.net/Page.aspx?pid=183 (accessed July 23, 2009); www.antislavery.org (accessed July 23, 2009).

[96] www.lastradainternational.org/?main=home (accessed September 16, 2008); http://www.endhumantraffickingnow.com/public/content/documents/155/FinalPressReleaseAthenRoudtable.pdf (accessed September 16, 2008).

[97] http://en.wikipedia.org/wiki/Visayan_Forum (accessed September 16, 2008); www.apneaap.org (accessed January 27, 2009).

[98] There have been such exceptions as in Ebbe and Das, *Global Trafficking in Women and Children*; Bales, *Disposable People*; Kathleen Barry, *Female Sexual Slavery* (New York: New York University Press, 1979); Katherine Farr, *Sex Trafficking: The Global Market in Women and Children* (New York: Worth Publishers, 2005); Kyle and Koslowski, *Global Human Smuggling*; Aronowitz, *Human Trafficking, Human Misery*.

[99] There are many articles and books from these perspectives. A representative collection of books includes: Beeks and Amir, *Trafficking and the Global Sex Industry*; Elizabeth Bernstein and Laurie Schaffner, eds., *Regulating Sex: The Politics of Intimacy and Identity* (New York and London: Routledge, 2005); Anna M. Agathangelou, *The Global Political Economy of Sex: Desire, Violence, and Insecurity in Mediterranean Nation States* (Houndsmills: Palgrave Macmillan, 2004); Claudia Aradau, *Rethinking Trafficking in Women: Politics Out of Security* (Houndsmills: Palgrave Macmillan, 2008); Heli Askola,

aspects of the problem.[100] Public policy works have focused on strategies to combat human trafficking and smuggling through legal strategies and citizen mobilization.[101] Yet most of these studies have provided little comparative analysis. Few have paid much attention to the role of organized crime in human trafficking, the economics of human trafficking, and the money laundering of the traffickers and smugglers, which this book addresses.[102]

Legal Response to Trafficking in Women for Sexual Exploitation in the European Union (Oxford-Portland, OR: Hart Publishing, 2007); Elina Penttinen, *Globalization, Prostitution and Sex-Trafficking Corporeal Politics* (London and New York: Routledge, 2008); Melissa Farley, ed., *Prostitution, Trafficking and Traumatic Stress* (Binghamton, NY: Haworth Maltreatment and Trauma Press, 2003); Melissa Farley, *Prostitution & Trafficking in Nevada: Making the Connections* (San Francisco: Prostitution Research and Education, 2007); Helen J. Self, *Prostitution, Women and Misuse of the Law Fallen Daughters of Eve* (London, Portland, OR: Frank J. Cass, 2003); Christien L. Van den Anker and Jeroen Doomernik, eds., *Trafficking and Women's Rights* (Houndsmill: Palgrave Macmillan, 2006); Thanh-Dam Truong, Saskia Wieringa, and Amrita Chhachhi, *Engendering Human Security Feminist Perspectives* (London and New York: Zed Books, 2006); Vidyamali Samarsinghe, *Female Sex Trafficking in Asia: The Resilience of Patriarchy in a Changing World* (New York: Routledge, 2008); Marie Seagrave, Sanja Milvojevic, and Sharon Pickering, *Sex Trafficking* (Cullompton and Portland, OR: Willan Publishing, 2009).

100 See these books produced within the last decade: Peter Andreas, *Border Games: Policing the U.S.–Mexico Divide* (Ithaca and London: Cornell University Press, 2000) and other works; Julia O'Connell Davidson, *Children in the Global Sex Trade* (Cambridge: Polity, 2005); Friman and Reich, *Human Trafficking, Human Security and the Balkans*; Ernesto U. Savona and Sonia Stafanizzi, eds., *Measuring Human Trafficking Complexities and Pitfalls* (New York: Springer, 2007); Soudijn, *Chinese Human Smuggling in Transit*; Anna M. Troubnikoff, ed., *Trafficking in Women and Children Current Issues and Developments* (New York: Nova Science Publications 2003), 94.

101 Recent books on responses to human smuggling and trafficking include: Rijken, *Trafficking in Persons Prosecution from a European Perspective*; Kevin Bales, *Ending Slavery How We Free Today's Slaves* (Berkeley and Los Angeles: University of California Press, 2007); Anthony M. De Stefano, *The War on Human Trafficking: U.S. Policy Assessed* (New Brunswick: Rutgers University Press, 2007); Kimberly A. McCabe, *Trafficking of Persons National and International Responses* (New York: Peter Lang, 2008); E. Benjamin Skinner, *A Crime So Monstrous: Face-to-Face with Modern-Day Slavery* (New York: Free Press, 2008); Cornelius Friesendorf, *Strategies Against Human Trafficking: The Role of the Security Sector* (Vienna: National Defence Academy and Austrian Ministry of Defence and Sport, 2009); Kevin Bales and Ron Soodalter, *The Slave Next Door: Human Trafficking and Slavery in America Today* (Berkeley and Los Angeles: University of California Press, 2009).

102 Exceptions include Phongpaichit, Piriyarangsan, and Treerat, *Guns, Girls, Gambling, Ganga*; Ron Weitzer, *Sex for Sale: Prostitution, Pornography and the Sex Industry* (New York and London: Routledge, 2000); Phil Williams, ed., *Illegal Migration and Commercial Sex: The New Slave Trade* (London: Frank Cass, 1999); Sheldon Zhang, *Smuggling and Trafficking in Human Beings: All Roads Lead to America* (Westport, CT: Praeger, 2007); Nancy Scheper-Hughes and Loïc Wacquant, eds., *Commodifying*

I relied on all the previous categories of written sources including books, newspapers, testimonies, analyses of national governments, and reports of multinational organizations and NGOs. Materials in many languages have been used including Russian, French, Spanish, and Italian. By reading these sources in the original, I have been exposed to many different analytical perspectives on the problem.[103] To overcome the problem of relying on secondary sources,[104] my research has been enriched by numerous interviews with law enforcement personnel, journalists, peacekeepers, policy makers, and activists in the human trafficking area and occasionally with a victim of human trafficking or member of a human trafficking organization. I have met journalists and NGO and law enforcement personnel who have gone undercover to penetrate trafficking networks, and have even met with professional criminals and brothel owners. I have occasionally advised law enforcement on the nature of the criminal organizations behind the trafficking cases they are investigating. At international conferences, I have met numerous scholars, practitioners, and policy makers from around the world addressing these issues. Preparation and participation in law enforcement training have permitted me to understand the difficulties in combating trafficking. I have also worked on asylum claims for trafficking victims in the United States and Canada and requests for T-visas (special visas) for trafficking victims in the United States.[105] The documents available from these cases have given me insight into the victims and the details of their victimization.

Organization of the Book

This book focuses particularly on human beings trafficked for sexual exploitation, although attention is paid to all aspects of the smuggling

Bodies (London: Sage, 2002); Siddhart Kara, *Sex Trafficking: Inside the Business of Modern Slavery* (New York: Columbia University Press, 2009).

103 Giovanni Fiandaca, ed., *Donne e mafia il ruolo delle donne nelle organizzazioni criminali* (Palermo: Universitá degli Studi di Palermo, 2003); readings of Mexican, Argentine, and other press on these issues.

104 di Nicola, "Researching into Human Trafficking."

105 T-visas are the visas provided to trafficking victims who agree to cooperate with law enforcement in the preparation of a trafficking case. They were introduced under the TIP legislation. Even though up to 5,000 can be issued a year, the number that are actually awarded is much less. In 2007 the number was 2009. Attorney General's Annual Report to Congress and Assessment of the U.S. Government Activities to Combat Trafficking in Persons Fiscal Year 2007, May 2008, http://www.usdoj.gov/ag/annualreports/tr2007/agreporthumantrafficing2007.pdf, 20.

and trafficking problem. The work provides a global perspective, examining how human smuggling and trafficking differ in diverse regions of the world. The book emphasizes aspects of human smuggling and trafficking that are less frequently discussed in the literature – the social, political, and economic consequences of human smuggling and trafficking, the role of organized crime, the business of trafficking, and the strategies needed to address these illicit trafficking networks.

Part I of the book addresses the broader issues raised by trafficking. The first chapter discusses the complex and diverse forces that have contributed to the phenomenal rise in all forms of trafficking in recent decades. The central role that globalization has played in increasing economic competition, international mobility of people and goods, trade, and communications is central to this analysis. At the same time that economic and demographic forces have created pressures for emigration, barriers to entry into the most affluent societies have increased. Criminals have been able to link those who cannot immigrate legally with the demand in richer locales for cheap labor and readily available and affordable sexual services.

Most individuals who are trafficked are the poor, uneducated, and the most vulnerable members of society. But those who are trafficked are not only disposable people.[106] Educated individuals may contract with smugglers to move them to countries where there are barriers to entry. Sometimes these elites become victims of labor trafficking where they work for years in terrible conditions, as has been seen with Chinese and Pakistanis in the United Kingdom.[107]

Other forces also explain the recent rise in human trafficking. These include the decline in border controls, the rise of regional conflicts, and the traumatic changes of post-socialist transitions. The rise of nonstate actors – transnational criminals and terrorists – who have increasingly used human trafficking to support their crime organizations and finance their terrorist activities is discussed.[108]

The second chapter focuses on the diverse consequences of human trafficking. Enormous attention has been paid in the scholarly community

[106] Bales, *Disposable People*.

[107] Khalid Koser, "The Smuggling of Asylum Seekers into Western Europe: Contradictions, Conundrums and Dilemmas," in *Global Human Smuggling: Comparative Perspectives*, David Kyle and Rey Koslowski, eds. (Baltimore and London: Johns Hopkins University Press, 2001), 58–73.

[108] Note the work of Susan Strange, *The Retreat of the State: The Diffusion of Power in the World Economy* (New York: Cambridge, 1996) and Saskia Sassen, *Cities in a World Economy*, 2nd ed. (Thousand Oaks, CA: Pine Forge Press, 2000).

and the mass media to the broader consequences of the drug trade, but this type of analysis has not been applied sufficiently to the phenomenon of human trafficking. Using a human security framework,[109] the chapter focuses on the diverse political, economic, medical, and social consequences of the rise of trafficking. With this perspective, the concept of victims of trafficking moves beyond the individual victim to a much broader societal level.

Part II of the book addresses the business of human trafficking and the role of organized crime groups, terrorists, and other nonstate groups such as insurgents and guerillas in the trafficking of human beings. The intersection of human trafficking with the legitimate world is analyzed. The third chapter discusses the characteristics of crime groups that traffic human beings and compares them to the better-known drug organizations, analyzing group structures and participants. It analyzes their routes, recruitment, and retention and control of victims. Trafficking involves many more small groups than does the drug trade, with fewer large organizations. Human trafficking is the only form of large-scale transnational crime in which women are significantly represented both as victims and perpetrators.

Chapter 4 addresses the business model of organized crime, showing that crime groups from different regions of the world operate differently. These group differences are explained by historical, economic, and social factors because the illicit trade mirrors long-term patterns of licit trade. For example, for more than a century, the smugglers operating between Mexico and the United States made their profits by volume and frequency rather than premium pricing for each item. Russian-speaking groups sell their victims as if they were natural resources such as fur, timber, oil, or gas. The Chinese, in contrast, have a trade and development model, seeing the trade in human beings as one more commodity in which to maximize profits and obtain long-term development capital. These differences in business models have important implications. They help to determine the extent of abuse of the trafficking victim, profit margins, and the laundering and investment of profits.

Part III consists of five chapters that provide regional case studies of human smuggling and trafficking. Each of these chapters focuses on the unique elements of trafficking in the region, its historical precedents, the predominant forms of trafficking and human smuggling, and

[109] Human Development Report 1994, http://hdr.undp.org/en/reports/global/hdr1994/ (accessed July 31, 2009).

the geographical variations within each region. The impact of the state response to smuggling and trafficking is analyzed.

The regional analysis reveals that there are important distinctions between developed, developing, and transitional countries in their trafficking and smuggling patterns. These differences are greater than the simple generalization that developed countries are part of the demand side of the equation and developing countries are part of the supply side of the relationship. There are developing oil-rich countries such as Russia, Azerbaijan, and many countries of the Middle East that are an important part of the demand equation and some that are also part of the supply. The United States, an advanced industrialized country, is a large supplier of trafficked people for its own domestic markets, an anomaly in the developed world. The collapse of the Soviet Union and the post-socialist transitions worldwide have amplified the trafficking problem as traffickers draw on a seemingly endless supply of women rendered destitute by the post-socialist transition, collapse of the social welfare system, and a process of privatization in many former socialist states that transferred the wealth of states into the hands of a limited elite, often comprised of former Communist officials. Women and children were the largest losers in this enormous redistribution of property, but many men lost their jobs in the transition, particularly in Central Asia, and were forced to migrate illegally to support their families. In their vulnerable and illegal status, many became victims of trafficking.

Human smuggling and trafficking in Asia is the focus of the fifth chapter. Despite the enormous religious, political, and economic diversity of the countries of Asia, all of them face significant problems of human trafficking. Asian crime groups derive significant revenues from trafficking women and children into prostitution, supplying individuals for forced labor, and promoting sex tourism. Economic growth in India and China is not reducing the problem of human trafficking. Rather, the growing economic disparities within these countries instead result in increased problems of human trafficking. Moreover, the transition away from the Communist system, not only in China but also in Southeast Asia, as in the former USSR, discussed in Chapter 6, has proved highly conducive to the growth in human smuggling and trafficking. In most Asian states, there is an absence of political will to address human trafficking, as there are long traditions of human exploitation. Moreover, trafficking is facilitated in many countries of Asia by high levels of corruption within the government and among ruling elites.

Eurasia, the successor states of the former Soviet Union, is the subject of Chapter 6. Although this region is most associated with the traffic of Slavic women to international sex markets, the victims of labor exploitation may now exceed the number of sex trafficking victims. Whereas the countries of Asia have had longstanding and continuous traditions of exploitation, labor exploitation was prohibited by Communist ideology, although millions were engaged in forced labor in the extensive Soviet labor camp system. Prostitution was outlawed and suppressed under communism. However, human smuggling and trafficking have skyrocketed in the last two decades since the collapse of the socialist system. Few of the post-Soviet states have shown the political will or the commitment of resources to address the widespread exploitation and victimization of women, children, and male laborers. Civil society is weak and unable to counter traffickers or provide much support for victims while corruption permeates the state and facilitates trafficking on a grand scale.

Chapter 7 focuses on the diverse sources and forms of human smuggling and trafficking in Europe. The countries of Eastern Europe have been major source regions for the large numbers of women trafficked into the lucrative sex markets of Western Europe. Women are also trafficked from Nigeria, Latin America, and Asia for sexual exploitation, often by crime groups from those regions collaborating with their European counterparts. Men are smuggled and trafficked from Africa and many parts of Asia for labor exploitation. Many desperate individuals trying to reach Western Europe die each year in flimsy boats that cannot support their human cargo. Despite European Community concern about the rise of illegal migration and trafficking, the Schengen Agreement, which reduces internal border controls within many European countries, has been an important facilitator of human trafficking.

Human smuggling and trafficking within the United States is analyzed in Chapter 8. No longer a problem confined to major urban areas, victims of human smuggling and trafficking are now found in rural areas, suburban communities, and along the extensive highways of the United States. Without the social welfare and support systems known for families and children in other Western advanced democracies, a significant share of the trafficking victims are American-born youth. The United States, with its numerous domestic trafficking victims and sex tourism within its borders, has trafficking patterns that resemble those of a developing or transitional country rather than an advanced Western democracy. In contrast, the American patterns of human smuggling have much in common with Western Europe, where large numbers of illegal immigrants are vulnerable to labor exploitation. Although both Democratic and Republican administrations have sought to combat human trafficking and hundreds of millions of dollars have been spent to address the problem both domestically and internationally, the United States remains a major center of trafficking. There is an absence of public consciousness of the severity of the problem within the United States, particularly a lack of awareness of the extent of victimization of its native-born and youthful citizens.

In Chapter 9, I discuss Latin America and Africa, two poor regions of the world where less is known about contemporary human trafficking. Latin America and Africa have common traditions of human exploitation; the largest numbers of victims of the African slave trade were sent to Latin America, in particular, Brazil.[110] While African slave traders sent many of their slaves to the new world, the Spanish and Portuguese colonists enslaved many of the indigenous populations in Mexico and Central and South America that survived the conquest. Similar problems of labor exploitation within Africa typified colonial rule, particularly in sub-Saharan Africa. Therefore, both regions have long-term traditions of exploitation of enslaved laborers. Compounding the likelihood of trafficking is the large number of conflicts in both regions, particularly a post-Cold War phenomenon. The absence of resources to support their growing populations compounds the risk of trafficking for many citizens.[111]

The large numbers of refugees and of internally displaced people, especially in Africa, have provided a ready supply of people to the traffickers. In both regions, children are trafficked to be child soldiers and beggars and are sexually exploited. Research from the International Labour Organization, as mentioned previously, has suggested that the profits from human trafficking are less in these regions. This fact is not explained by the absence of victims but the very low cost of human life and the small sums that are derived from exploitation of child laborers, trafficked women, or domestic servants. Little is being done in most countries in both regions to combat trafficking because of an absence of political will, financial resources, or state capacity to act. Only Brazil stands apart in vigorously addressing labor trafficking.

[110] The number of slaves sent to Brazil is estimated at 3.6 million http://portal.unesco.org/ci/en/ev.php-URL_ID=8161&URL_DO=DO_TOPIC&URL_SECTION=201.htm (accessed July23, 2009).

[111] Raymond Fisman and Edward Miguel, *Economic Gangsters: Corruption, Violence and the Poverty of Nations* (Princeton: Princeton University Press, 2008).

The Conclusion focuses on the policy implications derived from the previous analysis. The diversity of human trafficking means that not one single strategy can effectively combat human trafficking worldwide. Globalization, restrictions on movements of labor, economic disparities within countries and worldwide, as well as the rise of international conflicts, have all contributed to the rise of human smuggling. Greater legal labor mobility might lessen the extent of human smuggling but it would not eliminate the problem. The adoption of international conventions, the implementation of training, and public awareness and prevention programs have done little to stem the rise of human smuggling and trafficking. Present strategies are inherently limited by state sovereignty, the absence of harmonized legislation, the flexibility of the crime groups relative to state bureaucracies, and the economic imperative of many marginalized individuals internationally. Moreover, an economic approach must be much more central in strategies to address human smuggling and trafficking. Much more needs to be done to address the conditions that make individuals ready to pay large sums to smugglers or be susceptible to the ploys of traffickers. In the absence of fundamental change in the now globalized world, human smuggling and trafficking will grow dramatically for the rest of the twenty-first century. The global economic crisis that began in 2008 will make millions indebted to traffickers, as the crime groups have become major sources of credit in the financial crisis.[112] The consequences of this tragic trade in human beings will be long-term changes in the social, political, and economic life of many countries. There will also be "grave threats to individual rights, civil liberties, and human dignity."[113] Beyond this, there will be a decline of democracy and the rule of law in established democracies and increased authoritarianism in many potentially democratic states.

[112] Louise Shelley, "The Financial Winners of the Current Crisis," policytraccc.gmu.edu/.../Financial%20Winners %20of%20Current%20Crisis002.pdf (accessed July 23, 2009).

[113] Douglas Massey et al., *Worlds in Motion: Understanding International Migration at the End of the Millennium* (New York: Oxford University Press, 1998), 293.

PART I

THE RISE AND COSTS OF HUMAN TRAFFICKING

1

Why Has Human Trafficking Flourished?

Numerous root causes have been identified for the existence of human trafficking. They include lack of employment opportunities, poverty, economic imbalances among regions of the world, corruption, decline of border controls, gender and ethnic discrimination, and political instability and conflict. These push factors are contrasted with the pull factors of demand for workers, the possibilities of higher standards of living, and the perceptions of many in poor communities that better opportunities exist in larger cities or abroad.[1] Yet most of these conditions have existed for a very long time. They alone do not explain the phenomenal growth of human trafficking since the mid-1980s.

Trafficking has increased dramatically with globalization, the rise of illicit trade, and the end of the Cold War. Free markets, free trade, greater economic competition, and a decline in state intervention in the economy have been hallmarks of the globalizing process. Globalization is also characterized by greater mobility of goods and people and more rapid communications.[2] Remote parts of the world are now integrated into the global economy. Yet controls on entrance to the most affluent countries create barriers for those who seek to migrate. This is highly criminogenic because the limitations on labor clash with the demands of a global economy.[3] Many seek illicit means to enter countries where there is demand for labor.

[1] Alexis A. Aronowitz, *Human Trafficking, Human Misery: The Global Trade in Human Beings* (Westport, CT: Praeger, 2009), 11–12.

[2] Louise Shelley, Chris Corpora, and John Picarelli, "Global Crime Inc," in *Beyond Sovereignty*, 2nd ed., Maryann Cusimano Love, ed. (Belmont, CA: Wadsworth, 2003), 143–66.

[3] Karen Bravo, "Free Labor! A Labor Liberalization Solution to Modern Trafficking in Humans," *Journal of Transnational Law and Contemporary Problems* 18 (2009): 545–616.

Globalization alone does not explain the growth of human trafficking. With the end of the Cold War, there were revolutions in Eastern Europe, the demise of Soviet socialism, and the collapse of the USSR. The bipolar world ended. Greater international political instability resulted. After the breakup of the USSR, many new states sought sovereignty, and parts of larger states such as Chechnya in Russia, regions such as Nagorno – Karabagh in the Caucasus, and states in the Balkans sought greater independence. Apart from these conflicts, more than sixty national and regional conflicts have occurred since the early 1990s, leaving widespread devastation and many individuals vulnerable to exploitation by human traffickers.

Increasing and more severe natural disasters, possibly as a result of global warming, have also left millions displaced, homeless, and impoverished. Examples include the tsunami in Southeast Asia, Hurricane Katrina in New Orleans, drought in Sudan and the earthquake in Haiti. Assistance programs to aid disaster victims have often been insufficient, and needed aid too often has been diverted by corrupt officials. Deprived of their land and without increased opportunities in nonagricultural sectors,[4] these desperate people are often exploited by human traffickers.

Crime groups, particularly human smugglers and traffickers, have seized the opportunities created by the global economy. They have expanded their activities across borders and to new regions of the world; illicit trade has been transformed and has created "ravaging effects."[5] By the mid-1990s, the illicit economy already represented about 6 percent of the world's economy, and its share has increased since then because illicit money remains untaxed and areas of illicit trade such as human trafficking have expanded.[6] The most recent estimates of the illicit economy place the figure at $1 trillion to $1.5 trillion.[7]

Whereas the growth of legal trade is hindered by border controls, customs officials, and bureaucratic obstacles, transnational crime groups exploit the loopholes of state-based legal systems to extend their reach. Control of transnational criminals is difficult because legal systems are

[4] Asian Development Bank, *Combating Trafficking of Women and Children in South Asia Manila* (Philippines: Asian Development Bank, 2003), 40.

[5] Moisés Naím, *Illicit: How Smugglers, Traffickers and Copycats are Hijacking the Global Economy* (New York: Anchor Books, 2006), 8.

[6] Vito Tanzi, "Policies, Institutions and the Dark Sides of Economies," *Public Choice* 108, nos. 3–4 (August 2001): 387–90.

[7] Moisés Naím, "It's the Illicit Economy, Stupid," *Foreign Policy Magazine* (November/December 2005), http:/www.foreignpolicy.com/story/cms.php?story_id=3270 (accessed March 1, 2007).

state based whereas nonstate actors such as criminals and terrorists operate transnationally, violating the laws of numerous countries simultaneously, while often eluding the jurisdiction of any one.

Facilitating the growth of human trafficking has been the absence of a significant coordinated international effort to address the problem. Counter-trafficking strategies have been small and of limited effect. The coordinated law enforcement, intelligence, and prosecution response that has been applied to the drug industry has not been used against human traffickers. Further, trafficking is often treated as peripheral to the larger problem of resolving conflicts, fostering economic development, and delivering disaster relief. This has resulted in a response that is not commensurate with the scale or the rapid growth of human trafficking.

Demand for Human Trafficking

Demand fuels the growth of human trafficking. Many of the world's citizens would never buy illegal drugs or smuggled weapons, but consumers will use the products produced by trafficking victims without thinking about why they are available at such an affordable price. Instead, they are satisfied to have found a well-priced good in a global competitive economy. They will unknowingly buy clothes produced by the sweatshops where trafficked workers are employed, and buy the fruits and vegetables harvested by trafficked agricultural workers. Increasingly accustomed to the benefits of a consumer society, they will eat in restaurants where trafficked laborers are employed. With more women employed outside the home in developed countries, they hire domestic laborers to take care of their children and their homes, all too often forcing those employed to work for substandard wages and long hours, conditions often prohibited by the work laws in their countries. Men who purchase sexual services rarely think about the prostitutes with whom they have sexual relations. Instead, they happily hire the services of a younger woman who is compliant and affordable without thinking of why these services are so accessible. Sex slavery today, according to one financial analyst, has made sex services more available than a decade ago and thereby has increased demand.[8]

The business of human trafficking is built on widespread individual human suffering, yet human trafficking is hard to combat because it has

[8] Siddharth Kara, *Sex Trafficking Inside the Business of Modern Slavery* (New York: Columbia University Press, 2009), 37.

financial advantages for many legal businesses. Just as the slave trade of previous centuries financially benefited many participants beyond the actual slave traders, the contemporary trade in human beings also yields significant profits for many legitimate employers. Agricultural producers, manufacturers, and construction companies can pay trafficked workers subminimum or no wages. Moreover, they of course do not pay health or accident insurance, Social Security taxes, social benefits, or pensions that may cost their competitors significant sums. The nefarious sex traders who exploit women and children are not the only ones who profit from human trafficking.

Moreover, businesses enjoy other tangible advantages from exploiting trafficked labor. They use trafficked labor to ensure they have a compliant labor force. As American businesses tolerated the infiltration of organized crime into labor unions because the mobsters kept the workers passive, the same situation endures in contemporary trafficking.[9] Construction companies can meet deadlines, farmers can harvest their crops before they spoil, and sweatshops can produce competitive products because they employ compliant trafficked laborers who cannot resist the employers' demands.

Globalization

Many of those exploited are available because of globalization.[10] Globalization, as mentioned in the introduction, has facilitated the rise of human trafficking by marginalizing many rural communities, impoverishing women and children in many regions, and accelerating rural to urban migration.[11] Increased speed and ease of money movement, as will be discussed later, facilitate not only the laundering of traffickers' profits but grand corruption.

The increasing volume of international cargo has facilitated trafficking. Not all cargo leaving Hong Kong is inspected, enabling smuggled Chinese to travel in holds of boats to the United States without detection. The same "illusion of inspection" exists in the port of Rotterdam, which is also a human smuggling and trafficking hub.[12] Trucks and vans crossing

[9] James B. Jacobs, *Mobsters, Unions and Feds: The Mafia and the American Labor Movement* (New York: New York University Press, 2006).

[10] Joseph E. Stiglitz, *Globalization and Its Discontents* (New York: W.W. Norton, 2003).

[11] Shafqat Munir, "Trafficking South Asia and Pakistan," *HIMAL South Asian*, http://www.himalmag.com/2003/september/report_2.htm (accessed November 10, 2003).

[12] Carolyn Nordstrom, *Global Outlaws: Crime, Money and Power in the Contemporary World* (Berkeley: University of California Press, 2007), 159–62; M.R, J. Soudijn, *Chinese Human Smuggling in Transit* (Den Haag: Boom Juridische Uitgevers, 2006), 37.

borders throughout the world are also rarely inspected. Smuggled Indians were found in a specially constructed compartment of a truck crossing from Odessa, Ukraine, into Moldova.[13] We can safely assume that many such vehicles had moved with their human cargo before this one was finally detected. Sixty people from Afghanistan and the Indian subcontinent were killed in Turkey in early 2006 when the truck carrying them crashed far from their point of origin.[14]

Globalization has facilitated speedy, low-cost, and anonymous communications that are a boon to the activities of traffickers. Web sites advertise sex tourism overseas and internationally market child pornography and "brides" available for marriage, often a discreet cover for sexual trafficking. Behind the poor, vulnerable, and isolated trafficking victim often exists an elaborate communications system that links the human traffickers with the global market for their goods. Illustrative of this is a Russian trafficking ring from southern Russia near the Black Sea that sent its victims to Alaska, halfway around the world, arranging the whole operation through e-mail, a fact discovered only after the exploited girls were detained.[15] The Internet allows communication among buyers and sellers of trafficked people, chat rooms allow buyers to exchange information on sex tourism, and text messaging is used by traffickers to link with customers.[16] Cell phones are used even from prisons to manage trafficking rings, and instant messaging allows human traffickers to launder their proceeds without a trace. Internet chat rooms and Web sites allow pedophiles to distribute material of exploited children.[17] In 1998, 1 million downloads of child sexual pornography were executed within a six-month period from a Web site that was allegedly operating from Tajikistan.[18] Traffickers and their high-tech associates exploited a remote

[13] Interview with Ukrainian law enforcement official, Odessa, July 2004.

[14] Hacaoglu Selcan, "40 Illegal Immigrants Killed in a Turkey Road Accident," May 21, 2006, www.turkishdailynews.com.tr/article.php?enewsid=44026 (accessed April 10, 2007).

[15] Beatrix Siman Zakhari, "Legal Cases Prosecuted under the Victims of Trafficking and Violence Protection Act of 2000," in *Human Traffic and Transnational Crime: Eurasian and American Perspectives*, Sally Stoecker and Louise Shelley, eds. (Lanham, MD: Rowman and Littlefield, 2004).

[16] U.S. Department of State, *Trafficking in Persons Report, 2008* (Washington, DC: U.S. Department of State, 2009), 13.

[17] Steve Ragan, "British Police Break up Pedophile Ring, 31 Children Rescued," June 19, 2007, http://www.monstersandcritics.com/tech/news/article_1319658.php/British_police_break_up_pedophile_ring_31_children_rescued (accessed August 14, 2009).

[18] Interview with experts of the cybercrime center of U.S. customs in 1999.

locale now joined to the global economy that lacked any capacity to counter human trafficking.

Decline of Borders, Globalization, and the Post – Cold War Era

In recent decades, border controls have declined in many part of the world. Well-intentioned international agreements such as the North American Free Trade Agreement (NAFTA) and the Schengen Agreement in Europe, enacted to promote free trade and cross-border movement, have facilitated smuggling and trafficking.[19]

Reduced border controls in North America and Europe have been a result of deliberate policies as countries respond to the imperatives of free trade. In contrast, diminished border controls followed unintentionally from the collapse of the USSR, leaving a huge landmass reaching from the Pacific Ocean to Europe with only limited controls over population movement. Vast portions of Africa with limited governance, corrupt officials, and little prioritization of border controls have created a paradise for all forms of cross-border illicit trade, including human smuggling and trafficking.[20]

Land reform introduced in Mexico just before the adoption of NAFTA contributed to the privatization of land and the consolidation of land holdings, with larger owners displacing traditional farmers.[21] With the subsequent introduction of NAFTA in 1994, the number of individuals crossing the U.S.–Mexico border increased dramatically as the poverty and displacement of traditional Mexican farmers pushed citizens to leave. The ever-present demand for cheap labor in the United States serves as a strong attractor.[22]

[19] Peter Andreas, "The Transformation of Migrant Smuggling across the U.S.-Mexico Border," in *Global Human Smuggling Comparative Perspectives*, David Kyle and Rey Koslowski, eds. (Baltimore, MD: Johns Hopkins University Press, 2001), 107–25; Peter Andreas, *Border Games: Policing the U.S.-Mexico Divide* (Ithaca, NY: Cornell University Press, 2000).

[20] Nordstrom, Global Outlaws, Diana Wong, "The Rumor of Trafficking, Border Controls, Illegal Migration and the Sovereignty of the Nation State," in *Illicit Flows and Criminal Things States, Borders, and the Other Side of Globalization*, Willem van Schendel and Itty Abraham, eds. (Bloomington, IN: Indiana University Press, 2005), 69–100.

[21] Maria Teresa Vázquez Castillo, *Land Privatization in Mexico: Urbanization, Formation of Regions and Globalization in Ejidos* (New York: Routledge, 2004); Jessa Lewis, "Agrarian Change and Privatization of Ejido Land in Northern Mexico," *Journal of Agrarian Change* 2, no. 3 (July 2002), 402–20.

[22] "Rise, Peak and Decline: Trends in U.S. Immigration 1992–2004," Pew Hispanic Center 2005, http://pewhispanic.org/reports/report.php?ReportID=5 (accessed June 22, 2007); Jeffrey S. Passel, "Unauthorized Migrants: Numbers and Characteristics," background briefing prepared for Task Force on Immigration and America's Future (Washington,

With the introduction of the Schengen Agreement in 1985 and its subsequent amendments, it is now possible to move within twenty-five European countries without showing a passport.[23] Therefore, once a trafficker brings a woman or a forced laborer into the European community, that person can reach different markets without detection. Facilitating entry into Europe are the porous coasts of many Mediterranean countries exploited by many smugglers and traffickers.

The countries of the former USSR, with their limited border controls, are now important transit and destination countries for human smuggling and trafficking. Millions now reside illegally in Russia and Ukraine, and many victims transit through the region.[24] Some illegal migrants from China, the Indian subcontinent, and Afghanistan never reach their intended destinations in Western Europe and stay for years in the Slavic countries.[25]

Trafficking and smuggling are also facilitated in Europe, Asia, Africa, and Latin America by the increasing number of border regions outside the control of central state authorities. One of the most infamous is the Transdniester area between Ukraine and Moldova, a conflict region that declared itself independent from the Moldovan central government. The documentary *Sex Slaves* vividly captured the large-scale trafficking from the region that had been analyzed in numerous reports.[26] Women trafficked from Transdniester to Turkey and other international destinations, as citizens of a nonrecognized state, often receive no protection from any legal authorities.[27] The problem of statelessness and trafficking is discussed later in this chapter.

DC: Pew Hispanic Center, 2004), http://pewhispanic.org/files/reports/46.pdf (accessed January 30, 2007).

[23] Elizabeth Joyce, "Transnational Criminal Enterprise: The European Perspective," in *Transnational Crime in the Americas*, ed. Tom Farer (New York: Routledge, 1999), 99–115; http://www.answers.com/topic/schengen-area-1 (accessed August 15, 2009).

[24] Olena Braichevska, Halyna Volosiuk, Olena Malynovska, Yaroslav Pylnskyi, Nancy Popson, Blair A. Ruble, *Non-Traditional Immigrants in Kyiv* (Washington, DC: Kennan Institute, 2004); "Korruptsia i nezakonaia migratsiia," http://www.transparencykazakhstan.org/content/89.html (accessed July 31, 2009); James Rodgers, "Moscow 'to cut migrant workers," June 7, 2007, http://news.bbc.co.uk/go/pr/fr/-/2/hi/europe/6731059.stm (accessed June 7, 2007).

[25] Elena Tiuriukanova, *Prinuditel'nyi trud v sovremennoi Rossii* (Moscow: ILO, 2004).

[26] "Sex Slaves," Frontline documentary, http://www.pbs.org/wgbh/pages/frontline/slaves (accessed June 25, 2007).

[27] Mark Galeotti, "The Trandnistrian Connection: big problems from-a small pseudo-state," *Global Crime* 8, no. 3 and 4 (August – November 2004): 398–405; Kara, *Sex Trafficking*, 117–19 on Moldova.

In many Asian multiborder areas, there is also an absence of governmental control. In these locales, various crime groups and the smugglers are the dominant powers. Illustrative of this is the Golden Triangle region, in which human trafficking from Cambodia, Laos, Myanmar, and southern China flows into northern Thailand.[28]

Other examples of this dynamic are the India – Bangladesh and India – Nepal border areas, where a whole culture of human smuggling and organized crime has developed.[29] The same pattern exists on parts of the Afghan border, where drug smuggling rings have been adapted for human smuggling and trafficking.[30]

The problem also exists in the triborder area in South America where Paraguay, Brazil, and Argentina meet. Since 2000, the region has acquired a reputation as a major hub for human trafficking.[31] Young girls, especially from Paraguay, are brought to this region, where crime and terrorism have flourished. The Netherlands is a large hub for trafficked women from Europe, Africa, and the Balkans despite extensive efforts by the Dutch government to close down illegal brothels and prosecute traffickers.[32]

Globalization, Crises, and Unequal Economic Development

The global financial system has resulted in monetary crises of greater severity and frequency. The global crisis that began in 2008 is especially severe, but it is unfortunately not unique. There have been serious national and regional crises since the 1980s that have had a visible and direct impact on human trafficking. The wealthy in the developing world can usually weather these financial crises, but the poor often face disaster as the cost of basic necessities multiplies, leading to starvation or untenable debt, conditions ripe for exploitation by human traffickers.

[28] Kara, *Sex Trafficking*, 161–66.

[29] Ibid., 44–82.

[30] See *Trafficking in Persons Report 2006*, http://www.state.gov/g/tip/rls/tiprpt/2006/65988.htm (accessed April 20, 2007).

[31] "Tri-border Area of Argentina, Brazil and Paraguay Sees a Rise in Human Trafficking," January 29, 2008, http://www.humantrafficking.org/updates/830 (accessed July 31, 2009).

[32] Shared Hope International, "Netherlands" in *DEMAND: A Comparative Examination of Sex Tourism and Trafficking in Jamaica, Japan, the Netherlands and the United States*, http://www.sharedhope.org/files/demand_netherlands.pdf (accessed September 2, 2009); Conny Rijken, "EU's Human Rights Based Approach to Trafficking in Human Beings"; Rudolf E. H. Hilgers, "The Programmatic Approach of Trafficking in Human Beings in the Netherlands," paper presented at The Commodification of Illicit Flows: Labour Migration, Trafficking and Business, Centre for Diaspora and Transnational Studies, University of Toronto, October 9–10, 2009.

As Chapter 9 discusses, Nigeria was the first country identified where an economic crisis and the provision of structural adjustment loans by international financial bodies was associated with increased trafficking.[33] The bailout conditions imposed by the International Monetary Fund (IMF) and the World Bank included strict financial controls on government expenditures and significant cuts in social programs that reduced living standards dramatically for the poor and the middle urban class.[34] Women sought employment abroad but instead of finding enhanced opportunities, many became trafficking victims.

A similar situation was observed in the following decade with the financial crises of the late 1990s in Russia, Argentina, Thailand, and Indonesia. Economic policies adopted in response to IMF bailouts impoverished many women and children.[35] Desperate women in Russia and Argentina seeking to support families rather than finding greater work opportunities were exploited by traffickers.[36] Asian families made destitute by the crisis or faced with overwhelming debts often solved their economic problems by selling their children to traffickers.[37] Men seeking employment traveled to remote destinations. Instead of sending home remittances, the men all too often became trafficked laborers. These phenomena are unfortunately being repeated on a global scale in the financial crisis that started in 2008.[38]

Unequal development is also a hallmark of globalization. Capital moves to areas in which investors can make a profit, often regions where there is abundant human manpower, good transportation infrastructure, and communications. Chapter 5 on Asia analyzes how internal trafficking has grown within India and China to satisfy demand for sexual services in major cities such as Mumbai and Shanghai. Trafficking also occurs from neighboring states to India and China to meet the demand

[33] Kemi Asiwaju, "The Challenges of Combating Trafficking in Women and Children in Nigeria," in *Global Trafficking in Women and Children*, Obi N.I. Ebbe and Dilip K. Das, eds. (Boca Raton, FL: CRC Press, 2008), 181; Melissa Farley, "Prostitution, Trafficking, and Cultural Amnesia: What We Must *Not Know* in Order to Keep the Business of Sexual Exploitation Running Smoothly" *Yale Journal of Law and Feminism* 18 (2006), 112.

[34] Paola Monzin, *Sex Traffic Prostitution, Crime and Exploitation* (New York: Palgrave Macmillan, 2005), 64.

[35] Kara, *Sex Trafficking*, 26–29.

[36] Ibid., 26–28; meetings with women's groups and counter-trafficking organizations in Argentina in 2001.

[37] Bertil Lintner, "Asia's Sex Trap," http://www.asiapacificms.com/articles/fallen_angels/ (accessed January 20, 2004).

[38] *Trafficking in Persons Report 2009*, 32–40.

for prostitutes. Disparities in national economies also drive the sex trade in other parts of Asia. The lack of employment and economic development in Myanmar, Cambodia, and Laos has provided a steady stream of young girls and women for the Thai sex industry,[39] which serves customers from more prosperous countries of Asia as well as the Middle East, Europe, and North America.[40]

Unequal economic development between Latin and North America has also fueled smuggling and trafficking. This inequality has resulted in large numbers of laborers illegally crossing the U.S.–Mexican border, a passage facilitated by NAFTA and the greater movement of goods and people.[41] As discussed in more detail in Chapter 8, this smuggling all too often turns into trafficking as individuals are enslaved in agriculture, construction, and other menial forms of labor. Yet outright trafficking has also increased as young women, often unwitting victims of the traffickers, are transported from Mexico and Central America to serve the American market.[42]

Rise of the Illicit Global Economy, Globalized Corruption, and Human Trafficking

Both large- and small-scale corruption contribute significantly to the rise of human trafficking, as mentioned in the introduction. The role of small-scale corruption is most apparent and is the lifeline of the traffickers. But it may be less pernicious than the new and globalized large-scale corruption.

39 Asian Development Bank, *Combating Trafficking of Women and Children in South Asia*; World Vision, "Situation Analysis Report of Trafficking and Migration," http://www.adb.org/Documents/Books/Combating_Trafficking/ (accessed June 26, 2007); Bertil Lintner, "Betting on the Border," http://www.asiapacificms.com/articles/cambodia_casinos/ (accessed January 20, 2004).

40 Lintner, "Asia's Sex Trap."

41 Pew Hispanic Center, "Modes of Entry for the Unauthorized Migrant Population," May 22, 2006, http://pewhispanic.org/files/factsheets/19.pdf (accessed June 25, 2008).

42 Janice Raymond and Donna Hughes, "Sex Trafficking of Women in the United States: International and Domestic Trends," 2001, sponsored by U.S. Department of Justice http://www.ncjrs.gov/pdffiles1/nij/grants/187774.pdf (accessed June 22, 2007); lecture of Thomas Stack and Leland Wiley, "Latino Houses of Prostitution," at American University, February 27, 2007, and prior discussions with the investigators of this Montgomery county, Maryland case; Florida State University Center for the Advancement of Human Rights, *Florida Responds to Human Trafficking* (2003), 37–62, http://www.cahr.fsu.edu/H%20-%20Chapter%202.pdf (accessed June 22, 2007); Sarah Garland, "This Woman was Forced into Slavery ... in the U.S." *Marie Claire*, May 2006, 126–29.

Corruption is a fact of life in Latin America, Africa, Eurasia, and many countries of Asia and the Middle East as evidenced by Transparency International surveys.[43] Corruption results in distorted economic policies that benefit the elites and limit economic development. Civil servants such as border guards, police, and customs officials will facilitate trafficking by taking bribes to augment their low salaries, often not sufficient to provide a living wage. But in the cultures of corruption that prevail in many countries, trafficking rings are also able to bribe higher status officials such as consular officers, judges, and prosecutors without whom their businesses could not function.[44] Labor trafficking is also facilitated by corruption of labor and health inspectors, particularly in developed countries. Moreover, without corrupt health officials, a trade in organs could not persist in hospitals.

Yet this low-level corruption is not new. What has changed with the global economy is the speed and scale with which dictators can steal large amounts of money from their treasuries. Grand corruption consists of several components.[45] Political leaders siphon off national revenues, foreign assistance funds, and loans made by multinational organizations for structural adjustment and economic development. Lack of oversight in project loans and structural adjustment funds of such multilateral financial institutions as the IMF, the World Bank, and regional international banks has allowed billions of development assistance funds to be siphoned off by high-level corrupt officials while at the same time creating greater indebtedness for the citizens and the state.[46] Debt forgiveness has been provided to some countries with particularly corrupt leaders, but billions of debt is still owed. The cost of servicing these loans deprives countries of the capital needed for economic development, education, social services, and medical care.[47]

[43] Transparency International surveys are based on perceptions of corruption.

[44] Leslie Holmes, "Corruption and Trafficking: Triple Victimisation?," in *Strategies Against Human Trafficking: The Role of the Security Sector*, Cornelius Friesendorf, ed. (Vienna: National Defence Academy and Austrian Ministry of Defence and Sport, 2009), 89–121.

[45] Susan Rose-Ackerman, "The Political Economy of Corruption," in *Corruption and the Global Economy*, ed. Kimberly Ann Elliott (Washington, DC: Institute for International Economics, 1997), 31–34; Michael Johnston, *Syndromes of Corruption Wealth Power and Democracy* (Cambridge: Cambridge University Press, 2005).

[46] Paul Collier, *The Bottom Billion: Why the Poorest Countries Are Failing and What Can Be Done About It* (Oxford: Oxford University Press, 2007), 136

[47] Paolo Mauro, "Why Worry About Corruption," IMF, February 1997. http://www.imf.org/external/pubs/ft/issues6/index.htm (accessed August 3, 2009); Arvind K. Jain, ed., *The Political Economy of Corruption* (London: Routledge, 2001); Global Witness, "Undue Diligence: How Banks do Business with Corrupt Regimes," http://www.globalwitness.

Money once stolen is often hard to locate and even harder to recover.[48] The secrecy of much of the international banking system and the proliferation of offshore banking centers make the embezzlement of government funds and grand corruption ever easier. Both Nigeria and the Philippines, even after lengthy investigations, were able to repatriate only a small fraction of their stolen billions.

The growth of this grand corruption in recent decades appears to correlate very highly with trafficking. Many countries that are rated among the most corrupt in Transparency International's Corruption Perception Index, such as Indonesia, Russia, Ukraine, Nigeria, Bangladesh, Pakistan, and the Philippines,[49] are major suppliers of trafficked people, particularly women and children. Further, in a 2004 Transparency International report, many of these countries' past leaders were identified as the most corrupt politicians in the world. For example, the convicted money launderer Pavel Lazarenko, the former Prime Minister of Ukraine, stole in excess of one-half billion dollars from his country's treasury. Other egregious examples include the family of Sani Abacha in Nigeria, President Marcos of the Philippines, and first place President Suharto of Indonesia, whose familial corruption led to the phenomenal economic collapse of his country.[50]

Illustrative of the way this grand corruption contributes directly to human trafficking is the Philippines. There, corruption combined with crony capitalism has proven particularly pernicious.[51] With dismal economic opportunities at home, humans became a needed source of capital for the state as emigrants send home billions in remittances annually.[52] Hundreds of thousands of Filipino women labor overseas, often as

org/media_library_detail.php/735/en/undue_diligence_how_banks_do_business_with_corrupt (accessed August 15, 2009).

48 Global Witness, "Undue Diligence."

49 "Corrupt political elites and unscrupulous investors kill sustainable growth in its tracks, highlights new index," http://www.transparency.org/pressreleases_archive/2002/2002.08.28.cpi.en.html (accessed January 20, 2004); Global Corruption Report 2004, http://www.transparency.org/publications/gcr/gcr_2004 (accessed August 1, 2009), p. 13.

50 Global Corruption Report; Michael Johnston, "Public Officials, Private Interests and Sustainable Democracy: When Politics and Corruption Meet," in *Corruption and the Global Economy*, Elliott, ed., 61–82.

51 Andy Guth, "Human Trafficking in the Philippines: The Need for an Effective Anti-Corruption Program, *Trends in Organized Crime*, www.springerlink.com.mutex.gmu.edu/content/662 wp1450148jl85/fulltext.pdf (accessed November 29, 2009).

52 IOM – Philippines, http://www.iom.int/jahia/Jahia/pid/502 (accessed January 9, 2009); *Philippine Overseas Employment Administration 2007 Annual Report*. Philippine Overseas Employment Administration, http://www.poea.gov.ph/ar/ar2007.pdf (accessed October 4, 2008); International Organization for Migration, *Combating Trafficking in*

exploited domestic labor, and men perform hard physical labor in many Gulf states, sometimes becoming victims of trafficking, as discussed further in Chapter 5. Trafficking in the Philippines is, however, not restricted to the labor sector. Philippine trafficking also includes trafficking for the purposes of marriage, the local sex industry, commercial adoption, and sexual exploitation of children.[53]

Political Factors

End of the Cold War

The end of the Cold War contributed to the rise of trafficking by increasing the number and duration of intrastate and regional conflicts. These conflicts, as will be discussed, impoverished and displaced many. They eliminated families and communities, leaving individuals vulnerable to traffickers. The post-Communist transitions were particularly hard on women and children. With the collapse of the Communist political and economic systems, state-guaranteed employment ended and the social safety net disappeared; the demise of these supports was accelerated by an ideological commitment to eliminate all attributes of the Communist system. The corruption of long-term one-party rule led to highly corrupt law enforcement and crime groups closely linked to the state. Impoverished women and children in post-Communist countries from the Balkans to Vietnam became trafficking victims, as they lacked protection from their governments and were vulnerable to powerful and venal transnational crime groups. Their fates are discussed in greater depth in Chapters 5 and 6.

The demise of the USSR ended the world dominated by the two great superpowers – the United States and the USSR. Before the late 1980s, patron–client relationships existed between the great powers and countries in most regions of the world. This kept many conflicts in check. The bipolar world of the Cold War era broke down in the late 1980s and what unfortunately followed was the rise of numerous regional conflicts that have often been perpetuated by greed rather than grievance. Illicit trade, including human trafficking, has been key to the endurance of these conflicts.[54]

South-East Asia: A Review of Policy and Programme Responses, 2000, p. 51. http://www.unesco.org/most/migration/ctsea.pdf (accessed August 15, 2009).

[53] *Trafficking in Persons Report* 2009, 239–40;

[54] David Keen, "Incentives and Disincentives for Violence," in *Greed and Grievance: Economic Agendas in Civil Wars*, Mats Berdal and David Malone (Boulder, CO: Lynne Rienner,

Regional Conflicts and Trafficking

The proliferation of regional conflicts since the early 1990s has produced devastating situations conducive to human smuggling and diverse forms of trafficking.

Millions of refugees resulting from these conflicts are uprooted from their traditional societies with no viable means of support. Many are forced into the abysmal conditions of refugee camps. Having lost their livestock and their traditional lands, they are often dependent on the handouts of foreign aid organizations. Desperate and disoriented, they are ready to leave their camps but lack the resources to move, making them ripe for exploitation by traffickers. The more affluent in conflict regions pay smugglers to move them and their children to safer countries where they can seek political asylum but often they too become trafficking victims. Therefore, trafficking compounds their initial victimization.

Trafficking in men and women also provides financial support for regional conflicts in Africa, Europe, Latin America, and Asia,[55] as discussed in subsequent chapters on specific regions. Children are trafficked in many regions to provide soldiers for rebel armies.

Peacekeeping missions increasingly deployed in the last two decades to police conflicts have all too often exacerbated the problem of trafficking.[56] These missions are large and expensive, representing 25 percent of the UN budget and significant sums from other multilateral organizations and individual nations.[57] Numerous youthful male soldiers placed in dangerous conditions far from their homelands, without adequate oversight, become ready customers for the brothels

2000), 19–42; Michael L. Ross, "Oil, Drugs, and Diamonds: The Varying Roles of Natural Resources in Civil War," in *The Political Economy of Armed Conflict: Beyond Greed and Grievance*, Karen Ballentine and Jake Sherman (Boulder, CO: Lynne Rienner, 2003), 47–70.

55 German Agency for Technical Cooperation, "Armed Conflict and Trafficking in Women," (2004), 13–23, http://www2.gtz.de/dokumente/b (accessed June 22, 2007).

56 Corinna Csáka, "No One to Turn to: The Under Reporting of Child Sexual Exploitation and Abuse by Aid Workers and Peacekeepers," Save the Children, United Kingdom, 2008; Melanie O'Brien, "Prosecuting Peacekeepers in the ICC for Human Trafficking," *Intercultural Human Rights Law Review* 1 (2006), 281–83.

57 Presently, approximately 25 percent of the UN budget is spent on peacekeeping activities internationally, or $5 billion out of a total of $19 billion. Apart from the United Nations, other multilateral organizations such as NATO and the African Union send peacekeeping missions. In addition, individual countries send their own peacekeepers to the Balkans, to individual African countries such as the Ivory Coast and Cameroon, and to Asian conflicts in East Timor and Afghanistan.

filled with trafficked women that spring up as soon as peacekeepers arrive.[58]

With the governing military philosophy of these different peacekeeping forces all too frequently being "boys will be boys," the abuse of women in the bars and brothels around the missions is routine. Commanding officers of peacekeeping missions place primary attention on maintaining order. The fact that the prostitutes who serve the peacekeepers are trafficked women is ignored or seen as a peripheral concern.

Many powerful journalistic investigations of abuse of trafficked women in the Balkans focused attention on the linkage between peacekeeping and trafficking.[59] These exposés revealed that traffickers embed organized crime within the community. As a result, new policies were developed by the U.S. Department of Defense, NATO, and the United Nations intended to eliminate peacekeepers' exploitation of trafficked women. The problem, however, persists because enforcement of these policies has been sporadic and there has been an absence of political will to address the problem.[60]

Reports out of Afghanistan indicate that U.S. government contractors have allowed their employees to frequent brothels. Further, they have quashed investigations of this misconduct.[61]

Statelessness

The *Trafficking in Persons Report 2009* estimated that 12 million persons worldwide are at present stateless and unable to register a birth, educate their children, get health care, work, or travel legally.[62] Stateless people in all regions of the world, whether they are Hill Tribes in Northern Thailand, Roma in Europe, or Haitian migrants in the Caribbean, are particularly vulnerable to trafficking and forced labor. They can expect no protection from the police or recourse to any legal system.

[58] Sarah E. Mendelson, *Barracks and Brothels: Peacekeepers and Human Trafficking in the Balkans* (Washington, DC: CSIS, 2005); Owen Bowcott, "Report Reveals Shame of UN Peacekeepers," *The Guardian*, March 25, 2005, http://www.guardian.co.uk/itnernational/story/0,3604,1445537,00.html (accessed June 9, 2007).

[59] Sebastian Junger, "Slaves of the Brothel," *Vanity Fair*, July 2002; Victor Malarek, *The Natashas: Inside the New Global Sex Trade* (New York: Arcade, 2004).

[60] Mendelson, *Barracks and Brothels*; Jorene Soto, " 'We're Here to Protect Democracy, We're Not Here to Practice It': The US Military Involvement in Trafficking in Persons and Suggestions for the Future," *Cardozo Journal of Law and Gender* 13 (2007), 561–77.

[61] David Isenberg, "Sex and Security in Afghanistan," October 6, 2009 www.atimes.com/atimes/South_Asia/KJ06Df03.html (accessed November 29, 2009).

[62] *Trafficking in Persons Report 2009*, 31.

Social Factors

Labor and sexual trafficking have grown in response to changing social conditions of recent decades. Youthful populations have burgeoned in the developing world. Without capital and adequate job growth, rural to urban migration has undermined traditional values as well-established communities are destroyed, and long-standing discrimination against women, girls, and minorities has been amplified by the global economy.

Demographic Factors

Two important demographic forces have contributed to human trafficking – population growth and the increasing imbalance between the numbers of men and women in many countries. In the last forty years, the world's population has nearly doubled with the growth confined almost entirely to the developing world. Unemployed or underemployed youth and street children in the teeming cities of the third world are exploited by traffickers for labor and sexual exploitation.[63]

In Asia, the epicenter of human trafficking, women represent less than 50 percent of the population of China and all South Asian countries. In China, there are fewer women than men because many female fetuses are aborted because of the one-child policy and society's preference for males. Other forces explain this discrepancy in Nepal, India, Bangladesh, and other South Asian countries. "The negative sex ratio can be attributed to excess mortality of women and girls resulting from both direct and indirect discrimination in the provision of food, care, medical treatment, education, and above all physical and sexual violence."[64] In these countries, the gender imbalance is both a cause and a consequence of human trafficking. Women are trafficked from other Asian countries as wives for Chinese men. In South Asia, many trafficking victims die prematurely.

Rural to Urban Migration

Small-scale agriculture cannot compete in a global economy. Combined with explosive population growth in rural areas, small family plots can no longer support the enlarged families. Family members choose different

[63] *Trafficking in Persons Report 2008*, 9.

[64] Asian Development Bank, *Combating Trafficking of Women and Children in South Asia* (Manila, Philippines: Asian Development Bank, 2003), 49.

paths for survival. Some seek any opportunity to emigrate abroad whereas others migrate from rural to urban areas.[65]

Just as rural to urban migration was conducive to the growth of crime and prostitution in the nineteenth century, it has contributed to the growth of human trafficking in the late twentieth and early twenty-first centuries.[66] In their urban communities, formerly rural families lose their traditional ways of life just as they did in earlier periods. Long-held social and cultural values can be weakened by exposure to mass media, promotion of materialism, and the daily travails of survival in overpopulated cities. Families may adjust badly to the impoverished conditions they face in quickly growing and overcrowded cities. Family homelessness, familial breakdowns, parental illness, divorce, death of a parent, and abandonment by the father often follow rural to urban migration. Alcohol abuse often becomes more common within families, including violence and sexual exploitation of women and children who often run away. Familial exploitation often becomes a steppingstone to abuse by traffickers.[67]

Even when families do not deteriorate so severely, poor migrant families often have limited capacity to take care of their children in large cities. Children may run away or become street children. Both groups are vulnerable to traffickers.

Men often migrate alone to cities within their countries or move abroad. Far from their families or unable to afford marriage, they add to demand for the services of prostitutes. This is evident in the slums of India, among Mexican laborers in the United States, and in Chinatowns around the world.[68]

Gender and Ethnic Discrimination that Gives Rise to Trafficking

One scholar explained the recent growth of sex trafficking in South Asia, Eurasia, and East Asia after the fall of the Berlin Wall in these terms, "The

[65] The criminogenic element of this rural to urban migration was first discussed by the author in *Crime and Modernization: The Impact of Industrialization and Urbanization on Crime* (Carbondale: S. Illinois University Press, 1981).

[66] Ibid.

[67] Economic and Social Commission for Asia and the Pacific, "Sexually Abused and Sexually Exploited Children and Youth in the Greater Mekong Subregion: A Qualitative Assessment of their Health Needs and Available Services," St/ESCAP/2045 (New York: United Nations, 2000).

[68] See 1996 film of Ruchira Gupta, "Selling of Innocents," which won an Academy Award; Thomas Stack, Montgomery County Police Department, Maryland, Presentation on investigating human trafficking crimes in Washington Metropolitan area, American University, Washington, DC, November 6, 2006.

particular ascension of sex slavery resides at the intersection of the socio-economic bedlam promoted by economic globalization and a historic, deeply rooted bias against females."[69]

Trafficking most frequently occurs in societies where women lack property rights, cannot inherit land, and do not enjoy equal protection under the law. Yet trafficking also occurs on a significant scale in Eurasia, where women have legal rights and access to education but face discrimination in obtaining jobs, decent wages, and access to capital. During the 1990s, many job advertisements in post-Soviet countries read "only the young and the willing need apply."[70] This requirement forced women to provide sexual services in exchange for employment.

In contrast, in many societies in Africa, Latin America, and parts of Asia, fewer resources are provided for the education, medical care, or overall welfare of female children. Females are the first to be pulled out of school in financial crises such as occurred in the late 1990s and again starting in 2008. As a consequence, female children have fewer options. Frequently, girls and women can obtain employment only in sectors where they are most vulnerable to labor and sexual exploitation, including as domestic servants, carpet weavers, and child care providers.[71] In some countries, the route to prostitution is more direct as girls are viewed as a means for a family's economic advancement.[72] Trafficking their daughters is one way that Southeast Asian families generate funds to make capital improvements to their home and their land.[73]

Women of minority groups or low castes face even more intense discrimination. "Prostitution in South Asia is not primarily a criminal issue, but a social problem caused by extreme underdevelopment and caste discrimination in a strictly hierarchical society."[74] Compounding

[69] Kara, *Sex Trafficking*, 30.

[70] Sally Stoecker, "The Rise in Human Trafficking and the Role of Organized Crime," *Demokratizatsiya* 8, no. 1 (Winter 2000), 129–14; Donna Hughes, "The 'Natasha' Trade: The Transnational Shadow Market of Trafficking in Women," *Journal of International Affairs* 53 (Spring 2000), 625–51; Sally Stoecker, "Human Trafficking: A New Challenge for Russia and the United States," in *Human Traffic and Transnational Crime*, 13–28.

[71] International Labour Organization, *Gender Promotion Program, Preventing Discrimination, Exploitation and Abuse of Women Migrant Workers, An Information Guide: Booklet 6, Trafficking of Women and Girls* (Geneva: ILO); Human Rights Watch/Asia, "Rape for Profit: Trafficking of Nepali Girls and Women to India's Brothels," Human Rights Watch 12, no. 5 (A), 1995.

[72] Asian Development Bank, *Combating Trafficking of Women and Children*, 15.

[73] Interviews with human trafficking specialists in Thailand by author in 1998.

[74] Lintner, "Asia's Sex Trap."

their victimization is that once trafficked, women from low castes or minority groups are provided less assistance than other trafficking victims.[75] Moreover, the Supreme Court of India has failed to protect the rights of prostitutes even when court cases reveal that this exploitation is perpetuated by endemic police corruption.[76]

In Asia, the most vivid example of ethnic discrimination linked to trafficking is the Hill Tribes of Northern Thailand. Stateless and lacking Thai citizenship, they are not granted access to social services, education, or state employment. Compounding their problems is the fact that crop substitution programs introduced in Northern Thailand have failed to provide the income once gained from the cultivation of poppy. Daughters are often sold into prostitution because families cannot survive through legitimate means.[77]

The relationship between discrimination and trafficking is not confined to Asia. Traffickers in Europe also exploit the vulnerability of ethnic and racial minorities. A disproportionate number of the women and minors trafficked from Moldova, an epicenter of European trafficking, are members of the Gagauz and Roma minorities. The Gagauz are a Turkic population, and the Roma in Moldova, as elsewhere, are still subject to intense discrimination and are disproportionately victims of trafficking.[78]

Public Health Causes

The state of public health contributes directly and indirectly to human trafficking. The demographic boom in the developing world, mentioned previously, is a direct result of the control of many of the most deadly contagious diseases. Public health issues contribute to trafficking in more direct ways as well. The most notable impact on trafficking comes from the AIDS epidemic, but increased rates of violence and rising health costs also contribute to increased levels of trafficking.[79]

[75] Ruchira Gupta, "Interview," *Satya*, http://www.satyamag.com/jan05/gupta.html, (accessed June 5, 2006) and personal interviews with her while working as a consultant to her on a USAID project on Southeast Asia in 2004.

[76] Kumar Regmi, "Trafficking into Prostitution in India and the Indian Judiciary," *Intercultural Human Rights Law Review* 1 (2006), 373–406.

[77] David A. Feingold film, *Trading Women*, depicts this problem.

[78] Steve Harvey, "A Europol Perspective on criminal profits and money laundering linked to trafficking in human beings," OSCE-UNODC-Cyprus Regional Operation Meeting on Combating Human Trafficking and Money Laundering in the Mediterranean Region," September 18–19, 2008, Larnaca, Cyprus.

[79] Chris Beyrer and Julie Stachowiak, "Health Consequences of Trafficking of Women and Girls in Southeast Asia," *Brown Journal of World Affairs* 10, no. 1 (Summer/Fall 2003),

When a family cannot raise the money for medical care and medicines, female family members are sometimes trafficked. In the documentary *Sex Slaves*, a young woman from Ukraine is trafficked into prostitution with the hope of earning money to pay for the medical care of a brother suffering from cancer related to the Chernobyl explosion.[80] In the Mekong region of Southeast Asia, girls are sold to traffickers for a defined period of time to provide money for the health care of more senior family members.[81]

Public health problems such as familial violence and sexual abuse of young girls increase susceptibility to trafficking. As previously mentioned, these phenomena have become more frequent in recent decades with the displacements caused by regional conflicts and rural to urban migrations. The traumatic early transition years in the Soviet successor states were also noted by higher rates of familial violence, often directed at women and female children. In the United States, abused American children provide a significant percentage of juvenile trafficking victims. In many countries of North Africa and the Middle East, child prostitutes are seen as public goods and are subject to physical violence.[82] The brutalization of the girl in all societies is often a prelude to the trafficking that follows.[83]

The proliferation of HIV-AIDS has contributed in diverse ways to trafficking. Ironically, although the scourge of AIDS should have led to a decline in trafficking and use of prostitutes, the reverse has occurred. The large numbers of untreated AIDS victims in the developing world has produced many orphans or children with ill or single parents. The social stigma attached to AIDS has made many of these children pariahs within their communities. Children with no healthy family members to support them are ostracized within their communities, increasing their vulnerability to traffickers.

105–17; *Global Eye on Human Trafficking* 4 (2008), 1, http://www.iom.int/jahia/webdav/site/myjahiasite/shared/shared/mainsite/projects/showcase_pdf/global_eye_fourth_issue.pdf (accessed January 12, 2009).

[80] "Sex Slaves" Frontline documentary, http://www.pbs.org/wgbh/pages/frontline/slaves (accessed June 25, 2007).

[81] Economic and Social Commission for Asia and the Pacific, "Sexually Abused and Sexually Exploited Children and Youth in the Greater Mekong Subregion."

[82] Susanne Louis B. Mikhail, "Child Marriage and Child Prostitution: Two Forms of Sexual Exploitation," in *Gender, Trafficking and Slavery*, Rachel Masika, ed. (Oxford: Oxfam, 2002), 48.

[83] Melissa Farley, "Prostitution, Trafficking, and Cultural Amnesia: What We Must *Not Know* in Order to Keep the Business of Sexual Exploitation Running Smoothly," *Yale Journal of Law and Feminism* 18 (2006), 101–36.

The increasing problem of intergenerational prostitution has developed as a result of the spread of AIDS. Trafficked women who die of AIDS often leave behind young children. Orphaned without any contact with living family members, these children are dependent on brothel keepers for their support. Often the brothel keepers maintain the girls and then prostitute them even younger than the age of ten.[84] The sexual slavery of the mother therefore continues on to the succeeding generation. This is particularly common in the brothels of India but is by no means unique to that society.[85]

The spread of AIDS has also contributed to the demand for younger victims, as many customers believe that younger victims are less likely to be carriers of the infection.

The search for younger victims exacerbates the spread of the disease and compounds the probability of youthful victimization. Young trafficked girls are particularly vulnerable to lesions during sexual relations, thereby making them more likely to contract venereal diseases and AIDS.[86] As their symptoms become visible, they are no longer able to serve clients. Therefore, the brothel keepers need to continuously search for new girls to restock their brothels. As a consequence, in Asia trafficking is now extending into regions that previously had been untouched by the problem.[87]

Conclusion

Trafficking is now a preferred crime of both small-scale entrepreneurs and larger crime groups. Counter-trafficking strategies and programs have been insufficient to stem their growth. Traffickers too often can get away with their crimes and in some countries where they operate there are no laws criminalizing their heinous practices. Where laws exist, law enforcement has not prioritized human trafficking, international cooperation to combat this problem is insufficient, and protections are inadequate for victims.

Even though hundreds of millions have now been spent worldwide to support anti-trafficking programs focused on prevention, harmonization of laws, training of law enforcement, and victims' assistance, these are

[84] Gupta, "Interview," and personal interviews with her while working as a consultant to her on a USAID project on Southeast Asia in 2004.

[85] Ibid.

[86] IOM, *Combating Trafficking in South-East Asia*.

[87] Ibid., 17–18.

inadequate measures because trafficking results from deep-seated poverty, the low status of women, and such political forces as long-term violent conflicts. Job creation, especially in the developing world, is not keeping pace with the expanding youthful population. Privatizations such as seen in Mexico and the post-Soviet states left impoverished citizens vulnerable to traffickers.

The global economy with ever more ruthless competition heightens demand for cheap labor that can be obtained only through human exploitation. Human trafficking should continue to flourish because the forces that contributed to its rise continue unabated. Populations continue to grow in the developing world and resources needed to develop these countries and youthful populations still exit to the financial havens of the first world and offshore havens.[88] Far too many of the world's billions of citizens remain disposable people.[89]

Regional conflicts have not diminished. Millions are still displaced rapidly by conflicts as was seen in the Swat Valley in Pakistan in 2009, creating vulnerable people ripe for exploitation. Global warming continues displacing millions from low-lying lands. The trajectory for climate change suggests ever-greater human displacement, thereby aggravating human trafficking in the future.[90]

Human trafficking has flourished in the last two decades, and there is no end in sight. It is a defining problem of the twenty-first century and will reshape the world's populations and the quality of life and governance worldwide.

[88] Raymond W. Baker, *Capitalism's Achilles Heel, Dirty Money and How to Renew the Free-Market System* (Hoboken, NJ: John Wiley & Sons, 2005).

[89] As discussed by Kevin Bales, *Disposable People: New Slavery in the Global Economy* (Berkeley and Los Angeles: University of California Press, 1999).

[90] Kate Romer, "'Environmental' Refugees?" *Forced Migration Review* (May 25, 2006), 61; IOM Policy Brief, "Migration, Climate Change and the Environment," May 2009, http://www.iom.int/jahia/webdav/shared/shared/mainsite/policy_and_research/policy_documents/policy_brief.pdf (accessed August 15, 2009).

2

The Diverse Consequences of Human Trafficking

> No man is an island, every man is a piece of the continent, a part of the main; if a clod be washed away by the sea, Europe is the less, as well as if a promontory were, as well as any manner of thy friends or of thine own were; any man's death diminishes me, because I am involved in mankind. And therefore never send to know for whom the bell tolls; it tolls for thee.
>
> – John Donne

These lines written by Donne four hundred years ago are symbolic, but they capture the present reality of trafficking where many die in dinghies trying to reach the shores of Europe. As Donne understood, those who die are not only the individual victims. All of society is diminished by these losses.

Many analyses of human trafficking focus on the costs of trafficking to the victim. In contrast, this chapter also focuses on the larger societal and political ramifications of this heinous activity without denying the suffering of the victims. The costs of human trafficking are experienced on the individual, community, national, regional, and global level. They affect not only source countries but also transit and host countries. Trafficking impacts both democratic and authoritarian states and countries in transition and in conflict. Trafficking challenges states' control over their borders and their ability to determine who will reside on their territory. It undermines states because trafficking can survive only with the corruption and complicity of governmental officials. In some countries, as has been documented in Thailand, the profits from trafficking help fund political parties and campaigns.[1]

[1] Pasuk Phongpaichit, Sangsit Phiriyarangsan, and Nualnoi Treerat, *Guns, Girls, Gambling, Ganja: Thailand's Illegal Economy and Public Policy* (Chiang Mai: Silkworm, 1998).

Yet trafficking undermines human as well as political security. Human security, as defined by the United Nations, requires that citizens have security in their daily lives from such constant threats as "massive population movements, infectious disease and long term conditions of oppression and deprivation."[2] Yet victims of human trafficking often suffer hunger, are more frequently victims of HIV/AIDS and their very existence is defined by repression and every known form of deprivation. Therefore, human trafficking violates the defining elements of human security.

Enormous attention has been paid in the scholarly community and the mass media to the broader consequences of the drug trade, but this type of analysis has not been applied sufficiently to the phenomenon of human trafficking. This chapter looks at the violations of human security as well as the political, demographic, social, labor, and health costs associated with the rise of human trafficking. Some of these costs of human trafficking resemble those of the drug trade – widespread violations of human rights, the spread of disease, and the destruction of communities. But some consequences are distinctive including demographic decline, depression of wages, humiliation of women, and many forms of gender-based victimization.

Social Consequences

Impact on the Individual and the Community

The consequences of trafficking for the victims, their families, and communities are severe and diverse. Once trafficked, and thereby exploited and harmed, an individual's future opportunities in life are often very limited. Trafficked children are deprived of the opportunity of obtaining an education at a crucial age and they suffer psychological scars that may never heal and may prevent them from functioning in society as they mature. Teenagers and women trafficked for both sexual and labor exploitation are sometimes deprived of the opportunity of marriage or of having children. Men trafficked as laborers face years without family life and may suffer pain from work-related injuries. Trafficked males who cannot return or send money home place family members in a vulnerable situation, making remaining family members ripe for exploitation.

[2] Jan van Dijk, Officer in Charge, Human Security Branch, Vienna, April 1–2, 2004, Speech "Human Security: A New Agenda for Integrated Global Action," www.unodic.org/unodc/en/ about-unodc/speeches/speech_2004–04-01_1.html (accessed April 6, 2010).

Families that have lost children and youths to traffickers may be permanently traumatized and experience a profound sense of loss. Trafficking done by friends and family members, an all too frequent occurrence, weakens or destroys familial and community bonds, particularly in tight-knit communities. Those left behind feel betrayed. Close relatives suffer from guilt and despair at having failed to protect their offspring and from a fear that they will never see them again.

Families that have paid smugglers only to have the family member trafficked may experience financial and physical pressure from the trafficker that destroys family health and community solidarity. This occurs particularly among Chinese, with those smuggling the individual to the United States, Canada, or Europe closely linked to the family back in China.[3]

The importation of trafficked women into a community such as occurred in the Balkans after the arrival of the UN peacekeepers has many unforeseen repercussions. Sexual services become more available in the commercial market, affecting the quality of relations in the family and in couples who have yet to be married. As exemplified by the situation in Bosnia-Herzegovina, family breakdowns and divorces become more frequent.[4]

Increased numbers of illegal migrants and trafficked peoples in an area may result in increased discrimination and hostility toward ethnic and racial minorities. For example, trafficked workers from Central Asia who are in Russia doing construction work receive low or no pay and provide labor competition to domestic workers. Russian laborers at the low end of the pay scale perceive the migrants and trafficked workers as competition, fueling their already existing prejudice against these new arrivals from Moslem Central Asia. This antagonism all too often results in serious violence.[5] In the United States, Minutemen, a right-wing militia group, have shot migrants attempting to cross from Mexico into the United States.[6]

[3] Ko-lin Chin, *Chinatown Gangs: Extortion, Enterprise and Ethnicity* (New York and Oxford: Oxford University Press, 1996), 159.

[4] "Trafficking, Slavery and Peacekeeping: The Need for a Comprehensive Training Program," UNICRI, May 9–10, 2002, http://policy-traccc.gmu.edu/publications/TIP&PKO_EWG_Report_Final.pdf (accessed August 15, 2009).

[5] Jane Buchanan, "Are You Happy to Cheat US? Exploitation of Migrant Construction Workers in Russia," February 10, 2009, http://www.hrw.org/en/reports/2009/02/09/are-you-happy-cheat-us-0 (accessed August 18, 2009).

[6] http://www.minutemanproject.com/organization/about_us.asp (accessed August 18, 2008); Robert Lovato, "Minutemen Mobilizes Whites Left Behind by Globalization"

Today, few female victims of sexual trafficking are repatriated after being trafficked because of the limited chances of rescue and the significant costs for transport home. Those who do return may be an enormous burden to their communities. In Egypt, girls who were married to Middle East visitors and are returned to their villages cannot be supported or remarried. Many are retrafficked.[7] Victims return to many locales with severe psychological and health problems that their home communities cannot afford to treat. In Asia, girls and women return to their rural villages addicted to alcohol and drugs after a fast-paced urban life. Without treatment programs at home for their addictions, the victims often spread the problem of drug abuse to neighbors and family members.

Women and girls who are sexually trafficked suffer a wide range of victimization. Many young women who resist their traffickers die each year, as evidenced by the dozens of skeletons of young women found in a pit in 2007 in Nizhyi Tagil in the Urals region of Russia.[8] Before being sold to clients, women and girls may be beaten and tortured by their traffickers to break their will. In some countries, girls who refuse to serve sexual clients even though they are ill may be subject to torture, as discussed in Chapter 5 in reference to Cambodia. Eastern European criminals have tortured women and girls to death in front of others to induce compliance.

Other forms of victimization are common. Many are stigmatized by their communities even though their victimization is not their fault.[9] In one study, nearly all victims "reported being threatened by their traffickers with death, beatings, increased debt, harm to their children and families or re-trafficking."[10] The threat of being resold to a worse trafficker who

Public Eye Magazine (Winter 2005), http://www.publiceye.org/magazine/v19n3/lovato_fringe.html (accessed June 25, 2007); Bruce W. Nelan, "Racisme," *Time*, June 24, 2001, http://www.time.com/time/magazine/article/0,9171,157646,00.html (accessed June 25, 2007).

7 Interview with Egyptian representative at OSCE-UNODC-Cyprus Regional Operational Meeting in Combating Human Trafficking and Money Laundering in the Mediterranean Rim Region, September 18–19, 2008, Larnaca, Cyprus.

8 Na Urale nashli tainoe zahoronenie seks-rabyn," *Komsomolskaya Pravda*, 2 February 2007, http://kp.ru/daily/23848.4/62919/ (accessed February 5, 2007); Valentina Blinova, "Proshchanie," *Ogonek* 7 (February 12–18, 2007), 18–20.

9 Richard Danziger, Jonathan Martens, and Mariela Guajardo, " Human Trafficking and Migration Management in the Security Sector and Counter-Trafficking," in *Strategies Against Human Trafficking: The Role of the Security Sector*, ed. Cornelius Friesendorf (Vienna: National Defence Academy and Austrian Ministry of Defence and Sport, 2009), 289.

10 *Trafficking in Persons Report 2008* (Washington, DC: U.S. Department of State, 2008), 21.

would increase their debt is also often used to intimidate women and force compliance. Unfortunately, these threats are carried out with such frequency that the victims take them seriously.

Once engaged in prostitution, trafficked women and girls employed in brothels throughout the world are often forced to serve as many as thirty clients a day during a 12-to 14-hour work day. No days off are provided for menstruation or illness. Unlike the women working in the regulated brothels of some Western European countries who can require their clients to use condoms, trafficked women are often denied the right to protect themselves. In certain regions of the world, such as India and Africa, where rates of HIV transmission are particularly high among sex workers, mortality often occurs at a very young age.[11] Often the trafficked women leave behind young children whose mothers' early deaths leave the children no means of survival outside of the brothels where they are raised. Falling into the hands of the brothel keepers or pimps who controlled their now deceased mothers, these children have no futures outside of the world of begging, forced prostitution, or crime.

Many victims who have been sexually trafficked, if they survive, are permanently psychologically damaged, suffering posttraumatic stress, painful flashbacks anxiety, fear, incapacitating insomnia, depression, sleep disorders, and panic attacks as a result of the conditions described above.[12] For many others loss of appetite, uncontrolled aggression, self-blame, thoughts of suicide, self-harm, and constant crying are common symptoms. One woman articulately summed up her feelings "I feel like they have taken my smile and I can never have it back."[13]

The violent abuse is not limited to women trafficked into sexual servitude. Women sold into domestic servitude may be subject to severe beatings or food deprivation, and may be locked inside homes for years on end. They may be forced to work long hours without breaks. They may also be subject to sexual abuse by male family members of the households in which they work. In many parts of the world, they have no recourse

[11] Kathryn Farr, *Sex Trafficking: The Global Market in Women and Children* (New York: Worth Publishers, 2005), 228–30.

[12] *Trafficking in Persons Report 2005* (Washington, DC: U.S. Department of State, 2005), 14.

[13] Cathy Zimmerman et al. "Stolen Smiles: A Summary Report on the Physical Psychological Health Consequences of Women and Adolescents Trafficking in Europe," London School of Hygiene and Tropical Medicine, 2006, http://www.eaves4women.co.uk/POPPY_Project/ Documents/Recent_Reports/Stolen%20smiles-OSCE%20version%20Final.pdf (accessed May 19, 2008).

because there are no labor laws to protect them. In some countries, their illegal status deprives them of any legal rights.

Women may be trafficked into marriage to men they do not want to marry. For example, women who escape from North Korea into China may be trafficked into marriages with Chinese men,[14] and Hmong refugees import women to the United States as second wives.[15] In both the Chinese and the American cases, the women are not really wives but often merely domestic slaves who are vehicles for reproduction.

Women and men trafficked to work in factories can be locked in at night to prevent their escape. Physical abuse is meted out in these enterprises to those who fail to produce goods at the high production norms established by the factory owners. Compounding the victimization, many of the factories that abuse workers have unsafe equipment or toxic fumes that will later cause fatal illnesses.

Children are trafficked into particular industries where their small size allows them to perform more effectively. For example, in Nepal, girls and boys are trafficked into the carpet industry because their small fingers enable them to weave intricate designs. While engaged in carpet weaving, they may be sexually abused. Therefore, the labor trafficking may be only the initial form of exploitation, as the children may be subsequently trafficked into full-time sexual slavery.[16] Small boys in Ghana are trafficked to tend fishing nets.[17]

Children trafficked as beggars are beaten and deprived of food if they do not bring home sufficient money each day. In India, the beggar mafia deliberately maims children to make them better beggars, often with the complicity of members of the medical profession.[18] This phenomenon has

[14] UNFPA, "Women and International Migration," in *State of World's Population 2006*, http://www.unfpa.org/swp/2006/english/notes/notes_for_indicators2.html (accessed 9 June 2007).

[15] Minnesota Office of Justice Programs and Minnesota Statistical Analysis Center, "Human Trafficking in Minnesota: A Report to the Minnesota Legislature," September 2006.

[16] ILO/IPEC, "Helping Hands or Shackled Lives: Understanding Domestic Child Domestic Labour and Responses to It," Geneva, June 2004, http://www.ilo.org/public/libdoc/ilo/2004/104B09_138.engl.pdf (accessed January 11, 2009).

[17] Raggie Johansen, "Child Trafficking in Ghana," http://www.unodc.org/newsletter/en/perspectives/0601/page002.html (accessed August 7, 2009).

[18] "CNN-IBN and DIG exposed the Beggar Mafia in India," July 31, 2006, http://www.indiantelevision.com/release/y2k6/july/julyrel67.htm (accessed May 19, 2009); discussion of Indian doctors caught on film offering to maim children and adults for begging with payment offered by the begging mafia, http://www.bio-medicine.org/medicine-news/Maimed-Conscience – and-Maimed-Beggars–28Medical-Ethics-in-India-29–u2013-Part–12794–4 (accessed August 18, 2008).

also recently been observed in Great Britain with beggar children from Eastern Europe.[19]

In Africa and Latin America, children are trafficked as child soldiers. Forced to bear arms and even kill family members, they are traumatized by the violence to which they are exposed and in which they are forced to participate. In many conflict regions, young girls and women are forced into brothels to provide sexual services for the peacekeepers. In refugee camps in conflict regions, as previously stated, some children are forced to exchange sex with the peacekeepers to obtain food that they need for their daily survival, compounding their psychological trauma.[20]

Women and girls may suffer secondary victimization even if they are rescued from those who originally exploited them, as they may be treated badly even by advanced Western democracies. Often rapidly deported without medical or psychological treatment, they may quickly be retrafficked, a common fate in many source regions.

Demographic Consequences

Human trafficking has devastating demographic consequences in many regions of the world as it deprives societies of women of childbearing age. The situation is particularly acute in many of the former socialist states, which were already facing demographic crises and are epicenters of sexual trafficking. Moldova, Ukraine, and Russia have lost hundreds of thousands of women to sexual and labor trafficking.[21] Women from these post-Soviet states do not give birth to children in their own countries because they are trafficked abroad. Many of them are unlikely to return, but if they do, they may not prove to be suitable and effective mothers because of the psychological traumas they have experienced. In the villages of the Hill Tribes of Northern Thailand, sources of many trafficked women, there are many communities without any young women between 15 and 25. Yet demographic loss from

[19] Steven Harvey, "A Europol Perspective on Criminal Profits and Money Laundering Linked to Trafficking in Human Beings," OSCE-UNODC-Cyprus Regional Operational Meeting.

[20] UN Ousts Peacekeepers in Sex Case, *New York Times*, November 3, 2007, http://query.nytimes.com/gst/fullpage.html?res=9800E5D61439F930A35752C1A9619C8B63&fta=y (accessed May 19, 2009); "Peacekeeping and Sex Abuse: Who Will Watch the Watchmen?" *The Economist*, May 29, 2008, http://www.economist.com/world/international/displaystory.cfm?story_id=11458241 (accessed May 19, 2009).

[21] Donna Hughes, "The 'Natasha' Trade: The Transnational Shadow Market of Trafficking in Women," *Journal of International Affairs* 53 (Spring 2000), 625–51.

trafficking is not confined to women, as smuggling victims from Asia, Latin America, and Africa may become victims of trafficking. Whole villages in Southern China are literally drained of people, and parts of Mexico are without youthful males.[22] Those left behind often have difficulty surviving.

Political Consequences

The political consequences of human trafficking are many and diverse. Trafficking undermines democracy, rule of law, and accountability of governments. The corruption that facilitates trafficking undermines governance. Profits from the sale of human beings by warring parties in conflict regions, as previously mentioned, help perpetuate conflicts. Furthermore, the presence of illegal migrants and trafficked people can decrease the internal stability of countries. Traffickers can also pose a direct threat to national security by moving terrorists along with the people they seek to exploit.

Human trafficking not only undermines traditional concepts of human rights. An important and unrecognized consequence of trafficking is that it represents a new form of authoritarianism. Whereas in the past authoritarianism was based on the state's monopoly of violence, this new authoritarianism, resulting in coercion of individuals, does not originate from the state. Traffickers, unlike slave traders in the past, do not have charters or permits from the government.

Trafficking as a New Form of Authoritarianism

Trafficking represents a new form of authoritarianism in which individuals are subject to coercion and control outside of the state. State officials such as border patrol members, customs officials, law enforcement officers, and members of the security apparatus are often trafficking facilitators, but they participate in this repression for personal gain and not in the interests of the employers. States, as evidenced by their signature of the UN protocol against trafficking, have affirmed their opposition to trafficking. No state, other than North Korea, has a deliberate state policy to traffic their citizens, although some, through their inaction and complacency, facilitate trafficking.[23]

[22] Patrick Radden Keefe, *The Snakehead: An Epic Tale of the Chinatown Underworld and the American Dream* (New York: Doubleday, 2009), 249.

[23] North Korea is rated in the third and lowest tier by the U.S. State Department for failing to address trafficking. Russian government officials in the Far East stated that they would

This new authoritarianism is not the result of a state ideology such as fascism or communism or the personal authoritarianism of an individual dictator.[24] Rather, it is a consequence of the growth of the global illicit economy and the rise of powerful transnational crime groups, linked to but not part of the state. These groups are not, however, controlled by the states. Yet the consequences for the victims of sexual or labor trafficking are often the same as those in an authoritarian state – an absence of legal rights, a legal system that does not protect the individual, and often frequent and extreme mental and physical abuse of the person.

One of the central features of an authoritarian society is that the state has a monopoly on the forces of coercion and abuses this power to enforce compliance.[25] This coercion is exercised most often against individuals who oppose the political or economic interests of the state, or come from undesired minorities. It is the discretionary use of violence and the absence of available remedies that set democratic and authoritarian states apart.

Trafficking victims may resemble victims of state abuse, as they are subject to torture or other extreme forms of intimidation and are deprived of freedom of movement. Even though they are not intimidated by the state, they often have very limited means to counter the abuse they face. Defined as "others," "prostitutes," or "illegal migrants," they are stigmatized and denied equal rights, sometimes even in societies where they may be citizens.[26] Foreign victims are often deported from the country where they were trafficked, thereby denied recourse against those who have persecuted and exploited them. Therefore, like the residents of an authoritarian state, they have no ability to protect themselves from their abusers.

This new authoritarianism can occur even in democratic states that do not prioritize counter-trafficking, as these governments emphasize traditional national security concerns over those of human security.

not have more workers from North Korea as the government was not paying them and collecting all their wages for their work in Russia.

[24] Louise Shelley, "Transnational Organized Crime: The New Authoritarianism," in *Illicit Global Economy and State Power*, H. Richard Friman and Peter Andreas, eds. (Lanham, MD: Rowman and Littlefield, 1999), 25–51.

[25] Hannah Arendt, *Eichmann in Jerusalem: A Report on the Banality of Evil* (Hammondsworth, NY: Penguin, 1977).

[26] Jana Arsovska and Stef Janssens, "Policing and Human Trafficking: Good and Bad Practices," in Friesendorf, *Strategies Against Human Trafficking*, 203.

The Impact of Trafficking on Democracy

Trafficking destroys the central tenets of democracy. Illegal immigrants trafficked for sexual exploitation or labor are now pervasive throughout most of the developed world, including the United States and Canada, Western Europe, Japan, and Australia. These individuals, subject to terrible abuse and often outside the reach of both criminal and civil justice system, undermine the quality of democracy.

Democracies establish the right to protection under the law, guarantee human freedom, and establish rights of citizens. But human trafficking victims, by virtue of their status, are often not citizens of their country of residence. Although as Chapter 8 on the United States reveals, there are many youthful victims of sexual trafficking who are citizens. Yet many democratic societies, through their lack of protections for trafficking victims, have allowed mass violations of human rights to occur within their countries.

Despite the fact that all democratic countries are signatories of the UN protocol on trafficking that defines trafficked people as "victims," many democratic states have not changed their laws or procedures to protect the rights of trafficked persons.[27] Moreover, even in countries where needed laws have been adopted, the allocated resources or the enforcement mechanisms needed to protect trafficking victims are absent. In some countries, protection is predicated on the victim's agreement to participate in a criminal investigation against their traffickers. Yet many states have inadequate witness protection programs for the victims and have no provisions to protect the families of the trafficking victims in their home country who may be endangered by the testimony of the trafficking victim.[28] Therefore, with few countries granting residence permits to those who have testified against their traffickers, cooperation with law enforcement may mean a death sentence for the victim of his/her family members.[29]

Illustrative of this are the policies that operate in Italy. "In Italy, victims are granted a six-month permit to stay to consider their options and prepare themselves to go back to their homeland. But they often risk being detained and deported shortly after being discovered or coming

[27] http://www.unodc.org/unodc/en/treaties/CTOC/countrylist-traffickingprotocol.html provides a list of the countries that have signed the protocol on trafficking (accessed August 18, 2009).

[28] Cornelius Friesendorf, "Introduction," in Friesendorf, *Strategies Against Human Trafficking*, 27.

[29] Barbara Limanowska and Helga Konrad, "Problems of Anti-Trafficking Cooperation," in Friesendorf, *Strategies Against Human Trafficking*, 462–63.

forward."[30] Therefore, they face a double vulnerability. Cooperation can lead to immediate deportation. Yet, even with cooperation, there is only a six-month reprieve[31] from return to an environment where they may face life threats or retrafficking. Such treatment undermines the fundamental principles of a democracy – justice and accountability under the law – as traffickers can easily get away with their crimes.

Democratic societies do not allow residents to sell themselves into slavery. Yet slavery is perpetuated in democratic societies because trafficking victims have debts that are unenforceable under the civil legal system but that govern their lives. This is the case of both individuals who are smuggled who have a debt as a result of a consensual relationship with their smuggler and trafficking victims who are told that they have a debt to repay to their trafficker. These debts are so real to their victims that there are reported cases of Nigerian, Chinese, and other victims in democratic countries who return to their exploiters after having been liberated from their traffickers.[32] This occurs because the debts to traffickers are unfortunately enforceable because police and courts in democratic societies cannot protect trafficking victims from the international enforcement networks of the transnational criminals.

Democratic societies have made enormous efforts to develop labor, health, and occupational standards and policies to ensure the protection of workers at their workplace. This is particularly true of the mature Western democracies and, in particular, the social welfare states of Western Europe. The rise of human trafficking contradicts the values and interests of these societies by denying workers a healthy labor environment. An enormous discrepancy exists between the professed values of the democratic societies and the daily existence of trafficking victims who labor within them. Trafficking victims, as discussed later, rarely have access to the labor protections of the larger society.

Later chapters on Europe and the United States will provide many other illustrations of the principles of democracy contravened by human trafficking. These include analyses of widespread trafficking of women for sexual exploitation in Europe from Africa, Latin America, Eurasia,

[30] Francesca Bosco, Vittoria Luda di Cortemiglia, and Anvar Serojitdinov, "Human Trafficking Patterns," in Friesendorf, *Strategies Against Human Trafficking*, 75.

[31] Ibid.

[32] See, for example, Wenchi Yu Perkins, Congressional-Executive Commission on China, "Combating Human Trafficking in China: Domestic and International Efforts," March 6, 2006, http://www.cecc.gov/pages/hearings/2006/20060306/WenchiYuPerkins.php?PHPSESSID=a434a44f109dac260f724aadb19b802c (accessed July 1, 2008).

and Asia; gun battles in the United States to capture illegal immigrants and enslave them; and the forced begging by children in many cities of Europe.[33] All of these reveal the incapacity of democratic states to protect the principles of the society from the increasing violations of rights committed by human traffickers.

Trafficking, Conflict States, and Terrorism

As Chapter 1 revealed, regional conflicts provide many trafficking victims through destruction of communities, deprivation of land, and the death of family members. Yet human trafficking is key in the perpetuation of conflict, as captured children provide soldiers, kidnapped and trafficked girls are given as rewards to victors in battle, and the sale of victims helps provide funding to buy arms and maintain soldiers.

Different forms of violent political action are funded by human trafficking. Yet the role of human traffickers in funding insurgents, guerillas, and terrorists is much less known than in reference to their counterparts in the drug trade. The traditional practice of trafficking girls from Nepal to the brothels of India has been taken over by Nepalese insurgents to fund their insurgency against the state.[34] The ideology of these Marxist guerillas should preclude them from exploiting their fellow human beings. Yet their political objectives outweigh their ideology. The Nepalese situation has parallels with the situation in Taliban-dominated Afghanistan, where the mullahs for many of the Taliban years tolerated the drug trade because it supported their own goals, even though drug abuse violates the Koran.[35]

[33] See, for example, Pat Flannery, "Shootout over Migrants Shows Danger to Public: Last of Kidnappers Face Sentencing," *Arizona Republic*, July 9, 2001, http://usinfo.state.gov/eap/Archive_Index/reprint3.html (accessed June 25, 2007); Paul Charlton, Statement to the U.S. Senate, Committee on the Judiciary, March 1, 2006, http://kyl.senate.gov/legis_center/subdocs/030106_Kyl.pdf (accessed June 25, 2007).

[34] US. Department of State, Country Reports on Human Rights Practices – Nepal, http://www.state.gov/g/drl/rls/hrrpt/2005/61709.htm (accessed June 10, 2007); "Human trafficking has some link with terrorism," Ganguly, *The Hindu*, December 7, 2008 http://www.hindu.com/2008/12/07/stories/2008120760161000.htm (accessed August 8, 2009); Francisco E. Thoumi, *Political Economy and Illegal Drugs in Colombia* (Boulder, CO: L. Rienner, 1995); Rensselaer W. Lee III, *White Labyrinth: Cocaine and Political Power* (New Brunswick, NJ: Transaction Publishers, 1989); Bertil Lintner, *Burma in Revolt: Opium and Insurgency since 1948* (Boulder, CO: Westview Press, 1994); Kairat Osmonaliev, "*Developing Counter-Narcotics Policy in Central Asia: Legal and Political Dimensions*," Silk Road Paper, January 2005, http://www.silkroadstudies.org/Silkroadpapers/Osmonaliev.pdf (accessed June 26, 2007).

[35] Tamara Makarenko, "Crime, Terror and the Central Asian Drug Trade," *Harvard Asia Quarterly* 6, no. 3 (2002).

In northern Uganda, a terrorist insurgent group, the Lord's Resistance Army, abducted young children from villages to serve as soldiers and sex slaves. More than 12,000 children have been abducted since 2002, and many have fallen into sexual slavery. There is no effective state in this conflict region, which helps explain the unimpeded human trafficking.[36] In neighboring Sudan, "children are unlawfully conscripted, at times through abduction, and utilized by armed rebel groups – including all SLA factions, the Popular Defense Forces, Janjaweed militia, and Chadian opposition forces – in Sudan's ongoing conflict in Darfur, the Sudanese Armed Forces and associated militia also continue to exploit young children in this region,"[37]

In Europe as well, human smuggling and trafficking provide support for terrorist groups. The PKK out of Turkey funds much of its activities through such crimes as drug dealing, extortion, and human smuggling.[38] A member of Hezbollah confined in a Viennese prison was observed running a sex trafficking ring by means of his cell phone. Because the terrorist's true identity was disguised through false documentation, the criminal actors who procured the women would not know that the trafficker provided funding for a terrorist organization.

Trafficking and conflict intersect in other ways. The Taliban placed restrictions on Afghan women but preyed on minority women who were trafficked as rewards for fighters.

> ... the conquering Taliban. Now it is clear from the testimony of witnesses and officials of the new government that the ruling clerics systematically abducted women from the Tajik, Uzbek, Hazara and other ethnic minorities they defeated. Stolen women were a reward for victorious battle. And in the cities of Kabul, Mazar-i-Sharif, Jalalabad and Khost, women victims tell of being forced to wed Taliban soldiers and Pakistani and Arab fighters of Osama bin Laden's al-Qaeda network, who later abandoned them. These marriages were tantamount to legalized rape. "They sold these girls," says Ahmad Jan, the Kabul police chief. "The girls were dishonored and then discarded."[39]

[36] *Trafficking in Persons Report 2005*, 216–17.

[37] *Trafficking in Persons Report 2008*, 232.

[38] Abdulkadir Onay, "PKK Criminal Networks and Fronts in Europe." February 21, 2008, Policy Watch no. 1344. http://www.washingtoninstitute.org/templateC05.php?CID=2720 (accessed August 8, 2009).

[39] Tim McGirk "Lifting the Veil on Taliban Sex Slavery," *Time*, February 10, 2002, http://www.time.com/time/magazine/article/0,9171,1101020218-201892,00.html (accessed August 8, 2009).

This practice has not stopped with the resurgence of the Taliban as an IOM report from 2008 reveals. Human beings, particularly women, as in the past, are the spoils of war.[40]

There has been speculation that potential terrorists have used the human smuggling networks of the MS-13 who operate on the U.S.–Mexican border to facilitate their entry into the United States.[41] Serious corruption problems detected on the U.S.–Mexican border by the Inspector General's office of the Department of Homeland Security could help facilitate this movement that has grave national security implications for the United States.

Health Consequences

Trafficking victims die, become seriously ill, or are injured in many locales around the world each year as a result of the hazardous work conditions in which they labor, the abuse of their traffickers and their clients, and their sheer physical exhaustion. For many who are impaired, there are no effective treatments, as they are psychologically damaged for life, suffering frequent nightmares and flashbacks and manifesting suicidal tendencies.[42] The constant abuse, violence, and intimidation they have suffered make it nearly impossible for them to return to normal lives. As one official at the International Organization for Migration in Moldova explained, they can repair the broken jaws and bones but they cannot mend the often irreparable psychological effects.[43]

Research in Great Britain reveals that women who had stopped engaging in prostitution had the same levels of mental health problems (40 percent) and drug addiction (73 percent) as those who remained in the sex industry. This is consistent with posttraumatic stress disorder. These data affirm the insight of the IOM official in Moldova that the damage may be permanent, even in a society such as the United Kingdom, where those engaged in prostitution would have greater

[40] "Trafficking in Persons in Afghanistan Field Survey Report" Kabul, IOM, June 2008, 21, http://www.iom.int/jahia/webdav/shared/shared/mainsite/activities/countries/docs/afghanistan/iom_report_trafficking_afghanistan.pdf (accessed August 8, 2009).

[41] Thomas Davidson, "Terrorism and Human Smuggling Rings in South and Central America," November 18, 2005, *Terrorism Monitor* 3, no. 22, http://www.jamestown.org/single/?no_cache=1&tx_ttnews[tt_news]=611 (accessed August 8, 2009).

[42] Bosco, di Cortemiglia, Serojitdinov, "Human Trafficking Patterns," 75.

[43] Interview with IOM official employed in Moldova, interview in Chisinau, July 2004.

access to medical care than most trafficked into the sex industry.[44] Addiction to alcohol and drugs, sometimes imposed on the victim by the trafficker, impairs and shortens their lives. These conditions contribute to the untimely demise of youthful U.S. trafficking victims, who often survive only seven years after they have been trafficked into prostitution.[45]

Hundreds of victims die annually of dehydration while attempting to cross the deserts from Mexico into the United States. Others die in transit, as previously mentioned, in overcrowded vans or unseaworthy boats before they reach their destinations. Every year young women who resist their traffickers die, such as the Afghan girls who jump into wells rather than be trafficked.[46] Others die from HIV contracted through unprotected sex, as victims have no possibility to protect themselves in their sexual encounters, or access to life-prolonging drugs. In the trafficking culture, their lives are cheaper than the cost of medication. An unknown number of sex trafficking victims are killed by their customers.

Limited research has been done of the longevity of trafficking victims. But research conducted in the United States on mortality of prostitutes reveals a high likelihood of premature death. As researchers explained,

> To our knowledge, no population of women studied previously has had a crude mortality rate, standardized mortality ratio, or percentage of deaths due to murder even approximating those observed in our cohort. The workplace homicide rate for prostitutes (204 per 100,000) is many times higher than that for women and men in the standard occupations that had the highest workplace homicide rates in the United States during the 1980s (4 per 100,000 for female liquor store workers and 29 per 100,000 for male taxicab drivers).[47]

This fate is hardly unique. "A Canadian commission found that the death rate of women in prostitution was forty times higher than that of the general population. A study of Vancouver prostitution reported a

[44] H. Ward and S. Day, "What Happens to Women Who Sell Sex? Report of a Unique Occupational Cohort," *Sexually Transmitted Infections* 82 (2006), 413–17.

[45] FBI powerpoint, "Innocence Lost Initiative," http://courts.michigan.gov/scao/services/CWS/AWOLP/FBI.pdf (accessed August 17, 2008).

[46] IOM, "Trafficking in Persons in Afghanistan," Field Survey Report, Kabul, 2008. http://www.iom.int/jahia/webdav/shared/shared/mainsite/activities/countries/docs/afghanistan/iom_report_trafficking_afghanistan.pdf (accessed August 19, 2009).

[47] John J. Potterat, Devon D. Brewer , Stephen Q. Muth, Richard B. Rothenberg, Donald E. Woodhouse, John B. Muth, Heather K. Stites, and Stuart Brody, "Mortality in a Long-term Open Cohort of Prostitute Women," *American Journal of Epidemiology* (2004), 159, 778–85, http://aje.oxfordjournals.org/cgi/content/full/159/8/778 (accessed August 8, 2009).

36 percent incidence of attempted murder."[48]One can presume that the rates of mortality are higher among trafficking victims than those among all prostitutes, as trafficking victims have the least control over their fates and are harmed regularly by both their traffickers and their customers. The epidemiologists found that their research on the high death rates of prostitutes was consistent with work done by their colleagues in London and in Nairobi, Kenya.[49]

Human trafficking has other health costs for the victim that are enduring but not as permanent as death. Many victims of sex trafficking become pregnant. They are often forced by their traffickers to have abortions to continue serving clients without interruption and are frequently rendered sterile by the unsanitary conditions under which the abortions are performed or the frequency of their occurrence.[50]

Children maimed to be beggars suffer from injuries that cannot be repaired. Unset broken limbs may result in permanently crippled arms and legs. In more extreme cases, limbs that are surgically removed for children to be more pitiful beggars can never be reattached nor sight returned to blinded children. Handicapped children who are exploited as beggars may be forced to beg in the sun without water, causing dehydration and other serious strains on their already weakened bodies.[51]

Organ trafficking may benefit the rich, who can acquire organs, but it leaves those who have been deprived of organs a precarious future. Those whose organs are trafficked are the very poor, often women.[52] Individuals who agree to sell or are deceived into selling their organs face multiple health consequences. First, as the traffickers' interests are in extracting the organ for sale, they care little or nothing about the recovery of the voluntary or forced organ donor. Therefore, many who have lost their organs to organ traffickers are unpaid for their losses and, therefore, are unable to pay for needed postoperative care.[53] Moreover, the sources of

[48] Melissa Farley, "Prostitution, Trafficking, and Cultural Amnesia: What We Must *Not Know* in Order to Keep the Business of Sexual Exploitation Running Smoothly" *Yale Journal of Law and Feminism* 18 (2006), 107.

[49] Potterat et al.

[50] Bosco, di Cortemiglia, Serojitdinov, "Human Trafficking Patterns," in Friesendorf, *Strategies Against Human Trafficking*, 74; H. Ward and S. Day, "What Happens to Women Who Sell Sex? "

[51] This latter problem was observed by the author in St. Petersburg in the early 2000s.

[52] In India, those who sell organs are often street vendors. In Nigeria, they are from rural areas, Alexis A. Aronowitz, *Human Trafficking, Human Misery: The Global Trade in Human Beings* (Westport, CT and London: Praeger, 2009),116; Nancy Scheper-Hughes and Loïc Wacquant, eds., *Commodifying Bodies* (London: Sage, 2002.

[53] Aronowitz, *Human Trafficking, Human Misery*, 120.

the trafficked organs are provided totally inadequate postoperative care, often rendering those who have lost kidneys and other organs invalids for life. Some of them are plagued by postoperative infections that make them unable to return to work and a burden to their families and communities. Others face serious psychological problems after surgery.

Those who receive organs from criminal suppliers may receive diseased organs or organs that are an inappropriate match for their bodies. Still others may receive other life-threatening problems such as AIDS or blood diseases that accompany organs that are obtained outside of regulated channels. The World Health Organization estimates that 10 percent of the 70,000 kidneys used annually in transplants are obtained on the black market.[54] This figure suggests that as many as 14,000 donors and recipients annually may suffer severe health problems as a result of organ trafficking.

The rate of accidents among trafficked laborers is particularly high because they work in the most dangerous conditions and for very long hours. Therefore, their exhaustion and their work environment make trafficked workers particularly prone to serious accidents. In many societies, they cannot receive treatment and become invalids. In the United Arab Emirates, young boys who were trafficked to be camel jockeys died or were seriously injured from this dangerous work.[55] In the United States, uninsured trafficked laborers often arrive at the emergency rooms of hospitals. Their acute injuries often require expensive medical care that is not compensated by the employer of the illegal laborer.[56] In less affluent societies or countries without public hospitals that provide care to all, trafficking victims may be permanently incapacitated or simply die. Such victims are referred to as "disposable people" by Kevin Bales because there is no concern for keeping trafficked people functional or healthy.[57]

Human trafficking affects more than individual victims. It has far-reaching and underappreciated health effects that undermine global health. Trafficked individuals are often transported very long distances in abysmal conditions. For example, Chinese smugglers often ship their human cargo in the holds of vessels where there is inadequate ventilation and food. Many of those smuggled contract diseases such as tuberculosis

[54] *Trafficking in Persons Report 2009*, 17.

[55] *Trafficking in Persons Report 2005*, 218–20.

[56] Jennifer Gordon, *Suburban Sweatshops: The Fight for Immigrant Rights* (Cambridge, MA: Belknap Press of Harvard University Press, 2005).

[57] Kevin Bales, *Disposable People: New Slavery in the Global Economy* (Berkeley and Los Angeles: University of California Press, 1999).

and scabies. Neither in transit nor on arrival in their country of destination are they provided health care or access to the medicines needed to cure their diseases.[58] This is particularly problematic among smuggled Chinese, who are often forced to work off their debt through employment in Chinese restaurants, where they become vectors for the spread of disease in their new communities.

Chapter 1 discussed the role of AIDS in the growth of human trafficking. But trafficking also contributes to the spread of AIDS. The health consequences of human trafficking are particularly severe in the sexual arena. Many victims of sex trafficking, unlike those in government-regulated brothels, are not allowed to protect themselves in their sexual encounters. Consequently, trafficked women, girls, and boys are at great risk to contract venereal disease, which compounds the risk of becoming HIV positive. In one epidemiological study in San Francisco in the early 2000s, one-quarter of men and women selling sexual services had a form of venereal disease.[59] Those who control the sex trafficking victims are disinterested in providing any medical assistance to these sex slaves. Therefore, one can presume that trafficked individuals have an even higher rate of sexually communicable diseases. Therefore, as each trafficking victim has multiple customers daily, sexually transmitted diseases and HIV spread into the larger community, infecting many individuals, compounding health costs, and increasing premature mortality.

The spread of AIDS though human trafficking not only has great medical costs for the community but has also had a devastating demographic impact in Africa, Southeast Asia, and Latin America. In Africa, particularly, it has left many countries without teachers, doctors, and the trained professionals needed for future development.

Labor Consequences

The labor force consequences of human trafficking are diverse and often unrecognized. Intergenerational prostitution and bondage perpetuates

[58] Patrick Radden Keefe, "The Snakehead," *New Yorker*, April 24, 2006, 68–85; Ko-lin Chin, "The Social Organization of Chinese Human Smuggling," in *Global Human Smuggling*, David Kyle and Rey Koslowski, eds. (Baltimore: Johns Hopkins University Press, 2001), 216–34; Zai Liange and Wenzhen Ye, "From Fujian to New York: Understanding the New Chinese Immigration," in *Global Human Smuggling*, Kyle and Koslowski, eds., 187–215.

[59] D.Cohan, A. Lutnick, P. Davidson, C. Cloniger, A. Herlyn, J. Breyer, C. Cobaugh, D. Wilson, and J. Klausner, "Sex Worker Health: San Francisco Style," *Sexually Transmitted Infections* 82 (2006), 418–22, http://sti.bmj/cgi/content/abstract/82/5/418 (accessed August 10, 2009).

exploitation. Male bonded laborers sometimes sell their wives into prostitution to buy themselves out of bondage.[60] In this way, one form of labor exploitation leads to another. Individuals can free themselves only by enslaving who that are closest to them.

Trafficking depresses salaries, makes sexual services more accessible, and leads to increased work related injuries. Moreover, the costs of these exploitative labor practices are rarely assumed by individual businesses that profit but are costs borne by the larger society as injured trafficked laborers use expensive medical services in developed societies for which neither the hospital nor the state is compensated.

Trafficking undermines the financial welfare of low-income people who are free to sell their labor. Those trafficked into domestic servitude, agricultural labor, and construction reduce the salary levels of others and the quality of their work environment because employers know they have access to a cheaper and more malleable work force. Trafficked workers are often employed in the most dangerous sectors of the economy such as mines, kilns, and brick factories where scant attention is paid to health and safety conditions.[61]

The large pool of illegal workers leads to depressed wages and poor working conditions. Illustrative of this phenomenon are the Mexicans exploited in the southwest of the United States or the way that smuggled and trafficked workers depress wages in the case of the Chinese. Legal Chinese immigrants to the United States are deprived of the opportunity to earn a decent wage or are deprived of wages they have legitimately earned.[62] Enslaved workers often remain outside the protection of the labor law because of poor enforcement and the incapacity of inspectors to penetrate the tightly controlled communities in which the exploitation takes place. The same phenomenon is present in France and Italy, as discussed in Chapter 5.[63]

[60] Kevin Bales, *Disposable People*, 203.

[61] Kevin Bales, *Disposable People*, 25; *Trafficking in Persons Report 2008*, 8; Siddhart Kara, *Sex Trafficking: Inside the Business of Modern Slavery* (New York: Columbia University Press, 2009).

[62] Peter Kwong, "Impact of Chinese Human Smuggling on American Labor Market," in *Global Human Smuggling*, David Kyle and Rey Koslowski, eds. (Baltimore: Johns Hopkins University Press, 2001), 235–53.

[63] Gao Yun and Véronique Poisson, *Le Traffic et L'Exploitation des Immigrants Chinois en France* (Paris, France, ILO, 2005), http://www.ilo.org/public/french/support/publ/pdf/catalog.pdf (accessed June 20, 2007); interviews with Italian prosecutors from Milan and Florence at TraCCC in Washington, DC, 1999 and 2000; "People Smuggling," http://www.interpol.int/Public/THB/PeopleSmuggling/Default.asp (accessed June 25, 2007).

Trafficking of workers overseas also depresses wages and work conditions for fairly compensated employees. Often these exploited workers are children who cannot protest their exploitation.[64] Trafficked and bonded workers produce counterfeit sneakers, pocketbooks, and clothing, but also other consumer goods for which profit margins are often small. Manufacturers seeking to produce with fair trade practices cannot compete,[65] and there is pressure to pay lower wages for unskilled workers in the factories. Many retail sellers have bought these commodities because they are cheaper, but the presence of buyers intensifies the abuse of workers.

Trafficking depresses wages not only in labor markets for low-skilled workers but also for victims of sexual exploitation. The arrival of many trafficking victims to Great Britain from Eastern Europe since the end of the Cold War has depressed the pay of prostitutes. As Paul Holmes, a leading law enforcement specialist on human trafficking explained, in the decade after the fall of the Berlin Wall, there was no increase in the price of sexual services in London.[66] During this period, the price of housing, transport, and the overall cost of living had risen precipitously. But the greater availability of women had reduced the income of all prostitutes and made sex with a prostitute much more affordable than in the past. Abundant supply hurt domestic workers and increased human exploitation, neither a desirable outcome in the labor market.

Conclusion

The consequences of the international drug trade are so evident and significant that many countries and multinational bodies such as the European Union and the United States are ready to make countering the drug trade a top policy priority. The responses by states and international organizations are diverse because drug trafficking has been defined as a threat to national and global security. Yet apart from these threats, the problem is seen as a response to the absence of economic opportunities. Its role in increasing violence and crime, in spreading communicable diseases, and in destroying communities is also well known. Therefore,

[64] "Gap Pulls 'Child Labour' Clothing," http://news.bbc.co.uk/2/hi/south_asia/7066019.stm (accessed August 19, 2009).

[65] Discussions with officials of the counterfeiting program of U.S. Chamber of Commerce, September 2007; see also Moisés Naím, *Illicit: How Smugglers, Traffickers and Copycats Are Hijacking the Global Economy* (New York: Anchor Books, 2006), p. 126.

[66] Interview with Paul Holmes by the author in April 2000 in London.

the counter-trafficking response includes military and law enforcement efforts, often combined with alternative economic development strategies and assistance programs for addicts to reduce demand.

Yet human trafficking, as this chapter has discussed, also has far-reaching consequences as human trafficking for labor, sexual, and other forms exploitation is now a universal phenomenon. Countries in all regions are now part of a global market of trafficked individuals. Many think of trafficking as arising merely from the demand for cheap labor, but its consequences are so far-reaching that it has both serious and long-term conventional and human security consequences.

Trafficking undermines state security, as does the drug trade. Like the drug trade, it can perpetuate conflicts, facilitate the activities of terrorists, and undermine order and the principles of mature democracies. It may strain the social welfare capabilities of countries confronted with many trafficked individuals.

While the drug trade increases urban violence and homicide rates, contributes to the growth of gangs and organized crime, and increases corruption in both developing and developed societies, human trafficking has some but not all these consequences. Human trafficking, like the drug trade, contributes to the rise of organized crime and embeds organized crime in the state structures emerging in transitional and conflict societies. But as a more latent social phenomenon, it does not often contribute to greater rates of visible violence or the visible upheaval now evident in Mexico. The shoot-out on the Arizona highway in the southwest United States to kidnap smuggled aliens is exceptional.[67] Instead, much of the violence associated with human trafficking is on a personal level, as individual victims are frequently the brutalized and murdered.

Yet other forms of violence accompany trafficking in many regions of the world. Trafficking victims are subjects of violent attacks in Russia, reflecting the political tensions enhanced by the presence of minority groups. Political violence and conflict is prolonged as the profits from human trafficking are used, for example, to fund conflicts in the Balkans and violent insurgencies in Nepal and Uganda.

The human security consequences of the rise of international human trafficking transcend the rise in intrapersonal violence by creating serious health consequences for the global community thereby impacting the

[67] Pat Flannery, "Shootout over Migrants Shows Danger to Public: Last of Kidnappers Face Sentencing," *Arizona Republic*, July 9, 2001, http://usinfo.state.gov/eap/Archive_Index/reprint3.html (accessed June 25, 2007).

demographics of many regions and countries. Like the drug trade, human trafficking contributes to premature death and the spread of HIV/AIDS. The larger community suffers other health costs of human trafficking. Trafficking victims become vectors of disease through their work in the sex industry or in restaurants. Without access to medical care, they contribute to the spread of venereal diseases, tuberculosis, scabies, and other illnesses. Their victimization leads to larger health costs within society. Demographic crises result in source countries with low birth rates and high rates of human trafficking.

Women are repressed and vulnerable children are subject to exploitation, denying them a viable future. Families and communities suffer as members of their communities are trafficked – as the fate of the trafficking victims remains unknown. Or victims return to die or live in their communities with severe psychological and physical problems that place a protracted burden on the family.

Globalization has made the international labor market more competitive. While some poor peasants will cultivate narcotics to enhance family incomes, others in poverty become trafficked laborers in their home countries and abroad. Many exist for years in enforced, bonded, or enslaved labor situations in developed democracies, oil-rich states, or more affluent regions of their native country.

The political consequences of human trafficking are significant. The rise of organized crime groups, enriched by the proceeds of this new form of slavery, creates non–state-based authoritarianism. The corruption and collusion of government officials with human traffickers results in the absence of protections for trafficked individuals. But this corruption also undermines the quality of governance and rule of law.

The broad conventional and human security consequences of human trafficking need further recognition. Whereas many understand that drug trafficking victimizes both the drug abuser and the larger society, few realize that the victims of human trafficking are greater than those actually subject to exploitation. As John Donne wrote, all humanity suffers as a result of the human washed away by the sea. All aspects of human security suffer as a consequence of human trafficking. The true global costs of human trafficking may equal or exceed those of the international drug trade.

PART II

THE FINANCIAL SIDE OF HUMAN TRAFFICKING

3

Human Trafficking as Transnational Organized Crime

A diversity of actors participates in human trafficking, ranging from diplomats and employees of multinational organizations who traffic young women for domestic labor to small-scale entrepreneurs, to members of the large criminal organizations of Asia that specialize in human smuggling and trafficking.[1] This chapter focuses on organized smuggling and trafficking and criminal networks rather than on the exploitation committed by elite individuals.

Trafficking networks include both economically and politically motivated criminals. Both categories of traffickers often intersect with the larger world of transnational crime. They obtain false documents for their victims from criminal specialists, hire thugs from outside their network to intimidate women and traffic laborers, and move their proceeds through established money-laundering channels.

The trafficking networks also interact with the legitimate world as they advertise their products, move their victims through public transport, and secure visas from public officials.

[1] United Nations Office on Drugs and Crime (UNODC), "Trafficking in Persons: Global Patterns," 68, http://www.unodc.org/pdf/traffickinginpersons_report_2006–04.pdf (accessed July 28, 2009); Eurojust, "Human Trafficking the State of Affairs," October 2005, http://polis.osce.org/library/f/3273/2219/EU-NLD-RPT-3273-EN-Eurojust%20and%20Human%20Trafficking%20-%20The%20State%20of%20Affairs.pdf (accessed July 28, 2009); Cornelius Friesendorf, "Introduction: The Security Sector and Counter-Trafficking," in *Strategies Against Human Trafficking: The Role of the Security Sector*, Cornelius Friesendorf, ed. (Vienna: National Defence Academy and Austrian Ministry of Defence and Sport, 2009), 57.

Transnational Criminals Involved in Trafficking

Criminal trafficking groups are structured in a variety of ways. Few are large groups with pyramidal structures. Many traffickers outside of the large Asian crime groups operate as decentralized networks with loose connections between links in the trafficking chain.[2] These groups are frequently ethnically based, and they depend on diaspora communities in many countries for support. Yet cooperation of crime groups from other countries is essential if individuals are to be moved long distances, as the Tara case broken in the Balkans discussed later in the chapter reveals. Subgroups of criminal trafficking networks often specialize in a particular aspect of the business, such as recruitment, transport, and supply of false documents.[3]

Investigations have identified diverse network structures.[4] But as trafficking has developed over the last decades, trafficking groups have become more "professional, entrepreneurial and less visible."[5] Buyers and sellers coordinate closely. Their communications can be so secure that law enforcement has no prior warning of their activities. This explains how criminals in Britain could organize and execute public auctions of women at airports without prior detection.

Diversity of Actors

The commitment to trafficking as an activity differs among criminal actors. Some traffickers are opportunists. They will engage in any illicit activity that yields a profit, trafficking included. These criminals may recruit a few women for a trafficking ring one time and move drugs another. Other traffickers, particularly women, engage exclusively in human smuggling and trafficking.[6] As opportunists, they also capitalize on the human misery created by the financial crisis that began in 2008.

There are others who participate in segments of the business. For example, coyotes facilitate smuggling across the U.S.–Mexican border

[2] UNODC, "Trafficking in Persons," 69.

[3] Francesca Bosco, Vittoria Luda di Cortemiglia, Anvar Serojitdinov, "Human Trafficking Patterns, in Friesendorf," *Strategies Against Human Trafficking*, 67.

[4] John Picarelli, "Organised Crime and Human Trafficking in the United States and Western Europe" in Friesendorf, *Strategies Against Human Trafficking*, 124.

[5] Jana Arsovska and Stef Janssens, "Policing and Human Trafficking: Good and Bad Practices," in Friesendorf, *Strategies Against Human Trafficking*, 178.

[6] Alexis A. Aronowitz, *Human Trafficking, Human Misery: The Global Trade in Human Beings* (Westport, CT and London: Praeger, 2009), 52–55.

and are involved on only a short-term basis. They may not know the person they are transporting; they provide a service on a pay-as-you-go basis. On the other end of the spectrum are the Japanese tourist agencies that traffic women into the sex industry on a long-term basis.

The professions of the traffickers are diverse. They include former prostitutes; military, security, and law enforcement personnel; athletes, as well as typical criminals found in organized crime groups. They can also include mobilized military personnel employed by multinational peacekeeping forces or government contractors.

In addition, investigations in Russia and the United States reveal that many traffickers of women arrested for sexual exploitations had higher educations and no prior convictions.[7] The high social status and education of some human traffickers contrasts sharply with that of drug traffickers, often originating from poor families or criminal environments such as triad or mafia families.

Former and current members of security apparati and law enforcement, as well as military personnel, assume key roles in many trafficking rings of current and former communist states and current police are involved in many other societies as well. Former security personnel were present in approximately one-quarter of identified Balkan trafficking rings.[8] A major trafficking ring broken in Russia in March 2007 was run by law enforcement and security personnel.[9] On the Tajik-Afghan border, low-ranking military personnel who once supplemented their low salaries by trafficking in drugs now also facilitate the illicit movement of people.[10] In Cambodia in 2006, two military officers and a member of the military police were arrested for running brothels and trafficking.[11]

[7] Ministry of Internal Affairs (MVD) report at first conference sponsored by Elena Tiuriukanova under TraCCC anti-trafficking project in Russia, Moscow, September 28–29, 2006; Beatrix Siman Zakhari, "Legal Cases Prosecuted under the Victims of Trafficking and Violence Protection Act of 2000," in *Human Traffic and Transnational Crime: Eurasian and American Perspectives*, Sally Stoecker and Louise Shelley, eds. (Lanham, MD: Rowman and Littlefield, 2004).

[8] Johan Leman and Stef Janssens, "An Analysis of Some Highly Structured Networks of Human Smuggling and Trafficking from Albania and Bulgaria to Belgium," www.soc.kuleuven.be/immrc/pdf%20artikelen/human%20smuggling.pdf (accessed June 9, 2007).

[9] The nature of the personnel was discussed with the author during her visit in mid-March 2007. The case had been investigated by the Federal Security Service of Russia.

[10] IOM Tajikistan in cooperation with Sharq Scientific Research Center, "Labour Migration from Tajikistan, 2003," http://www.iom.tj/publications/labour_migration_2003.pdf (accessed June 22, 2007).

[11] *Trafficking in Persons Report 2007* (Washington, DC: U.S. Department of State, 2007), 74, http://www.humantrafficking.org/countries/cambodia (accessed July 29, 2009).

Law enforcement officials, as mentioned in the introduction, are deeply implicated in human trafficking in many parts of the world. In Bangladesh within two years in the mid-2000s, Bangladesh charged eight security officials for complicity in trafficking.[12] In 2006, "the former Deputy Director of the Police Anti-Human Trafficking and Juvenile Protection Department in Cambodia was convicted for involvement in trafficking and sentenced to five years imprisonment."[13] Law enforcement officials in Latin America and West Africa are also implicated in human smuggling and trafficking, as discussed in Chapter 9.

Human traffickers, like their associates in the illicit narcotics trade, are aided by an array of facilitators. These include not only the officials discussed later in the chapter who procure visas and passports for traffickers but also travel agents, hoteliers, operators of safe houses, night club owners and managers, apartment owners, and newspaper publishers. Adoptions out of Central America are facilitated by midwives, registry officials, lawyers, notaries, doctors, and even judges.[14] Language schools and professors have even facilitated visas to disguise trafficked women as students.[15]

Comparing Drug and Human Traffickers

Human trafficking can be differentiated in many respects from the narcotics trade. There are many large named organizations such as the Cali and Medellin cartels that engage in drug trafficking. Although the *yakuza* and triads traffic people, it is not possible to identify a large named multinational crime group that engages solely in human trafficking.

Large-scale drug traffickers can be extraordinarily violent to gain market entry, punish informants, or murder investigative journalists. The violence of human traffickers is usually more restricted to reprisals against the victims and their immediate families rather than directed against their criminal rivals. There have, however, been cases in Mexico and in the Russian Far East where journalists writing on human trafficking have

[12] Leslie Holmes, "Corruption & Trafficking: Triple Victimisation," in Friesendorf, *Strategies Against Human Trafficking*, 97.

[13] *Trafficking in Persons Report 2007*, 74.

[14] Francesca Bosco, Vittoria Luda di Cortemiglia, Anvar Serojitdinov, "Human Trafficking Patterns," in Friesendorf, *Strategies Against Human Trafficking*, 57.

[15] Phil Williams, "Combating Human Trafficking: Improving Governance Institutions, Mechanisms and Strategies," in Friesendorf, *Strategies Against Human Trafficking*, 421; Los Angeles Police Department Press Release, "Operation White Lace," www.lapdonline.org/press-releases/2002/12/pr02726.htm (accessed July 20, 2006).

been attacked and severely injured or killed. Yet journalists writing on human trafficking are much less frequently attacked than their colleagues investigating drug trafficking or official corruption.

Balkan groups, as discussed in the next chapter, have broken into European markets by using extraordinary violence, but this is the exception rather than the rule. The market for trafficked people is growing so rapidly and the business is so globalized that trafficking groups can coexist rather than kill each other off, as occurs regularly in the drug trade.

The links between drug traffickers and insurgents, guerillas, and terrorists have been identified in many parts of the world. These relationships have been analyzed in Colombia, Myanmar, and Afghanistan as well as other countries.[16] Such nonstate actors have also been linked to human trafficking in many locales. Pakistani terrorists buy children to serve as suicide bombers and Marxist guerillas in Nepal traffic girls to India to fund their political cause.[17] Rebels in Africa trade in children to fund their conflicts and obtain child soldiers. Yet much less is known about the relationships between these nonstate political groups and human traffickers than is the case with drug traffickers.

Most human traffickers have a commodity that they can exploit repeatedly whether it is a human being sold for labor exploitation, a woman sold into sex slavery, or a child's exploitation that results in pornography that can be sold to multiple buyers. The exceptions are organs and children trafficked for adoptions that can be bought and resold for a profit only once. This contrasts with the narcotics trade, where drug traffickers must constantly restock their product, as their commodity may be sold only once.

Large drug trafficking organizations are run exclusively by men. Women, if they have a role in the drug trade, usually serve at the lowest and most vulnerable levels, as drug couriers or as money launderers

[16] Francisco E. Thoumi, *Political Economy and Illegal Drugs in Colombia* (Boulder, CO: L. Rienner, 1995); Rensselaer W. Lee III, *White Labyrinth: Cocaine and Political Power* (New Brunswick, NJ: Transaction Publishers, 1989); Bertil Lintner, *Burma in Revolt: Opium and Insurgency since 1948* (Boulder, CO: Westview Press, 1994); Kairat Osmonaliev, "*Developing Counter-Narcotics Policy in Central Asia: Legal and Political Dimensions*," Silk Road Paper, January, 2005, http://www.silkroadstudies.org/Silkroadpapers/Osmonaliev.pdf (accessed June 26, 2007).

[17] "Rape for Profit: Trafficking of Nepali Girls and Women to India's Brothels," *Human Rights Watch/Asia* 12, no. 5(A) (1995); Augustine Anthony, "Pakistan Rescues boys trained as Suicide Bombers," July 28, 2009, http://www.reuters.com/article/asiaCrisis/idUSISL90520 (accessed August 23, 2009).

removed from operations. In contrast, in human trafficking, women assume a larger role as recruiters and even directors of significant smuggling organizations such as Sister Ping, discussed in this chapter.

Human trafficking organizations are more prominent in Asia, particularly China, Japan, India, and Thailand and the former socialist countries of Eastern Europe and the Soviet Union. Drug traffickers have been particularly prominent in Latin America, Nigeria, the Golden Triangle (Laos, Thailand, and Myanmar), and the Golden Crescent (Iran, Afghanistan, and Pakistan). Yet the areas where drug crime networks are well established are increasingly important growth areas for human trafficking.

Narcotics trafficking has high profits and some risks. Prisons throughout the world are filled with drug traffickers, and many countries have found ways to deprive them of their profits. In contrast, few human traffickers are incarcerated and almost none have lost the proceeds of their crime.

Table 3.1 elucidates the differences between the trade in humans and drugs:

Women as Traffickers

Women in every culture assume a significant role in human trafficking. But only in China has a woman been found at the top of a major transnational trafficking organization. Sister Ping was sentenced to thirty-five years' imprisonment by an American court for conspiracy to commit alien smuggling, other smuggling charges, and money laundering after many Chinese died on her vessel the *Golden Venture* off the East Coast of the United States.[18] Before this tragedy, she had run a highly successful multimillion-dollar criminal empire that stretched across several continents. Sister Ping rationalized her role in human smuggling in that she believed she was providing a public service for migrants who could not enter the United States without her services. Members of the Chinatown community where she resided for many years reinforced this perception of her as a service provider to the community.[19]

[18] ICE news release, "Sister Ping Sentenced to 35 Years in Prison for Alien Smuggling, Hostage Taking, Money Laundering and Ransom Proceeds Conspiracy," http://www.ice.gov/pi/news/newsreleases/articles/060316newyork.htm (accessed March 16, 2006); http://www.usdoj.gov/usao/nys/pressreleases/March06/sisterpingsentencingpr.pdf (accessed July 26, 2009).

[19] P. R. Keefe, "The Snakehead," *New Yorker*, 24 April 2006, 68–85; Patrick Radden Keefe, *The Snakehead: An Epic Tale of the Chinatown Underworld and the American Dream* (New York: Doubleday, 2009).

TABLE 3.1. *A Comparison of Drug and Human Trafficking*

	Drug Trafficking	Human Trafficking
Perpetrators	Many large-scale organizations, some smaller Mostly male; women's role limited to couriers Criminals, guerillas, insurgents, and terrorists	Full range of traffickers from small-scale entrepreneurs to major organizations Many female perpetrators, functioning as heads of organizations and recruiters Some high-status individuals, as well as guerillas, insurgents, and terrorists
Commodities	Marijuana, heroin, cocaine, opium, synthetic drugs Produced and sold one time	Humans for sexual and labor exploitation Children for adoptions, begging, pornography, child soldiers Trade in body parts Many bought and resold Continuous source of profit
Regions	Every part of the world involved Prominent in Latin America, United States, Europe, Africa, Afghanistan, Middle East and South East Asia	Every part of the world involved Particularly prominent in crime groups from Asia, former socialist countries, Balkans, Mexico and Nigeria
Risks	High profit but some risk	High profit but low risk

Women are important recruiters in Eurasia and Africa. Latin American, Asian, African, and Eurasian women run brothels and sex trafficking rings as many international investigations have revealed. Many women traffickers were once prostitutes but enter the business because they can earn more than in the legitimate economy. Becoming a human trafficker requires the acquisition of certain skills. Some women exploited by a

Eurasian trafficker in Los Angeles, according to the police investigators, were carefully studying the complex skills needed to be successful traffickers.[20] These skills include recruitment, transportation, procurement of false documents, marketing, and money laundering.

The now-imprisoned leader of the Los Angeles organization, Rima Fetissova, trafficked her own daughter, a minor, into prostitution, a phenomenon unfortunately not unique to this case. A Thai trafficking case in Washington, DC was uncovered when a young Thai girl solicited an Immigration and Naturalization Service agent while her mother applied for the renewal of her visa. The subsequent investigation revealed that the mother, who recruited girls for a brothel approximately three miles from the White House, would stop at nothing to provide for her customers. Her young teenage daughter had been compelled to work in the brothel.[21]

In some countries such as India, the role of women is so institutionalized that there is a specific name for the women who control brothels, *nayikas*.[22] Nayikas both recruit women from their own region and community and manage the brothels, cutting off their victims' contact with the outside world. As Indian commentators explain:

> The *nayika*, a term equivalent to boss lady, occupies a role absolutely pivotal to the brothel system. Usually older ex-prostitutes, they have survived by saving money and gradually acquiring girls of their own. Several *nayikas* might rent space in one brothel; the organizational effect of this is akin to cell structures used in spy networks to isolate individual operatives and frustrate outside penetration...
>
> *Nayikas* pay the go-betweens, the *dalaals* who know where the vulnerable families are – whose crops have failed, whose breadwinner has died – and inveigle daughters away from gullible parents and arrange transport to Delhi. Little room for compassion exists in the relation of a *nayika* to the girls she controls. A veteran of a brutalizing system, she knows all their motives and evasions; her livelihood depends on working the girls relentlessly.[23]

European investigations have also revealed a key role for women in trafficking. For example, Albanian gangs make use of Belgian or Dutch

[20] Interview with "Operation White Lace" investigators in Los Angeles in 2005.

[21] Ibid., and interview with former INS investigator in 1999. In the White Lace case in Los Angeles discussed subsequently, the ringleader also trafficked her own minor age daughter.

[22] This is ironic, as the name "*nayika*" was formerly used for the type of female lover and heroine modeled on Radha in the classic Indian love poem, the *Rasikapriya* (1591) of Keshav Das.

[23] Michael Parker, "India's Other Virus Human Trafficking and the Spread of AIDS," http://www.un.org/Pubs/chronicle/2006/issue2/0206p14.htm (accessed July 28, 2009).

women because they are less likely to arouse law enforcement's suspicion than the tough Albanians. The Albanian pimps and traffickers live in one city while the Dutch or Belgian "madams"– appointed by the traffickers to control the prostitutes – live in another. The Albanians come occasionally to check their business and to collect the money while the "madams" act as the main pimps. The Albanians also use the same madams, or other women with EU passports, as drug couriers.[24]

Nigerian women trafficked to Italy replicate the exploitation to which they have been exposed. In other words, Nigerian trafficking is characterized not only by female leadership, but also by a self-reproducing organizational structure. Women trafficked for sexual exploitation must abide by a pact with their trafficker.[25] This pact determines how much she must repay and is sealed with Nigerian rituals or voodoo. Once the pact has ended, it is common for a victim to work for a madam as a supervisor of other prostitutes, and eventually become a madam herself. In Italy, madams are usually between 25 and 35 years old. In the Netherlands, where many Nigerians prostitutes arrive as minors, some become madams around the age of 20. The prospect of upward mobility in the trafficking organization is a strong incentive to comply with the pact.[26]

Participation in trafficking may seem a rational choice for a woman in a desperate situation. A Georgian brothel keeper in Antalya, Turkey, explained to me that she had traveled regularly between her hometown and the seaside resort for a decade.[27] Her work began in the most desperate years of the post-socialist transition. The women in her brothel sent some of their wages home, a fact that distinguished them from others in the male-run brothels in Antalya, where the trafficked women were enslaved and uncompensated.[28]

[24] Arsovska and Janssens, "Policing and Human Trafficking," 184.

[25] Esohe Aghatise, "Trafficking for Prostitution in Italy: Possible Effects of Government Proposals for Legalization of Brothels," *Violence Against Women* 10 (2004), 1136.

[26] Jørgen Carling, "Migration, Human Smuggling and Trafficking from Nigeria to Europe," produced for IOM, http://www.prio.no/sptrans/1326102309/file48438_carling_2006_migration_human_smuggling_and_trafficking_from_nigeria_to_Europe.pdf (accessed July 17, 2009).

[27] Interview with a trafficker in Antalya in March 2004. For a fuller discussion of trafficking in Turkey, see Anna M. Agathangelou, *The Global Political Economy of Sex: Desire, Violence, and Insecurity in Mediterranean Nation States* (New York: Palgrave Macmillan, 2004), 130–36 and Stef Janssens and Jana Arsovska, "Human Trafficking Networks in Turkey," *Jane's Intelligence Review* 20, no. 12 (2008).

[28] What was observed in 2004 subsequently changed; a police crackdown in Antalya in spring 2007 did not eliminate the pervasive prostitution, but the women appear now to be compensated for their services. This may be a reaction of the traffickers who face imprisonment for their activities and do not want the women to testify against them.

The Routes of the Traffickers

Humans trafficked for labor exploitation often travel long routes, as their ultimate destinations are locales with greater demand for labor, which may be far from their homes in sub-Saharan Africa, Afghanistan and Pakistan, southern China, or the mountainous communities of southern Mexico. Illustrative of this are the large numbers of Filipinos, Thais, and Ethiopians who are trafficked as domestic laborers to the Middle East.[29] Hundreds of thousands of Fujian Chinese are in New York and Paris, many of them indentured servants or trafficked laborers. Tajiks and Vietnamese are trafficked as laborers to Moscow, Siberia, and all of Russia in between.[30] Trafficked Vietnamese in the United Kingdom help cultivate a large-scale home-grown cannabis crop.[31]

Traffickers are logistics specialists who can move individuals across vast distances. They often require numerous safe houses along the way where they can lodge their human cargo until it is safe to move them further. Frequently the route is not the most direct because the traffickers knowingly avoid policed roads, border checkpoints, and jurisdictions where there is efficient and honest law enforcement. Traffickers require a military-like intelligence capacity to successfully avoid these obstacles. Their intelligence capabilities may not be as developed as that of large-scale narcotics traffickers, but they are needed to organize routes successfully and deliver the human product. The end destination for the trafficking victim is often one where a diaspora community can absorb the trafficked people, or where an allied crime group can receive and distribute the trafficked laborers.

Affluent countries are particular destination countries, as are oil-rich states of the Middle East. Trafficking is also particularly pronounced in countries with significant domestic organized crime problems, such

[29] Aronowitz, *Human Trafficking, Human Misery*, 81; for discussion of Ethiopians, *Trafficking in Persons Report 2009*, 239. http://www.humantrafficking.org/countries/thailand (accessed July 30, 2009).

[30] Liudmila Erokhina, "Trafficking in Women in the Russian Far East: A Real or Imaginary Phenomenon?" in *Human Traffic and Transnational Crime*, Stoecker and Shelley, eds., 79–94; "50,000 Illegal Chinese Immigrants Miserable in Paris," June 24, 2005, reporting on the ILO report, "Chinese Immigrants Victims of Labor Exploitation in Paris," http:///english.people.com.cn/200506/24/eng20050624_192189.html (accessed June 9, 2007); Ko-lin Chin, *Chinatown Gangs: Extortion, Enterprise and Ethnicity* (New York and Oxford: Oxford University Press, 1996).

[31] Interview with members of Serious Organized Crime Agency, Washington, DC, May 2009.

as Nigeria, the countries of the former USSR, the Balkans, Japan, and Mexico.[32]

A crisscross of routes traverses the globe illustrating the truly global dimensions of the trade. Women from the former Soviet Union are trafficked to Europe, the Middle East, Asia, Latin America, and North America.[33] Similarly, women from the Dominican Republic are trafficked to Spain and elsewhere in Europe.[34] Italy is the primary recipient country of women trafficked from Nigeria, while women from the Balkans are trafficked throughout Western Europe.[35]

In further illustration of the global dimensions of human trafficking, Chinese trafficking groups are significantly involved in the sex industry in Thailand and neighboring countries.[36] Thai women are trafficked by Thai and other Asian crime groups to Japan and the United States; and Japanese organized crime groups are major actors in the Asian sex trade,[37] arranging sex tourism to Thailand and importing girls from Thailand, the Philippines, and Russia to Japan.[38] Not as well known in the international crime literature is Indian organized crime, which traffics girls from Nepal and Bangladesh to major urban centers, particularly Mumbai.[39]

The global dimensions of the problem have been analyzed by the UNODC, revealing that no region of the world has remained untouched by the phenomenon. Almost all countries are involved in human trafficking as source, transit, and destination countries.[40] The presence of

[32] UNODC, "Trafficking in Persons."

[33] Bertil Lintner, "The Russian Mafia in Asia," http://www.asiapacificms.com/articles/russian_mafia/ (accessed January 31, 2004); interviews with Russian law enforcement personnel.

[34] IOM Migration Information Programme, "Trafficking in Women from the Dominican Republic for Sexual Exploitation," excerpted in *Trends in Organized Crime* 3, no. 4, (1998): 26–29.

[35] N. Lindstrom, "Regional Sex Trafficking in the Balkans: Transnational Networks in an Enlarged Europe," *Problems of Post-Communism* 53, no. 4 (2004); Aghatise, "Trafficking for Prostitution in Italy," 1129–55.

[36] Bertil Lintner, *Blood Brothers: The Criminal Underworld of Asia* (New York: Palgrave MacMillan, 2003), 222–23.

[37] David Kaplan and Alec Dubro, *Yakuza: Japan's Criminal Underworld* (Berkeley: University of California Press, 2003).

[38] A. Fukumoto, M. Gaffney, and M. Rabaa, "Deception and Exploitation: Human Trafficking from Thailand to Japan," www.american.edu/traccc/resources/studpubs.html (accessed June 22, 2007).

[39] S. P. Singh, "Transnational Organized Crime: The Indian Perspective," Annual Report for 2000 and Resource Material Series, No. 59 (Tokyo: Unafei, 2002), http://www.unafei.or.jo/pdf/no59/ch.29/pdf (accessed January 31, 2004).

[40] UNODC, "Trafficking in Persons."

trafficked Baltic women in the strip houses and massage parlors of Iceland reveals that even a remote and lightly populated country can be a destination for traffickers who continuously seek new destinations for their human cargoes.[41]

Methods of the Traffickers – Recruitment, Transport, and Control

Traffickers must recruit their victims, transport them to the locale where they can be exploited, and then maintain control. The variety of recruitment techniques, modes of transport, and forms of exploitation are limited only by the imaginations of the traffickers. Their flexibility, opportunism, and brutality ensure that they have a constant supply of victims. Human smugglers and traffickers often operate through diaspora communities but this pattern is more characteristic of Asian, African, and Latin American groups than of Slavic groups.

Recruitment

Trafficking victims are recruited in a variety of ways. No single source supplies a large number of victims. However, recruitment is easiest during economic crises, natural disasters, and conflicts when there is a ready supply of potential victims. Only at this time does human trafficking resemble the drug trade. At most times, unlike in the narcotics trade, traffickers cannot find an ample supply at one source, as do the drug suppliers who ship tons of raw materials from Afghanistan and Colombia.

Human smuggling, in contrast to trafficking, may indeed attract hordes of people. Illustrative of this are the television reports showing large numbers of desperate Africans attempting to disembark from flimsy boats that have transported them from Africa to the Canary Islands or Lampedusa, close to the Italian shore. According to the UNODC, this massive smuggling business operating from Mauritania, Gambia, Senegal, and Morocco to Europe nets the criminal groups 300 million euros annually, an enormous amount considering the limited financial resources of those being smuggled.[42]

[41] See the United States Human Rights report www.state.gov/g/drl/rls/hrrpt/2006/78817.htm (accessed June 9, 2007).

[42] Caroline Brothers, "Criminal Gangs Profit from Smuggling of Illegal Immigrants from Africa into Europe," March 20, 2007, http://www.iht.com/articles/2007/03/19/news/crime.php (accessed June 10, 2007).

Human trafficking, in contrast to Chinese or African human smuggling, has no such ready supply. Significant time and effort must be spent by the traffickers to recruit the individuals they will subsequently exploit.

Traffickers prey on the vulnerable. Individuals without parents or with ailing parents, single mothers seeking ways to support their children, the desperately poor, and refugees from conflicts are common victims. In the Netherlands, Moroccan and Turkish teens, known as "Lover Boys," recruit young girls and it does take time to "season" the girls and break them down until they are willing to be prostituted.[43] But as actual cases in the chapters that follow illustrate, trafficking victims can also include well-educated individuals looking for greater opportunities who are deceived and coerced by their traffickers. College students looking for summer employment, women looking for suitable marriage partners, and educated individuals from poor countries seeking work abroad to help educate family members and provide remittances have all been victimized by traffickers.

Initial victimization of the trafficked person is usually by a member of his own ethnic group. For example, Chinese, Mexican, Nigerian, and Russian groups recruit in their own countries. Recruitment may be even more concentrated. Chinese smugglers operate primarily out of their home communities in the southern Fujian province.[44] Nigerian traffickers recruit their victims primarily from their state of Edo in the south central part of the country.[45]

There are many reasons that recruitment occurs within one's own group. Proximity and access are important. But equally important is trust.[46] Trust is important because people often contract with smugglers to move them to a particular locale, to pay them a certain amount of money, or to keep them in bondage for a particular period. Trust is more easily established with someone from one's own ethnic, language, or cultural group. The violation of this trust, which occurs in every

[43] Shared Hope International, *DEMAND: A Comparative Examination of Sex Tourism and Trafficking in Jamaica, Japan, the Netherlands, and the United States*, p.50, http://www.sharedhope.org/files/demand_netherlands.pdf (accessed September 3, 2009).

[44] For a discussion of Fujian province as a source, Keefe, "The Snakehead," 20–35, 113–15.

[45] Jørgen Carling, "Migration, Human Smuggling and Trafficking from Nigeria to Europe," produced for IOM, 8, 25–26, http://www.prio.no/sptrans/1326102309/file48438_carling_2006_migration_human_smuggling_and_trafficking_from_nigeria_to_europe.pdf (accessed July 29, 2009).

[46] See Valerie Braithwaite and Margaret Levi, eds., *Trust and Governance* (New York: Russell Sage Foundation, 1998).

trafficking case, may be as devastating to the individual as the physical or psychological abuse.

A wide variety of recruitment techniques are used.[47] The techniques used depend on the levels of education, the expectations of the victims and their families, and their financial situation. The widely used techniques in Eastern Europe and the former Soviet Union – advertisements and websites – are utilized less frequently in the poorer countries of Asia, Africa, and Latin America. In regions with poorly educated victims, recruitment most frequently occurs on a personal basis. All too often, the victim is previously acquainted with his trafficker.

Trafficking victims are often recruited by people they know – friends, family, acquaintances, and sometimes boyfriends. Some men deliberately befriend vulnerable young women, pretending to be their boyfriends and then selling them into prostitution. This was accurately depicted in the Swedish film *Lilya 4-Ever*, in which a boyfriend sold her, and in the Indonesian film, *Chants of Lotus*, in which a junior high school student is trafficked by a family friend.[48] In India, procurers for brothels look for lost children, befriend them, and sell them into prostitution.[49]

In the Cadena case in the southern United States, a group of minor girls was entrusted by family members to a known family from their Veracruz community. The parents were assured that the girls would be working with families as domestic helpers, a story that seemed credible to their families, as many young Mexican girls travel to the United States for employment. The girls understood that their situation was different only when they crossed the Mexican – U.S. border and were driven to a store to try on lingerie.[50]

Such complete deception of the victim is not always the rule. Prostitutes recruited from Lithuania, Russia, and Ukraine who became part of the While Lace Case agreed to work in California because of the prospect of earning more money. But the U.S. courts defined some of the women as trafficking victims because they had been deceived as to the conditions of their transport and of their employment. Some were

[47] Aronowitz, *Human Trafficking, Human Misery*, 55–56.

[48] "Chants of Lotus" was produced in 2007 and shown at the Freer/Sackler Museums, Washington, DC, September 28, 2008.

[49] Interview with Ruchira Gupta, 2004.

[50] Florida State University Center for the Advancement of Human Rights, "Florida Responds to Human Trafficking," http://www.cahr.fsu.edu/H%20-%20Chapter%202.pdf (accessed July 20, 2006).

smuggled into the United States after experiencing extreme hardship in Mexico and then were forced to work by the head of the trafficking ring even while ill.[51]

Recruiters often inform the adult victims that they have a contract and a debt to the traffickers. But they are told that once this debt is paid off, they will be free to earn their own money. In some cases, women are informed that they will work in nightclubs as dancers, but are never informed that they are expected to perform sexual services for the customers. The reality always differs from the presentation made to the victim; the extent of deception differs by region and the nature of the traffickers.

Some women trafficked into prostitution return to their home communities with tales of their superior earnings. As remittances have provided for improved living standards in Nigeria and Senegal, the Philippines, and many communities in Latin America, such tales are often credible to poorly educated neighbors. The recruiters talk their friends and acquaintances into joining them or sending their children by lying about the conditions of the work and the amounts to be derived from employment abroad. These women get recruiting bonuses from the traffickers who paid for their trips home. Or, as previously mentioned, the older prostitutes establish themselves as trafficking entrepreneurs, enslaving the women and girls they have recruited.

Traffickers also travel to rural areas of many poor countries to recruit victims. This can be as likely in the north of Thailand, the mountainous communities of Nepal, or the villages of Central Asia. The traffickers will find the poorest families, those with drug or alcohol abuse or serious medical problems. They will assure the family that they can provide a better future for the child, and many offer some nominal payment in return.

In some cases, the recruitment is not so benign. Families may also be directly offered money for the child. This method has been used successfully with alcoholics and drug addicts in Russia. But paying parents to sell children also works in other cultural contexts. In a vivid scene captured on film in *Selling of Innocents*, a young Nepalese girl is sold by her father to a trafficker and the child is instructed by her parents to do whatever the trafficker demands.[52]

[51] Interview by author with investigators of this case, Los Angeles December 2006.

[52] For more information on the film see http:// movies.nytimes.com/movie/296002/Selling-of-Innocents/overview (accessed July 29, 2009).

Often these impoverished families, with more children than they can support, face no alternative other than reducing the numbers of mouths they have to feed. Selling off their children is not seen as a malicious act but rather is motivated by the possibility of saving their other children. Some researchers in Thailand and Nigeria contend that these sales are motivated by growing consumerism.

Organ sales are motivated by the same contrasting reasons – familial obligation and a desire for consumer goods. A trafficker will locate a potential provider of a kidney that will be extracted in an operation outside of the seller's home country. The money derived from the organ sale may be used to support a starving family, to provide medical care for an ill relative, or provide investment capital for the family. Or, the mother, as in an actual case, will buy expensive clothes for her child with the proceeds of the kidney sale.[53] In general, the donors will be poorly compensated and provided insufficient postoperative care.[54] The person may be deceived or coerced.[55] For example, "a person is told that he will be donating blood and is then coerced into selling a kidney."[56]

Many ploys are used to recruit more educated victims, including advertisements and the establishment of marriage and employment agencies in the countries of origin. They also create fake model agencies and film production studios.[57] Well-paid jobs and opportunities to study abroad are offered.[58] These latter forms of deception are particularly pervasive in Eastern Europe and the former Soviet Union, where levels of education are higher and trafficking victims are highly literate. Web and newspaper advertisements for matchmaking services and marriage bureaus may prove to be covers for trafficking networks. Newspapers carrying advertisements for employment abroad as nannies, hotel maids, or providers of care for the elderly may be covers for traffickers as advertisers are rarely vetted.[59] As women from the region sometimes obtain valid

53 This situation was told to me by a colleague in the U.S. government working on transnational crime.

54 Michele Goodwin, *Black Markets: The Supply and Demand of Body Parts* (Cambridge and New York: Cambridge University Press, 2006), 12; Aronowitz, *Human Trafficking, Human Misery*, 119.

55 *Trafficking in Persons Report 2009*, 74.

56 Aronowitz, *Human Trafficking, Human Misery*, 117.

57 Bosco, di Cortemiglia, Serojitdinov, "Human Trafficking Patterns," 52.

58 Ibid.

59 Sally Stoecker, "Human Trafficking: A New Challenge for Russia and the United States," in *Human Traffic and Transnational Crime*, Stoecker and Shelley, eds., 20.

employment as chambermaids and on cruise ships, the advertisements carry some credibility.

Newspaper advertisements and employment agencies in recipient countries are also conduits for trafficking. Stranded women in the United States have answered advertisements and fallen into trafficking situations. Likewise, Russian-speaking unregistered employment agencies in New York do not bother to differentiate whether an individual is a legal or illegal immigrant. They place individuals in exploitative labor situations with inadequate pay and working hours, conditions that violate existing labor laws. These victims may be highly educated. Research conducted among Kyrgyz and other Central Asian immigrants from poor Soviet successor states revealed that many placed by these agencies in exploitative labor situations with Russian-speaking families were formerly members of the educated elite of Central Asia now residing illegally in the United States. They endured this exploitation because they earned more than they could at home and needed to support family members in their countries.[60]

Other circumstances, such as the failed post-socialist transitions, provide a fertile ground for trafficking recruiters. Citizens of countries under sanctions, individuals residing in conflict zones, and those stranded after large-scale natural disasters are ready prey. In preinvasion Kurdish Iraq, a whole street of human smugglers in Sulaimaniya and Arbil sold their services to those who sought to leave the country.[61] Families would sell their large homes and move to much smaller quarters to pay the large fees demanded by the smugglers. With this volume of smuggling, many Kurds failed to reach their ultimate destination and instead became trafficked laborers in transit countries. Others who reached their destinations were caught and imprisoned, unable to support their families who had sacrificed much to facilitate their move. Smuggling and trafficking out of postwar Iraq and neighboring unstable countries continue as revealed by arrests in Croatia in 2009 following a multinational investigation.[62]

In the prewar period, the victims of traffickers were exclusively male but in the postwar period, Iraqi women have been trafficked as prostitutes

[60] Saltanat Liebert, *Irregular Migration from the Former Soviet Union to the United States* (London: Routledge, 2009).

[61] Reported by a student of mine whose cousin worked as a human smuggler in Sulaimaniya, in Kurdish, Iraq; see also University of California, March 31, 2003, "Scholar in Iraq Scholar to Monitor Conditions of Displaced Civilians," www.universityofcalifornia.edu/news/article/5282 (accessed January 27, 2009).

[62] For a discussion of the Tara case, see http://www.secicenter.org/p450/02+April+2009 (accessed July 29, 2009).

in Syria, Lebanon, and neighboring states.[63] The fate of Iraqi women is unfortunately not unique, as the following regional chapters discuss. Women from the war-torn countries of the Balkans have been trafficked to Western Europe, and the victims of violent conflict in the Democratic Republic of the Congo and Rwanda have been trafficked as laborers, combatants, and sex slaves.[64]

Large-scale disasters such as earthquakes in Central America and South Asia displaced people who become vulnerable to trafficking middle men and recruiters, For example, many children were trafficked as bricklayers, domestic servants, and brides after monsoons and major flooding in Eastern India in summer 2008.[65] An adoption freeze was introduced after the tsunami in 2004 because past experience led aid workers to anticipate large-scale trafficking of orphaned and displaced children.[66]

Transport and Entry

Traffickers face important logistical challenges in moving people long distances. These challenges are similar to some faced by narcotics traffickers – they must coordinate transport, evade border and customs controls, and ensure entry of the product into the market. But human trafficking poses unique challenges. The human cargo must be fed and housed in transit and delivered in "serviceable" condition. Small shipments of drugs can be readily moved by couriers but a shipment of human beings cannot be easily disguised.

Investigated trafficking cases reveal every known form of transport from feet to airplanes. In some cases individuals travel in horrendous conditions – in the holds of cargo vessels, in small boats with no protection from the sun or rain, or in specially constructed and poorly ventilated compartments of trucks. Many become ill, but the traffickers, seeking to minimize costs, rarely provide medical care. The conditions of transport recall the abysmal conditions in which slaves were transported in past centuries to the new world.[67]

[63] Hugh Macleod, "Despair of Baghdad turns into a life of Shame in Damascus," *Guardian*, October 24, 2006, http://www.guardian.co.uk/Iraq/Story/0,,1929893,00.html (accessed June 22, 2007); correspondence with former TraCCC student employed in the U.S. embassy in Damascus; *Trafficking in Persons Report 2009*, 273.

[64] *Trafficking in Persons Report* 2005, 86, 186.

[65] Nita Bhalla, "Traffickers Prey on Disaster-hit Children in India," 23 March 2009, http://www.reliefweb.int/rw/rwb.nsf/db900SID/KHII-7QFA5W?OpenDocument (accessed July 28, 2009).

[66] Ibid.

[67] H. S. Klein, *The Middle Passage: Comparative Studies in the Atlantic Slave Trade* (Princeton: Princeton University Press, 1978).

A Balkan human trafficking ring case named "Tara" with 52 identified participants dismantled through regional coordination reveals the complexities of illegally transporting large numbers of people across different borders. Four criminal groups, each in a different country, cooperated to move at least 192 people from the Near and Far East, charging those seeking to enter the European Union 1000 to 1500 euros each.

> The smugglers were very careful about their business, trying to cover up their tracks by all means, i.e. to stay below the radar. The groups from Croatia were connected with smugglers from other countries. The persons transported across the border with regular transport lines, in personal vehicles, taxis or vans. The persons were accommodated at secret locations before the transport and payments were conducted via messengers – drivers of regular bus routes or Western Union ... The arrested criminals often used illegal border crossings and a guide.[68]

This case is not exceptional. The Chinese who died in the van crossing the English channel had been initially transported by Snakeheads, a Chinese crime group, by plane from Beijing to Belgrade. Then with the efficiency of a well-coordinated international business, they were moved by auto through Hungary, Austria, France, and the Netherlands before the group was loaded for their last fateful leg to the United Kingdom.[69] Traffickers use an enormous variety of techniques to move people and to facilitate their entry into their destination countries. Corruption, as previously mentioned, is often an integral part of the transport process as border guards, customs officials, consular officers, and other diplomatic personnel must be bribed or extorted.[70] Collusive relationships are established with real or bogus travel agencies to facilitate the trafficking.

In one example in Bulgaria, in the mid-1990s a former senior Bulgarian intelligence official opened a travel agency. By establishing close relations with a Western embassy in Sofia, official tourist visas were delivered en masse to the travel agency for travel to Western Europe. This allowed the

[68] For a discussion of the case see http://www.secicenter.org/p450/02+April+2009 (accessed July 29, 2009), for the specific quote see "Smuggled 200 people to EU via Croatia," April 2, 2009, http://www.javno.com/en-croatia/smuggled-200-people-to-eu-via-croatia_248077 (accessed July 29, 2009).

[69] Reuters, "Britain's Straw Says Truck Deaths a Warning," June 19, 2000; Warren Hoge, "Trucker Found Guilty in Death of Immigrants," *New York Times*, April 5, 2001, A6.

[70] John Pomfret, "Bribery At Border Worries Officials: Mexican Smugglers Intensify Efforts to Entice U.S. Agents," *Washington Post*, July 15, 2006, A01.

agency to facilitate human smuggling and trafficking, activities it combined with money laundering.[71]

In other parts of the world, smuggling and trafficking victims suffer enormously. Thousands of trafficking victims illegally cross the U.S.–Mexican border in tiny boats, or walk through huge and specially constructed subterranean tunnels. Others cross hundreds of miles of desert on foot. Hundreds die each year of starvation and dehydration, having been deceived or abandoned by their traffickers. In 2008, 54 women from Myanmar perished in a freezer truck used to transport seafood.[72]

More secure are the individuals who travel on overcrowded and uncomfortable buses across large distances. This was the case of a group of Georgian trafficking victims who had traversed a large expanse of Russia before entering Finland, which was only a transit point to their ultimate destination of Italy.[73]

Moving significant numbers of individuals is challenging, but moving them across guarded borders can be even more difficult. Fortunately for the smugglers and traffickers, vast parts of Africa, Latin America, Asia, the former Soviet Union, and the Middle East can be traversed with relative ease. Border posts can be crossed in exchange for small payments, large stretches of border are uncontrolled and can be easily traversed by knowing traffickers, and the illicit movements of people can be disguised easily within licit movements. As in the aforementioned Tara case, illegal border crossings are used.

Yet indifference of officials can make the job of traffickers easier. A traveler arriving at Istanbul's international airport is greeted by warning signs in Russian advising entrants of the dangers of exploitation by traffickers. But at the same time, I observed young Central Asian women heavily made up and clearly employed as prostitutes who entered Turkey through passport control amidst long lines of tourists.

Traffickers use particular ingenuity to facilitate the movement of their "commodities." In most consulates around the world, foreigners attempting to obtain visas complain of the enormous obstacles. To overcome these roadblocks, traffickers often do more than bribe officials. Examples

[71] Arsovska and Janssens, "Policing and Human Trafficking," 190.

[72] "Myanmar Migrants Suffer in Lorry," August 10, 2008, http://antidictatorship.wordpress.com/2008/04/10/54-burmese-illegal-immigrants-die-inside-container-van/ (accessed July 27, 2009).

[73] Tamar Mikadze, "Human Trafficking Won't Go Away in Georgia," *CACI Analyst*, June 15, 2005, http://www.cacianalyst.org/newsite/?q=node/3112 (accessed June 22, 2007); interview with International Law Enforcement advisor in Georgia in 2005.

of corrupt consular officials facilitating trafficking by providing visas have been discovered by American, Swiss, Belgian, and German investigations. Many cases of corruption in visa and passport issuance can be traced to India and Pakistan, Latin America, as well as the Balkans and Eastern Europe.

A U.S. State Department official was arrested in 2000 in Guyana after having amassed more "than $1.3 million in cash and gold in a conspiracy to sell U.S. visas to foreigners.[74]" In 2005, another visa bribery scheme was detected in the embassy in Mexico City, and dozens of port of entry and border patrol officials were arrested for corruption.[75]

Insights on how officials are corrupted can be gained from a 1990s case investigated by the U.S. Immigration and Naturalization Service that resulted in the ruin of the career of a young consular officer stationed in India. Just as the security police in the Soviet era looked for diplomats whom they could blackmail to do their bidding, the Indian crime groups were on constant alert for the same vulnerabilities. Demoralized by the heavy workload and the constant strain of turning down visa applicants, the recently stationed American diplomat proved to be an excellent target for the human smuggling/trafficking network. Placed in a compromising position by the organized crime group, he was subsequently blackmailed by the criminals. He provided visas to the crime ring, which in turn received large sums for their ability to move their clients into the United States. But the Indian crime operation went sour and the facilitating role of the American visa officer was disclosed while he was still in India.[76]

Swiss authorities had similar problems with their embassy in Pakistan in 2006. Swiss officials in the Department of Foreign Affairs reported that criminal gangs "involved in human trafficking had almost certainly infiltrated the visa section of the Islamabad embassy and corrupted officials." As in the Bulgarian case, Pakistani travel agencies were complicit in the visa fraud.[77]

In the Indian subcontinent, officials are corrupted in any type of foreign embassy that can aid the smugglers/traffickers, not only those of western states. A group of Indians transited through the Erevan airport in the 1990s on Armenian passports. They obtained the passports after

[74] John Allen Williams and Richard E. Friedman, "The Intersection of Immigration and National Security," *American Bar Association National Security Law Report* 30, no. 4 (Nov/Dec. 2008), 17.

[75] Ibid.

[76] This case was investigated by an INS agent with whom the author worked closely.

[77] Holmes, "Corruption & Trafficking," 103.

smugglers bribed high-level embassy officials or "stole" the passports from the Armenian embassy in India.[78] At the end of the Shevardnadze era in Georgia in summer 2004, a high-level border guard official watched a group of Indians exiting from a Moscow flight move through a special line at passport control in Tbilisi, where no passport checks were made.[79] Both of these cases reveal the cross-border linkages of the criminals, the careful preparation of the human smugglers, and the complicity of officials that facilitate this movement.

Organized crime groups from Eastern Europe and Eurasia are also often associated with visa fraud. In the 1990s, a trafficking network infiltrated the visa section of the U.S. embassy in Prague. Despite the intense scrutiny over local national employees, a Czech criminal in the consular division was able to recommend to his superiors the issuance of numerous visas to young women that his organization sought to traffic to the United States. The traffickers were able to operate successfully for several years until one of their unwilling victims escaped from their clutches in the United States. The criminal investigation revealed that the trafficked women had entered on legitimate visas. Eventually, the investigation narrowed to the criminal plant within the embassy who was prosecuted for his role in the criminal conspiracy.[80]

At the same time period, a Belgian employed in the protocol service of the Belgian Ministry of Foreign Affairs arranged the distribution of diplomatic passports and "sold at least 300 residence permits to people associated with the Russian mafia. One of the accomplices in this case was an important figure in a large Russian company engaged in money laundering."[81]

Traffickers are unsurpassed in their ingenuity to overcome the obstacles to entering a destination country. In the White Lace case in California, a group of high-end prostitutes had been brought to Los Angeles from Lithuania, Russia, and Ukraine. The trafficking ring ran an advertisement in the Yellow Pages that cost $7,000 a month. Some of the trafficked women had initially entered the country as members of sports and religious delegations originating in their home countries.

[78] This was part of a well-documented asylum case in which the author served as an expert witness in June 2003.

[79] The border official who reported this worked closely with the TraCCC center in Georgia.

[80] The case was discussed with TraCCC staff by investigators of consular corruption in the U.S. Department of State in the early 2000s.

[81] Arsovska and Janssens, "Policing and Human Trafficking," 190.

Others entered through Mexico illegally after having stayed in safe houses in Mexico. For the ones who entered the United States more directly, the traffickers had located sports and religious delegations that the women could join and through deception or corruption had added the women to these groups, thereby ensuring they received visas with facility.[82] The same situation was found in research among irregular Kyrgyz migrants residing on the east coast of the United States, some of whom had entered the country as members of designated travel groups.[83]

The farcical dimensions of the abuse of delegations and foundations is provided by an investigation undertaken by the American consular official in St. Petersburg who investigated the city's Spina Bifida Foundation after at least a dozen young women had separately requested visas for study trips to learn about this rare genetic disorder. Sensing something wrong, the official visited the foundation address listed on the applications, finding an actual nameplate for the foundation on the door. But the veracity of the foundation ended there. Its director was not even aware that spina bifida was a disease. Instead of being alarmed that his bogus operation was unmasked, he became afraid that he might contract this awful malady. His risk of contracting the disease, a malady inherited at birth, was as minimal as his risk of prosecution.[84] In the late 1990s when this scam was unmasked, Russian law enforcement did nothing to prosecute trafficking facilitators.

Securing Residence

The subterfuge of traffickers allows victims' entrance, often on seemingly legitimate visas, but securing long-term residence for those they seek to exploit poses other challenges. A variety of methods are used by the traffickers, including the provision of false documents, retention of the services of visa mills, false marriages, and other subterfuges to allow their victims to stay.

Trafficking victims are provided false documents giving them new identities. A particularly ingenious method was used by the traffickers in the White Lace case. The prostitutes were registered as students at a language school that did not ask questions of its prospective students

[82] Interview with vice squad investigators Los Angeles Police Department, December 2005.

[83] Saltanat Liebert, *Irregular Migration*.

[84] Interview in 1999 with the consular official who unmasked this trafficking ring.

or monitor their class attendance. Unfortunately for the criminals, this particular visa mill had also provided visas for two of the 9/11 hijackers, a fact that brought the traffickers under particular scrutiny.[85] It also illustrates the fact that the service providers for transnational crime can intersect with the world of terrorists.

Lawyers are also hired by smugglers and traffickers to obtain residence permits. The fees paid to the lawyers are often the largest cost to the traffickers. In one case in the mid-1990s investigated in the United States, a small New York law firm was engaged in visa fraud, concocting applications for permanent residence to aid an Indian smuggling operation. A more famous case involved a Harvard-educated lawyer, Mr. Robert Porges, and his wife, Sherry Lu Porges, who together gained $13 million between 1993 and 2000 from filing false political asylum claims for large numbers of Chinese smuggled to the United States by a Chinese crime ring.[86] Documents seized from the traffickers revealed that one-quarter of the proceeds of the crime group were spent on legal fees.[87]

Traffickers arrange falsified documents to show that the women they are trafficking to Israel are Jewish. This can be arranged easily in many countries of the former Soviet Union, where officials can be bribed to produce or sign any document. On arrival in Israel, the "Jewish" women obtain citizenship under the law of return. With an Israeli passport, they can be moved to many other countries around the world, where Israelis can enter without visas.

In some countries, traffickers arrange marriages between their victims and local residents. Although subsequent investigations may eventually unmask these marriages as bogus, traffickers have thus managed to prolong the time that the victim can work before deportation. Marriages can also be used to trap women. For example, a Brazilian woman entered Switzerland thinking she would study and married a Swiss man to stay. Her plans did not materialize as her husband trafficked her, along with her aunt, who arranged her travel.[88]

[85] Interview with the investigator, December 2005, Los Angeles.

[86] These two cases were discussed with the author by INS investigators in 1998 and 1999; Graham Rayman, "Human Smuggling Lawyer charged in schemes to sneak Chinese into country," *Newsday*, September 21, 2000, http://www.friends-partners.org/lists/stop-traffic/1999/1159.html (accessed January 9, 2009).

[87] Discussion with INS agents and analysts examining the financial flows in the case.

[88] Benjamin S. Buckland, "Smuggling & Trafficking: Crossover & Overlap, in Friesendorf," *Strategies Against Human Trafficking*, 156.

Controlling the Victim

Victims of trafficking are controlled by acute violence, psychological intimidation, and threats to the families of the victims. Many of the dehumanizing practices that were used during the Holocaust to produce passive victims are replicated by the traffickers. Trafficking victims are deprived of their identities, moved vast distances away from their families, languages, and cultures in inhumane conditions, and are tortured to induce compliance. Some have their arms and bodies tattooed indicating they are the possessions of the traffickers. Individual victims who resist the traffickers are tortured in front of other victims. Women who continue to resist can be thrown to their deaths from windows of apartment buildings or left to die from gangrene of the wounds inflicted by the traffickers.[89]

An important difference exists between the facilitators of the Holocaust and the traffickers. Many who supervised the execution of the Holocaust victims believed they were serving the state. Their bureaucratic approach to their work led Hannah Arendt to characterize Eichmann on trial as the "banality of evil."[90] But there is nothing banal about the heads of trafficking organizations. Wiretaps on traffickers and interviews with investigators who have conducted surveillance of traffickers reveal that many are among the most vicious of criminals. They never identify with the suffering of their victims, recalling the brutal guards who loaded the boxcars of humans to deliver to the concentration camps. The discourse of traffickers recalls that of slave traders of previous centuries who referred to their commodities as "ignorant savages," meriting the brutal treatment they received.

Traffickers routinely confiscate the passports and documents of those trafficked. Without these documents, the trafficked have no legal status. Loss of identity is central to the dehumanization of the victim. It also has very practical implications. If a trafficking victim escapes, he or she often cannot even command the protection of his own country's embassy, as he has no proof of citizenship. Criminal investigators in the recipient countries cannot investigate the trafficking network if they are unaware of the country of origin of the victim. For example, around the millennium Turkish criminal investigators found a group of forty

[89] Interviews with law enforcement and intelligence sources who have worked on these cases with fatal outcomes.

[90] Hannah Arendt, *Eichmann in Jerusalem: A Report on the Banality of Evil* (Hammondsworth, NY: Penguin, 1977).

stranded Indians in Istanbul without passports or any identification. Speaking a dialect that was unknown to any Indian diplomats in Turkey, the well-intentioned investigators could not locate the trafficking network or determine to which part of India these people, abandoned by their smugglers, should be returned. The cost of returning forty Indians by air to India was something neither the Indian embassy nor the Turkish government wanted to assume.[91] These anonymous victims remained in lengthy limbo whereas their traffickers eluded any sanctions or financial penalties.

The central element of trafficking is coercion and deception. Victims rarely comply immediately with the wishes of their traffickers. Or they subsequently resist. Attempts at escape are brutally punished so that other trafficking victims will not follow. To coerce the victims in these situations, traffickers may retain the services of particularly violent criminals to rape and beat the women repeatedly after they have been brought to their destination. One might think that the customers would not appreciate having sex with a woman with bruises all over her body, but this does not appear to be a liability. As a vice investigator in London with decades of experience explained, "I have yet to see a customer turn in a trafficker for providing him with an abused woman. Rather, if the client objects to the woman's condition, he merely asks the trafficker to provide him another woman who is not damaged."[92]

The "violence specialists" retained by the traffickers are a special subset of the business, comprised often of demobilized soldiers, veterans of civil wars and regional conflicts; they are the pure thugs of organized crime networks. In some cases, their violence toward trafficking victims represents a form of revenge on enemy women. Illustrative of this is the case of Chechens who are used by traffickers to "break in" Slavic women.[93] Chechens, brutalized by years of repression by Russians, are key figures in post-Soviet organized crime. Traffickers, exploiting their hatred of Russians and their traditional desire for revenge, retain these criminals to terrorize the women under their control. Chechens now are the largest community of political refugees in Western Europe. Within the legitimate community of refugees are criminals whose services are available to traffickers in most European cities.

[91] This case was described by one of the Turkish National Police officers from the anti-smuggling unit in a class at American University in 2005.

[92] Interview in London in April 1998.

[93] An asylum case on which the author worked illustrated this phenomenon in Italy.

The international links of the traffickers allow them to deploy violence at all stages of their network. Their ability to intimidate both the victim and the family at home differentiates contemporary trafficking from the slave trade of earlier centuries. Victim compliance is achieved by threatening family members.[94] The threats against loved ones are not idle but are often carried out, adding veracity to the traffickers' words "If you do not do what we want, we will hurt your family."

One asylum case granted in Canada illustrates the violence applied to a trafficker's loved one. A boyfriend who tried to protect a returned Russian trafficking victim to Estonia in the late 1990s had his ribs broken and his life threatened. Having been provided no protection by local Estonian law enforcement, he and the former trafficking victim fled to Canada.[95]

Similar threats are made in labor trafficking cases. International communications facilitate the delivery of threats from long distances. In the late 1990s, the family of a Chinese individual smuggled to Canada had not made expected payments. Phone calls were repeatedly made to the family in China during which the screams of the tortured trafficking victim were heard. Canadian law enforcement sought to break up the ring but could not trace the phone calls, which were routed from Canada through the United States to China. Seeking the cooperation of American law enforcement, the calls of the traffickers in Canada were traced back to their home base in China. With this proof, diverse elements of the criminal organization that terrorized the victim and his family in China could finally be arrested.[96]

Victims of traffickers rarely seek assistance. The reasons for inaction are multiple. Often they do not have the language or the capacity to reach law enforcement. Other victims have such engrained fear of law enforcement from their countries of residence that they do not expect to obtain any assistance in the country to which they are trafficked. Others know from the experience of their fellow trafficking victims that their appeals

[94] Cathy Zimmerman, Mazeda Hossain, Kate Yun, Brenda Roche, Linda Morison, and Charlotte Watts, "Stolen Smiles: a Summary Report on the Physical and Psychological Health Consequences of Women and Adolescents Trafficked in Europe," London School of Hygiene and Tropical Health, 2006, 10, http://www.lshtm.ac.uk/hpu/docs/StolenSmiles.pdf (accessed July 29, 2009).

[95] The author was an expert witness in this case.

[96] Case of a Washington-based federal prosecutor reported by him November 30–December 1, 2000 "Transnational Crime, Corruption and Information Technology," American University, Washington, DC, http://www.american.edu/traccc/events/attended.html (accessed June 22, 2007).

to the police are hopeless. Law enforcers in league with the traffickers will resell the victim, and the victim may be subjected to intense violence as punishment for the escape attempt.

Victims often believe that it is selfish to appeal for help. They have been repeatedly told by their traffickers that there will be violent retaliation against family members if they attempt to escape. The international ties of the traffickers make this a viable threat in many situations. Those that have "incurred a debt to their traffickers" may, as a result of their escape, place inordinate debt on their family at home, who will be visited by the traffickers' network demanding payment. Therefore, European authorities who have rescued Nigerian women report that they return to their traffickers to fulfill their obligations.[97] Likewise, police in New York report that some Chinese immigrants located in police raids do not want "to be freed" because of the burden that will be placed on family members in China. A similar situation in the Midwest is discussed in Chapter 8.

Conclusion

Human trafficking is a large and rapidly growing component of transnational crime. The recent growth has been characterized by the entrance of a large range of groups into this trade. No longer is trafficking dominated by Asian criminals. Rather, trafficking groups operate on every continent and even in remote locales. Much of trafficking is within individual countries, but increasingly victims are trafficked long distances to reach their destinations to face sexual or labor exploitation. In conflict regions, youths may be trafficked as child soldiers.

Traffickers have well established international logistics networks to move their victims across vast distances. Many uneducated victims often do not even know the name of the country of their destination. Moreover, many trafficking victims are moved so far from their homes that there is no prospect of return.

Traffickers succeed because groups from different parts of the world cooperate. Traditional animosities among ethnic groups are often ignored to obtain a profit. Yakuza operate successfully in many parts of Asia

[97] For a discussion of what binds Nigerian trafficking victims see Jørgen Carling, "Migration, Human Smuggling and Trafficking from Nigeria to Europe," produced for IOM, 29, 55, http://www.prio.no/sptrans/1326102309/file48438_carling_2006_migration_human_smuggling_and_trafficking_from_nigeria_to_europe.pdf (accessed July 17, 2009).

where Japanese are still hated for their World War II atrocities. Arabs and Israelis work together in the Sinai trafficking women from the former Soviet Union.

As in other forms of organized crime, violence, intimidation, and corruption play key roles. Unfortunately, the violence is directed almost exclusively at the trafficking victims or their families rather than criminal rivals, as is the case in drug trafficking. Therefore, victims feel compelled to stay in their trafficked situation even if there are ways to extract themselves from the exploitative situation. In some cases, this is the Stockholm Syndrome at work.

Just as all organized crime needs corruption to operate, trafficking organizations bribe all kinds of officials to execute their operations.[98] The ultimate corruption may be when members of the police and security apparati play key roles in trafficking networks, unfortunately an all too frequent occurrence in many communist and post-communist states in Eurasia and Asia.

[98] Holmes, "Corruption & Trafficking," 89–121.

4

The Business of Human Trafficking

Organized crime, like all businesses, is focused on making a profit, ensuring supply, and meeting demand. What sets an organized crime business apart is that violence and corruption are innate to its business operations. As the previous chapter has shown, human trafficking is very much part of organized crime because the criminals who traffic people rely on coercion, deception, corruption, and brute force at every stage of the business. Human trafficking businesses worldwide share these common features.

Yet analyses of international business and trade reveal that there are great variations in the business practices of entrepreneurs in different regions of the world. This helps explain great differences in trade data and in economic rates of growth. For example, the Chinese have focused on trade to foster development. In the worldwide recession that started in 2008, China experienced a decline in growth but not a national economic meltdown. Rather, the Chinese were among the first to show signs of recovery from the global economic crisis. In contrast, Russia and some other post-Soviet states experienced significant economic growth after the year 2000 as a consequence of the rise in prices for the sale of natural resources such as oil and gas that provided the core of their economy.[1]

The 2008 global financial crisis had a much more negative impact in this region. Four Soviet successor states suffered the greatest decline in gross domestic product because they were natural resource dependent

[1] Shimelse Ali, Uri Dadush and Lauren Falcao, "Financial Transmission of the Crisis: What's the Lesson," http://www.carnegieendowment.org/publications/index.cfm?fa=view&id=23284& prog=zgp&proj=zie (accessed August 22, 2009).

and lacked diversified economies that could survive well in a difficult environment. In the United States, the economy is driven by consumer consumption; the American economy contracted in the global crisis, as Americans could not spend as in the past.

These economic comparisons are very relevant to this analysis of human trafficking. The illicit trade in humans mirrors the legitimate economy. As this chapter analyzes, Chinese human traffickers treat their business as a form of trade and a means of generating capital for economic development. Groups from the Soviet successor states treat the trade in women as an exploitable natural resource, such as oil, gas, and timber that is sold without regard to the future. American pimps who trade in women consume almost all their profits and engage in conspicuous consumption, a pattern of behavior associated with American life before the very deep recession that began in 2007.

Distinctive regional differences in trafficking are not a contemporary phenomenon. In the past, there was no single model of slavery. Slavery was different in the American colonies, Brazil, and the Horn of Africa.[2] Just as the trade in humans was shaped in the past by cultural, geographic, and economic forces, today's human trafficking is also shaped by these forces as well as by historical traditions.

Some groups specialize in human trafficking whereas others commit diverse crimes simultaneously.[3] Others make more use of corruption and technology. Still others exploit the absence of effective state controls in their home country, whereas others use underground banking or commodities to launder their money. These distinctions are essential in understanding the business operations of human trafficking groups in different regions of the world.

[2] David Northrup, *Indentured Labor in the Age of Imperialism 1834–1922*, Studies in Comparative World History (New York: Cambridge University Press, 1995), 156–57; Hugh Tinker, *A New System of Slavery: The Export of Indian Labour Overseas, 1830–1920* (London: Oxford University Press, 1974), 114.

[3] Kevin Bales and Stephen Lize, "Trafficking in Persons in the United States," National Institute of Justice report, November 2005, Award Number: 2001-IJ-CX-0027, 5, http://www.ncjrs.gov/App/Publications/abstract.aspx?ID=233446 (accessed September 3, 2009). In the White Lace case, the post-Soviet group engaged in identity theft. Los Angeles Police Department Press Release, Operation White Lace, http://www.lapdonline.org/press-releases/2002/12/pr02726.htm (accessed July 20, 2006). This information was obtained from interviews in 2005. Mexican drug groups move both drugs and people simultaneously as do Balkan groups. See Jana Arsovska and Stef Janssens, "Policing and Human Trafficking: Good and Bad Practices," in *Strategies Against Human Trafficking: The Role of the Security Sector*, Cornelius Friesendorf, ed. (Vienna: National Defence Academy and Austrian Ministry of Defence and Sport, 2009). But Chinese appear to be more unidimensional, focusing only on people.

Understanding the nature of the organization is not an intellectual construct. It is essential if there is to be success in combating human trafficking. As the great anti-mafia judge Giovanni Falcone explained, he was able to combat La Cosa Nostra in Sicily only when he profoundly understood its nature.[4] Judge Falcone's understanding of the mafia is unfortunately not very helpful to the counter-trafficking effort because the mafia has made its money primarily in other areas of criminal activity. Yet his insight that one must understand the tradition, cultures, and norms of a criminal group in order to fight them effectively should be at the core of any rational policies to counter the business of human trafficking.

Categorization of Trafficking Groups as Different Business Types or Criminal Enterprises

Six different business models of traffickers drawn from each of the regions discussed in Chapters 5 through 9 are analyzed. The business models of Chinese, post-Soviet, Balkan, American, Hispanic, and Nigerian groups are analyzed. These are ideal types, and not every crime group from a particular region fits within a particular model. For example, significant differences could be identified within Asia as Japanese and Indian traffickers differ greatly. Each group is analyzed in terms of many criteria including business strategies, advertising, profit margins and goals, use of violence and corruption, and the educational level of the traffickers. These models are not confined to the country or region of origin because the smugglers and traffickers cross continents. Chinese and post-Soviet groups are the most geographically far-reaching in their trafficking operations, followed by the Nigerians.

Groups often cooperate along transit routes and countries of destination. Yet these distinctive features strongly influence these interactions.

Trade and Development Model – Chinese Traffickers

The Chinese trade and development model[5] is most applicable to the smuggling of men for labor exploitation but also applies to the trafficking

[4] Alexander Stille, *Excellent Cadavers: The Mafia and the Death of the First Italian Republic* (New York: Pantheon, 1995).

[5] This analysis of Chinese organized crime and trafficking is based on a variety of law enforcement sources in addition to the academic sources and the materials from prosecuted cases. The evidence from actual investigations of the business side of Chinese organized crime has been made available to the researcher. These include economic analyses of the crime based on the findings of criminal investigations. In addition, information has

of women, who may represent as much as 10 percent of the total human trade conducted by Chinese groups, judging from confiscated ship logs and recent investigations.[6] Chinese smuggling organizations operate as businesses that are integrated from start to finish. They record their expenses in minute detail, listing the costs of bribes and even of the $20 bus fares for transfer between Chinatowns of the Northeast on so-called Chinatown buses.[7] They control those smuggled from recruitment through debt bondage. Corruption is an integral part of the business from start to finish. As in the former Soviet states, state controls are eliminated as Chinese government officials in southern China are bribed or are directly implicated in the trafficking networks.[8] Seized ledgers and investigations reveal that corruption costs are an integral cost at every stage of the business. This is their largest expense, except in cases where they incur legal expenses.[9] Without such payments, smugglers could not move tens of thousands of people out of the tightly controlled territory of China.[10] Officials are bribed at the source and in transit countries in the Americas; even at high levels of the U.S. Citizenship and Immigration Services corruption has facilitated this trade.[11] Chinese smugglers, however, save

been obtained from Interpol's organized crime division, which analyzed the relationship among different Chinese trafficking organizations operating in Europe. Also Ko-lin Chin, *Chinatown Gangs Extortion Enterprise & Ethnicity* (New York and Oxford: Oxford University Press, 1996); Willard H. Myers III, "Testimony, 21 April 1994, Willard H. Myers, III, Founder/Director, Center for the Study of Asian Organized Crime," in Senate Foreign Relations/Terrorism, Narcotics and International Operations, U.S. Law Enforcement and Foreign Policy, Federal Document Clearing House, 1994; Peter Kwong, *Forbidden Workers: Illegal Chinese Immigrants and American Labor* (New York: New Press, 1997).

6 UNODC, "Trafficking in Persons: Global Patterns," http://www.unodc.org/pdf/traffickinginpersons_report_2006ver2.pdf (accessed July 27, 2006).

7 Chinatown buses provide a cheap form of intracity transport between Chinatowns in the major cities of the American East coast. The buses have been cited for numerous violations but continue to function and are used by economy-minded travelers as well as smugglers.

8 "Interview with Peter Kwong," http://usinfo.state.gov/eap/Archive_Index/Interview_with_Peter_Kwong.html (accessed June 28, 2007).

9 But the largest expenses were the legal fees incurred in the filing of phony asylum claims for the smuggled Chinese. The lawyers received almost 25 percent of the sixty million dollars generated by the trafficking ring. Interview with the law enforcement analyst in Washington, DC, conducting a complex, computerized analysis of the seized financial records of the Chinese smugglers, 1999.

10 Ko-lin Chin, *Smuggled Chinese: Clandestine Immigration to the United States* (Philadelphia: Temple University Press, 1999), 42

11 Ibid., 42–45; Patrick Radden Keefe, *The Snakehead: An Epic Tale of the Chinatown Underworld and the American Dream* (New York: Doubleday, 2009), 283–85; discussions with investigators of the Asian Cruise case.

on advertising costs, as they do not need to publicize their businesses to recruit or sell the services of the smuggled humans. The smugglers' links ensure a steady flow of human beings from the source communities with guaranteed placement upon delivery. Although as the Fujian area has become more prosperous, there is less desire to incur large debts to emigrate, and smugglers have to look to other parts of China for others who will pay for their services.[12]

Men are required to work long hours in restaurants, sweatshops, and other businesses controlled by the Chinese diaspora community. Girls and women are required to work in sweatshops or brothels.[13] In Asian Cruise, a large-scale investigation by the Immigration and Naturalization Service (INS) of Chinese smuggling to the United States, smuggled migrants were tied to 400 Chinese restaurants or take-outs in the Washington, D.C., area.[14] The conditions of employment, according to analysts of their work environment, often resembled those of trafficked rather than smuggled people.[15]

Young girls who are forced into prostitution are controlled from recruitment to assignment to a brothel. In one brothel in Washington, D.C.'s Chinatown, a five-minute walk from the national headquarters of the Citizenship and Immigration Services, young girls were found chained to the walls. Wiretaps on a brothel in a typical suburban Virginia home revealed the links between the girls and their home communities in Fujian, from where the traffickers also originated.[16]

The control of the trafficked humans from recruitment through exploitation results in significant and long-term profits. This illicit trade in people resembles other Chinese trade that is integrated across continents and in which the significant profits are repatriated for investment in southern China.

Assets are sometimes laundered home through wire transfers, but multimillions of dollars are returned through the system of Chinese underground banking, which launders money through gold shops and

[12] Keefe, *Snakehead*.

[13] Jenny W. Hsu, "Dozens of Smugglers Captured," *Taipei Times*, June 19, 2009, http://www.taipeitimes.com/News/front/archives/2009/06/19/2003446547 (accessed August 19, 2009).

[14] Bertil Lintner, *Blood Brothers: The Criminal Underworld of Asia* (New York: Palgrave MacMillan, 2003), 222–23; discussions with U.S. investigators of Chinese organized crime.

[15] M. R. J. Soudijn, *Chinese Human Smuggling in Transit* (Den Haag: Boom Juridische Uitgevers, 2006); "Interview with Peter Kwong."

[16] Interview with an INS investigator in 2000.

other long-established techniques.[17] Money generated from human smuggling and trafficking can be moved extremely rapidly through the underground banking system. After the arrest of the lawyer-facilitator Mr. Porges, mentioned in Chapter 3, tens of millions of dollars was moved through the underground banking system back to China before law enforcement investigators in Washington could freeze the accounts of the smugglers.[18]

Chinese are smuggled and trafficked not only into the United States but also into Europe, Australia, and many parts of Asia, as well as parts of the former Soviet Union as the following chapters will discuss. Much of the 13th arrondissement in Paris has been taken over by Chinese, a large percentage of them smuggled migrants. The International Labour Organization (ILO) estimates that there are now 50,000 illegal Chinese immigrants in France, 70 percent of them in Paris.[19] Great Britain is also filled with large numbers of smuggled Chinese, as the tragic deaths in the van crossing the Channel and the deaths of 20 smuggled cockle workers in 2004 made the public realize.[20]

Illegal Chinese work in horrendous labor conditions in the Italian textile and leather industry that investigators there find difficult to penetrate. In a bizarre case, Chinese smugglers formed an alliance with the IRA, a terrorist organization, in order to enter Northern Ireland.[21]

Smuggled Chinese have different fates depending on their destinations. Smugglers of Chinese citizens to the United States free those they have smuggled after they have worked off their debt, whereas prosecutors in Italy report that the individuals trafficked there often remain enslaved even after their contracted period of bondage is over. Part of the reason for this divergent treatment is that Chinese migrants cannot be readily absorbed into the legitimate economy. Therefore, freed Chinese cannot

[17] For an understanding of different forms of underground banking see Nikos Passas, "Informal Value Transfer Systems, Money Laundering and Terrorism," January 2005 http://www.ncjrs.gov/pdffiles1/nij/grants/208301.pdf (accessed June 29, 2007).

[18] Interview with investigators of Asian Cruise Case.

[19] "50,000 Illegal Chinese Immigrants Miserable in Paris," June 24, 2005, reporting on the ILO report, "Chinese Immigrants Victims of Labor Exploitation in Paris," http:///english.people.com.cn/200506/24/eng20050624_192189.html (accessed June 9, 2007).

[20] James Meek and Jonathan Watts, "Two days before the disaster, Yu phoned his wife. He said his life was terrible. I told him to leave. He said without this job I can't eat,"http://www.guardian.co.uk/world/2004/feb/20/china.ukcrime (accessed May 17, 2009).

[21] John Cassidy, "UFV Link to Triad Gang; RUC probes attack on Chinese Immigrants," *Sunday Mirror*, June 2, 2000, http://findarticles.com/p/articles/mi_qn4161/is_20000702/ai_n14513648ehead-IRA connection (accessed June 29, 2007).

then pay the smugglers to move other family members as frequently as occurs in the United States.[22] Furthermore, smugglers have greater difficulty delivering replacement workers to Italian sweatshops. The underground factories that exploit the workers are therefore reluctant to free them. In the United States, it is in the financial interests of the smugglers to uphold their contracts with those smuggled, but that is not always the case in Italy.

The Chinese model results in less significant violations of human rights than the post-Soviet model because the Chinese smugglers and traffickers have an interest in gaining long-term profits from those whom they have smuggled. They need to keep them healthy to ensure that they can work and perpetuate the cycle of smuggling. Furthermore, the fact that the smugglers' success in recruiting future clients within the closely knit communities of southern China depends on the experience of those they have previously smuggled sets limits on the abuse that this human cargo can suffer. Violations may be greater in Europe than in the United States, where smuggled migrants have less chance of succeeding financially in their new country and therefore are of less long-term benefit to their smugglers.

Natural Resource Model – Post-Soviet Organized Crime

Post-Soviet crime groups, ranging from a few individuals to multifaceted crime groups, traffic women and exploit laborers, but do not operate with an integrated business model. Their focus is on short-term profits, with little concern for the maintenance of supply and the long-term durability of the business. Post-Soviet organized criminal groups sell people as if they were a readily available natural resource such as timber or furs. In this respect, this business reflects the pre-revolutionary Russian trade in natural resources and the new Russian trade emphasis on the sale of oil and gas.[23]

[22] Willard Myers analyzes the system by which those freed from bondage pay for the transport of others, testimony of Willard H. Myers III. This process, according to Khalid Koser, also exists among Pakistani irregular migrants to the UK. Reported in a talk at American University, April 23, 2007.

[23] "Paznoobraznye posledstviia torgovli liud'mi," (Diverse Consequences of the Trade in People) in *Vne Tolerantnosti. Torgovliia liud'mi i rabskii trud:metamorfozy starykh prestuplenii i novykh metody ikh preodoleniia*, Liudmila Erokhina, ed. (Vladivostok: Izdvo TGEU, 2009), 23–45.The information for this model is based on more than a dozen years of research conducted by scholars in Russia and Ukraine under the sponsorship of TraCCC (Transnational Crime and Corruption Center). The TraCCC researchers have had significant access to law enforcement personnel and records. As both countries have increased their commitment to fight human trafficking, much more information has become available for analysis. This analysis is based also on interviews with individuals

Post-Soviet trafficking groups are most pronounced in the Slavic regions of Russia but also thrive in the Baltics and Moldova. They are less prevalent in the Caucasus and Central Asia, which have more traditional societies. Often comprising individuals with higher educations, they frequently use former military personnel as their enforcers. Russian soldiers brutalized by the wars in Afghanistan, Yugoslavia, or Chechnya, including Chechens themselves, often use extreme violence against the women who resist working as prostitutes or are suspected of withholding money from their traffickers.

In the late 1980s and early 1990s, small-scale entrepreneurs assumed a larger role in human trafficking in the Soviet successor states. Larger crime groups focused more on grabbing the prime jewels of the Russian economy then being privatized. Only after major crime groups solidified their hold on the larger economy did they expand into sexual and labor trafficking on a significant scale.[24] This is exemplified by the infamous Uralmash crime group that acquired key businesses and natural resources during privatization in and around Ekaterinburg, the third largest city of Russia. Only in the late 1990s did splinter groups of Uralmash begin to participate in significant human trafficking, often based in the nightclubs and casinos they owned.

The post-Soviet traffickers recruit girls from children's homes, and use advertisements and fake employment agencies to secure other victims. Infants sold for adoptions are acquired from hospitals and children's homes and sometimes purchased from alcoholic parents. Children who will be forced to be beggars are found in institutions, on the street, or in railway stations where abandoned and street children gather.[25] Web sites and the Internet are used extensively, as post-Soviet groups are the most technologically advanced and reliant of any of the diverse trafficking

who had been trafficked and with those who were involved in recruiting women to be trafficked. Additional insights were obtained by TraCCC interviews with Western law enforcement investigators and prosecutors who have conducted investigations of trafficking cases in the United States and in Europe. See also *Torgovliia Liudmi*, Elena V. Tiuriukanova and Liudmila D. Erokhina, eds. (Moscow: Akademia, 2002); Louise Shelley, "Post-Communist Transitions and the Illegal Movement of Peoples: Chinese Smuggling and Russian Trafficking in Women," *Annals of Scholarship* 14, no. 2 (Fall 2000), 71–84.

24 Stephen Handelman, *Comrade Criminal: Russia's New Mafiya* (New Haven: Yale University Press, 1995), 72–92; Research by TraCCC-affiliated scholars in the Urals.

25 Clementine K. Fujimura, Sally W. Stoecker and Tatyana Sudakova, *Russia's Abandoned Children: An Intimate Understanding* (Westport, CT: Praeger, 2005); Sally Stoecker, "The Rise in Human Trafficking and the Role of Organized Crime," *Demokratizatsiya* 8, no. 1 (Winter 2000), 129–214.

organizations. With these systems of recruitment, current victims are not linked to the next, as is the case in Chinese smuggling and trafficking where recruitment goes on within communities.

Women are often acquired for resale to intermediaries who will exploit their services in lucrative markets. Most often, the women are sold to nearby trading partners (usually the most proximate crime group). For example, women are sold to crime groups from the Balkans, Turkey, or Israel. Corruption is employed in every phase of their operations, but particularly by buying protection or so-called *kryshas* from local law enforcement, bribing officials at borders, and penetrating the consular branches of diverse embassies.[26]

London police discovered diverse techniques used by post-Soviet groups to repatriate profits. Trade based money laundering was key. Groups operated export – import businesses, directly acquiring commodities such as cars or galoshes that could be resold in their home countries at a profit. These businesses also engaged in over- and under-invoicing, widespread techniques used by other illicit businesses for laundering money.[27]

This model does not maximize profits, as the business is not integrated from start to finish, as is the Chinese. But the traffickers' analytical capacity helps them retain their profits. They have determined that the safest method to launder their profits is to use couriers and transfer profits in the name of the trafficked women, for example, through wire transfer businesses. Money orders are also used. In the White Lace case mentioned in the previous chapter, the police in Los Angeles found piles of the carbon copies of $20 money orders strewn all over the floor.[28]

Often, significant shares of the profits are disposed of through conspicuous consumption. Yet they are also used to purchase another commodity with a rapid turnover, for example, buying shops in Western Europe to sell counterfeit goods and acquiring food service and travel businesses at home. These forms of money laundering reveal how human

[26] A discussion of the *krysha* can be found in Frederico Varese, *The Russian Mafia: Private Protection in a New Market Economy* (New York: Oxford University Press, 2005). Research by the TraCCC team found that protection of different crime groups that traffic women in some regions was divided among the police and the security police.

[27] Interview by author with Paul Holmes, London, 1998.

[28] This was the money laundering associated with the White Lace case. Los Angeles Police Department Press Release, "Operation White Lace," http://www.lapdonline.org/press-releases/2002/12/pr02726.htm (accessed July 20, 2006). The money laundering patterns were learned through interviews in Los Angeles in 2005.

trafficking converges with other crimes. Selling counterfeits is another form of illicit trade, and ownership of travel agencies facilitates movement for criminals and continual money laundering of funds through manipulation of ticketing.[29]

The post-Soviet business model results in very significant violations of human rights because the traffickers have no interest in wresting long-term profits from the women and have no connections to their families. Therefore, there are no constraints on their behavior, as in the Chinese case. Repatriation efforts are often unsuccessful because the women are frequently broken by their experiences and their home communities lack adequate social support services.

Violent Entrepreneur Model – Balkan Crime Groups

The Violent Entrepreneur Model pertains almost exclusively to the trafficking of women.[45] These crime groups do not traffic laborers, although they traffic drugs and arms along the same routes and sometimes move all of these commodities simultaneously. Their human victims are large numbers of women from Balkan states, as well as women from the former Soviet Union and Eastern Europe sold to Balkan crime groups. These criminal groups initially made their profits by offering the women to peacekeepers stationed in Kosovo. They also developed extensive international networks, running an integrated business by controlling the women from the time of "acquisition" in the Balkans through their exploitation in the brothels of Western Europe.

This is an opportunistic model in both the source and recipient countries. The civil conflict and subsequent instability in the Balkans in the 1990s resulted in large numbers of vulnerable women. Female victims were often those whose families had died or women seized as part of blood revenge by one family against another. The women had already been traumatized by the violence of war or that of internecine feuds among families and clans.

Balkan traffickers operate within family groups. Therefore, although the organizations are controlled by men, there are cases in which operations in a particular country or region are controlled by female family members or by outsiders. For example, French police, through wiretaps, discovered that a sister of one of the French-based Balkan traffickers

[29] Johan Leman and Stef Janssens, "The Albanian and Post-Soviet Business of Trafficking Women for Prostitution: Structural developments and Financial Modus Operandi," *European Journal of Criminology* 5, no. 4 (2008), 445.

was operating a cell in Belgium.[30] As the previous chapter pointed out, Balkan criminals maintain control across several neighboring countries. Belgian and Dutch women, as mentioned in Chapter 3, have been hired by Balkan clans to help run day-to-day operations because they arouse less police suspicion.[31]

The reach of Balkan trafficking groups is much less than that of post-Soviet or Chinese operations. The intended market for the women they traffic is Western and Eastern Europe. When they entered this trade, this market was dominated by established groups that traded in women. To market their commodity, Balkan groups used extreme force to oust competitors from existing markets in Continental Europe and Great Britain, hence the model name of "violent entrepreneurs."[46] Once entrenched in these markets, they cooperated with post-Soviet and Eastern European groups to provide them women and with well established Turkish organized crime groups that control the Dutch markets of the illicit sex trade.[32] For example, police investigations in Belgium revealed that the Balkan trafficking group in their country worked with 10 organized crime groups in Bulgaria.[33]

Law enforcement professionals initially investigating these criminals sometimes became targets of the crime groups that were often run by past and present members of the police and security apparati. In a sample of identified networks, one-quarter contained a former member of security person. The deep involvement of those entrusted to uphold state security reveals the depth of corruption and explains the concomitant incapacity of many Balkan states to combat trafficking.

The profits of these groups are large because they exploit women in some of the most active and lucrative markets in the world. Their expenses were particularly low in the 1990s, as they controlled the street walkers and did not need to spend much on rent or facilities for the women. They did link with the legitimate economy as they interacted with transport companies and financial institutions. The transport company allowed them to move women to Western Europe, and the banks and wire transfer businesses such as Western Union allowed them to repatriate assets.[34]

30 Arsovska and Janssens, "Policing & Human Trafficking," 213.

31 Ibid., 184.

32 Shared Hope International, *DEMAND: A Comparative Examination of Sex Tourism and Trafficking in Jamaica, Japan, the Netherlands, and the United States*, p. 48, http://www.sharedhope.org/files/demand_netherlands.pdf (accessed September 3, 2009).

33 Arsovska and Janssens, "Policing & Human Trafficking," 213.

34 Ibid., 213; testimony of Jean-Michel Colombani, April 25, 2001 in Assemblée Nationale, *L'esclavage, en France, aujourd'hui* Document 3459, 2001, 27–37.

Traffickers' handsome profits are transferred to their families or clans either through wire transfers as mentioned or through cash couriers.[35] With such substantial profits, the head of a trafficking "network in Bulgaria owned a chain of restaurants, several cafés, a pawn shop, and a taxi company."[36] Profits were also used to finance other illicit activities, to gain political power, and for investment in property and businesses such as car dealerships and travel agencies.

This model results in very significant violations of human rights and terrible violence against trafficked women. The model's reliance on violence in all stages of its operations makes it the most serious violator of human rights. Threats to family members at home are combined with terrible physical abuse of the women.

American Pimp Model – High Consumption and Small Savings

The pimp model operates exclusively within the United States and applies only to female sexual trafficking. Pimps make significant profits by trafficking small numbers of American girls and women who remain under the control of the trafficker for extended periods.

The pimps are U.S.-born traffickers, entrepreneurs operating often in loose but mutually supportive networks. They seek out vulnerable young women and runaway, homeless, or throwaway children in "a society in which children in crisis can go unnoticed."[37] The pimps find the girls at malls or bars, or find runaways on the street, who they initially manipulate by psychological means. As many of these young women have already been subjected to sexual abuse, they are recruited through offers of affection. As a federal case discloses the world of pimps, "To persuade underage females to prostitute for them, the Defendants ... presented a vision of ostentatious living, promising fame and fortune. Pimps perpetrated this myth with their own flamboyant dress, flashy jewelry, and exotic, expensive cars."[38] They then subjected the girls to the coercion that defines trafficking.

Psychological manipulation and drugs are the main tools by which the pimps keep control over their victims, forcing the women to be totally subservient and relinquish all of their earnings to their pimps.

[35] Leman and Janssens, "The Albanian and Post-Soviet Business of Trafficking Women," 445.

[36] Arsovska and Janssens, "Policing and Human Trafficking," 213.

[37] Shared Hope International, *DEMAND*, 90.

[38] U.S. of America vs. Charles Floyd Pipkins a.k.a. Sir Charles, Andrew Moore, Jr. a.ka. Batman, August 2, 2004, http://www.ca11.uscourts.gov/opinions/ops/200214306.pdf (accessed September 3, 2009).

But physical violence is also used. As the case documented, "Prostitutes endured beatings with belts, baseball bats, or 'pimp sticks' (two coat hangers wrapped together). The pimps also punished their prostitutes by kicking them, punching them, forcing them to lie naked on the floor and then have sex with another prostitute while others watched, or 'trunking' them by locking them in the trunk of a car to teach them a lesson."[39] Approximately a third of their victims suffer broken bones and half-broken teeth. Young girls are also tattooed with phrases and images indicating that they are the property of a specific pimp.[40]

In the technologically sophisticated United States, pimps used their own films to train the prostitutes under their control. They also use the Internet. For example, many pimps place their girls on craigslist. Others established a Web-based escort service that allowed customers to select particular girls.[41]

The pimps control their victims from recruitment through exploitation. Limited investment is made in the business as the women are provided little and often operate from the streets rather than apartments or other facilities requiring an expenditure by the pimp. Pimps minimize expenses by having the prostitutes they control live either in the "pimp's home or in a room at a motel or boarding house paid for by the pimp. Prostitutes turned tricks in adult clubs, in parking lots, on mattresses behind local businesses, in cars, in motel rooms, or in rooming houses. Despite these difficult conditions, prostitutes are forced to charge $30 to $80 for each client served and must turn over all her money to her pimp." Pimps engage in price-fixing to establish uniform pricing.[42]

The pimps operate as small-scale entrepreneurs who work together within networks. Federal prosecutors in Atlanta linked 14 pimps in one indictment.[43] Illustrative of their interactions are the annual conventions held in major American cities in which annual prizes are awarded for outstanding pimps.[44] The Chicago pimp ball has operated for thirty

[39] Ibid.

[40] Nicholas D. Kristof, "The Pimps' Slaves," March 16, 2008, *New York Times*, http://www.nytimes.com/2008/03/16/opinion/16kristof.html?_r=1&adxnnl=1&adxnnlx=1251986531-f+6Xe7ZylYVkdg04ixK2Zw (accessed September 3, 2009).

[41] U.S. of America vs. Charles Floyd Pipkins.

[42] Ibid.

[43] Josh Tyrangiel and Amy Bonestee, "Justice: The U.S. Attorney: Pinch On The Pimps," March 19, 2001, http://www.time.com/time/magazine/article/0,9171,999516,00.html (accessed September 3, 2009).

[44] Lessley Anderson,"Muni's Mack Daddy," *San Francisco Weekly*, June 4, 2003, http://www.sfweekly.com/2003–06–04/news/muni-s-mack-daddy (accessed January 5, 2009).

years, at times with corporate sponsorship. American popular culture, through song, videos, newspaper reports, and myth, has romanticized the pimp.[45] Until recently, there has been no attempt to reveal the pimp as an exploiter of girls and women.

The pimp model is characterized by high consumption and the absence of savings that has characterized contemporary American life. The pimps dissipate their large incomes of several hundred thousands of dollars annually on expensive clothes, jewelry, and automobiles rather than saving their money or laundering it into the legitimate economy.

The model of trafficking is characteristic of contemporary American economic life in which large incomes are expended in conspicuous consumption with no thought of saving for the future. In this model, vulnerable human beings are the source of the easy profits of the traffickers. Women, particularly minority women, are devalued. The commodification of women is part of the materialism of American life. This *sui generis* American trafficking model conforms to general Americans patterns of consumption and investment.

Supermarket Model – Low Cost and High Volume – U.S.-Mexican – Trade

The Supermarket Trade Model is based on maximizing profits by moving the largest numbers of people with relatively low costs for each individual moved.[46] Before 2001, smugglers often charged as little as several hundred dollars for their services. The increased controls on the U.S.–Mexican border since September 11th have raised the costs of transiting the border to thousands of dollars in many cases. In the period since 2001, drug organizations that previously confined their activities to moving narcotics have diversified to facilitate human smuggling.[47] Also, violent and multimember gangs such as MS-13 have entered the human smuggling business because large profits

[45] Janice Show Crouse, "Protesting the Pimps' Party," December 7, 2005, http://www.cwfa.org/articles/9621/BLI/dotcommentary/index.htm (accessed January 5, 2009).

[46] See Peter Andreas, *Border Crimes: Policing the U.S.–Mexico Divide* (Ithaca, NY: Cornell University Press, 2000). Analysis of this phenomenon is also based on interviews with American and Mexican law enforcement personnel. TraCCC has had excellent access to the U.S. border patrol because it developed training curriculum for them over many years.

[47] Mark Wuebbel, "Demystifying Human Smuggling Operations Along the Arizona – Mexico Border," http://www.american.edu/traccc/resources/publications/wuebbe01.pdf (accessed June 29, 2007).

can be made by moving hundreds of thousands of men and women annually.[48]

This model is applicable to the smuggling of both men and women. The trade in women is part of a much larger trade that involves moving large numbers of people across the border at low cost. In most cases, the smugglers only facilitate the cross-border trade, a feat that may require multiple attempts. According to a Government Accountability Office report, "From 1994 through 2004, Border Patrol records indicate that between 0.9 and 1.7 million migrants were apprehended in the nine southwest Border Patrol sectors each year" with the figure peaking in 2000.[49] In a small percentage of cases, after entry, traffickers exploit particularly vulnerable individuals such as deaf mutes forced to beg or young girls, as will be discussed in more detail in Chapter 8 on the United States.[50] Most of the Mexican "people movers" benefit from a trade that is based on large-scale supply, and, until 2007 seemingly endless demand.

The ongoing trade requires significant profit sharing with local border officials. Estimates by American law enforcement officials policing the U.S.–Mexican border suggest that as many as 90 percent of their Mexican counterparts may be taking bribes.[51] Corruption of their American counterparts is a constant and growing concern, and the inspector general's office of Homeland Security has documented numerous cases.[52] This corruption is believed to be rising because of the enormous financial

[48] Ibid.; statement of Chris Swecker, U.S. House of Representatives, Committee on Homeland Security, Subcommittee on Management, Integration and Oversight, March 8, 2006.

[49] Government Accountability Office, "Illegal Immigration: Border-Crossing Deaths Have Doubled Since 1995; Border Patrol's Efforts to Prevent Deaths Have Not Been Fully Evaluated," August 2006, p.42, http://www.gao.gov/new.items/d06770.pdf (accessed June 11, 2007).

[50] Louise Shelley, "Corruption and Organized Crime in Mexico in the Post-PRI Transition," *Journal of Contemporary Criminal Justice* 17, no. 3 (August 2001), 226; Florida State University Center for the Advancement of Human Rights, *Florida Responds to Human Trafficking* (2003), 37–62, discusses the Cadena case, http://www.cahr.fsu.edu/H%20-%20Chapter%202.pdf (accessed November 15, 2006).

[51] Interviews with U.S. border patrol officials while doing curriculum development for the U.S. border patrol between 2003 and 2005.

[52] "For the nature of its mission, Customs and Border Patrol (CBP) is vulnerable to corruption. In most instances, we found that CBP officials were involved with smugglers and drug traffickers," said Carlton Mann, Assistant Inspector General for Inspections, in an interview conducted on July 22, 2009, cited in Carmen Apaza, "The Importance of Bureaucratic Oversight Mechanisms: The Case of the Inspector General of the Department of Homeland Security," doctoral dissertation, August 2009.

temptations and the close kinship ties that exist between the Mexican and the American border officials.[53]

As security has increased at the border, the payments to smugglers on the border have escalated. Therefore, many individuals entering the United States owe thousands to the human smugglers. Smugglers also extort money from family members already in the United States by threatening to do grave physical harm to those they have transported across the U.S. border.

The increased cost of cross-border facilitation means that the likelihood of trafficking increases as individuals cannot pay their debts to the smugglers. With the economic contraction since 2007, many illegal individuals are in limbo. They are unable to obtain work to repay their debts and yet they cannot return home and rejoin their families because their earnings in Mexico will never allow them to repay their smugglers. Indentured servitude often follows.

Hispanic trafficking organizations have lower advertising costs than other trafficking groups. Business cards advertising the availability of sexual services with code words and symbols understandable only to members of the Hispanic community are distributed in shops and eating places where legal and illegal immigrants congregate. One world of illegality exists within another. Newspaper advertisements, Web sites, or other commercial services are not used to communicate with possible clients. Yet these traffickers do intersect with the legitimate economy as they rent apartments to use as brothels.[54]

Hispanic trafficking rings engage in price-fixing similar to that once done by legitimate organizations before it was outlawed. Women under the command of different trafficking organizations in the eastern United States each charge customers $30 for fifteen minutes and the amount is split 50–50 between the prostitute and the managers of the prostitution ring. At the end of the week, the women must hand over the chits, which are then totaled by a simple numerical system of lines and cross – hatches, a method necessitated by the women's low educational levels. If a woman appears to be withholding chits from the ring operators, she is punished, often brutally.[55]

[53] Randal C. Archibold and Andrew Becker, "As Border Efforts Grow, Corruption is on the Rise," *New York Times*, May 27, 2008, http://www.nytimes.com/2008/05/27/us/27border.html?_r=1&scp=1&sq=Border%20patrol%20May%2027,%202008&st=cse (accessed January 5, 2008).

[54] Shared Hope International, *DEMAND*.

[55] Lecture of Thomas Stack and Leland Wiley, "Latino Houses of Prostitution," at American University, February 27, 2007.

This bookkeeping system of Latin American trafficking rings in the eastern United States is primitive, a sharp contrast with the accounting of the most sophisticated Colombian and Mexican drug organizations.

The large number of clients that the women must serve, up to 30 a day, is reflective of the supermarket model in which the traffickers make their money – on the quantities of people served rather the quality of service. A cell of the trafficking network may net the traffickers a million dollars annually but this is far less than that netted by a comparable sized organization from the post-Soviet Union, where there is a broader and more select clientele.

Traffickers launder their money in traditional ways, returning millions of dollars in profits to Mexico, where it is invested in land and farms. Traffickers' investment patterns resemble those of migrants rather than those of drug traffickers, who often stockpile cash or buy businesses. Just as individuals smuggled to the United States send home remittances to buy land or to build and improve homes, the traffickers follow the same pattern but on a larger scale. Traffickers of even limited numbers of women or workers could invest millions in Mexican farms because they made enormous profits from their human exploitation.[56]

This model results in many significant violations of human rights and even fatalities of those smuggled and trafficked. Because there is little profit to be gained from each individual who is moved, smugglers are not always concerned about the safe delivery of those smuggled to their ultimate destination. Crossing the deserts that lie on the U.S.–Mexican border requires providing significant water to those being moved, an obligation that is not always fulfilled. Traffickers also prey on the most vulnerable sectors of Mexican society such as the deaf, minors, and those from areas of the highest unemployment. The debts incurred to organized crime by many workers in the economic crisis that started in 2007 may enhance their vulnerability in the future.

Traditional Slavery with Modern Technology – Trafficking out of Nigeria and West Africa

Nigerian organized crime groups are multifaceted; trade in women is only one part of their criminal profile.[57] Trafficking groups that trade

[56] See, for example, John Bowe, *Nobodies: Modern American Slave Labor and the Dark Side of the New Global Economy* (New York: Random House, 2008), 64–67; Shared Hope International, *DEMAND*.

[57] Information on this model is based on European analyses in government reports and interviews with law enforcement personnel from France, Italy, and the Netherlands,

in women have mixed drugs and women in the same delivery chain.[58] Members of the Nigerian diaspora community facilitate the trade, especially in Italy, which has the largest Nigerian immigrant community and the greatest number of enslaved women in Europe of Nigerian nationality.

On-the-ground recruitment in Nigeria occurs on a large scale in one region, Edo, which has also been a source of labor migrants. Yet as Chapter 9 discusses, Nigerian trafficking networks have tentacles all through West Africa, drawing women from many neighboring countries. Female recruiters conclude contracts with girls and women, and use voodoo to force compliance through psychological as well physical pressures. Many of the women who serve as recruiters were previously victims of sex trafficking. They use the modern transport links of present-day Nigeria, and are very effective because they "combine the best of both modern and older worlds by allying sophisticated forms of modern technology to tribal customs."[59] Exploiting the vulnerability of uneducated women, this trade model resembles a form of traditional slavery modernized to the global age.

Corruption is endemic in Nigeria, and state control of illicit activity is insignificant because government officials are direct beneficiaries. Nigerian traffickers exploit the corrupt and ineffective bureaucracy to obtain genuine passports with partial or incomplete information. In much

which receive a disproportionate share of the trafficking victims from Africa, as well as the limited academic research available on the topic. For further reading see Obi N. I. Ebbe, "The Political-Criminal Nexus: The Nigerian Case," in *Trends in Organized Crime* 4, no. 3 (1999), 29–59; Testimony of Zohra Azirou, Celine Manceau, and Georgina Vaz Cabral, 25 April 2001, in Assemblée Nationale, *L'esclavage, en France, aujourd'hui*, Testimony, vol. 1, Document 3459, 2001, 38–56; Assemblée Nationale, *L'esclavage, en France, aujourd'hui*, Report vol. 1, Document 3459, 2001, 12–14; IOM, "Trafficking in Women to Italy for Sexual Exploitation," 1996, http://www.iom.int/DOCUMENTS/PUBLICATION/ EN/MIP_Italy_traff_eng.pdf (accessed January 4, 2006); Jørgen Carling, "Trafficking in Women from Nigeria to Europe," *Migration Information Source*, July 1, 2005; Jørgen Carling, "Migration, Human Smuggling and Trafficking from Nigeria to Europe," produced for IOM, http://www.prio.no/sptrans/1326102309/file48438_carling_2006_migration_human_smuggling_and_traffiking_from_nigeria_to_europe.pdf (accessed July 17, 2009); Esohe Aghatise, "Trafficking for Prostitution in Italy: Possible Effects of Government Proposals for Legalization of Brothels," *Violence Against Women* 10 (2004), 1130.

[58] Francesca Bosco, Vittoria Luda di Cortemiglia, Anvar Serojitdinov, "Human Trafficking Patterns," in Friesendorf, ed., *Strategies Against Human Trafficking*, 53.

[59] "European Union Organised Crime Situation Report," Europol, 2000, http://www.europol.eu.int/index.asp?page=EUOrganisedCrimeSitRep2000 (accessed January 4, 2005).

of the 2000s, Transparency International's ranking of Nigeria as one of the most corrupt countries in the world means that trafficking rings can operate with impunity.[60]

The human rights violations of Nigerian traders are significant. Children are abandoned in recipient countries and women are pressured to work in the most physically dangerous conditions at the lowest end of the prostitution market. No money need be spent on advertising, as the women are forced to be very assertive in selling their services. Nigerian women are highly visible as streetwalkers in Italy. In the United Kingdom and Norway, Nigerian women work outdoors, even in the harsh climate.[61] Physical violence is common, and contracts with the family, which are seen by the victim as enforceable, are used to obtain compliance. Many women are unwilling to leave their traffickers because of the voodoo that is used and the coercion that is applied on family members by the transnational Nigerian criminal networks.

African crime groups make high profits, as human trafficking to Europe has grown significantly since the late 1990s. Small profits are returned to the local operations of the crime groups and occasionally to family members of the girls and women. Much of the profits are believed to flow to other illicit activities and are laundered into the legitimate economy.[62] Large homes in Edo, the source of the majority of trafficked women, are built with the proceeds of this trade.[63] Development is not fostered by the significant proceeds of this transnational crime. Even though the proceeds generated by trafficking in Western Europe would go far in Nigeria, the funds generated from the human trade, just like those resulting from the drug trade, are not used for development. Rather, they are more often used to buy political influence and buy corrupt officials at home.

The following models have distinct ways of moving their profits and preferential forms of laundering their proceeds.

[60] Nigeria was in 121st place after a courageous anti-corruption campaigner headed their agency, http://www.transparency.org/policy_research/surveys_indices/cpi/2008 (accessed September 3, 2009). Before that the situation was quite different. Nigeria in the 2006 Corruption Perceptions Index is 142 out of 163, http://www.transparency.org/policy_research/surveys_indices/cpi/2006 (accessed June 29, 2007), as well as interviews with Nigerian NGOs and retired and current Nigerian law enforcement.

[61] See Ana Jonsson, ed., *Human Trafficking in the Baltic Sea Region* (London: Routledge, 2009).

[62] IOM, "Trafficking in Women to Italy for Sexual Exploitation," 1996.

[63] Carling, "Trafficking in Women from Nigeria to Europe"; Carling, "Migration, Human Smuggling and Trafficking from Nigeria to Europe."

TABLE 4.1. *Profitability of Business Models of Trafficking*

Categorization by Profits			
Profits	**High**	**Medium**	**Low**
Model 1	X		
Model 2	X		
Model 3		X	
Model 4			X
Model 5			X
Model 6		X	

- Model 1 Chinese Groups – Very significant capital for development, large quantities returned home primarily through underground banking system, investment in land, homes, infrastructure, hotels, and a range of businesses
- Model 2 post-Soviet Groups – Much disposed of immediately in high consumption; some invested in other illegal businesses at home as well as those with high cash turnover such as restaurants, nightclubs, travel agencies, and car dealerships, investment overseas in property and trade businesses
- Model 3 Balkan Groups – Large-scale investments overseas and in international organized crime activity. Some profits returned home for investment in the economy through wire transfers and couriers. Investments made at home in cash-reliant business such as restaurants, cafés, taxi companies, car dealerships, and travel agencies. Profits also used to finance other illicit activities and to gain political power.
- Model 4 American Pimp – Little capital saved. Profits spent on clothes, expensive cars, and jewelry.
- Model 5 Mexican Groups – Capital repatriated, invested in homes, land, and farms
- Model 6 Nigerian Groups – Some profits returned to criminals' home base and to the community. Much of the profits go to other illicit activities and are laundered with proceeds of other illicit activity

Applying the Insights of the Business Models of Trafficking

The *Trafficking in Persons Report* classifies countries according to three different components of a counter-human trafficking strategy – prevention, prosecution, and protection. There has been criticism of the specific tier classifications of individual countries, yet very few have criticized this three-pronged approach to countering human trafficking.

Examining the diverse business models of the major regions of the world illustrates that the same prevention, prosecution, and protection strategies will not work everywhere. Human trafficking is so diverse that it requires multifaceted solutions tailored to the cultures and the nature of the dominant trafficking patterns. Yet in designing strategies to stem the growth of trafficking, few have applied Judge Falcone's profound insight or those of the corporate world wherein companies deeply analyze the business operations of their competitors to compete more effectively. Rather, counter-trafficking has far too often focused on uniform counter-trafficking strategies rather than those that would drive trafficking entrepreneurs of different regions out of business.

The following analysis shows why we must understand different business modes of operation and the realities of the markets where they operate. Only with this understanding can we begin to identify their vulnerabilities.

Any counter-trafficking must start with prevention. Preventing the recruitment of children, men, and women is the best way to reduce the number of victims. Some anti-trafficking advocates press for more education for girls, stating that if there is greater investment in females, they will have the opportunity to support their families and will not be vulnerable to traffickers.[64] This prevention model may work well in Asia, where crime groups prey on the uneducated and economically marginalized people,[65] but it does not work in preventing post-Soviet trafficking, where orphanage directors hand over their 18-year-old girls to traffickers on their graduation from the institutions. Moreover, post-Soviet groups capitalize on this recruitment strategy because there is a demand for young and more educated prostitutes in Western European markets. Men having more educated prostitutes feel they are getting a high-level prostitute such as a "call girl" at an accessible

64 See Nicholas D. Kristof and Sheryl Wu Dunn, "The Women's Crusade," http://www.nytimes.com/2009/08/23/magazine/23Woment.html?_r=1&scp=1&sq=kristof%20women&st=cse (accessed August 31, 2009).

65 See the work of Ruchira Gupta and her NGO, Apne aap, http://www.apneaap.org/activity.htm (accessed September 4, 2009); Judith Gilmore, "Evaluation Report of the Microsoft Unlimited Potential Anti-Trafficking Program in Asia," September 25, 2008, http://cis.washington.edu/depository/publications/researchpapers/antitrafficking.pdf (accessed September 4, 2009).

price.[66] Therefore, education may prevent trafficking in one region but may be exploited by crime groups in another. When directors of children's homes are corrupt, education is not a palliative. Rather, countering corruption and respect for children's rights must be at the core of a counter-trafficking strategy there.

Prosecution is integral to counter-trafficking because without certainty of punishment, criminals will migrate to any form of criminal activity where risks are low. Low prosecution rates have increased numbers of human traffickers. But many investigations have failed to dismantle trafficking networks because too few investigators understand that they must tailor their investigations to address regional differences in trafficking businesses. Often law enforcement does not have the language skills to perform adequate investigations. Moreover, many times the investigation of human trafficking is assigned to the vice squad or the morals branch of the police, law enforcement groups that lack resources and have a mandate that does not allow them to address the convergence of human trafficking with other illicit forms of criminal behavior.

Yet providing investigators the resources to unravel the international dimensions of the trafficking business is essential if there is to be a meaningful impact on the organization. Skilled investigators, understanding the integrated nature of the Chinese trafficking business, knew that a wiretap placed on a brothel in suburban Virginia would lead back to the criminal organization in China. This same approach might not work with post-Soviet groups that at the first opportunity sell women to other trafficking organizations. Therefore, the current exploiter may have no link with the source of the victim. Other techniques must then be used to reconstruct the network that trafficked the victims, as was done in the Girasole operation in which multiple European countries worked together to analyze the system of travel agents and hotels that facilitated the trafficking of women from the Balkans and Ukraine, resulting in the arrest of 80 criminals.[67]

Some crime groups, such as the Chinese ones, keep extensive records of their smuggling/trafficking operations down to the cost of a ticket on a Chinatown bus, whereas Hispanic trafficking groups keep much more primitive records. Therefore, dismantling a Chinese human trafficking

[66] Interviews with Dutch trafficking specialists in Washington, DC, 1999–2000.

[67] "Albania Report," http://www.protectionproject.org/human_rights_reports/... /albania.doc (accessed August 30, 2009); Phil Williams, "Combating Human Trafficking: Improving Governance Institutions, Mechanisms and Strategies," DCAF, Geneva, 2009, 417–22.

network needs to be predicated on the search for the organization's financial records, whereas dismantling a Latino trafficking organization requires a different law enforcement approach that relies on confiscating the material evidence of a case such as the payment chits and the condoms as a way of calculating the number of customers and the finances of a trafficking network.[68]

Advertising strategies exist almost exclusively to market trafficked people in the sex industry, where premium prices are paid for their services. It is rare to advertise the availability of trafficked laborers, beggars, or child soldiers. Trafficking groups in Europe and the United States rely heavily on newspaper advertisements, as mentioned previously.[69] Sex tourism in third world countries is advertised frequently through Web sites on the Internet. Latin American prostitution-trafficking groups in the United States advertise apartments where women work as prostitutes through business cards distributed with symbols such as cowboy boots and ropes understandable only to the possible clientele.[70]

Trafficking groups employ diverse advertising strategies that can be a key to identifying and prosecuting the group. Often these advertisements are places where the crime group intersects with the legitimate economy, allowing for a more effective law enforcement response. Asian groups, post-Soviet groups, and American pimps rely heavily on the Internet, whereas Hispanic and Balkan trafficking groups do much less.[71] Cooperation with Internet service providers and other undercover techniques in cyberspace must be tailored to address Web-reliant groups. Post-Soviet groups, with their flair for the big and showy, may take out a full-page ad in the phone book that costs $7,000 monthly, whereas some Asian groups take out much more discrete ads in newspapers promoting

[68] Shared Hope International *DEMAND*, 88–89.

[69] The involvement of newspapers in the sex trade is hardly new. More than two decades ago, Mort Rosenblum, then the editor of the *International Herald Tribune* (*IHT*) told his publishers that he thought it inappropriate for the newspaper to publish advertisements for escort services. The owners of the *IHT*, located in Paris, were prestigious American newspapers, the *New York Times* and the *Washington Post*. At that time, the small but expensive escort advertisements brought the newspaper approximately two million dollars in revenues annually. The editor's refusal to run such advertisements was sufficient for the publisher to dismiss the editor. The publishers were ready to pay a significant settlement to Rosenblum rather than discontinue these advertisements. Mort Rosenblum, *Who Stole the News?: Why We Can't Keep Up with What Happens in the World and What We Can Do About It* (New York,: John Wiley & Sons, 1993); private conversations with Mort Rosenblum.

[70] Shared Hope International, *DEMAND*, 88.

[71] Shared Hope International, *DEMAND*.

their "massage services." Diverse investigative techniques are needed to find the traffickers behind these different advertisement strategies in order to dismantle the trafficking organizations.

Following the money trails of human trafficking organizations is imperative and all too rarely done. It is a requisite because it can deprive criminal organizations of not only their profits but also their working capital. Moreover, understanding the finances of a crime organization allows the reconstruction of the criminal organization, a prerequisite to dismantling the crime group. This approach is routine in fighting drug organizations, but is all too rarely applied to traffickers.

Strategies to protect victims should vary depending on the nature of the trafficking organizations. Chinese, post-Soviet, and Nigerian victims have refused to cooperate with law enforcement abroad because of the long reach of the trafficking organization and their capacity and readiness to harm relatives abroad. Retrafficking is frequently a problem with Balkan trafficking groups that have such good intelligence that they meet planes of deported victims from Western Europe and immediately retraffick the women. Mexican traffickers hold captive for ransom individuals they smuggle across the U.S.–Mexican border. They then extort money from their relatives, illegal immigrants in the United States, whom they believe will pay up rather than jeopardize their illegal status in the United States by contacting U.S. law enforcement.[72] Protection of a victim requires understanding of the capacity of the trafficking organization to retaliate. Without this, the victim and the family may suffer more and the criminals may continue to generate more revenue from this human exploitation.

Conclusion

Trafficking businesses have many features common to large-scale legitimate transnational businesses – the retention of specialists, the divisions of functional responsibilities, and the need to use advertising and modern day communications to market their services.[73] The flexibility of these illicit businesses, their exploitation of advanced technology, and expert use of corruption make them highly viable and profitable. Trafficking

[72] Josh White and Dagny Salas, "Better to Be Deported Alive than to be Dead," *Washington Post*, August 23, 2009, A1.

[73] See Susan Strange, who places transnational corporations and crime groups within the same intellectual framework, *The Retreat of the State: The Diffusion of Power in the World Economy* (New York: Cambridge University Press, 1996).

organizations have experienced greater growth than most other transnational businesses because they have successfully combined the characteristics of illicit businesses with the practices of successful multinational corporations. The networked structures of the human smugglers and traffickers allow their trade to continue even if a particular division such as an accounting unit or a logistics cell is disrupted.

Human trafficking is also growing because there are financial advantages for many participants beyond the actual criminals who move and exploit human beings. Many legitimate enterprises such as nightclubs, newspapers, and transport companies make significant profits by turning a blind eye to this pervasive phenomenon.

Despite the common characteristics of human traffickers, their businesses closely resemble the trade patterns and cultures of the region from which they emanate. Trafficking is not its own *sui generis* business model but closely mirrors the trade in legitimate commodities. The trade patterns of the regional crime groups discussed in this chapter reflect patterns of trade that are centuries old. The trafficking out of Africa bears much in common with the slavery of the past, with local communities involved in the recruitment and export going through a West African hub. Russian trafficking resembles the trade in natural resources, and Chinese trade seeks to fuel economic development. The Chinese model is based on family ties whereas the Russian model, where historically there has been less reliance on the extended family, is more focused on the individual. Low-cost cross-border smuggling has characterized the situation on the U.S.–Mexico border for more than a century. The American pimp model combines the American patterns of high consumption with the exploitation of minorities that is one consequence of American racism.

An important correlation exists between the violation of human rights and the types of business models in existence. Not all slavery in the new world was the same.

Slavery in eighteenth and nineteenth century Brazil was significantly different than that in the United States. In past centuries, the extent of human trade was affected by the life expectancy of the slaves. Slaves transported to and exploited in Brazil had a much shorter life expectancy than in the United States, resulting in the transport of more people to Brazilian slave markets.[74] Today as well, in those regions where

[74] Philip C. Curtin, *The Atlantic Slave Trade: A Census* (Madison, WI: University of Wisconsin Press, 1969), 2777; Herbert S. Klein, *The Middle Passage: Comparative Studies in the Atlantic Slave Trade* (Princeton: Princeton University Press, 1969), 55, 84.

conditions are particularly harsh, such as in the Balkans, more women are trafficked because within a short time period they cease to be marketable. Therefore, the volume of contemporary trafficking is shaped not only by demand but also by the treatment of the victims.

Human rights violations such as torture and deprivation of liberty[75] are greater when those trafficked are repeatedly passed from one set of owners to another. This is particularly true in the case of women from the former socialist states. Violations are also worse when there is little relationship between past and present victims of trafficking and the recruitment of future victims is not dependent on those previously recruited by the trafficker. With the increasing transnational nature of organized crime, traffickers can threaten victims' families at home, increasing compliance of trafficking victims.

The profits of the trafficking business are enormous. Trafficking organizations, especially from Asia, invest in the tourism sector. They buy hotels, golf courses, and restaurants. Profits from trafficked Chinese labor help buy restaurants, and other Chinese laborers make the restaurants profitable. Japanese *yakuza* use the profits of their diverse businesses to buy golf courses and resorts in Thailand and then gain further profit by marketing vacations there that combine resort amenities and sex tourism. Profits from trafficking can be invested in the development of other illicit businesses such as gambling establishments and the drug trade or can be used to acquire legitimate businesses. In some cases, they fuel development and support families without other means of support. The remittances sent home by the trafficking victim, however small, may maintain a child or family in a precarious situation. Understanding that trafficking sometimes serves an important economic function not only for the smuggler but also for the communities in which they operate is crucial to explaining its endurance.

Many smuggling and trafficking groups repatriate profits to buy political influence, to neutralize law enforcement and prevent future prosecutions. Trafficking groups in the Balkans and Asia are the most ready to influence the political process but Mexican smugglers, emanating from the large-scale drug trade, have also shared this objective. For many traffickers, the acquisition of political influence is the best use they can make of their profits. This allows the criminals to become embedded in the power structures of their home communities.

[75] Freedom from these abuses is codified in the United Nations' International Covenant on Civil and Political Rights.

Trade in human beings has recently been one of the fastest growing forms of transnational crime and is now estimated at $10 to $32 billion in annual profits.[76] Yet not enough is being done to go after the profits of this crime or the money laundering associated with it. Therefore, the criminals are able to enjoy or invest their profits with little concern of their seizure. Most traffickers launder their profits outside the traditional banking system.[77] Instead, as previously mentioned, they use wire remittance services, cash couriers, and elements of underground banking. The money flows often follow the same trajectory as the people. There is one important distinction – the money and people often flow in opposite directions.[78]

The phenomenal growth of human smuggling and trafficking is explained by more than the criminals' ability to respond to supply and demand.[79] Smuggling and trafficking groups have been major beneficiaries of globalization because they have simultaneously exploited advanced technology, the diminution of state control over territory and citizens, and the growing international illicit economy. Consequently, their rapid growth is not a transient phenomenon. The business acumen,[80] marketing strategies, and expert use of facilitators by the crime groups discussed in this and the previous chapter, unfortunately portend significant future growth in the number of human traffickers and smugglers for these organizations.

[76] "UNICEF Says Human Trafficking a $10 Billion Business," 4 April 2005, http://www.voanews.com/english/archive/2005–04/2005–04–04-voa11.cfm?moddate=2005–04-04 (accessed September 11,2009); "New ILO Global Report on Forced Labor," in 2005 estimated profits of $32 billion from forced labor, http://www.ilo.org/public/english/region/afpro/addisababa/pdf/coercionqanda.pdf (accessed September 11, 2009).

[77] Council of Europe, Select Committee of Experts on the Evaluation of Money Laundering Measures (Moneyval), "Proceeds from Trafficking in Human Beings and Illegal Migration/Human Smuggling," Strasbourg, May 31, 2005; Leman and Janssens, "The Albanian and Post-Soviet Business of Trafficking Women." It is rare that a suspicious financial transaction report from the banking system triggers a human trafficking investigation. It occurs in a limited percentage of cases in Europe and the United States. The famous case that led to the resignation of Governor Eliot Spitzer of New York was a rare example of a bank report that triggered a criminal investigation.

[78] Gerhard Mild, Moneyval, "The work of the Council of Europe to fight money laundering with a special view to the combat against human trafficking," presented at OSCE-UNODC-CYPRUS Regional Operational Meeting on Combating Human Trafficking and Money Laundering in the Mediterranean Rim Region, September 18–19, 2008, Larnaca, Cyprus.

[79] Khalid Koser, "Why Migrant Smuggling Pays," *International Migration* 46, no. 2, (2008), 3–26.

[80] Leman and Janssens, "The Albanian and Post-Soviet Business of Trafficking Women," 445–48, make this point.

PART III

REGIONAL PERSPECTIVES

5

Asian Trafficking

The majority of the world's human trafficking victims live or originate in Asia, including, as mentioned in the introduction, three-fourths of the world's victims of forced labor.[1] Asian trafficking victims are exploited in all regions of the world, especially other Asian countries, Europe, the Middle East, Australia, and North America.[2] The trafficking business in Asia is more often dominated by organized crime than in other parts of the world.

Asian crime groups, both large and small, specialize in human smuggling and trafficking, in contrast with their counterparts in Latin America, North America, or Western Europe, who profit more significantly from the drug trade. The well-known crime groups of China and Japan participate in the trade, but also lesser known Korean, Thai, Indian, and other groups.[3] Crime groups became key actors in both domestic and transnational trafficking earlier and on a larger scale than their criminal counterparts in other parts of the world. Crime groups alone are not the sole facilitators. Government officials in most regions of Asia assume important roles in perpetuating the trafficking. Corruption is not

[1] Roger Plant, head of ILO's Special Action Group on Forced Labor at U.S. Hearing, "Combating Human Trafficking in China: Domestic and International Efforts," March 6, 2006, Congressional-Executive Commission on China, http://www.cecc.gov/pages/hearings/2006/20060306/RogerPlant.php (accessed August 18, 2008); *Trafficking in Persons Report 2009* (Washington, DC: U.S. Department of State, 2009), 33.

[2] United Nations Office on Drugs and Crime, *Trafficking in Persons: Global Patterns*.

[3] Bertil Lintner, *Blood Brothers: The Criminal Underworld of Asia* (New York: Palgrave Macmillan, 2003); Vidyamali Samarsinghe, *Female Sex Trafficking in Asia: The Resilience of Patriarchy in a Changing World* (New York: Routledge, 2008), 107.

confined to border areas but also involves police in the cities and officials in ports, airports, and many other parts of state bureaucracies. In some parts of Asia, such as the Philippines, elites are also traffickers.[4] In the most extreme case of North Korea, the state contracts out its citizens for employment abroad in exploitative conditions, as is seen in the Russian Far East.[5]

Human smuggling and trafficking provide a significant share of the profits of many Asian organized crime groups in Japan, China, and Southeast Asia as well as in India. Not only is profit made by moving the men, women, and children, but the exploitation of human labor and the investment of the profits from this trade are sources of funds for economic development, as was discussed in the Chinese trafficking model in the previous chapter.

All forms of human trafficking exist in Asia – sexual, labor, forced marriages, trafficking of children for adoptions, child soldiers, organ trafficking, trafficking for begging, and debt bondage.[6] Sexual and labor trafficking are the most significant components of the problem. Debt bondage is pervasive and has been for centuries. In India and China before the Communist revolution, generations of a family might remain in debt bondage without being able to free themselves.[7] Intergenerational prostitution, particularly in India, also keeps successive generations of its victims in the sex trade. As Ruchira Gupta, a leading Indian anti-trafficking activist, analyzes this phenomenon,

[4] John T. Sidel, *Capital, Coercion and Crime Bossism in the Philippines* (Stanford, CA: Stanford University Press).

[5] See the work of the Vladivostok Center on Transnational Crime that includes work on human trafficking, http://www.crime.vl.ru January 13, 2009). Also see Vladivostokskii tsentr po izucheniiu organizovannoi prestupnosti, *Obraztsy nekotoryykh protsessual'nykh dokumentov po ugolovnomu delu, vozbuzdennomu po faktu torgovli liudmi, sopriazhennomu s peremeshcehniem ikh cherez gosudarstvennuiu granitsu rossiiskoi ferderatsii: Uchebno-metodicheskoe posobie* (Vladivostok: Iztvo VGUES, 2007). In an interview with a vice-governor of the Russian Far East in summer 2007, he told me that they were limiting employment of North Korean workers because they believed they were enslaved in Russia despite the interest of North Korea in sending more workers.

[6] For an excellent discussion of baby and child trafficking for adoptions in Cambodia and diverse states in India see David M. Smolin, "Child Laundering: How the Intercountry Adoption System Legitimizes and Incentivizes the Practices of Buying, Trafficking, Kidnapping, and Stealing Children." *Wayne Law Review*, vol. 56 (2006) 135–59.

[7] John Picarelli, "Historical Approaches to the Trade in Human Beings," in *Human Trafficking*, Maggy Lee, ed. (Cullompton, Devon: Willan Publishing, 2007), 33.

"That is really dangerous; when a woman's children and her children's children are also sold into prostitution, it becomes institutionalized ... none of the mothers want their daughters to get into prostitution ... but when they become older and disease-ridden, and their earning capacity comes down, they push their daughters into prostitution, because otherwise they starve.[8]

Men frequenting prostitutes is deeply engrained in the culture of many Asian societies. Therefore, brothel keepers and those running entertainment businesses secure trafficked women to meet the demand, often by procuring women through human traffickers. Women who were once trafficked often themselves become traffickers.[9]

Trafficking of children in Asia assumes a more significant proportion of overall trafficking than in other regions of the world. Increasingly younger children are found in the sex industry as customers seek to avoid AIDS, and much Asian sex tourism features children and minors of both sexes.[10] Children in India are maimed to be more effective beggars.[11] Babies are trafficked within China for adoptions abroad, with boys commanding more than girls.[12] Young boys were trafficked from Pakistan and Bangladesh to the United Arab Emirates (UAE) to perform the dangerous work of camel jockeys.[13]

[8] Interview with Ruchira Gupta, http://www.satyamag.com/jan05/gupta.html (accessed August 18, 2008).

[9] Ruchira Gupta, NGO Briefing on Release on Trafficking in Persons Report, June 6, 2008, U.S. State Department, Washington, DC.

[10] Pratima Poudel and Jenny Carryer, "Girl Trafficking, HIV/AIDS, and the Position of Women in Nepal," *Gender and Development* 8, no. 2 (July 2000) 74–9; Samarsinghe, *Female Sex Trafficking in Asia*, 79.

[11] Discussion of Indian doctors caught on film offering to maim children and adults for begging with payment offered by the begging mafia, http://www.bio-medicine.org/medicine-news/Maimed-Conscience – and-Maimed-Beggars–28Medical-Ethics-in-India-29 –u2013-Part–12794–4 (accessed August 18, 2008).

[12] Chinese girl trafficking for adoptions. In one case, dozens of children were taken from the poorer state of Yunnan and sold in the wealthier state of Shandong. A higher price was commanded for boys than for girls, http://gvnet.com/humantrafficking/China.htm (accessed June 8, 2008); Francesca Bosco, Vittoria Luda di Cortemiglia, Anvar Serojitdinov, "Human Trafficking Patterns," in *Strategies Against Human Trafficking: The Role of the Security Sector*, Cornelius Friesendorf, ed. (Vienna: National Defence Academy and Austrian Ministry of Defence and Sport, 2009), 57.

[13] Steven Nettleton, "The Hard Road Home for Young Camel Jockeys from Bangladesh," http://www.unicef.org/infobycountry/bangladesh_35935.html (accessed August 18, 2008). Since 2005 UAE has forbidden camel jockeys younger than 16; see report on Bangladesh human rights group on this problem Govind Prasad Thapa, "Plight of Trafficked Women in Nepal," in *Global Trafficking in Women and Children*, Obbe N. I. Ebbe and Dilip K. Das, eds. (Boca Raton, FL: CRC Press, 2008), 97.

As in other regions of the world, not all child trafficking is for financial profit. Children are trafficked as child soldiers in conflict regions within Sri Lanka, Myanmar, and the Philippines.[14]

Rapid economic development in India and China is not decreasing trafficking. In the large and populous countries of Asia such as India, China, and Indonesia, internal trafficking may be a more significant part of the problem than its cross-border component. For example, in China, badly injured minors and adults work as slaves in precarious work conditions at pottery kilns. The demand for production at low cost provides an incentive to exploit laborers.[15] Increasing economic disparity within countries also fuels trafficking, as mentioned in Chapter 1. For example, rapid development has occurred in the state of Bangalore and the city of Mumbai in India, including rapid growth in the number of highly proficient computer and technology specialists. The same can be said for Shanghai and parts of China where significant foreign investment has been made in infrastructure projects. Sex trafficking has increased in Mumbai and Shanghai to satisfy increased consumer demand. Girls from poorer regions of India and Nepal are brought to the brothels of Mumbai, whereas women are trafficked from poorer regions of China and Southeast Asia to satisfy the demand in Shanghai and other larger cities where many male migrants live on their own far from their families for extended periods.

Chinese economic development, combined with the controls of the central Communist state, create distinct conditions for trafficking. Some speculate that China may replace Thailand as the sexual trafficking hub for Asia.[16] Within China, there is also much domestic trafficking providing forced or bonded laborers for factories. The policy of one-child families means that unwanted girls are sometimes trafficked for adoptions abroad in order that parents may have a prized son. The resulting gender imbalance fuels other trafficking as women are trafficked from North Korea and the poorer states of Southeast Asia such as Myanmar, Cambodia, and

[14] United Nations Office on Drugs and Crime, *Global Report on Trafficking in Persons 2009*, http://www.unodc.org/documents/Global_Report_on_TIP.pdf (accessed July 18, 2009), 52–53.

[15] Simon Elegant, "Slave Labor in China Sparks Outrage," June 20, 2007, http://www.time.com/time/world/article/0,8599,1635144,00.html (accessed August 18, 2008); *Trafficking in Persons Report 2008* (U.S. Department of State, 2008), 8.

[16] Statement of Chris Smith, "Combating Human Trafficking in China: Domestic and International Efforts," March 6, 2006, Congressional-Executive Commission on China, http://www.cecc.gov/pages/hearings/2006/20060306/ChrisSmith.php (accessed August 18, 2008).

Vietnam to China to provide brides for Chinese men who cannot find them within their own society.[17] Often North Korean women are lured by crime groups or cross into Northeast China hoping to escape the difficult conditions at home.[18] Therefore, state policies to limit population growth can inadvertently lead to new forms of trafficking.

Human trafficking in Asia, particularly the forced labor component, was exacerbated by the global financial crisis, which began in 2008. The consequences of this crisis have been experienced most acutely in Asia where the preponderance of the world's forced labor victims reside.[19]

Human trafficking persists in many parts of Asia because of the indifference of many countries and the absence of political will.[20] In authoritarian Asian countries, leaders are more interested in maintaining political power than in serving their citizens and providing for their welfare. In democratic societies like Japan, the failure to address trafficking is explained more by enduring cultural norms such as the entitlement to sex by Japanese "salarymen" and an unwillingness to recognize the extent of the problem and intimidation by the *yakuza*.

Historical Precedents

Trafficking in human beings has significant historical precedents in Asia. Asia has a long history of exploitation of labor, although it lacked the large-scale slave trade that unites North America, Europe, and Africa. In most countries of Asia, there was a rigid caste or class system in which those at the bottom performed hard physical labor, often without or with only minimal compensation. Indentured servitude and other forms of unfree labor throughout Asia were always present. Furthermore, there was significant export of Asian populations to foreign countries in the 19th century when European colonial powers ruled many Asian countries. This led to the influx of many residents of Indian origin into the

[17] Statement of Ambassador John Miller, "Combating Human Trafficking in China: Domestic and International Efforts," March 6, 2006, Congressional-Executive Commission on China, http://www.cecc.gov/pages/hearings/2006/20060306/ JohnMiller.php (accessed August 18, 2008).

[18] http://gvnet.com/humantrafficking/NorthKorea.htm (accessed July 14, 2007).

[19] *Trafficking in Persons Report 2009*, Washington, DC: U.S. Department of State, 2009), 33.

[20] Kevin Bales, *Disposable People: New Slavery in the Global Economy* (Berkeley and Los Angeles: University of California Press, 1999); Pasuk Phongpaichit, et al., *Guns, Girls, Gambling, Ganja: Thailand's Illegal Economy and Public Policy* (Chiang Mai: Silkworm Books, 1998).

Caribbean, Guyana, and South Africa; of Javanese to the Netherlands West Indies; and of early Chinese settlers to the United States.[21]

Colonial Western European powers in Asia capitalized on the demands for labor in the United States, the Caribbean and South America, and Africa when it was no longer possible to procure slaves. Indians were not only forced into virtual slavery within their own countries, for example, in tea plantations,[22] but also were shipped to many other parts of the British empire where they served as indentured servants. Almost a million Indians went to Mauritius, British Guyana, and Trinidad alone and those who signed a contract as laborers faced a criminal penalty for breach of contract, even though recruitment was often the result of deception and coercion.[23]

China had an active trade in human beings from Southern China, particularly in the second half of the nineteenth century. Those who controlled this trade were more often Chinese, rather than colonial powers (as was the case in India). The Chinese unskilled workers or "coolies" sent off from the Southern ports of China were treated differently than those who went to the New World as indentured servants. These coolies were subject to deception and often loaded on to the boats with great force.[24] An active trade in coolies from China replaced the slave trade in the rapidly industrializing Western half of the United States, where they helped build the transcontinental railroad. The number of Chinese shipped to both North and South America and the Caribbean as indentured laborers, however, was far smaller in number than the millions of Africans who arrived as slaves in the New World.

Labor trafficking is not confined to these examples but they provide an idea of both the geographical dimensions of Asian human trafficking in the 19th century and the diversity of actors who engaged in the trade. A strong tradition of trafficking for sexual exploitation also existed in Asia, but much of the trafficking was confined to the region with the exception of Chinese women who were trafficked to brothels on the Pacific coast of the United States, where they provided sexual services for the single

[21] Wilhelmina Kloosterboer, *Involuntary Labour Since the Abolition of Slavery: A Survey of Compulsory Labour Throughout the World* (Westport, CT: Greenwood Press 1976).

[22] Nelson Mandela, *The Long Walk to Freedom: The Autobiography of Nelson Mandela* (Boston: Little Brown, 1994); Roy Moxham, *Tea: Addiction, Exploitation and Empire* (New York: Carroll and Graf, 2003).

[23] Kloosterboer, *Involuntary Labour*, 8–9.

[24] Sterling Seagrave, *Lords of the Rim: The Invisible Empire of the Overseas Chinese* (New York: G.P. Putnam's Sons, 1995).

Chinese laborers. This problem was reduced after the Chinese Exclusion Act in 1882, when immigration from China was curtailed. Public hearings in 1876 revealed the trafficking of women and the control of illicit activity by Chinese tongs, Chinese fraternal organizations, but bribes to police officers ensured that laws were not enforced.[25]

Asian organized crime groups have long historical traditions and have deep roots in their societies dating back hundreds of years. Their involvement in human trafficking is not a recent development. Japanese organized crime was always associated with water – ports and spas. They provided women for visitors to spas and facilitated their shipment abroad through the ports where they oversaw the flow of goods. In 19th and early 20th century Japan, women were trafficked from poor rural communities to domestic brothels as well as the sex industries of Borneo, China, and other Asian locales. The book, and subsequently distinguished movie, *Sandakan Brothel No. 8*, is based on the life of a young Japanese woman sold into prostitution by her family in the early nineteenth century. Trafficked as far as North Borneo, she eventually bought her freedom and returned home, but was an outcast in her society when her past was revealed.[26]

The enslavement of Asian women as sex slaves for the invading Japanese army during World War II has affected Japan's relationships with its Asian neighbors up until the present, particularly because the Japanese government still refuses to apologize for its conduct or provide compensation to most of these abused women.[27] Historians estimate there were between 80,000 and 200,000 of these "comfort women" during World War II. Of these, most were from the Korean peninsula but also from China, Indonesia, Malaysia, and the Philippines.[28]

The Korean War and the subsequent conflict in Vietnam, in which the French and subsequently the Americans participated, resulted in the creation of many brothels that served the soldiers of these conflicts. Elderly

[25] Ko-Lin Chin, *Smuggled Chinese and Clandestine Immigration to the United States* (Philadelphia: Temple University Press, 1999), 28.

[26] Yamazaki Tomoko, *Sandakan Brothel No. 8: An Episode in the History of Lower-Class Japanese Women* (Armonk, NY: M.E. Sharpe, 1999).

[27] At the Ritsumeikan Conference on Human Trafficking in December 2004 in Kyoto, members of the law faculty reported testifying on behalf of the so-called comfort women but could receive no compensation for them. See discussion in U.S. State Department Country Reports on Human Rights Practices Japan, 2006, http://www.state.gov/g/drl/rls/hrrpt/2006/78775.htm (accessed August 19, 2008), on provision of assistance to 285 former comfort women.

[28] "Comfort women protest texts," *UPI*, 2 May 1997, http://www.catwinternational. org/factbook/philippines.php (accessed July 14, 2007).

Korean women forced into prostitution have accused the Korean government and American military in complicity in facilitating the brothels. The government saw the provision of prostitutes as a way to ensure that the American military stayed in Korea.[29]

The brothels that arose to serve the servicemen were not confined to Vietnam but proliferated in Thailand and the Philippines as well.[30] After the wars, the presence of peacekeepers and soldiers added to the demand for prostitutes near the bases. At the present time, women trafficked by organized crime are found near U.S. military bases in South Korea and in Okinawa, Japan.[31] As Japan and South Korea have become more affluent, it is less likely that the prostitutes near the bases are local women. Instead, they are often trafficked women from elsewhere in Asia such as the Philippines, Thailand or Vietnam or even the former Soviet Union. Recent research conducted in South Korea discovered that the presence of these foreign troops has only added to the demand that already existed in the strong domestic prostitution markets throughout Asia.[32]

The Distinctiveness and Diversity of Asian Trafficking

The economies of Asia range in size from that of Japan (the second largest economy in the world), to China (which is a growing economic titan), to the extremely poor countries of Bangladesh, Nepal, Cambodia, Laos, and Indonesia. There is a thriving legitimate export economy in Japan and China, whereas the illegitimate economy in Thailand and Myanmar contributes significantly to the overall economy.

Japan is a highly developed democracy, but many other Asian countries have authoritarian governments, ruled by entrenched and corrupt clans and elites, military dictators, and communist rulers. Many countries have known peace and stability since World War II, whereas others have suffered serious internal conflicts such as Korea, Vietnam, Laos, and Cambodia, and more have known regional conflicts such as a Maoist

[29] Choe Sang-Hun, "Ex-Prostitutes Say South Korea and U.S. Enabled Sex Trade Near Bases," *New York Times*, January 8, 2009, A6.

[30] http://www.catwinternational.org/factbook/philippines.php (accessed July 14, 2007).

[31] Isabelle Talleyrand, "Military Prostitution: How the Authorities Worldwide Aid and Abet International Trafficking in Women," *Syracuse Journal of International Law and Comparative Law* 27 (2000), 151–76.

[32] Dong-Hoon Seol and Geon-Soo Han, "Foreign Women's Life and Work in the Entertaining Sector of Korea from the Human Trafficking Perspective," in *Human Security ,Transnational Crime and Human Trafficking: Asian and Western Perspectives*, Shiro Okubo and Louise Shelley, eds. (New York: Routledge, 2010 in press).

insurgency in Nepal and terrorist violence in Pakistan, India, Sri Lanka, the southern Philippines, and southern Thailand. Despite this enormous diversity in politics, religion, and economics, all countries in Asia face serious and diverse problems of trafficking.

Many of the forces that contribute to human trafficking in Asia were identified in Chapter 1. These include globalization, economic differentiation, weakening of border controls, high levels of corruption, and the presence of regional conflicts. Ethnic discrimination and discrimination against lower castes and the disruptions caused by rural to urban migration all contribute to trade in humans. Within these low-caste communities, it is the girls who have the most limited opportunities to obtain education or training and exit their familial poverty. There are such long traditions of debt bondage, forced marriages, and trafficking into prostitution that in many Asian countries neither the victim nor the trafficker is significantly stigmatized, helping perpetuate these practices.[33]

The enormous diversity defies easy classification. Asia is a host, source, and transit region for human trafficking, and some countries are active in all three stages of trafficking. Crime groups from one country support the sex business in others. For example, Yakuza now organize sex tours for Japanese and other Asian businessmen to other parts of Asia. Whereas crime groups export Thai women to Japan, trafficked women from other poorer Southeast Asian countries such as Myanmar, Cambodia, and Laos transit through Thailand for exploitation elsewhere or work in the significant Thai sex industry.[34]

The densely populated countries of Bangladesh and India are major sources of trafficking victims, but the concentration of the population is not sufficient to explain the pervasiveness of trafficking. Almost all the countries of Asia, even such prosperous ones as Korea, are source countries of trafficking victims. Pakistani laborers toil in Saudi Arabia, Chinese babies are trafficked for adoption overseas, and girls from Nepal are found in the brothels of India.[35]

33 Bales, *Disposable People*, 34–79, 149–231; John Frederick, *Fallen Angels: The Sex Workers of South Asia* (New Delhi: Roll Books, 2000).

34 Human Rights Watch/Asia, *Owed Justice: Thai Women Trafficked into Debt Bondage in Japan* (New York, 2000).

35 Human Rights Watch/Asia, "Rape for Profit: Trafficking of Nepali Women and Girls to India's Brothels," *Human Rights Watch* 12, no. 5A, 1995; *Trafficking in Persons Report 2004*; Samarsinghe, *Female Sex Trafficking in Asia*, 78; Govind Prasad Thapa, "Plight of Trafficked Women in Nepal," in Ebbe and Das, *Global Trafficking*, 99.

Many point to gender inequality as the reason that so many Asian women and girls are trafficked into prostitution in Asia and throughout the world. But sexual trafficking and sex tourism is just one component of the human trafficking that is widespread throughout Asia. In addition, forced labor in factories and workshops, domestic labor, forced begging, debt bondage as well as organ trafficking are important elements of the Asian trafficking problem.

High levels of corruption among the rulers of Asian countries appear to be highly correlated with human trafficking. Citizens of the Philippines, Indonesia, and Pakistan have suffered greatly as their countries have been drained of much of their national resources by Marcos, Suharto, and Bhutto, who have been identified as among the world's leading kleptocrats.[36] But other countries such as Korea and Japan that have much lower levels of corruption have serious problems of human trafficking, although the victims may not as often be domestic as in the most corrupt Asian societies.

Not all trafficking in Asia is facilitated by organized crime groups. Much trafficking is done by or with the direct collusion of corrupt state structures, military, police, security elites, and sometimes even with the direct involvement of elite families, as was mentioned previously in regard to the contemporary Philippines and also applies to many Southeast Asian countries including Indonesia.

Human trafficking persists not only because of historical traditions but also because there is an enormous demand for cheap labor and sexual services within the region. Moreover, Indian, China, and Japan are major actors in the global economy; therefore, the impact of globalization is felt acutely there. The labor law framework that exists in the United States and Europe to protect against exploitation does not exist in many Asian countries facilitating the trafficking of human labor throughout Asia.[37] The more affluent countries of Asia may have minimal forced labor on their territory, but South Korea has been accused of using forced or enslaved labor in its enterprises in Bangladesh.[38]

[36] Transparency International survey on largest kleptocrats was released in 2004; see http://www.spiritus-temporis.com/kleptocracy/transparency-international-ranking.html (accessed August 18, 2008).

[37] "Child Labour and Responses in South Asia," http://www.ilo.org/public/english/ region/asro/newdelhi/ipec/responses/index.htm (accessed August 18, 2008); "Always on Call Abuse and Exploitation of Child Domestic Workers in Indonesia," http://hrw.org/reports/2005/indonesia0605 (accessed August 18, 2008).

[38] http://gvnet.com/humantrafficking/SouthKorea.htm (accessed July 23, 2008).

Trafficking also persists because there is the expectation within many parts of Asia that members of the family will work in demeaning or exploitative conditions to provide for the welfare of the rest of the family members. The sale of family members to traders is done to relieve the family of a member they cannot afford to feed or to provide much needed capital for a project that may sustain the family. In India, girls are sold into prostitution to finance the medical treatment of a family member.[39] In Japan, women can be pressured into prostitution to pay off a debt for a family member to the *yakuza*, Japanese organized crime groups that control gambling and the popular entertainment industry in Japan.[40]

An analogous situation also can exist in the human smuggling that often leads to labor trafficking. Chinese families will pay significant sums to human smugglers and ensure that members of the family work under extremely hard conditions to provide for the smuggling fees of the next member of the family.[41] Likewise, in Pakistan, families that can afford university educations for their children will pay smugglers to move their children who have graduated with advanced degrees to England, consigning these members of the family to hard manual labor for years with the expectation that the money earned will provide for the smuggling fees of the next family member.[42] Money earned abroad will also pay for the education of family members in the home country.

Magnitude of the Problem and Regional Differences

Every region of Asia has a significant problem of human trafficking. Religious, economic, social, and political differences as well as historical

[39] Economic and Social Commission for Asia and the Pacific, "Sexually Abused and Sexually Exploited Children and Youth in the Greater Mekong Subregion: A Qualitative Assessment of their Health Needs and Available Services," St/ESCAP/2045 (New York: United Nations, 2000), Foreword, Rukhmini Rao, "Bonded by Caste and Gender: The Feminization of Poverty in Rural India," July 16, 2006, http://www.cwpe.org/nb (accessed August 19, 2008).

[40] U.S. State Department Country Reports on Human Rights Practices, Japan, 2005 identifies domestic trafficking as a problem, http://www.state.gov/g/drl/rls/hrrpt/ 2005/61610.htm (accessed August 18, 2008). From Japanese specialists I have learned of the problem of family debt that can lead to this victimization.

[41] Willard Myers, "Of Qinqing, Qinshu, Guanxi and Heiyu: The Dynamic Elements of Chinese Irregular Population Movement," *Trends in Organized Crime* 2, no. 2 (Winter 1996): 44–47; Peter Kwong, *Forbidden Workers: Illegal Chinese Immigrants and American Labor* (New York: New Press, 1997).

[42] Khalid Koser, "Why Migrant Smuggling Pays," *International Migration* 46, no. 2 (2008), 3–26, as well as conversations with the author.

precedents, however, explain the enormous diversity of human trafficking in Asia. Not all the countries of Asia were colonized by Western powers, but the colonization of the past helps explain the trafficking routes of the present.

Although the following section tries to establish certain distinct characteristics among regions of Asia, all regions are linked. Women are imported into the Japanese sex industry by the *yakuza* from Thailand and other Southeast Asian countries.[43] Laborers from Vietnam and China are exploited in the Far East parts of Russia, and Chinese women are found in the brothels of Pakistan.[44]

The chapter divides Asian human trafficking into different subregions including Northeast Asia, Southeast Asia, and South Asia including the Himalayan countries, Bangladesh, Pakistan, India, and Afghanistan. In each of these regions, the relative contribution of sex and labor trafficking to the overall trafficking problem is different. Moreover, different criminal actors participate in the trade in each region. Northeast Asia for this analysis includes North and South Korea, Northern and Central China, Japan, and the Russian Far East, which is very much integrated into the human trafficking of this region. Southeast Asia includes Thailand, Myanmar, Laos, Cambodia, Vietnam, the Philippines, Indonesia, and parts of Southern China whose trafficking is more integrated into the trafficking of this region than that of North Asia.

Northeast Asia

Northeast Asia is the most affluent part of Asia, with the exception of North Korea. Japan, Korea, China, and the Russian Far East, all in Northeast Asia, receive large numbers of human trafficking victims from abroad. But these countries are also integrated into the global human trafficking market and are also the source and transit countries for sexual, labor, and other forms trafficking. Not all trafficking requires transit to another country. Slaves rescued from forced labor in China reinforce the fact that there is much domestic trafficking.

[43] Protection Project, *International Child Sex Tourism: Scope of the Problem and Comparative Case Studies* (Washington, DC: Protection Project, Johns Hopkins University, 2007), 31, 106–7; Human Rights Watch/Asia, *Owed Justice: Thai Women Trafficked into Debt Bondage in Japan* (New York, 2000).

[44] Tarique Niazi "China, Pakistan and Terrorism," Foreign Policy in Focus, http://www.fpif.org/fpiftxt/4384, July 17, 2007 (accessed July 23, 2008); Elena Tiuriukanova, *Prinuditelnyi Trud v Sovremenoi Rossii: Nereguliremaya migratsiya i torgovliia liudmi* (Moscow: International Labour Organization, 2004).

Japan is no longer an exporter of prostitutes, but the long tradition of men frequenting prostitutes continues.[45] Instead, with Japan's postwar affluence, however, the pattern has reversed, with more than 100,000 women from Thailand and the Philippines trafficked into the Japanese sex industry each year to work in the large entertainment districts that exist in major Japanese cities and in resort areas.[46] The majority of Filipino women in Japan were assisted by recruiters, agents, or intermediaries.[47] The exploitation of some Thai women has been so severe that they have murdered their exploiters, a shocking level of violence in a country with generally low rates of crime and violence.[48]

In Kyushu, the southern island of Japan with huge hot spas associated with organized crime, almost all of the women in the brothels are Japanese, as there has been a crackdown on the trafficking of foreign women.[49] This is not the case in Tokyo, where trafficked women from every continent can be found as the *yakuza* have established links with Colombian, Nigerian, as well as Russian and Thai groups to procure women for the massive internal sex industry. Chinese and Hungarian trafficked women have been found along with women from Southeast Asian countries.[50] These women often enter on entertainment visas that are not available to ordinary categories of foreign workers. The women then work in a variety of establishments ranging from bars, snack bars where customers meet women and leave for sexual services, as well as health clubs and restaurants that serve as covers for brothels. Escort services are also vehicles for exploitation of trafficked women. As in other developed countries, the Internet and cell phones are used to provide anonymity.[51]

The trafficking links in North Asia are evidence of the new ties between the *yakuza* and Russian organized crime in the Far East. These ties facilitate illegal trade in fish and lumber but also in humans.[52] The

[45] See discussion of the past in Sayo Masuda, *Autobiography of a Geisha* (New York: Columbia University Press, 2003).

[46] Samarsinghe, *Female Sex Trafficking in Asia*, 40; Shared Hope International, *Demand: A Comparative Examination of Sex Tourism and Trafficking in Jamaica, Japan, the Netherlands, and the United States* (Washington, DC: Shared Hope International, 2007), 124.

[47] Samarsinghe, *Female Sex Trafficking in Asia*, 142; Peter B. E. Hill, *The Japanese Mafia: Yakuza, Law, and the State* (Oxford: Oxford University Press, 2003), 113–16.

[48] Yuriko Saito, "The Trafficking of Thai Women to Japan and Countermeasures of the Thai Government," forthcoming in *Human Security, Transnational Crime and Human Trafficking*, Okubo and Shelley, eds.

[49] Field visit by the author in December 2006.

[50] Shared Hope International, *Demand*, 115–20; Saito, "Trafficking of Thai Women."

[51] Ibid., 130.

[52] Analysis of Vladivostok Center as well as observation by author in July 2007.

numerous houses of prostitution in the Far East of Russia near Japan provide an easy new destination for Japanese sex tourists seeking non-Asian women.[53]

The profits that the *yakuza* make from its involvement in the sex trade are considerable. Therefore, efforts to address human trafficking have resulted in death threats from the *yakuza* to Japanese government officials, journalists, and researchers.[54]

Even though South Korea is now the world's 13th largest economy, according to the World Bank,[55] there are still Korean women trafficked both within Korea and abroad. With growing economic prosperity in Korea, there are, however, fewer Korean women available to serve as prostitutes and many women are imported either from Russia or the Philippines. In 2001, 8,500 mostly Russian and Filipina women entered the country on "entertainment" visas, the majority of them working around the bases where tens of thousands of American military personnel were stationed.[56]

As in Japan, labor trafficking is a much smaller part of overall Korean trafficking than in other parts of Asia. Korean women are trafficked into Japan, the United States, and many were trafficked to Canada through exploitation of the Canadian entertainment visa. Chapter 8 on the United States discusses Korean women trafficked to brothels near U.S. military bases.[57] Moreover, there are many women trafficked from abroad into Korea's brothels. The relative ease of getting a visa for Korea as compared with Japan has often made this an attractive alternative for women intending to migrate as entertainers. In addition, recruiters and managers often tell the foreign women that Korea is similar to, or better than, Japan.[58] A growing number of these foreign victims are trafficked to South Korea for sexual or

[53] Ibid.

[54] Mention of these threats were made in the speech of a Japanese immigration official at a conference on human trafficking at Ritsumeikan University in Kyoto, Japan in December 2004; discussion of threats against NGO, Shared Hope International, *Demand*, 113; Jake Adelstein, "The Mob Is Big in Japan," *Washington Post*, May 11, 2008, B2, describes threats while doing research.

[55] http://en.wikipedia.org/wiki/List_of_countries_by_GDP_(nominal) (accessed August 18, 2008).55 June J. H. Lee, *A Review of Data on Trafficking in the Republic of Korea*, IOM Migration Research Series no. 9, IOM, 2002.

[56] Katharine Moon, *Sex among Allies: Military Prostitution in U.S.–Korea Relations*, (New York: Columbia University Press, 1997).

[57] Seol and Han, "Foreign Women's Life and Work," in *Human Security, Transnational Crime and Human Trafficking*, Okubo and Shelley, eds. (2010).

[58] Ibid.

labor exploitation through brokered international marriages to South Korean men.[59]

Women from Russia, Uzbekistan, Kazakhstan, the People's Republic of China (P.R.C.), the Philippines, Thailand, and other Southeast Asian countries are trafficked for sexual exploitation to South Korea.[60] There is a segmentation of the market; different nationalities serve different clienteles.

Women from the former Soviet Union serve both an American and Korean clientele whereas Filipinos are forced to work at the clubs that serve American servicemen because of their knowledge of English.[61] In addition, Korea is a transit country for Chinese women who reach the United States by air and those who are trafficked by ship. Korean men are a significant source of demand for child sex tourism in Southeast Asia and the Pacific Islands.[62]

The situation in North Korea contrasts dramatically with that in South Korea. The highly authoritarian government of North Korea has very tight controls over its population. North Korea is not integrated into the global licit economy, but human trafficking is one way that it is integrated into the illicit economy. Just as the North Korean state produces counterfeit money and cigarettes distributed throughout the world, the North Koreans use the trade in humans as a way of generating hard currency for the state.[63] North Korean women are also trafficked as wives to China, where the one-child policy has resulted in an absence of women to marry. Often these women are lured by crime groups or cross into Northeast China hoping to escape the difficult conditions at home. These women are then subject to both sexual and labor exploitation.[64]

China manifests trafficking problems associated with a transitional socialist economy whose patterns are fully identified in Chapter 6 on Eurasia. China, with its large population and increasing economic and regional inequality regions, possesses almost every form of trafficking.

59 "Marriage vs. Trafficking," http://www.koreatimes.co.kr/www/news/art/2008/04/202_22150.html (accessed August 19, 2008); *Trafficking in Persons Report*, June 2007 (Washington, DC: U.S. Department of State, 2007), 129.

60 Seol and Han, "Foreign Women's Life and Work," in *Human Security, Transnational Crime and Human Trafficking*, Okubo and Shelley, eds. (2010).

61 Samarsinghe, *Female Sex Trafficking in Asia*, 141.

62 Protection Project, *International Child Sex Tourism*, 29, 105–6.

63 Rafael Perl and Dick Nanto, "North Korea Counterfeiting of US Currency," March 22, 2006, http://www.fas.org/sgp/crs/row/RL33324.pdf (accessed August 19, 2008).

64 *Trafficking in Persons Report 2007*, 161.

It is a source, host, and transit country for trafficking. Despite the great publicity concerning Chinese human smuggling, the most acute trafficking problems in the People's Republic of China (PRC) consist of forced and bonded labor, trafficking for marriage, and sexual trafficking.[65] The acuity of this problem is particularly striking in a society that had an ideological commitment to equality. But the period of the Cultural Revolution and other tumultuous times in Communist Chinese history in which its citizens were compelled to work under the hardest of conditions in rural areas laid the groundwork for the labor exploitation and trafficking that often occurs within the context of legitimate businesses.

Apart from these more conventional forms of trafficking, the IOM has reported that organ trafficking is also on the rise.[66] There have been reports of trafficking of the organs of Chinese inmates on death row.[67] As organ trafficking indicates, trafficking in China is not exclusively a problem associated with crime groups but also occurs with the complicity of state officials.

Within the country, trafficking of individuals can be small scale as babies are sold for adoption, trafficked brides are found for rural men, and managers enslave trafficked workers. "International organizations report that 90 percent of internal trafficking victims are women and children, trafficked primarily from such poorer regions as Anhui, Henan, Hunan, Sichuan, Yunnan, and Guizhou Provinces to prosperous provinces"[68] along the east coast. In richer areas, most trafficked women are sold to commercial sex businesses, hair salons, massage parlors, and bathhouses.

Despite the one-child policy and the enormous attention paid by parents to their children, among the poor, China has a problem of internal trafficking of children for sexual and labor exploitation. Estimates on the total number of victims range from 10,000 to 20,000 each year, of which 90 percent are women and children.[69] Children in the poorer areas are also sometimes recruited by traffickers who promise their parents that their children can send remittances back home. Illustrative of this problem is the noted case of the exploitation of children at a brick factory. In

[65] *Trafficking in Persons Report* 2009, 104–5.

[66] *Trafficking in Persons Report 2009*, 104–5. "Rising Trade in Human Organs is Alarming: IOM," http://www.reuters.com/article/worldNews/idUSMAN28233220070607, June 7, 2007.

[67] Michele Goodwin, *Black Markets: The Supply and Demand of Body Parts* (Cambridge and New York: Cambridge University Press, 2006), 11.

[68] http://www.humantrafficking.org/countries/china (accessed July 31, 2009).

[69] *Trafficking in Persons Report 2007*, 80.

2007, numerous children as well as adults were found in slave labor conditions in Northern China. More than 160 people were arrested, accused of forcing men and young children into slave labor in illegal mines and brick factories. The liberated slaves included 570 people, 50 of them children, including one as young as 8, who were forced to work long hours without any compensation.[70]

The high unemployment rate in many provinces in China is a contributing factor to the problem of Chinese trafficking overseas. In one Jilin province alone, there are 5 million unemployed people out of a population of 27 million.[71] With this large-scale unemployment, desperate individuals become victims of labor trafficking not only within the country but also overseas. Organized crime groups control most of the international smuggling, as discussed in the previous chapters, but these groups cannot function without the complicity of government officials, particularly in the South of China far from Beijing's controls.[72] Chapters 3 and 4 discussed the business of Chinese smuggling and trafficking to the United States and Europe, but P.R.C. citizens are also smuggled to other regions of the world such as Africa, Latin America, Australia, and the Middle East. Chinese women and children are also trafficked for sexual and labor exploitation to other parts of Asia such as Malaysia, Thailand, Japan, Singapore, and Taiwan.[73]

This trafficking thrives in China because of the impunity of government officials complicit in the trade. Chinese authorities seldom if ever "prosecute officials for corruption relating directly to trafficking, as distinct from people smuggling." A rare exception occurred in Hong Kong rather than mainland China when a police officer was sentenced in 2005 for warning an organized crime-controlled brothel of impending police raids.[74]

Southeast Asia

There are many reasons that Southeast Asia is a hub of human trafficking, particularly sexual trafficking. The years of conflict in the region, the

70 "Former Slave Labor Tells of Brick Kiln Ordeal," June 21, 2007, http://www. chinadaily.com.cn/china/2007–06/21/content_899048.htm (accessed August 19, 2008); *Trafficking in Persons Report 2008*, 8.

71 Roger Plant at U.S. Hearing.

72 Chin, *Smuggled Chinese*, 49–93.*Trafficking in Persons Report 2008*, 91–92.

73 *Trafficking in Persons Report 2008*, 91–92.

74 Leslie Holmes, "Corruption & Trafficking: Triple Victimisation," in *Strategies Against Human Trafficking*, Friesendorf, ed.95.

high levels of corruption, and the transitions away from the Communist system have left many in very vulnerable positions. Therefore, there are many who are susceptible to being trafficked into the sex industry, forced marriages, and labor situations.

The geography of the region is also conducive to human trafficking. Crime groups and smugglers are the dominant powers in the multiborder areas of the region without clearly defined jurisdictions and an absence of governmental control and high levels of corruption. Illustrative of this is the Golden Triangle region, in which human trafficking from Cambodia, Laos, Myanmar, and southern China flows into northern Thailand.[75] Another example is the no man's land between Cambodia and Thailand where no one takes responsibility for law enforcement. In this area of Cambodia four hours from Bangkok, a casino industry second only in scale to Macao has developed with the brothels to go with it.[76]

Familial and cultural traditions also play a major role in perpetuating trafficking. Vidya Samarsinghe refers to this as the resilience of patriarchy in her work on Asian sex trafficking.[77] Evidence of this patriarchy are ongoing problems of lack of access to education, little investment in education for girls, and often a strong preference given to the education of male children over female. All these conditions are conducive to trafficking. Unsafe school environments, prevalent in many areas of Southeast Asia, also increase vulnerability to sexual exploitation.[78]

Unique historical and political conditions contribute to the trafficking in the different countries of Southeast Asia. For example, the legacy of the Marcos years and of subsequent corrupt Filipino leaders has been a country that sees its citizens as a source of support for the state rather than seeing the state as responsible for the support of its citizens. There has been a significant export of educated and less educated human beings, as will be discussed later. Those subject to exploitation abroad are just part of a larger policy of the export of people for the benefit of the state.

75 "Traffic Report: Thailand," http://www.worldvision.com.au/Libraries/3_3_1_Human_rights_and_trafficking_PDF_reports/Trafficking_Report_Thailand.sflb.ashx (accessed December 5, 2009); Bertil Lintner, "Illegal Aliens Smuggling to and through Southeast Asia," 2000, http://www.asiapacificms.com/papers/pdf/gt_alien_smuggling.pdf (accessed January 20, 2004).

76 Bertil Lintner, "Betting on the Border," http://www.asiapacificms.com/articles/cambodia_casinos/ (accessed January 20, 2004).

77 Samarsinghe, *Female Sex Trafficking in Asia*.

78 Economic and Social Commission for Asia and the Pacific, "Sexually Abused and Sexually Exploited Children and Youth in the Greater Mekong Subregion," Foreword. http://www.humantrafficking.org/countries/cambodia (accessed August 19, 2008).

The transitions away from the authoritarian systems of Southeast Asia have proved as traumatic for the populations of these countries as their counterparts in Eurasia discussed in Chapter 6.

> The International Labour Organization argues that the aftermath of the Khmer Rouge regime is still felt both psychologically and economically and plays a direct role in labor and sexual exploitation arising from ill-prepared migration. The upheavals caused by the conflict and lack of opportunities in rural areas have fueled a return to the cities and urban areas, all but emptied during the Khmer Rouge period. With well over half the population below the age of 20, Cambodia faces a growing problem of providing decent work for its young population, further increasing the drive toward cross-border migration for employment, and perpetuating the cycle of vulnerability to human trafficking.[79]

Exacerbating the trafficking situation in Cambodia, as well as in other of transitional communist states, is that the leadership itself is helping to supply and run the brothels. In Cambodia, police and military personnel are also deeply involved in the protection of the brothels and the associated human trafficking.[80] In Cambodia alone, the police estimated in 2003 that more than 50,000 girls were in brothels in their country. "The World Human Rights Organization and UNICEF estimate that one-third of the prostitutes in Cambodia are under the age of 18, the majority of whom are Vietnamese."[81] Vulnerable children in Cambodia who become victims of the domestic sex trade are abused and often then killed.[82] Girls are subjected to torture by electric shock in underground dungeons under the brothels to keep them compliant and ready to work even when in intense pain. In a publicized case of victimization in Cambodia, a woman trafficker poked out an eye of a young girl who would not have sex immediately after a painful abortion. Torture chambers housed underneath the brothels were used by the madams to keep the girls smiling for customers. [83]

The feminization of poverty in the states of Cambodia, Laos, and Vietnam and in the Yunnan region of China helps explain the increasing

[79] http://www.humantrafficking.org/countries/cambodia (accessed August 19, 2008).

[80] Samarsinghe, *Female Sex Trafficking in Asia*, 117, http://www.humantrafficking.org/countries/vietnam (accessed August 19, 2008).

[81] http://www.humantrafficking.org/countries/vietnam (accessed August 19, 2008).

[82] Interview by author with IOM officer who had served in Cambodia, September 2006.

[83] Nicholas D. Kristof, "The Evil Behind the Smiles," *New York Times*, January 1, 2009, A 21; Niklos Kristof, If this Isn't slavery, What Is?" *New York Times*, January 3, 2009, www.nytimes.com/2009/01/04/opinion/04kristof.html?_r=1 (accessed January. 12, 2009).

number of girls and women trafficked from these countries and regions.[84] Moreover, the social dislocations caused by the communist transitions have contributed to trafficking in a myriad of ways. Not only has there been a weakening of national border controls, thereby permitting the flow of girls and young women to more affluent countries in the region, but there has also been a very lopsided economic development, with a privileged minority gaining financially but with the vast majority facing greater poverty. In the socialist states of Southeast Asia, just as in Eastern Europe and the former Soviet Union, large-scale trafficking is occurring in countries that had made enormous efforts to stamp out prostitution.[85]

Cambodian babies were also sold on a large scale for adoptions until investigations by the United States Immigration Service and the prosecution of facilitators ended this international trade in babies. Between January 1997 and December 2001, the majority of more than 1,600 babies adopted by Americans from Cambodia had been "Obtained from their birth families by illicit child-buying, fraud and child-stealing."[86] According to U.S. investigators of this criminal enterprise, the babies were held in appalling conditions surrounded by feces and urine before their adoption.[87] The traffickers sought to maximize profit; they would not make the minimal expenditures to keep "their products" in sanitary conditions.

The long-term conflict in Vietnam in which both the French and Americans participated led to significant trafficking in Vietnam and in Thailand where many soldiers went for rest and recreation. The foreign customers merely compounded the domestic demand for prostitutes, often fulfilled by trafficked women. In the Philippines, near the Subic and Clark Air Force Bases of the U.S. military, there were 55,000 registered and unregistered prostitutes before these bases were closed in 1992.[88] After the base closures, there was a decline of women trafficked into the sex industry. But when the Philippines was declared a second front in the war on terrorism in early 2002, the number of prostitutes increased to satisfy the demand.[89] According to the Trafficking in Persons Report for

[84] International Organization for Migration, *Combating Trafficking in South-East Asia A Review of Policy and Programme Responses* (Geneva, 2000), 37–50.

[85] Louise Shelley, "Post-Communist Transitions and the Illegal Movement of People: Chinese Smuggling and Russian Trafficking in Women," *Annals of Scholarship* 14, no. 2 (2002), 71–84.

[86] Smolin, p. 137.

[87] Ibid., pp. 139–40.

[88] Samarsinghe, *Female Sex Trafficking in Asia*, 133.

[89] Ibid., 134.

2008, in Indonesia "complicity in trafficking of individual security force members and corrupt officials involved in prostitution and sex trafficking remain unchecked."[90] Peacekeepers in Indonesia are also thought to have exacerbated the trafficking problem.[91] Therefore, conflicts and the presence of soldiers in the region have contributed to the rise of trafficking in diverse countries of the region.

The financial benefits of sex trafficking are one of the main reasons it continues. The clients are not only military personnel but also foreign tourists from the Middle East, Europe, North America, and Asia who travel to Southeast Asia to have sex, often with minors. Illustrative of this is that 51 percent of Cambodian girls in one study had lost their virginity to a tourist or foreign client, indicating the important role that sex tourism plays in the growth of trafficking.[92] As Colligan-Taylor notes, "An alliance is formed between local governments in search of foreign currency, and both local and foreign businessmen willing to invest in the sex-travel industry."[93] The sex industry, particularly in Thailand, is viewed as a form of development capital.[94] Many parts of Asia have sought development capital often without concern as to its source. Japanese *yakuza* have purchased golf courses in Southeast Asia, thereby establishing the underlying foundation for sex tourism.[95] There has not been an attempt to discourage the investment of this criminal capital, which has distorted economic development and has contributed to a rise in trafficking.

The Thai sex industry employs approximately 150,000 to 200,000 girls and women.[96] Pedophilia tourism exists and is run by *triads*, often

[90] *Trafficking in Persons Report* June 2007 on Indonesia, 118–19.

[91] For a fuller discussion of trafficking in Indonesia see, Ruth Rosenberg, ed. *Trafficking of Women and Children in Indonesia* (Jakarta: U.S. Agency for International Development, 2002).

[92] Samarsinghe, *Female Sex Trafficking in Asia*, 110.

[93] Karen Colligan-Taylor, Introduction to *Sandakan Brothel No. 8* (Armonk and London: M.E. Sharpe, 1999), xxvii. *Sites along the Thai-Burmese Border* (World Vision Foundation of Thailand and Myanmar, January 2002).

[94] Interview with the president of Mahidol University, March 1992, when the author was part of a USIA-sponsored program and a curriculum was being instituted at the university on crime, including combating trafficking. He commented on the difficulties of instituting this program and was subsequently removed from his position for statements such as these.

[95] David Kaplan and Alec Dubro, *Yakuza: Japan's Criminal Underworld* (Berkeley: University of California Press, 2003).

[96] World Health Organization STI/HIV, *Sex Work in Asia*, July 2001, 17, http://www.wpro.who.int/NR/rdonlyres/D01A4265-A142-4E19-99AE-6CC7E44F995C/0/Sex_Work_in_Asia_July2001.pdf (accessed August 20, 2008).

in conjunction with *yakuza*.[97] Pasuk Phongpaichit, in her courageous book, *Guns, Girls, Gambling and Ganja*, points out the integral role that human trafficking plays in the Thai economy.[98] Human trafficking is a major revenue source for the police, who share the proceeds of this large-scale activity with the politicians and the political parties. Therefore, in contrast with the situation that exists in North Asia, where crime groups are clearly responsible for the human trafficking, the Thai situation is more closely tied to corrupt police, domestic groups, and networks tied to the government. Therefore, there is cooperation between corrupt state structures and foreign crime groups such as the *Yakuza* but the Thai sex industry is not the consequence of large well organized crime groups but rather of networks of criminals working with government officials who assume a key role in the trafficking.

As the Thai economy has developed, there are fewer Thai women to traffic and the traffickers find that they can command more money for the services of Thai women in international markets such as in Japan and the United States. Members of the Hill Tribes in Northern Thailand who lack Thai citizenship and their tribal kinsmen in neighboring countries are subject to ethnic discrimination and are trafficked into Southern Thailand's sex markets and beyond.[99] Those who are trafficked are the least educated. In the triborder area near Thailand, 22 percent of surveyed prostitutes had never attended school and 41.5 percent had some exposure to primary education.[100] Sex and labor traffickers have searched for women in the neighboring countries of Southeast Asia – Myanmar, Cambodia, Laos, and Vietnam as well as farther in the transitional countries of China, Russia, and Uzbekistan.[101] Many of the women in these countries are extremely poor relative to their counterparts in Thailand. The lack of employment and economic development in the neighboring countries has provided a steady stream of young girls and women for the

[97] Martin Booth, *The Dragon Syndicates: The Global Phenomenon of the Triads* (New York: Carroll and Graf Publishers, 1999), 233; Phongpaichit et al., *Guns, Girls, Gambling, Ganja*.

[98] Phongpaichit et al. *Guns, Girls, Gambling, Ganja*.

[99] *Trafficking in Persons Report*, June 2008, 243. Also, the noted David Feingold film *Trading Women* discusses the trafficking of girls from the Hill Tribes.

[100] John Whan Yoon, "Situation Analysis Report of Trafficking and Migration in World Vision Foundation Thailand's Three Border Sites along the Thai-Burmese Border," World Vision Foundation of Thailand and of Myanmar, Bangkok, Thailand, January 2002.

[101] *Trafficking in Persons Report*, June 2008, 243. Also, the noted David Feingold film *Trading Women* discusses the trafficking of girls from the Hill Tribes.

Thai sex industry.[102] Counter-drug programs without effective alternative economic development programs resulted in poverty and an increase in tribal groups in prostitution.[103] Ironically, it is these former communist countries that were supposed to have eliminated labor exploitation that are now major sources of trafficked women.

These transitional communist states also have large numbers of youth and women engaged in prostitution within their borders. As previously mentioned, Cambodia has large numbers of women and girls from Vietnam, but Vietnam and Laos have their own internal trafficking problems. The number of women engaged in prostitution in Vietnam is estimated at 300,000.[104] In addition, women from these countries are trafficked to nearby Malaysia and across from Singapore.

The victims of sex trafficking in Malaysia are just a component of the large illegal foreign work force.[105] Large numbers of Indonesians work illegally in Malaysia, many subject to acute labor exploitation. Malaysia cracked down on an estimated 600,000 illegal laborers in 2007, and further deportations continued with the worldwide global recession.[106]

"UNICEF estimates that 100,000 women and children are trafficked annually for commercial sexual exploitation in Indonesia and abroad, 30 percent of the female prostitutes in Indonesia are below 18, and 40,000–70,000 Indonesian children are victims of sexual exploitation." An independent estimate suggests that these figures are even higher. The East Java Children's Protection Agency estimates that at least 100,000 women and children are trafficked annually from, through, and to just this single region of Indonesia.[107] Many are trafficked to the Middle East

[102] Asian Development Bank, *Combating Trafficking of Women and Children in South Asia;* Asia Development Bank, World Vision, "Situation Analysis Report of Trafficking and Migration."

[103] For discussion of the impact of the counter-drug strategy, see http://www.yale.edu/seas/TradingWomen.html (accessed August 20, 2008). The author observed villages in Northern Thailand in 1998 depleted of young girls that had occurred since the decline of the drug trade in the region.

[104] World Health Organization STI/HIV, *Sex Work in Asia*, 20.

[105] Zarina Othman, "Human (in)security, Human Trafficking, and Security in Malaysia," in *Trafficking and the Global Sex Industry*, Karen Beeks and Delila Amir, eds. (Lanham, MD: Lexington Books, 2006), 47–60, 99–100.

[106] Soraya Permatasari, "As Malaysia Deports Illegal Workers, Employers Run Short," *New York Times*, September 13, 2007 http://www.nytimes.com/2007/09/13/business/worldbusiness/13iht-labor.4.7496516.html, accessed July 25, 2009); "Indonesian Workers in Malaysia to be Repatriated in Stages," February 6, 2009, http://www.themalaysianinsider.com/index.php/business/17764-indonesian-workers-in-malaysia-to-be-repatriated-in-stages (accessed July 25, 2009).

[107] http://www.humantrafficking.org/countries/indonesia (accessed July 1, 2008).

where their labor exploitation is combined with sexual abuse. Because of the national desire for remittances, repatriated victims who complain of their treatment are often retrafficked with the complicity of government officials.[108]

The pervasiveness of the sex trafficking and the related problem of sex tourism is just one component of a diversified trafficking problem in the region that includes slave labor, domestic servitude, and mail-order brides. Chapter 8 on the United States discusses how Hmong, a Southeast Asian tribal group, are brought to the United States as mail-order brides and subsequently enslaved. Vietnamese women are also enslaved as the result of fraudulent marriages. The Vietnamese government estimates that in approximately 10 percent of the arranged marriages of Vietnamese women with Chinese, the women become trafficking victims – raped and abused by their husbands and in-laws. In some cases, they are sold off to other men.[109]

Throughout the region, women and men are trafficked for forced labor in factories and construction or as domestic servants.[110] Vietnamese trafficking victims are recruited through fraudulent marriages and false promises of employment from licensed and unlicensed migrant labor recruiting agencies. In one case reported by Vietnamese courts, a Taiwanese couple and 73 associates were tried for trafficking Vietnamese women to Taiwan, Malaysia, and Singapore for forced labor or brokered marriages.[111] Men are trafficked for forced labor in the agriculture, fishing, and construction industries. Women are trafficked for sexual exploitation and forced labor in factories or as domestic servants. Children in Cambodia are trafficked for sexual exploitation and forced labor in organized begging rings, soliciting, street vending, and flower selling.[112] In neighboring Thailand, Burmese adults and children who voluntarily migrate are subsequently coerced into exploitative conditions in agriculture, factories, construction, commercial fisheries industries, begging, or as domestic servants.[113] In one Thai police raid of a shrimp-processing factory in 2008, 300

108 Interviews with law enforcement officials working in Indonesia, November, 2009.

109 http://www.humantrafficking.org/countries/vietnam (accessed August 20, 2008).

110 See Christina Wille, "Thailand-Lao People's Democratic Republic and Thailand-Myanmar Border Areas Trafficking in Children into the Worst Form of Child Labour: A Rapid Assessment, Asian Research Center for Migration," prepared for International Labour Organization, November 2001.

111 http://www.humantrafficking.org/countries/Vietnam (accessed August 20, 2008).

112 http://www.humantrafficking.org/countries/Cambodia (accessed August 20, 2008).

113 *Trafficking in Persons Report*, June 2007, 197.

workers from Myanmar were found imprisoned.[114] The traffickers were a loosely organized group, with Burmese, Laotian, Cambodian, and Thai individuals having transported the victims along the Thai border for forced labor.[115]

In the Philippines as in China, labor trafficking is a very important component of the trafficking problem. Filipino women work throughout the world, often as nurses and domestic servants. Women represent approximately half of the million Filipinos working overseas.[116] Their remittances are an important part of the Philippine economy. Total remittances in 2007 were U.S. $14.4 billion, which represented approximately 10 percent of the GDP.[117]

But not enough attention is paid to the conditions of their employment overseas. Many Filipino women go abroad as domestic servants and all too often wind up in situations of forced labor, particularly in the Middle East. Filipino domestic servants in the Gulf States are, however, better compensated and treated than women from Thailand and neighboring Southeast Asian countries.[118]

Human smugglers operate nodes in Kuala Lumpur, Malaysia, Jakarta in Indonesia and Bangkok in Thailand, where they attempt to smuggle individuals to Western Europe and Australia. Some of their clients have been men who resisted living under the Taliban in Afghanistan as well as others from Iraq, Iran, and Pakistan. With crackdowns on refugees, many of these individuals get abandoned by their smugglers when they cannot reach their intended destinations.[119]

Another trafficking problem in Southeast Asia is the trafficking of organs. According to the IOM, this problem is increasing in the poorest countries in the region such as Cambodia, Indonesia, Laos, Myanmar, the Philippines, and Vietnam.[120]

[114] *Global Eye on Human Trafficking*, no. 7, 2009, 3, www.iom.int/jahia/webdav/site/myjahiasite/shared/shared/mainsite/projects/showcase_pdf/global_eye_seventh_issue.pdf, (accessed December 4, 2009).

[115] http://www.humantrafficking.org/countries/Thailand (accessed July 25, 2009).

[116] IOM – Philippines, http://www.iom.int/jahia/Jahia/pid/502 (accessed January 9, 2009); *Philippine Overseas Employment Administration 2007 Annual Report*. Philippine Overseas Employment Administration, http://www.poea.gov.ph/ar/ar2007.pdf (accessed October 4, 2008).

[117] Philippine Overseas Employment Administration (POEA), 12.

[118] Author's interviews conducted in UAE, November 2008.

[119] Bertil Linter, "People Smuggling, the Crime of Flight," www.asiapacificms.com/articles/people_smuggling (accessed January 11, 2009).

[120] "IOM Says Alarmed over Rising Trade in Human Organs," June 7, 2007. http://in.reuters.com/article/idINIndia-30192020070607 (accessed July 25, 2009); *Global*

South Asia

Many of the countries included in this region (India, Bangladesh, Pakistan) are among the most densely populated countries in the world. Only India among them is enjoying a growing middle class and economic development. However, much of the Indian population, as well of the preponderance of citizens of the neighboring countries of Bangladesh, Nepal, and Pakistan, remains in intense poverty, with many children and adults at great risk of being trafficked into the sex industry, forced marriages, and different forms of forced labor. In several states in India, stolen or bought children were adopted by American and German families, the process facilitated by the corruption of legal officials.[121] With advanced medical facilities in the region, trafficking of organs from the poor to those who can pay for them and the accompanying expensive transplant operations is a reality of the region. According to the IOM:

> In India, police recently cracked down on an undercover transplantation ring where donors, initially lured by the promise of profit, found themselves kept at gunpoint. In South Asia live donations also occur among indentured labourers who sell their kidneys in order to repay debt, often under the coercive tactics of unscrupulous employers.[122]

A similar crackdown in Pakistan since the outlawing of transplants to foreigners in 2007 has led to a reduction in the number of kidney transplants from 2000 to 700 annually.[123]

Also contributing to the problem of Indian trafficking, as discussed in Chapter 1, is the caste system that has institutionalized disparities and kept untouchables as well as members of other lower castes in forced bondage for generations with no prospects of exit.[124] Advocacy groups estimate that 20 to 65 million are in bonded labor in India alone.[125]

Eye on Human Trafficking, no. 4, 2008, 1, www.iom.int/jahia/webdav/site/myjahiasite/shared/shared/mainsite/projects/showcase_pdf/global_eye_fourth_issue.pdf, (accessed January 12, 2009).

121 Smolin, 146–59.

122 *Global Eye on Human Trafficking*, no. 4, 2008, 1, www.iom.int/jahia/webdav/site/myjahiasite/shared/shared/mainsite/projects/showcase_pdf/global_eye_fourth_issue.pdf, (accessed Jan.12, 2009).

123 Geoffrey Cain, "Asia's Kidney Bazaars," *Far East Economic Review*, January 6, 2009, http://www.feer.com/economics/2009/january/Asias-Kidneys-Bazaars (accessed January 11, 2009).

124 http://edition.cnn.com/2007/US/06/12/human.trafficking/index.html (accessed June 28, 2008).

125 Bales, *Disposable People*, 195–231.

In South Asia, as elsewhere, a very strong correlation exists between familial poverty and the likelihood of being trafficked.[126] "The Ministry of Home Affairs (MHA) estimates that 90 percent of India's sex trafficking is internal. Women and girls are trafficked internally for the purposes of commercial sexual exploitation and forced marriage.[127] There are several reasons that girls are drawn into prostitution, including poverty, domestic violence, divorce, and desire for easy money.[128]

Organized crime plays a notable role in the region's trafficking, especially in India, a fact that is not widely acknowledged because of the absence of research on South Asian organized crime. Indian human traffickers may also sell drugs and arms.[129]

Crime groups in India have a clear division of responsibilities, as discussed in Chapter 3, with women, *nayikas*, controlling the girls in the brothels and the *dalaals* recruiting girls from vulnerable families whose crops have failed or breadwinners have died.[130]

Indian crime groups connect with traffickers in neighboring countries to procure girls for the sex industry, forced labor, and marriages. As a result, India has become a magnet for girls from less economically developed countries such as Nepal and Bangladesh, whose young women are increasingly found in the huge red light districts of many large Indian cities.[131] Some Nepalese girls are sold to the brothels after their sexual exploitation as child laborers in the carpet industry.[132] The age of the Nepalese trafficking victims is declining. Many Nepalese girls younger than 10 years of age are now being forced into the sex trade. In the 1980s, trafficked girls were most frequently 14 to 16 years of age. By 1994, they were even younger, ranging in age from 10 to 14.[133] Once sold to the brothels, Indian or foreign young women have no way out. When

[126] Suzanne Williams and Rachel Masika, "Editorial," in *Gender, Trafficking and Slavery*, ed. Rachel Masika (Oxford: Oxfam, 2002), 5–6.

[127] *Trafficking in Persons Report 2007*, 115.

[128] http://www.un.org/Pubs/chronicle/2006/issue2/0206p14.htm (accessed June 30, 2008).

[129] Interview with Kailash Satyarthi, a distinguished Indian activist against child trafficking, who was severely injured while trying to free children trafficked into the circus by criminals who also dealt in drugs and arms, November, 2009 in Dubai.

[130] Ibid.

[131] Bertil Lintner, "Asia's Sex Trap," http://www.asiapacificms.com/articles/ fallen_angels/ (accessed January 19, 2004).

[132] ILO/IPEC, *Helping Hands or Shackled Lives: Understanding Domestic Child Labour and Responses to It* (Geneva, June 2004), www.ilo.org/public/libdoc/ilo/2004/104B09_138.engl.pdf (accessed July 31, 2009).

[133] *Telugu Portal*, October 3, 2007, New Delhi, India, http://www.giftasia.in/index. php?-option=com_content&task=view&id=235&Itemid=353 (accessed June 30, 2008).

they are too sick to work any more, they are left to die in the streets of AIDS, tuberculosis, or other terminal diseases.[134]

Once the girls enter the brothels, they are sold several times over ... their ... debt ... increases exponentially as ownership changes hands – it's a contrived inflation. With little prospect of paying off, the girls are locked into years of servitude. To unravel the money nexus is to begin to comprehend the vested interests feeding off this system that block effective control of trafficking. After haggling down the starting price, a customer finds himself importuned over again for baksheesh, but the baksheesh is about all the girl will keep for herself. The rest of the money is entered into meticulously kept chits held against each girl's name: half will go to the owner, who has accounts to settle with building owners and to buy off police and other officials to disregard the illegalities of the trade; the other half goes to the *nayika*.[135]

Labor exploitation in India and Nepal is even more widespread than sexual exploitation. Children from South Asia also work in bonded labor or are trafficked as domestic servants, agricultural workers, beggars, and even in factories, often in hazardous situations. Since 1980, more than 76,000 children have been freed from "brick kilns, stone quarries, domestic labor, hotels, carpet looms, agriculture and allied work" by a well developed anti-child trafficking movement with more than 70,000 members.[136] Involuntary servitude of adult men and women often occurs in similar locales "in brick kilns, rice mills, agriculture, and embroidery factories."[137]

Indians and Nepalese migrate willingly to the Arab countries in the Gulf for work as domestic servants and low-skilled laborers. Many face nonpayment of wages and restrictions on mobility, and are forced to relinquish their passports. Others face these problems as well as physical and/or sexual abuse.[138]

In a tragic case, 13 Nepalese workers were trafficked from Nepal to Iraq, believing that "they were going to work at hotels in Jordan and elsewhere, but were instead taken against their will to work for a U.S. military contractor in Iraq. Unfortunately, the 12 men were captured by insurgents and killed on the way to the U.S. base where they were to work." Their families and the surviving laborer filed suit against the contractors, KBR and Daoud & Partners, in the United States, under the

[134] Interviews with Indian anti-trafficking activists, 1999–2004.
[135] http://www.un.org/Pubs/chronicle/2006/issue2/0206p14.htm (accessed June 30, 2008).
[136] http://www.bba.org.in/whatwedo/index.php, accessed December 4, 2009.
[137] *Trafficking in Persons 2007*, India, 115.
[138] Ibid.

American anti-trafficking law, and the case against the corporation was upheld by the U.S. court.[139]

Bangladesh, one of the poorest countries in the world, is the source of many different kinds of trafficking victims including forced marriage, domestic servitude, virtual enslavement in factories, and sexual exploitation of women and children. Forced labor occurs internally as some foreign owned enterprises exploit Bangladeshis. Ironically, this exploitation is occurring in an environment in which wages are already among the lowest in the world. Exploitation of Bangladeshis occurs in the nearby countries of India and Pakistan as well as in the Gulf States.[140]

South Asians seeking work in the Middle East also find themselves in trafficked labor situations. "Many Bangladeshi and Nepali men and women are trafficked through India for involuntary servitude in the Middle East."[141] Some employed in the Middle East face severe abuse. Conditions are so bad that Bangladeshis, not accustomed to workers' rights, have protested their treatment in factories. Bangladeshis in Jordan protested their slave-like work conditions and the severe beatings they have received. Some have been repatriated after these protests without receiving their wages.[142]

Despite a ban on the use of child camel jockeys in UAE in 2002, the problem continued to be observed until 2005 when robots were substituted for children.[143] In 2007, a UAE-UNICEF program was set up to repatriate boys to Bangladesh, Pakistan, and countries in Africa. The program provides training, psychological and financial support, and medical assistance to those who were injured. Since the ban on youth camel jockeys in UAE, "735 young men were returned to their families in Pakistan and 17 criminal gangs that trafficked the young boys have been arrested."[144]

Pakistan has also been a destination and transit country for trafficked women from outside the country including Bangladesh and Myanmar. Chinese women worked as prostitutes in a mosque near Islamabad until they were kidnapped by Islamic militants in 2007. In the

[139] http://www.cmht.com/cases/215/nepali-trafficking (accessed December 4, 2009).

[140] *Trafficking in Persons* 2007, 61.

[141] *Trafficking in Persons* 2007, 115.

[142] Jordan: Bangladeshi workers protest against abuse, IRIN Middle East, October 2, 2006, http://www.irinnews.org/report.aspx?ReportId=61858 (accessed January 7, 2009)

[143] "UAE Government Fails to Stop Child Camel Jockey Use," http://www. antislavery.org/archives/press/PressRelease 2004-UAE.htm (accessed January 11, 2009).

[144] *Helping Camel Jockeys: Pakistan*, http://www.helpingcameljockeys.org/solution/ pakistan_story/asp (accessed January 10, 2009).

mid-1990s, Amnesty International reported that the Mujaheddin allegedly "sold" Afghan women and girls to criminal networks in neighboring Pakistan.[145]

But not all who leave Pakistan do so involuntarily. As previously mentioned, there is also a male population that can pay to be smuggled abroad to obtain more income.[146]

Conclusion

There is no reason that the Asian countries should lose their preeminence in international human trafficking. Economic development in the most populous countries of India and China is not leading to a diminution of the number of trafficking victims. The locus of victimization of trafficking may, however, change in the future. Thailand may no longer be the center of the sex trade in Asia, as its primacy may be challenged by China and India, economic powerhouses with enormous income disparity. Rather, the numbers of victims of both sexual and labor trafficking appear to be increasing in these two giants of Asia and in many of the transitional communist countries of Asia that no longer have closed borders and have begun to receive tourists. Moreover, the development of Internet and of computer technology in Asia has rarely provided a route out of trafficking but has instead facilitated the international sex trade and the international proliferation of child pornography.

Those looking for explanations for the pervasiveness of human trafficking in Asia will have trouble in explaining the number of trafficking victims and the severity of trafficking by trying to examine religious practice and historical or political institutions. Trafficking is present in all Asian countries whether they are Moslem, Buddhist, Christian, or Hindu. Trafficking is also highly problematic in atheistic China and North Korea. Sexual trafficking appears to be less frequent in Moslem Pakistan than in predominantly Hindu India, but the presence of Chinese prostitutes near the Red Mosque in Pakistan suggests that even a holy Moslem site is not exempt from trafficking.[147] No religious faith in Asia has curtailed human trafficking.

145 Amnesty International, "Women in Afghanistan: A Human Rights Catastrophe," 11/3/95, http://www.rawa.org/ai-women.htm#6 (accessed January 10, 2009); Koser, "Why Migrant Smuggling Pays."

146 Koser, "Why Migrant Smuggling Pays."

147 Suzanna Koster, "The Red Mosque and the Talibanisation of Pakistan," July 10, 2007. http://www.militantislamonitor.org/article/id/3040 (accessed January 12, 2009).

Those looking to identify variations in trafficking based on histories of these countries' governance will not be able to identify strong variations. For example, Thailand and Japan that were not colonized and the Philippines that endured centuries of colonial rule all suffer from very serious problems of trafficking. The domination of a country and its citizens by a foreign power in past centuries does not necessarily contribute to significantly different levels of trafficking.

The political systems of countries affect the response but not the extent of trafficking. Therefore, trafficking may be as prevalent in democratic India and Japan as well as in the authoritarian one party state of the People's Republic of China. It is in the response to trafficking where one finds differences. More democratic countries with more developed civil societies have more evident anti-trafficking activity by community members.

Few Asian democracies have a deep commitment to individual and minority rights, as do Western democracies influenced by ideas of the Enlightenment. Therefore, in India, members of lower castes are disproportionately victims of trafficking. In Japan, minorities such as Koreans who lack citizenship despite long-term residence in Japan and foreigners are also disproportionately victimized. The same is true of the Hill Tribes of Northern Thailand, whose young girls are disproportionately represented in brothels.

Why is the problem of trafficking so pervasive throughout the diverse countries of Asia? Many countries in Asia have had forms of bonded labor for centuries, but the region never knew the large-scale slave trade that linked the Americas, Europe, and Africa. Therefore, there was no large-scale antislavery movement as developed in Europe and North and South America. There is no history of mass mobilization of citizens on behalf of the rights of others, as was the case of the slave emancipation movement of nineteenth century Europe and the Americas. Instead, in many parts of Asia, human beings are subordinated to the state, the community, and the family. As Professor Samarsinghe discusses, the endurance of patriarchy is central in explaining the proliferation of sex trafficking in such diverse countries of Asia as Bangladesh, Nepal, and the Philippines. Her analysis is also applicable to understanding the pervasiveness of other forms of trafficking. Therefore, individual expressions of rights have not been part of the political, economic, or cultural framework of most Asian countries.

Asia is home to the most populous countries in the world – India and China as well as some of the most densely settled countries such as

Bangladesh and Indonesia. With such large populations, often living in close proximity in terrible slums, individual life has less meaning than in societies with much smaller populations. Many of those trafficked in Asia are disposable people whose identities are of no concern to those who exploit them, and their sole utility is to their families or employers who achieve financial gain from their labor.

Compounding the likelihood of trafficking are other factors identified elsewhere as conducive to trafficking – extreme poverty, great economic differentiation within societies, wars and conflicts, high levels of corruption, and institutionalized discrimination against ethnic minorities.

Asian trafficking has many distinctive features apart from its sheer scale and diversity. Organized crime groups, particularly the *yakuza* and *triads*, as well as the less known Thai, Korean, and Indian crime groups, are key actors in the smuggling and trafficking of human beings. Trade in people is a more important part of their commercial activity than other major international crime groups. The Chinese and Pakistani smugglers, those who initially have a consensual relationship with the person moved, enjoy an acceptance by their community as providing a service even if their activity subsequently results in severe exploitation overseas.

Unlike in other parts of world, the sex trade and human capital is seen as a source of development capital. Particularly in Thailand and in other Southeast Asian countries, the ability to attract tourists because of the available sex industry is seen by some as a positive way to generate foreign investment and income for the country. Human smuggling is favored by Chinese and Pakistani because the profits of the smugglers will be reinvested in their home communities, as the trafficking model of trade and development reflects. Remittances of some of the individuals smuggled will provide for education of family members and community infrastructure needs.

Only India, which has a long history in the twentieth century of social and political activism dating back to Gandhi, is there a large-scale anti-trafficking movement supported by a developed civil society and elements of the business community. There has been mass mobilization against human trafficking as tens of thousands of citizens representing a broad coalition of organizations marched for days in 2007 across Northern India against child labor and trafficking.[148]

Despite this, India is on the Tier 2 Watch List of the U.S. State Department's TIP report in 2009. India is not alone; the presence of so

[148] http://www.globalmarch.org/childtrafficking/index.php (accessed December 4, 2009).

many Asian countries on the Tier 2 Watch List and Tier 3 is evidence of the limited mobilization of most Asian governments to aid victims of trafficking or prosecute traffickers.[149] Limited financial resources of many Asian societies help explain why countering trafficking is not a high priority. But even such a wealthy society as Japan, with a well functioning state bureaucracy, has chosen not to commit much of its resources to combat trafficking. With such limited state effort in the face of such massive problems of enslaved and bonded labor, Asia remains an epicenter of trafficking worldwide.

[149] Tier 2 Watch List: Countries whose governments do not fully comply with the TVPA's minimum standards, but are making significant efforts to bring themselves into compliance with those standards AND: (a) the absolute number of victims of severe forms of trafficking is very significant or is significantly increasing; or (b) there is a failure to provide evidence of increasing efforts to combat severe forms of trafficking in persons from the previous year; or (c) the determination that a country is making significant efforts to bring themselves into compliance with minimum standards was based on commitments by the country to take additional future steps over the next year.

Tier 3 Countries whose governments do not fully comply with the minimum standards and are not making significant efforts to do so, http://www.state.gov/g/tip/rls/tiprpt/2009/123132.htm (accessed August 25, 2009).

6

Human Trafficking in Eurasia and Eastern Europe

The collapse of the Soviet Union has been identified in this book as one of the major events explaining the recent rise in human trafficking. The end of the Cold War had its greatest impact in the former Soviet Union and the former socialist bloc of Eastern Europe. Human trafficking proliferated in the final years of the Soviet period, in the 1980s. At first, trafficking victims were primarily women, but after the dissolution of the USSR, diverse forms of trafficking developed, facilitated by the rise of organized crime, the decline of borders, high levels of corruption, and the incapacity of the transitional states to protect their citizens. Also contributing to human susceptibility to traffickers were the social and economic collapse, discrimination against women and minorities, and the conflicts that accompanied the demise of the socialist system. Millions were unemployed, disoriented, displaced, and vulnerable to exploitation. This chapter focuses on trafficking in the Soviet successor states and the countries of Eastern Europe that are not part of the European Union (EU).

This region, which spans Europe and Asia, is characterized by enormous cultural, political, economic, and religious diversity. Parts of the former Soviet Union such as the Baltic States have standards of living approximately 40 percent of the level of long-time members of the EU, whereas income levels in the impoverished countries of Central Asia and Moldova in the worst periods averaged as little as $50 monthly. These economic differences are accompanied by equally significant political differences. As EU members, the Baltic States are becoming stable democracies, whereas other regions, particularly Belarus and Central Asia, are even more authoritarian than in the final years of the Soviet period. Although all lived in the atheist USSR, religion has resurged in the post-Soviet period among both Christians and Moslems.

Despite the great differences in this region, all countries share a serious problem of human trafficking. They serve as source, transit, and host states for human trafficking.[1] Russia now hosts the second largest number of migrants in the world after the United States.[2] Russia, unlike the United States, had no tradition of migration apart from the enormous internal migration and exploitation within the former USSR,[3] under Stalin. Victims from Southeast and South Asia now traverse the immense territory of the former USSR trying to reach Western Europe, a destination that remains a dream rather than a reality for many smuggled people. Many people from diverse parts of Asia are left stranded in the Soviet successor states, ripe for exploitation. The number of individuals vulnerable to exploitation is small relative to the millions of laborers from Central Asia who are all too often enslaved or severely mistreated. Their migration to Russia represents a reverse migration from regions once colonized by the Soviet state. In this respect, Russia now resembles other former colonizers that receive migrants from states they once occupied.

The trafficking problem has persisted despite significant assistance programs from the EU, the United States, individual donor countries, and multilateral organizations such as the International Organization for Migration (IOM) and the Organization for Security and Cooperation in Europe (OSCE). Extensive resources have been dedicated to fighting trafficking, establishing law enforcement and victims' assistance programs, and supporting nongovernmental organizations (NGOs) to combat trafficking. But the traffickers still enjoy impunity, and millions of people are still trafficked annually. There is no prospect of a sharp curtailment in human trafficking in the near future, as the fundamental conditions that gave rise to the problem still persist. As in most parts of the world, the counter-trafficking response is inadequate compared to the

[1] Donna Hughes, "The 'Natasha' Trade: The Transnational Shadow Market of Trafficking in Women," *Journal of International Affairs* 53 (Spring 2000), 625–51; Phil Williams, ed., *Illegal Immigration and Commercial Sex: The New Slave Trade* (London: Portland, OR: Frank Cass, 1999).

[2] Aleksandr Bastrykin, "Migratsiia:Iz sveta – v ten'" *Itogi*, July 6, 2009, 19.

[3] According to the World Bank, Russia now ranks second in the world after the United States in terms of its migrant population. James Rodgers, "Moscow to Cut Migrant Workers," http://news.bbc.co.uk/go/pr/fr/-/2/hi/europe/6731059.stm June 7, 2007 (accessed June 7, 2007).

scale of the problem.[4] Moreover, human trafficking may even increase in the future because there is a structural imbalance between the demographically declining but richer Slavic states and the poor Central Asian states with growing youthful populations.

Persistence of the Problem

Russia has a long history of enslavement of its population, as the etymology of the word slave comes from *Slav*.[5] Russians were frequently enslaved abroad. From the Roman period to the Middle Ages, Slavs were highly represented in European slave markets. The Mongolian invasion resulted in further enslavement of the population by the conquerors.

Slavery persisted in Russia until the rule of Peter the Great,[6] although the population was not freed from slavery. Instead, their status shifted from that of slave to serf. Serfs were denied mobility and tied to their landowners. Serfdom persisted in the Russian empire much longer than in Western Europe, and approximately one-third of the population were still serfs when serfdom was officially ended under Alexander II in 1861. This is explained by the fact that the Russian empire remained outside the enlightenment and never adopted the concepts of individual rights that are at the basis of Western societies.[7] Russian occupation of Central Asia merely left the authoritarian rule and the subjugation of citizens by their rulers in place.[8]

The legacy of slavery, serfdom, and long-term authoritarian rule shapes contemporary trafficking. This was shown in Chapter 5 in reference to

[4] Lauren McCarthy, "*Sravnitelnyi analiz praktiki rossiiskikh i amerikanskikh pravookhranitel'nykh institutov v protivodeistvii torgovle liud'mi*," in *Vne tolerantnosti torgovliia liud'mi i rabskikh trud: novye metamorfozy starykh prestuplenii*, L. D. Erokhina, ed. (Vladivostok: Izdatelstvo TGEU, 2009), 186–203.

[5] http://www.scribd.com/doc/16205754/Slavs-Slaves (accessed August 20, 2009).

[6] See, for example, these works of Richard Hellie: "Muscovite Slavery in Comparative Perspective," in *Russian History* 6, part 2 (1979), 133–209, reprinted in *Articles on Russian and Soviet History 1500–1991*, vol. 1, Alexander Dallin, ed., and *Major Problems in Early Modern Russian History*, Nancy Shields Kollmann, ed. (New York and London: Garland, 1992), 291–367; "Women in Muscovite Slavery," in *Russian History* 10, part 2 (1983), 213–29; "Slavery Among the Early Modern Peoples on the Territory of the USSR," in *Canadian-American Slavic Studies* 17, no. 4 (Winter 1983), 454–65; *Slavery in Russia, 1450–1725* (Chicago: The University of Chicago Press, 1982).

[7] James H. Billington, *Icon and the Axe: An Interpretive History of Russian Culture* (New York: Knopf, 1966).

[8] Douglas Northrop, *Veiled Empire Gender & Power in Stalinist Central Asia* (Ithaca and London: Cornell University Press, 2004).

the bonded laborers of India and is illustrated more amply in Chapters 8 and 9, which discuss trafficking in North and South America and Africa. The passivity of citizens of post-Soviet states in the face of severe exploitation results from centuries of oppression combined with the realities of the recent Soviet past. Human freedom had no place in their life experience as Communist ideology made citizens subordinate to the interests of the state.

The past century and a half provided more direct precedents for contemporary slavery. The large-scale sex trafficking between the southern regions of the former USSR and Turkey was presaged by an earlier trade. In 1869, in *The Innocents Abroad*, Mark Twain reported that "Circassian and Georgian girls are still sold in Constantinople by their parents, but not publicly."[9] In another passage that explains the origin of the trade that now exists among Moldova, Russia, Ukraine, and Turkey, he wrote,

> Prices are pretty high now and holders firm, but two or three years ago, parents in a starving condition, brought their young daughters down here and sold them for even twenty and thirty dollars, when they could do no better, simply to save themselves and the girls from dying of want.[10]

But today, the sellers in the markets of Turkey are not parents but human traffickers who may have "acquired" their human commodities from alcoholic or otherwise dysfunctional parents. Or today's victims may also originate from the hundreds of thousands of youths in children's homes and orphanages. The absence of programs to help deinstitutionalized youth after age 18 return to their communities has made many of the females susceptible to sex traffickers. Even worse, some recruiters in Russia and other post-Soviet states have an ongoing relationship with specific orphanage directors who regularly deliver 18-year-old "graduates" of the children's homes into the hands of the traffickers.[11]

An international slave trade operating from Eastern Europe and Russia foreshadowed the long-distance trade of contemporary trafficking. From the 1880s through the 1930s, a white slave trade flourished among the Baltic States, Ukraine, and what is now Moldova to North and South America.[12]

[9] Mark Twain, *The Innocents Abroad* (New York: Literary Classics, 1984), 290.

[10] Ibid., 291.

[11] Clementine K. Fujimura, Sally W. Stoecker, and Tatyana Sudakova, *Russia's Abandoned Children: An Intimate Understanding*, (Westport, CT: Praeger, 2005); interview in Dubai with those who assist trafficking victims in the UAE, November 2009.

[12] Edward Bristow, *Prostitution and Prejudice: The Jewish Fight Against White Slavery 1870 –1939* (New York: Schocken Books, 1982); Isabel Vincent, *Bodies and Souls: The*

Poor women, as discussed in later chapters, were recruited by means of false promises of a better life by transnational organized crime groups. This trade lasted fifty years, ending only with the worldwide depression of the 1930s.

Even though the socialist system had an ideological commitment to end labor exploitation, millions were enslaved under the Soviet system. All exploitation was done by the state because no private enterprises were allowed in the Soviet period.[13]

Prostitution was outlawed and suppressed under communism, but it did not disappear entirely. Instead, prostitutes were forced to serve as secret police informers, and ships of Soviet prostitutes were sometimes sent abroad to provide "services" for Russian naval crews to ensure that they did not associate with local women at ports of call.[14] Moreover, millions of Russian citizens were in forced labor during the Soviet period until Stalin's death in 1953. Most were enslaved as political prisoners in labor camps whereas others toiled as slave laborers, building the subways of Moscow and major Soviet industrial projects.[15] Even after Stalin's death, the USSR had one of the largest inmate populations, with most prisoners confined to labor colonies where inmates worked under grueling and dehumanizing conditions.[16] Socialist ideology made work a central feature of punishment and rehabilitation.

Abusive labor was not confined to labor camps. During the Soviet era, demands on Uzbekistan to grow cotton resulted in forced child labor to harvest the cotton crop. Today in Uzbekistan, children are still exploited as cotton pickers as they were in the Soviet Union, a consequence of state policy to increase the number of available workers for the agricultural sector.[17]

Trafficking continues to exist on a large scale in former socialist states because of the same conditions that once facilitated the white slave

Tragic Plight of Three Jewish Women Forced into Prostitution in the Americas (New York: William Morrow, 2005).

13 Louise I. Shelley, "The Changing Position of Women: Trafficking, Crime and Corruption," in *The Legacy of State Socialism and the Future of Transformation*, David Lane, ed. (Lanham, MD: Rowman and Littlefield, 2002), 207–22.

14 IOM, "Trafficking in Women and Prostitution in the Baltic States: Social and Legal Aspects," 2001, 163.

15 Robert Conquest, *Great Terror: Stalin's Purge of the Thirties* (Hamondworth: Penguin, 1971); Aleksandr I. Solzhenitsyn, *Gulag Archipelago, 1918–56: An Experiment in Literary Investigation* (New York: Harper Perennial, 1991).

16 Anne Applebaum, *Gulag: A History* (New York: Doubleday, 2003).

17 "Child Labor in Uzbekistan Cotton Fields," http://us.oneworld.net/article/363578-in-brief-child-labor-uzbekistan-cotton-fields (accessed December 4, 2009).

trade – absence of respect for individual rights, the low status of women, corruption, deeply embedded organized crime groups, and ineffective law enforcement. The absence of political will in many Soviet successor states and in parts of the Balkans to counter-trafficking also explains its persistence. In some countries of Central Asia, the state actually encourages citizens to labor abroad under any conditions because of the absence of available employment at home. Many who are trafficked willingly submit to this exploitation, if only to receive limited payments, because this is superior to their possible earnings at home.

Diversity of Trafficking

All forms of trafficking exist in the vast territory of the former USSR and Eastern Europe. Sex trafficking has received the most publicity, as the exploitation of Slavic women from the Balkans and the former USSR has been widely publicized in newspaper exposes, documentaries, and feature films. But at present there are more post-Soviet victims of labor than of sex trafficking. An International Labour Organization (ILO) report in 2004 estimated that 20 percent of the 5 million illegal immigrants in Russia were victims of forced labor. They are often exploited in dangerous construction work,[18] in depopulated rural areas, and in heavy labor.[19] Those most likely to be exploited are men from Central Asia, the poorest regions of the Caucasus, and Belarus,[20] although some come from as far as Vietnam. Kazakhstan, with its natural resource wealth, is also a magnet for workers, legal and illegal, from Kyrgyzstan, Uzbekistan, and Tajikistan.[21]

[18] Elena Tiuriukanova, "Social, Economic and Criminal Effects of Migration in Russian Megalopilises," www.american.edu/traccc/resources/publications.html (accessed June 27, 2007).

[19] *Trafficking in Persons Report 2004*, www.state.gov/g/tip/rls/tiprpt/2004/33192.htm (accessed June 27, 2007); Elena Tiuriukanova, *Prinuditel'nyi Trud v Sovremmnoi Rossii: Nerugliermaya migratiia i torgovliia liudmi* (Moscow: International Labour Organization, 2004), www.american.edu/traccc/resources/publications.html (accessed June 27, 2007).

[20] IOM Migration Research Series no. 36, Rebecca Surtees, "Trafficking of Men: A Trend Less Considered: The Case of Belarus and Ukraine," http://www.iom.int/jahia/webdav/site/myjahiasite/shared/shared/mainsite/published_docs/serial_publications/MRS-36.pdf (accessed August 24, 2009).

[21] Liz Kelly, *Fertile Fields: Trafficking in Persons in Central Asia* (Vienna: IOM, 2005);Liz Kelly, "A Conducive Context: Trafficking of Persons in Central Asia," in *Human Trafficking*, Maggy Lee, ed. (Cullompton and Portland, OR: Willan Publishing, 2007), 73–91.

Child trafficking is all too common. Child labor is not confined to Uzbekistan. In Tajikistan, children are trafficked for forced labor and begging as well as commercial sexual exploitation.[22]

In Russia, forces other than state policy explain the pervasiveness of child exploitation. There are large numbers of abandoned, street, and institutionalized children whose parents have left them or who have been declared incompetent because of alcoholism, drug abuse, domestic violence, and child sexual exploitation.[23] Street children are a problem more often associated with poor third-world countries than a former superpower, but it is an ever more present reality in the post-Soviet countries, even more since the onset of the financial crisis in 2008. Before the financial crisis, the number of homeless or abandoned children was estimated to be at the same level as after World War II. Russia alone is estimated to have 700,000 orphans and 2 million illiterate youths.[24]

The reluctance of Russians to adopt children exacerbates the number of institutionalized children. There are now fifty transit homes throughout Russia. These are intended to provide temporary shelter for children who are found abandoned or begging in the streets. Yet many children do not enter the children's homes because they are forced by organized crime to beg or prostitute themselves. Even though the police are supposed to turn these children over to facilities where they will be cared for, this sometimes does not happen. Collusion between the criminals and the police prevents children from being brought to the transit homes.[25]

Migrants from Central Asia and the Caucasus often are forced to abandon the children they cannot sustain in Russia, exacerbating the numbers of abandoned and homeless children. Many of these children have no identity papers, and with a poor knowledge of Russian are even more vulnerable to exploitation.[26] Even if they arrive at transit shelters, which are supposed to provide only temporary support, there is no way for authorities to find the undocumented children's parents or return them to their home communities.

[22] Ibid., and *Trafficking in Persons Report 2009* (Washington, DC: U.S. Department of State, 2009), 276, 296.

[23] Fujimura, Stoecker, and Sudakova, *Russia's Abandoned Children*.

[24] V Rossii, *'tretiia volna" bezprizonosti, beznadzornosti, negramotnosti, i prestupnost' podrostov (statistika)*, June 1, 2005, http://www.newsru.com/russia/01jun2005/generation.html (accessed October 30, 2008).

[25] Discussion by Marina Ryabko, Director of the "Priyut-Tranzit" government-funded shelter for children and teens in St. Petersburg. The event was entitled "Child Trafficking and Exploitation in Russia: Scale and Scope," held on September 24, 2008, George Mason University, Arlington, VA.

[26] Ibid.

Children obtained by traffickers are exploited in numerous ways as prostitutes, in the production of child pornography, sold for adoptions, and forced to beg on the streets.[27] Commercial sexual exploitation of children is recognized as an increasing problem, although the Russian State parliament (Duma) has not yet passed adequate legislation to combat all aspects of this phenomenon. Much of the production of child pornography marketed internationally on the Internet is produced in Russia, using trafficked children. Russia now assumes second place in the production of marketed pornography worldwide, contributing 23 percent of international production.[28] Russia's distinct role in this form of exploitation reflects the high technological capacity of its criminals.

In Eastern Europe and the Soviet successor states, children in orphanages and children's homes are also sold by administrators for adoption. Organized crime groups serve as the intermediaries between the parents and the adoption agency.[29] Notaries are bribed to certify that parents have surrendered their parental rights. Criminally assisted adoptions do not always have happy endings. The failure of oversight of potential adoptive parents has resulted in children being placed in totally unsuitable families. Physical and sexual abuse has followed, and in the most extreme cases has led to death. In the United States between 1990 and 2005, thirteen adopted Russian children died in the custody of their American parents as a result of physical abuse or negligence by the parents. In the worst abuse case, the adoptive mother received a significant prison term.[30] Russian authorities did not crack down on the trafficking networks but instead curtailed adoptions to the United States.[31]

In Eastern Europe, pregnant mothers are trafficked so that their babies can be adopted. In a publicized trial in France, pregnant Romany women

[27] "Second Annual Report on Victims of Trafficking in South-Eastern Europe," 2005, www.iom.int/jahia/Jahia/cache/offonce/pid/1674?entryId=10161_101k (accessed June 27, 2007); Elena Tiuriukanova, *Prinuditel'nyi Trud v Sovremmnoi Rossii.*

[28] U.S. Attorney's Office of Eastern District of Wisconsin, http://www.usdoj.gov/usao/wie/LECC/Newsletter/July_2008.pdf (accessed October 30, 2008).

[29] Confirming the involvement of organized crime in Russian adoptions were the experiences of one Midwestern American family I met who described their grandson's adoption in the mid-1990s. Their son traveled to Russia with a significant amount of cash. Before his son's adoption, he was escorted by the adoption agency to some shady criminal figures and told to give them thousands of dollars in cash. The family was aware that their grandchild had been acquired through criminal practices, but justified the family complicity in terms of the better life they believe they had provided the child.

[30] J. Pomfret, "Bribery at Border Worries Officials," *Washington Post*, July 15, 2006, 1.

[31] Wendy Koch, "Russia Curtails American Adoptions," April 11, 2007 http://www.usatoday.com/news/nation/2007–04–10-russia-adoptions_N.htm (accessed July 29, 2009).

were trafficked to France because French Romany families could not adopt children because they lacked the prerequisite for a French adoption – a permanent place of residence. Once the children were born, French Romany families adopted the children and the women were sent home with payment.[32]

Children from the former socialist bloc are forced to beg both at home and abroad. The author in 2001 observed crippled children in wheelchairs in St. Petersburg being forced to beg in the heat of summer without being provided water. Child beggars such as those would be beaten if they did not return home with enough money.

Not only crippled children were exploited by organized crime groups. In the late 1990s, invalids who had lost arms and legs in war were forced in Moscow and other large cities to move among heavy traffic on small, square wood frames with wheels below to beg money from drivers. Like the children, they faced starvation and beatings if they did not return with money.[33]

The Albanian crime groups, especially those from Kosovo, have also trafficked children for begging and illegal adoptions.[34] In addition, trafficked Albanian children have been forced to steal and participate in more serious crimes. Young people were also forced to be facilitators of smuggling, transporting migrants across the sea from Albania to Italy in often-dangerous speedboats.[35]

Minorities subject to discrimination are especially vulnerable to exploitation as beggars. Many Romany children are forced into begging in Eastern Europe and others travel farther. In 2005, 700 Roma children were trafficked from Bulgaria to Austria to beg.[36] More recently, Romany child beggars have been found in the United Kingdom, some having been deliberately maimed to be better beggars.[37]

[32] "French Baby-smuggling Case Begins," January 22, 2007, http://news.bbc.co.uk/2/hi/europe/6286059.stm (accessed June 27, 2007).

[33] Robert G. Kaiser cites the legless veterans in "Letter from Russia: In Moscow, Playing a Brand-New Tune," *Washington Post*, May 5, 1999, http://www.cdi.org/russia/johnson/3271.html (accessed June 27, 2007).

[34] Vasilika Hysi, "Organised Crime in Albania: The Ugly Side of Capitalism and Democracy," in *Organised Crime in Europe Concepts, Patterns and Control Policies in the European Union and Beyond*, Cyrille Fijnaut and Letizia Paoli, eds. (Dordrecht: Springer, 2004), 546–51.

[35] Ibid., 548–51.

[36] *Trafficking in Persons Report 2006* (Washington, DC: U.S. Department of State, 2006), 78.

[37] Steve Harvey, "A Europol Perspective on Criminal Profits and Money Laundering Linked to Trafficking in Human Beings," OSCE-UNODC-CYPRUS Regional Operational

Child soldiers have been used in many conflicts in the region. "The majority of child soldiers in Europe have fought in opposition groups … serving in Chechnya, Daghestan, Kosovo, Macedonia and Nagorno-Karabagh."[38] Even farther east, child soldiers were used in the conflicts in Azerbaijan and Tajikistan.[39] All the named conflicts except for Kosovo and Macedonia occurred in the former USSR. In some cases, the children wanted to fight, as an interview with a former child soldier in Bosnia-Herzegovina indicates.[40] But often child and youth participation in these conflicts was coerced.

Despite the extensive victimization of youth, many more adults in the former USSR and Eastern Europe are victims of trafficking. Those exploited are not only migrants, as trafficking prosecutions in the Far East point to other dimensions of the problem. Russian military officers in the Far East were prosecuted for enslaving conscripts under their command, forcing the soldiers to work on their personal property as slave laborers. Senior members of a ship's crew were also successfully prosecuted after enslaved Ukrainian sailors were liberated from their traffickers while the vessel was docked in the Russian Far East.[41]

Organ trafficking is not widespread in Eastern Europe and the former Soviet Union because those seeking organs would not want medical care in the post-Soviet medical system. Instead, victims from the region travel to other countries to have a kidney removed. The "organ donors" are recruited by crime groups.

Distinctiveness of Human Trafficking

The distinctiveness of post-Soviet and Eastern European trafficking is the speed with which it grew and globalized. In contrast with Asian trafficking, discussed in Chapter 5, there was no long-existing trade in human beings or established networks to facilitate this business. Instead,

Meeting on Combating Human Trafficking and Money Laundering in the Mediterranean Rim Region, September 18–19, 2008, Larnaca, Cyprus.

38 P. W. Singer, *Children at War* (New York: Pantheon Books, 2005), 18.

39 Ibid., 21.

40 Jason Chudy, " From Bosnian Child Soldier to U.S. Army Leader," August 17, 2004, http://www.military.com/NewContent/0,13190,SS_081704_Bosnian,00.html (accessed August 21, 2009).

41 This information was presented at a training session in Khabarovsk entitled "Combating Human Trafficking at the Federal and Regional Levels," March 15–16, 2007, for representatives from the media in the Far East; conversations with MVD (Ministry of Interior) expert K. A. Volkov from Khabarovsk.

the conditions of the transitional societies created the ideal conditions conducive to trade in human beings. In less than a decade during the transitional period, the former Soviet states transformed from states with limited labor exploitation to worldwide symbols of trafficking in women. Now, years after the initial transition, all forms of human trafficking are endemic in the region, a result of poverty, ineffective counter-measures, the frequent collusion of government officials in this trade, and the rise of criminal entrepreneurship. The following analysis focuses on the unique conditions that contributed to the rapid rise of human trafficking and the post-Soviet model of human trafficking identified in Chapter 4.

Human trafficking proliferated in the mid-1980s in Eastern Europe and the former Soviet Union as the controls and social supports of the socialist system disappeared. At that time, the coercive apparatus of the communist states began to disintegrate and frequently they and their assets were privatized to organized crime.[42]

At first, the trafficking was internal but quite rapidly it became transnational as Balkan traffickers as well as those from Slavic states and Moldova capitalized on their proximity to the lucrative and extensive Western European markets.[43] Trafficking was initially less common from the Caucasus and Central Asia, where tight social and familial structures limited the phenomenon. But trafficking of women and men subsequently spread to the Caucasus and Central Asia as its citizens were trafficked to Soviet successor states, the Middle East, and occasionally beyond.[44]

Explaining the rise in trafficking are the feminization of poverty, the decline of social protections for family, increased intrafamilial violence, child abuse and alcoholism,[45] rise of serious regional conflicts, and increasing economic differentiation among social classes and successor states of the former USSR. Ever-present discrimination against women was an important facilitator.[46] Illicit trade in people could also be easily hidden

[42] Maria Łos and Andrzej Zybertowicz, *Privatizing the Police-State: The Case of Poland* (New York: St. Martin's Press, 2000); see also Louise I. Shelley, *Policing Soviet Society: The Evolution of State Control* (London and New York: Routledge, 1996).

[43] Kathryn Farr, *Sex Trafficking: The Global Market in Women and Children* (New York, : Worth, 2005).

[44] Beatrix Siman Zakhari, "Legal Cases Prosecuted Under the Victims of Trafficking and Violence Protections Act of 2000," in *Human Traffic and Transnational Crime: Eurasian and American Perspectives*, Sally Stoecker and Louise Shelley, eds. (Lanham, MD: Rowman & Littlefield, 2005), 140–42; *Trafficking in Persons Report 2009*, 174, 191, 296.

[45] Igor Kon and James Riordan, eds., *Sex and Russian Society* (Bloomington, IN: Indiana University Press, 1993), 6.

[46] Sally Stoecker, "Human Trafficking: A New Challenge for the United States and Russia," in *Human Traffic and Transnational Crime*, 13–28.

within the large shadow economies of all the post-socialist states.[47] An exacerbating vulnerability was the rise of organized crime outside the control of the state yet closely linked to its corrupt officials.[48] For these violent entrepreneurs, women became an important commodity,

Initially, women were the primary victims of the traffickers, having lost the most with the collapse of the socialist system.[49] The feminization of poverty was a consequence of an economic transition that prioritized the dismantling of the Soviet system. In a few years, many post-Soviet economies moved from total state ownership to a greater degree of private ownership than existed in several Western European countries. Little consideration was given to the long-term consequences of economic "reform" on women and children.

In the undoing of socialism, women lost their guaranteed employment, child subsidies, and support system. The financial crisis that followed the Soviet collapse in the early 1990s led to the demise of the social safety net attached to many enterprises, a problem exacerbated by Western policy advisors who advocated that socialist enterprises drop these benefits in the name of economic efficiency.[50] Childcare, summer camps, and other programs that benefited women and children were dropped. Unfortunately, eliminating those social benefits was rarely a prelude to more efficient enterprises or greater women's rights, but instead allowed for even more assets being stripped from enterprises by greedy management and greater female impoverishment.

Women were at a disadvantage at all stages of the privatization process in post-Soviet states. Women had little chance of acquiring any valuable assets because privatization in Russia and elsewhere gave managers a disproportionate share of former state property. Therefore, the Soviet legacy

[47] Svetlana Glinkina, "The Role of the Non-socialized Sector in Perestroika," in *Privatization and Entrepreneurship in Post-Socialist Countries*, Bruno Dallago, Gianmaria Ajani, and Bruno Grancelli, eds. (Houndsmills, UK: Macmillan Press, 1993), 341; Friedrich Schneider, "The Size of Shadow Economies in 145 Countries from 1999 to 2003," *The Brown Journal of World Affairs* 11, no. 2 (winter/spring 2005), 113–43.

[48] Vadim Volkov, *Violent Entrepreneurs: The Use of Force in the Making of Capitalism* (Ithaca, NY and London: Cornell University Press, 2002); Frederico Varese, *The Russian Mafia Private Protection in a New Market Economy* (Oxford: Oxford University Press, 2001).

[49] Sally Stoecker, "Human Trafficking: A New Challenge for the United States and Russia," in *Human Traffic and Transnational Crime*, 13–28.

[50] See, for example, Alena Heitlinger, "The Impact of the Transition from Communism on the Status of Women in the Czech and Slovak Republics," in *Gender Politics and Post-Communism: Reflections from Eastern Europe and the Former Soviet Union*, Nanette Funk and Magda Mueller, eds. (New York and London: Routledge, 1993), 98–101.

of male management was translated into the structure of post-Soviet property distribution. Very few women in the post-Soviet period acquired more than an insignificant share of the enterprises in which they had worked.

Factories were privatized to employees. Yet this aspect of privatization also worked to the disadvantage of women. Many women factory workers were employed in feminized industries such as textiles, food production, and processing, which were not competitive in a more open economy. Therefore, women disproportionately acquired stakes in industries without value, whereas men were more likely to acquire shares in extractive resource industries, which were more profitable.[51]

Voucher privatization also delivered nothing of value to women. The stock funds in which citizens could invest the vouchers were unregulated and riddled with fraud.[52] Auction privatizations also left women at a disadvantage. Women were often physically barred from many auctions of state property by the enforcers of organized crime.

Women could have been successful entrepreneurs of small businesses, if given access to capital, but often the only available creditors were organized crime. Women, less able than their male associates to retain protection services, all too often had their businesses expropriated by criminals using extortion and force.[53] In even worse cases, the criminals demanded the youthful daughters as payment for the debt.[54]

The corrupted privatization process in which valuable properties were transferred to insiders for relatively small sums deprived the state of much-needed revenues. Compounding the cash-flow problem was the export of capital on a massive scale from all former Soviet states. Starved for capital, the state could not pay wages.[55] Everyone suffered, but those

[51] For a discussion of the process, see Joseph R. Blasi, Maya Kroumova, and Douglas Kruse, *Kremlin Capitalism Privatizing the Russian Economy* (Ithaca, NY and London: Cornell University Press, 1997), 17–49. See also Janine Wedel, *Collision and Collusion: The Strange Case of Western Aid to Eastern Europe* (New York: St. Martin's Press, 1998) for a discussion of the corruption of the HIID (Harvard Institute for International Development) in administering grant assistance to the Russian privatization process. Harvard was subsequently fined $40 million by the U.S. Justice Department for this misconduct.

[52] Louise I. Shelley, "Privatization and Crime: The Post-Soviet Experience," *Journal of Contemporary Criminal Justice* 11, no. 4 (December 1995), 244–56.

[53] Ibid.

[54] The author participated in an asylum case in the mid-2000s in which a woman fled from Chelyabinsk, Russia, with her daughter because the criminals demanded the daughter when she could not repay the debt.

[55] N. A. Lopashenko, *Begstvo kapitala peredel sobstvennoisti ekonomicheskaia amnistiia* (Moscow: ANO: Iuridicheskie programmy, 2005).

most affected were women who were disproportionately represented on state payrolls as teachers, doctors, nurses, and office personnel. Desperate women sought any available work abroad in the absence of legitimate opportunities at home, increasing their vulnerability to trafficking.

Capitalizing on the vulnerability of women and children were the numerous organized crime groups whose emergence accompanied the collapse of the USSR. The collapse of the USSR destroyed formal governmental relations but not the informal relations that existed among criminals and officials across the former USSR. Human trafficking became a core crime activity of these transnational criminals as well as small networks of entrepreneurs.

The crime groups from the Balkans and the former Soviet Union, as discussed in previous chapters, have been among the most flexible in adapting to the globalized environment. They have altered their routes, structures, and methods to adjust to market conditions and new laws and enforcement techniques.

Their flexibility and adaptability is explained by their past work experience and high educational levels. Trafficking organizations consisted not only of inmates released from Soviet labor camps but also of decommissioned military personnel and present and past members of the security apparatus, as well as sportsmen. The professional backgrounds of many in the operations side of intelligence gave them the skills to produce fraudulent documents, utilize advanced communications technology, launder money, and operate successfully across borders.

Many of the criminals from the former USSR obtained a foothold in the countries of Eastern Europe in the early years of the transition, giving them a broader base of operations. Illustrative of this is a major transnational criminal enterprise run by Semyon Mogilevich that operated out of Moscow and Budapest, implicated in the trafficking of women, often from the former USSR to Eastern Europe.[56] This crime network as well as many others had working relationships with crime groups from Europe, the Middle East, and Asia, as well as North and South America. The famous Tarzan case, in which Ludwig Fainberg used Slavic women to lure Colombian drug traffickers to his strip joint near the Miami airport, epitomizes these relationships. Fainberg and his Colombian associate went to

[56] See "The 'Natasha Trade,'" Transnational Sex Trafficking, National Institute of Justice, January 2001, 13, http://www.uri.edu/artsci/wms/hughes/natasha_nij.pd (accessed June 22, 2007); The FBI set up an office in Budapest to help pursue him and his organization. Misha Glenny, *McMafia: A Journey Through the Global Criminal Underworld* (New York: Alfred A. Knopf, 2008), 72–77.

Russia to buy submarines and missile launchers from a Russian military base in the North that could be used to ensure delivery of drugs.[57]

The organized crime embedded in post-Soviet states creates other distinctive patterns. Trafficking victims increasingly are the offspring of trafficked victims. Intragenerational trafficking is a known phenomenon in India, where the trade in women and minors has gone on for a long time, but it is not seen in other industrialized societies prior to the departure abroad of mothers seeking to find a better life or send remittances home to their families. Unfortunately, the children left behind are often unsupervised and vulnerable to traffickers, as the film Lilya *4-Ever* accurately conveys. In this film, based on a true-life story, an Estonian mother leaves with a man for a foreign country. Her abandoned daughter, approximately 16 years of age, is trafficked to Sweden, where she commits suicide. Unfortunately, other examples of second-generation prostitution exist in other spheres of trafficking as children of trafficked women, especially from Moldova, are trafficked for adoptions or as beggars, or become victims of labor exploitation.[58]

Migration and crime are linked differently in Russia than in Western Europe. In many Western European countries, as much as a third of the prison population is composed of foreigners.[59] This is not the case in the former Soviet states. Foreigners, mostly from Soviet successor states, increased their crime commission in 2008 by 7.5 percent, to 54,000 crimes.[60] But this is a small percentage of total crimes committed, although there are many public complaints that migrants are highly criminal.[61] Labor migrants are much more frequently victims of crime than they are perpetrators of criminal acts.[62] According to the SOVA Center for Information and Analysis, a Moscow-based NGO that monitors hate

57 Robert L. Friedman, *Red Mafiya: How the Russian Mob Has Invaded America* (Boston: Little, Brown, 2000), 141–69 and interviews by the author with the undercover agent and the prosecutors in this case.

58 IOM Counter Trafficking Service, "Changing Patterns and Trends of Trafficking in Persons in the Balkan Region," July 2004, 9–10, http://www.iom.hu/PDFs/Changing%20Patterns%20in%20Trafficking%20in%20Balkan%20region.pdf (accessed August 23, 2009).

59 Alessandro de Giorgi, *Rethinking the Political Economy of Punishment: Perspectives on Post-Fordism and Penal Politics* (Aldershot, England and Burlington, VT: Ashgate, 2006), 101.

60 Aleksandr Bastrykin, "Migratsiia:Iz sveta – v ten'" *Itogi*, July 6, 2009, 19.

61 Ibid.; see some of the official speeches presented at the 3rd WAAF meeting held at the Russian Duma, September 27, 2006, http://waaf.ru/cgi-bin/index.cgi?r=7&r_1=3 (accessed June 27, 2007).

62 "Crime and Corruption Related to Migration in Russian Megalopolises," September 30, 2005, www.american.edu/traccc/events/hosted.html (accessed June 27, 2007).

crimes, from January to November 2008, there were at least 348 racially motivated attacks, and 82 victims died as a result. On December 5, 2008, assailants attacked two workers from Tajikistan, stabbing and decapitating 20-year-old Salokhiddin Azizov."[63]

Regional Variations in Trafficking

There are significant regional differences in trafficking explained by the vast geographical reach of the former USSR, the different cultural traditions, and the enormous economic discrepancies. Postconflict regions in Russia have their own distinctive trafficking patterns.

The territory discussed in this chapter reaches from the borders of China and Korea to the Baltic Sea and the boundaries of Western Europe. Although victims are transported great distances to their destinations, as with other commodities, extended transport adds additional costs. Therefore, sex trafficking victims from the Russian Far East and Siberia are more likely to be trafficked to Japan, Korea, and China than women in the far western parts of Russia. In Japan, Korea, and China, there is a significant demand for women from the former Soviet Union.[64] In Korea, women trafficked into the sex industry serve not only a local clientele but also American servicemen on the bases there.[65] In Japan, Russian women often enter on entertainment visas and are subsequently exploited by the *yakuza*. In such affluent Chinese cities as Harbin, Shanghai, and Hong Kong, there is also a strong demand for Russian women.[66]

In contrast, women from western Russia, Ukraine, and Moldova are more often trafficked to Western and Eastern Europe, the Balkans, and

[63] *Human Rights Watch Report*, "Are You Happy to Cheat Us?" http://www.hrw.org/en/reports/2009/02/09/are-you-happy-cheat-us-0 (accessed August 25, 2009), 14–15; see Web site of SOVA center for more general information, http://sova-center.ru/194F418 (accessed August 24, 2009).

[64] Liudmila Erokhina, "Trafficking in Women in the Russian Far East: A Real or Imaginary Phenomenon?" in *Human Traffic and Transnational Crime*, 79–94.

[65] Dong-Hoon Seol and Geon-Soo Han, "Foreign Women's Life and Work in the Entertaining Sector of Korea from the Human Trafficking Perspective" in *Human Security, Transnational Crime and Human Trafficking: Asian and Western Perspectives*, Shiro Okubo and Louise Shelley, eds. (Routledge, forthcoming 2010).

[66] M. Iu. Buriak, "Pravovaia Bor'ba s Torgovlei Liud'mi" in *Transnational'naia organizovannaia prestupnost':definitsii i real'nost,'* ed.V. A. Nomokonov (Vladivostok: Izd-vo DVGU, 2001), 209–22; L. D. Erokhina and M. Iu. Buriak, *Torgovliia zhenshchinami v tseliakh seksual'noi ekspluatatsii: teoriia i praktika bor'by* (Vladivostok: DVGU, 2001); see also bibliography on trafficking at Vladivostok Web site http://www.crime.vl.ru/index.php?cat=22 (accessed August 24, 2009).

Turkey. In the cold northern regions of Lapland, women from northwest Russia, Moldova, and Ukraine are trafficked to the wealthy neighboring Scandinavian countries. "The women from the Murmansk region are trafficked to Finland, or across Finland to Norway, on Thursdays through Ivalo and picked up on Sundays and brought back."[67] A sex trade also exists in the opposite direction as men take week-end cruise ships from Sweden to visit prostitutes in Estonia, a response to the Swedish policy that provides criminal sanctions for men who use prostitutes.[68]

At the southern border of the former USSR, Turkey is an important target destination for women from Southern Russia, Ukraine, Moldova, and the Caucasus. Women enter by plane or by boat from the port of Odessa, Ukraine, on the Black Sea, and across land from Georgia.

Slavic and Moldovan women are also trafficked to the Middle East, including Israel, UAE, and Egypt.[69] Yet cultural and religious links explain why many women from the Moslem countries of the Caucasus and Central Asia are also trafficked in significant numbers to Arab countries and to Turkey.[70] A Kyrgyz diplomat posted in an Arab country in the mid- to late 1990s reported that he was summoned by officials of his host government to collect Kyrgyz women jailed for prostitution. To his amazement, one had been such a talented musician that she had studied at the preeminent Moscow Conservatory on scholarship. He was filled with sadness that this brilliant former music student had been the victim of trafficking and faced a terrible future as there was no possibility of reintegration on return to Kyrgyzstan. Her case is not exceptional. Ironically, many Central Asian women seek work abroad specifically to aid their families and unfortunately fall into the hands of traffickers, thereby disgracing the families they sought to assist.[71]

[67] Elina Penttinen, *Globalization, Prostitution and Sex Trafficking: Corporeal Politics* (London and New York: Routledge, 2008), 94.

[68] Anna Jonsson, ed., *Human Trafficking and Human Security* (London and New York: Routledge, 2008).

[69] Rita Chaikin, "Fight Against Trafficking in Women in the North of Israel" in *Trafficking and the Global Sex Industry*, Karen Beeks and Delila Amir, eds. (Lanham, MD: Lexington Books, 2006), 201–16.

[70] See *Trafficking in Persons Report 2009*, 276, 296; Saltanat Sulaimanova, "Migration Trends in Central Asia and the Case of Trafficking of Women," *In the Tracks of Tamerlane: Central Asia's Path to the 21st Century*, Daniel L. Burghart and Teresa Sabonis-Helf, eds. (Washington, DC: National Defense University, Center for Technology and National Security Policy, 2004), 377–400.

[71] Interview with Kyrgyz diplomat by the author, Washington, DC, 2004. See also IOM, 2001, "Deceived Migrants from Tajikistan: A Study of Trafficking in Women and

Enormous economic differences among Soviet successor states help explain the problem of trafficking within the Commonwealth of Independent States (CIS).[72] The extreme wealth of many in Moscow and the presence of many others with significant disposable incomes have provided a large market for sexual services. The same situation also exists in Baku, Azerbaijan, where the oil market and the presence of highly paid oil workers results in trafficking of women from other parts of the USSR to satisfy the local demand for sexual services.[73]

Women are trafficked into Moscow from poorer areas of Russia, Ukraine, Moldova, and elsewhere to provide sexual services for all levels of customers. There are an estimated 100,000 prostitutes working in Moscow, 10 times the number in New York and London, only slightly smaller cities with much larger numbers of tourists. The economic recession contributed to a drop in the prices charged but not in the supply of women.[74]

Sex trafficking, as mentioned earlier, is the most publicized but not the most pervasive form of trafficking. The victims of labor trafficking are much greater. Most labor migrants come to Russia from nine successor states with which Russia maintains a visa-free regime[75] but most labor trafficking victims originate from Uzbekistan, Tajikistan, and Kyrgyzstan, former conflict regions, which are among the poorest countries in the world.[76] One-third of Tajik households now have a family member working outside of their country, most often in Russia or Kazakhstan.[77] The social and economic indicators of these Central Asian countries for infant

Children," www.iom.int/.../mainsite/published_docs/brochures_and_info_sheets/counter_trafficking_activities.pdf (accessed June 27, 2007).

72 The Commonwealth of Independent States is a regional organization founded in 1991 that included all the Soviet successor states except for the Baltic countries. Georgia ceded from the CIS in 2009.

73 Visit by the author to Azerbaijan in 2005 sponsored by the U.S. embassy in Baku where the author met with leading NGOs on the trafficking issue.

74 "Recession-hit Russian men turn to prostitutes for.. a chat and Shoulder to Cry on," *Daily Mail*, May 4, 2009, http://www.dailymail.co.uk/news/worldnews/article-1177164/Recession-hit-Russian-men-turn-prostitutes – chat-shoulder-on.html (accessed August 24, 2009).

75 These are all the countries of the former USSR except the Baltic states, Georgia, and Turkmenistan.

76 International Crisis Group, "Conflict History: Kyrgyzstan." http://www.crisisgroup.org/home/index.cfm?action=conflict_search&l=1&t=1&c_country=60 (accessed August 22, 2009); "Another Conflict Reported on the Tajik-Uzbek Border," http://enews.ferghana.ru/article.php?id=2226 (accessed August 25, 2009).

77 IOM Tajikistan in cooperation with Sharq Scientific Research Center, "Labour Migration from Tajikistan, 2003," http://www.iom.tj/publications/labour_migration_2003.pdf (accessed June 22, 2007); Intergovernmental Commission of the Government of the

mortality, levels of employment, and GDP are on or close to the level of African countries.[78]

The enormous economic discrepancies among the Soviet successor states explain the high rate of labor trafficking. The living standard in Russia in 2007 was estimated to be 16 times that in Tajikistan. The World Bank estimated Russia's gross national income that year at $7,560 whereas Tajikistan's was $460 per capita.[79] These discrepancies are perpetuated by acute levels of corruption. The 2008 corruption perception survey of Transparency International revealed that Central Asian countries have even lower ratings than Russia, which stands at 147th in the world. Kyrgyzstan and Uzbekistan are tied for 166th place, fourteenth from the bottom.[80] This rating was recorded even after the Tulip Revolution in Kyrgyzstan where citizens protested the corruption and criminality of the president.[81]

Approximately a million workers are in some form of labor exploitation. Their exploitation lies along a continuum. Exploitation ranges from 60- to 70-hour work weeks with no days off, to total nonpayment of wages and harsh working conditions of extreme cold or filth. In Karelia, near Finland, only 6 percent of surveyed migrant workers could not leave their jobs whereas in Astrakhan, near the Caspian Sea, almost one-third of migrants were bound to their workplace by their employers by being deprived of their passports,[82] recalling the serfdom of the pre-revolutionary period.

This level of exploitation is not surprising considering the complicity by government officials in trafficking illustrated by the following case.

Republic of Tajikistan on fight against trafficking of human beings in cooperation with NGO "Modar" Friedrich Ebert Foundation, Roundtable, "Prevention and Combating Human Trafficking – Exchange of Experience, Development of Strategic Approaches and Strengthening of Cooperation," Dushanbe, September 15–16, 2006, attended by the author, as well as conversations with Tajik government officials, September 2006.

78 Martha Brill Olcott, "Asia's Overlooked Middle," *International Economic Bulletin* (June 2009), http://www.carnegieendowment.org/publications/index.cfm?fa=view&id=23288&prog=zgp,zru&proj=zie (accessed August 23, 2009).

79 *Human Rights Watch*, "Are You Happy to Cheat Us?" 11.

80 http://www.transparency.org/news_room/in_focus/2008/cpi2008/cpi_2008_table (accessed August 23, 2009).

81 Erica Marat, "Criminal State of Play – An Examination of State-Crime Relations in Post-Soviet Union Kyrgyzstan and Tajikistan," published in *Jane's Intelligence Review*. March 1, 2007, http://www.silkroadstudies.org/new/docs/publications/2007/0702JIR.htm (accessed June 22, 2007).

82 E. V. Tiuriukanova, "*Torgovliia liud'mi raznye liki ekspluatatsii migrantov*," in *Vne tolerantnosti torgovliia liud'mi i rabskii trud: novye metamorfozy starykh prestuplenii i novye metody protivodeistviia* Erokhina, ed., 211–12.

Migrants on a train in transit from Central Asia to Moscow were forcibly removed and transported to a nearby factory where they were enslaved. The perpetrators were Chechen factory owners operating in collusion with local law enforcement. The collusion between Chechen criminals and law enforcement, two groups supposedly in conflict, is certainly strange as MVD troops are sent to fight in Chechnya. But it illustrates that the profits made from human trafficking outweigh larger political concerns.[83]

Deception as well as coercion is used to deprive migrants of pay. For example, some employers send prostitutes infected with venereal disease on payday to deliberately infect their employees. Then the worker has to work longer to pay for the medicines sold by his employer to cure his illness.[84]

Tajiks are exploited not only by Russian employers but also by fellow Tajiks who organize their fellow citizens into work brigades. The Tajik "protector" confiscates the passports of those he supervises, houses them in miserable living conditions of too many people to a room, feeds them too little food for laborers doing heavy physical labor, and often pays them a pittance or nothing. This exploitation continues because the Tajik who controls the work brigade pays off the police and thereby prevents imprisonment or deportation of the migrants who are violating Russian labor laws.[85]

Many victims of labor trafficking are injured or crippled; some die or simply disappear. Tajik activists suggest that as many as 800 laborers die yearly in Russia as a result of their labor exploitation.[86]

The geography of trafficking is also very much shaped by the regional conflicts that followed the end of the Cold War. These conflicts occurred disproportionately in the Caucasus and Central Asia, which still have unresolved conflicts and continuing violence.[87] Conflicts between

[83] "Combating Human Trafficking at the Federal and Regional Level," report of MVD investigator from Astrakhan, at first TraCCC anti-trafficking training led by Elena Tiuriukanova, Moscow, September 28–29, 2006. Such collusion was also reported by researchers in Siberia.

[84] Intergovernmental Commission of the Government of the Republic of Tajikistan on Fight Against Trafficking of Human Beings in Cooperation with NGO "Modar" Friedrich Ebert Foundation.

[85] IOM Tajikistan in cooperation with Sharq Scientific Research Center, "Labour Migration from Tajikistan, 2003," http://www.iom.tj/publications/labour_migration_2003.pdf (accessed June 22, 2007).

[86] See TraCCC Moscow-based trafficking conference entitled "Combating Human Trafficking at the Federal and Regional Level," September 28–29, 2006.

[87] Scott A. Jones, "Introduction" in *Crossroads and Conflict: Security and Foreign Policy in the Caucasus and Central Asia*, Gary Bertsch, ed. (London: Routledge, 2000), 2.

Armenia and Azerbaijan, between Russia and Georgia, between Moldova and Transdniester (a breakaway region from Moldova near the Black Sea and bordering Ukraine), and among and within countries in Central Asia, contributed to the rise of child soldiers, but also to impoverishment and displacement of millions.

Direct links between the rise of sexual trafficking and unresolved conflicts are clearest in the former Yugoslavia where Bosnia-Herzegovina and Kosovo have been and remain major sources of trafficked women.[88] In the former Soviet Union, the links between conflict and sexual trafficking are less apparent except in the Transdniester region, where many trafficked women originate.[89]

Much clearer links can be seen between conflict regions and labor trafficking. As previously discussed, many trafficked laborers are Uzbek, Kyrgyz, and Tajik, all countries that have had civil wars or conflicts.[90] A whole generation of Tajiks was deprived of education and has no possibility of employment in their country. The rise of conflict in Afghanistan has also aggravated both sexual and labor trafficking between Tajikistan and Afghanistan.[91]

The regional conflicts have not only provided male and female trafficking victims but the criminalized conflict regions of the Balkans, Transdniester, the Caucasus, and Central Asia have also allowed traffickers to operate with full impunity.[92]

The vast expanse of the former USSR and the Balkans is a major transit region for smugglers from Asia to Western Europe. Three of the four main smuggling routes to Europe traverse the former USSR and Bulgaria. The most northerly route goes through Russia and the Baltic states, and

[88] IOM Counter-Trafficking Service, "Changing Patterns and Trends of Trafficking in Persons in the Balkan Region, Assessment Carried Out in Albania, Bosnia and Herzegovina, the Province of Kosovo, the Former Yugoslav Republic of Macedonia and the Republic of Moldova," 2004, www.iom.int/documents/publication/en/balkans%5Ftrafficking.pdf (accessed June 27, 2007).

[89] Mark Galeotti, "The Transdnistrian Connection: Big Problems from a Small Pseudo-state," *Global Crime* 8, nos. 3 and 4 (August – November 2004): 398–405; interviews with law enforcement personnel in Moldova, summer 2004.

[90] IOM Tajikistan in cooperation with Sharq Scientific Research Center, "Labour Migration from Tajikistan," 2003, http://www.iom.tj/publications/labour_migration_2003.pdf (accessed June 21, 2007).

[91] Ibid.; author's interviews with personnel of the Ministry of Internal Affairs and the analytical unit of the national drug administration in Dushanbe, Tajikistan, September 2006.

[92] *Trafficking in Persons Report 2009*, 50, lists many of the countries from these regions on the Tier 2 Watch List that do not comply with the TVPA's minimum standards.

then Poland. To the south is a route through Ukraine, the Balkans, and the Czech and Slovak Republics. The third route goes through Bulgaria, Romania, and the Balkans.[93] Every year migrants who are smuggled from Asia and Africa do not make it to their destination and become illegal migrants in the Soviet successor states. Without alternatives, some of them become victims of labor trafficking in Russia and Ukraine.[94]

The Global Recession of 2008 and Human Trafficking

The global recession has hit the states of the former Soviet Union particularly hard, in part explained by the dependence of Russia and Kazakhstan on natural resources whose prices have collapsed. According to the Carnegie Endowment, the Ukrainian economy was the hardest hit in the world. Three other countries – Russia, Kazakhstan, and Bulgaria – are also in the top ten most negatively affected economies.[95] The financial crisis has affected trafficking in several ways including reducing demand for workers, depressing wages and remittances, and increasing debt. Czech police reported a decline in customers for prostitutes, often trafficked women from the former Soviet Union.[96] Moscow prostitutes report a decline in rates charged customers.

In 2008, before the crisis, remittances accounted for 47 percent of Tajikistan's GDP.[97] Tajikistan has the largest proportion of remittances in the world relative to its GDP, followed by Kyrgyzstan in fourth place. In the last quarter of 2008, Tajik and Kyrgyz banks reported remittances declining by half.[98]

93 J. Salt and J. Stein, "Migration as a Business: The Case of Trafficking," *International Migration*, 35, no. 4 (1997), 474–75.

94 It was estimated that there were 8,500 such illegal migrants in Kyiv alone. See Olena Braichevska, Halyna Volosiuk, Olena Malynovska, Yaroslav Pylynski, Nancy Popson, and Blair Ruble, *Nontraditional Immigrants in Kyiv* (Washington, DC: Woodrow Wilson International Center for Scholars, 2004), 10.

95 Shimelse Ali, Uri Dadush and Lauren Falcao, "Financial Transmission of the Crisis: What's the Lesson," http://www.carnegieendowment.org/publications/index.cfm?fa=view&id=23284&prog=zgp&proj=zie (accessed August 22, 2009).

96 Dan Bilefsky, "World's Oldest Profession, Too, Feels Crisis" *New York Times*, December 8, 2008, http://www.nytimes.com/2008/12/08/world/europe/08ihtsex.4.18500177.html?_r=1&scp=1&sq=prostitution%20in%20Czech%20republic%20delcines&st=cse, (accessed August 22, 2009).

97 IMF Survey: "IMF Chief Visits Central Asia Amid Sharp Slowdown," June 12 2009, http://www.imf.org/external/pubs/ft/survey/so/2009/new061209a.htm (accessed August 25, 2009).

98 Erica Marat, "Shrinking Remittances Increase Labor Migration from Central Asia," February 11, 20009, http://www.cacianalyst.org/?q=node/5035 (accessed August 25, 2009).

The number of migrants from those countries did not decline as the Central Asian economies collapsed and there was no employment at home. But trafficking increased as Central Asian workers were left unpaid or enslaved. Tajik workers in the main market of the Russian city Mytishi were left without employment or money–"some claiming that their employers have not paid their wages for several months. Others said that police took their passports and demanded a bribe before they would be returned. The Tajiks said that special police (OMON) come to the market at night and force some migrants to work without pay, sometimes cleaning streets, chopping firewood, or cooking at a prison."[99] Thousands of Kyrgyz and Uzbeks have found themselves in the same situation.[100]

The crisis will have long-term consequences, including even further growth of the illicit economy as many of the unemployed can find work only in the burgeoning illicit drug trade in the region. In the absence of income, others may become indebted to traffickers who will exploit them and their family members when the financial situation improves.

Combating Human Trafficking

Human trafficking persists on a massive scale in the CIS and non-EU member states of Eastern Europe because governments have not shown the political will to address this problem. Year after year, a significant share of the countries from this region are listed on the U.S. State Department's Tier 2 Watch List or on Tier 3 as countries that do not full comply with Trafficking Victims Protection Act minimal standards or are not making significant efforts to comply.[101] The countries of Eurasia have successfully prosecuted very few trafficking cases.[102] Almost all of the prosecutions have focused on sexual rather than labor trafficking.

With limited free and investigative media and with no traditions of civil society, there are limited capabilities within those societies to expose trafficking or advocate for changes in trafficking policy.[103] Although

99 "Unemployed Tajik Migrants Stuck in Russia," January 29, 2009, http://www.rferl.org/content/Unemployed_Tajik_Migrants_Stuck_In_Russia/1376505.html (accessed August 25, 2009).

100 Ibid.

101 See explanation of Tier 2 Watch List and Tier 3 at the end of the last chapter.

102 *Trafficking in Persons Report 2009*, 53, 55; McCarthy, "*Sravnitelnyi analiz praktiki rossiiskikh i amerikanskikh pravookhranitel'nykh institutov v protivodeistvii torgovle liud'mi.*"

103 In the early 2000s, a journalist in the Russian Far East was severely beaten and required hospitalization after reporting on the trafficking research of Liudmila Erokhina. L. S. Vasil'eva reports on the efforts to establish an anti-trafficking NGO, "*Formirovanie*

many of the authoritarian societies of the region are more tolerant of anti-trafficking NGOs than other manifestations of civil society, NGOs trying to combat trafficking are perennially underfinanced and all too often viewed with suspicion.[104]

Governments have failed to allocate resources to fight trafficking, and with pervasive corruption of law enforcement and often the high level complicity of officials, there is little chance of effective countermeasures. After the ouster of President Akayev of Kyrgyzstan, his wife was found to have derived significant profits from her role as a facilitator of labor trafficking.[105] High-level complicity in human trafficking is not confined to Kyrgyzstan. Corruption is also pervasive at the level of customs, border services, the police, and other parts of government in many Soviet successor states. In Ukraine, NGOs reported that "corruption was particularly a problem, at times involving prosecutors or judges though the government reported no investigations, prosecutions, or convictions of government officials complicit in trafficking."[106] Corruption of foreign officials in the region also undermines counter-trafficking as the diplomatic immunity of these officials precludes prosecution by local governments. "In August 2001, the French Ministry for Foreign and European Affairs confirmed that investigations were underway in eight French embassies after it was acknowledged that thousands – some claim up to 25,000, though this figure sounds unrealistically high – of visas had been issued in Sofia to Bulgarian prostitutes."[107]

Compounding the problems of combating human trafficking are the absence of viable witness protection programs for victims and their families in this region, the difficulties in collecting evidence against transnational trafficking networks, the absence of intelligence-led policing, and

innovatsionnykh podkhodov k resheneniu problemy treffika posredstvom mezhvedomstvennogo vzaimodeistviia predstavitelei gosudarstvennykh, nekomercheskikh organizatsii i pravookhranitel'nykh struktur," in *Vne tolerantnosti Torgovlia liud'mi i rabskikh trud: novye metamorfozy starykh prestuplenii*, 239–57.

104 At one point, the bank account of the mother of a leading official of the NGO "Sestry" was frozen as Russian officials tried to link the organization to an identified spy in the British embassy. "Russia: 'Spy-Rock' Scandal Has NGOs Worried," January 24, 2006, http://www.rferl.org/content/Article/1065018.html (accessed August 25, 2009).

105 Saltanat Liebert, *Irregular Migration from the Former Soviet Union to the United States* (London and New York: Routledge, 2009), 68.

106 *Trafficking in Persons Report* 2009, 291.

107 Leslie Holmes, "Corruption & Trafficking: Triple Victimisation," in *Strategies Against Human Trafficking: The Role of the Security Sector*, Cornelius Friesendorf, ed. (Vienna: National Defence Academy and Austrian Ministry of Defence and Sport, 2009, 2009), 102.

the segmentation of trafficking activities across many countries requiring cooperation from numerous jurisdictions. In Ukraine, Russia, and many Eastern European countries, special units have been formed to fight human trafficking. But these branches of the police are not considered high priorities or prestigious and receive limited funding and are often not assigned the most capable or ambitious personnel.

Yet other problems also impede trafficking prosecutions, as the following 2006 case from Saratov, a southern Russian city along the Volga, reveals. German law enforcement arrested a Russian man for sexual trafficking and deported him back to Saratov, providing Russian law enforcement with detailed information on the man's exploitation of women from the region. The Saratov courts had difficulty mounting a prosecution because the women did not want to testify against their "trafficker." They were grateful to him for having transported them to the lucrative markets of Western Europe.[108]

Administrative measures rather than criminal law have also been used to limit trafficking. Russia and Kazakhstan have established legal mechanisms to provide migrant workers legal status. In Russia, the adoption of a registration system for three-month work permits increased the legal part of the labor migration from 5 to 10 percent of the total in 2000 to 25–30 percent in 2007.[109] Yet bureaucratic obstacles impede many laborers from obtaining temporary work permits.

Conclusions

For seventy years, the Soviet Union was characterized by an ideology that outlawed worker exploitation, prohibited prostitution, and was committed to economic equality. Its borders were closed to the world by what came to be known as an "Iron Curtain" as guards were stationed around the entire perimeter of the former Soviet Union prohibiting entry and exit.

The USSR did not live up to its ideals. Millions were exploited by the state in labor camps, prostitution did not disappear, and economic differences existed. But private exploitation of labor was largely eliminated and social differentiation was much less than in the pre-revolutionary period.

[108] Elena Lvova reported on this case in the panel presentation, "Human Trafficking in Russia: Perspectives from Law and Justice," November 8, 2006, TraCCC, American University, http://www.american.edu/traccc/events/events.html (accessed June 22, 2006).

[109] Elena Tyuryukanova, "Irregular Migration and Criminal Gains (case of Russia),"OSCE-UNODC-CYPRUS Regional Meeting, September 8–19, 2008, Larnaca, Cyprus.

Within a few years of the collapse of the USSR, the Slavic successor states were major suppliers of prostitutes to world markets, Russia became the second largest recipient of migrants in the world, and post-Soviet states were major transit routes for labor migrants from China, Afghanistan, India, and many other parts of Asia to Western Europe. After inequitable privatizations, all countries in the region were characterized by enormous discrepancies in wealth. Russia, for example, had a wealth distribution on the level of Brazil and Mexico, two of the most economically differentiated countries in Latin America. Many of the Central Asian successor states, once part of a world superpower, now had indicators close to those of Africa and became dependent on remittances provided by citizens who worked abroad, willing to work in the most exploitative conditions in order to provide for their families. These radical changes occurred within years of the Soviet Union's collapse.

Human trafficking will be a defining problem of the Soviet successor states and of Eastern Europe outside of the European Union. Little can be done to prevent trafficking when it results from deeply rooted economic, political, and social problems within these societies. Compounding the problems are corrupt government officials, incompetent and ineffective law enforcement and legal systems, powerful organized crime groups, and the absence of respect for individual and human rights.

There is not a single solution to human trafficking. Reduction in all forms of human trafficking will take decades of focused effort to achieve. But that concerted effort is not yet visible as there is an absence of political will as evidenced by the presence of the majority of CIS states (7 out of 11) on the U.S. State Department's 2009 Tier 2 Watch list.[110]

Solving the human trafficking problem is not merely in the hands of the source countries. For example, although the EU has emphasized preventing trafficking of women from Moldova, its economic policies run counter to these efforts. Moldova is still a highly agricultural society but many of the farmers cannot market their products in Europe because of the trade barriers established by the EU. Although the contributing role of these economic trade barriers to the rise of sexual trafficking have been acknowledged within the OSCE, nothing has been done to address the economic policies that are highly conducive to trafficking.[111]

[110] The Baltic states and Georgia are not part of the CIS. Of the remaining 11 countries, Azerbaijan, Moldova, Russia, Tajikistan, Turkmenistan, Ukraine, and Uzbekistan are on the Tier 2 Watch List. *Trafficking in Persons Report 2009*, 50.

[111] Eleventh OSCE Economic Forum on "Trafficking in Human Beings, Drugs, Small Arms and Light Weapons: National and International Economic Impact," Prague, May 20–23, 2003.

Consequently, it is hardly surprising that many Moldovan women are found in the sex trade in Western Europe, Turkey, and the Middle East.

To achieve change, demand must be reduced as well as supply. The proliferation of sex trafficking has been facilitated by an enormous demand for young Slavic women throughout the world. A world market for child pornography spurs its production. The desire for cheap labor has fueled the trafficking of workers in the wealthiest Soviet successor states.

Reducing corruption and improving the rule of law must be given higher priority in anti-trafficking programs. The corruption of the police, border and customs services, and the judiciary are important facilitators of trafficking. Insufficient priority is given to international law enforcement cooperation by both the host and source countries.[112]

Many source and host countries in the Soviet successor states fail to provide adequate support for trafficking victims, seeing them instead as criminals rather than individuals in need of assistance. Anti-immigrant sentiment is growing in contemporary Russia, which is now home to at least five million illegal migrants. The backlash against foreigners, seen particularly in Russia but by no means confined to that country, does not portend well for the future treatment of trafficking victims. With the suppression of civil society under socialist rule, NGOs are still weak and poorly financed. They try to help victims, but they can provide no substitute for effective government-supported assistance programs, which are not available at present.

The former USSR region is characterized by a very high level of migration. As countries seek to curb this migration, trafficking is likely to grow as desperate migrants seeking to avoid state controls resort to the assistance of criminal facilitators. Whereas the world has associated the former USSR region with sexual trafficking, in the future trafficking in the region will increasingly be for labor exploitation.

[112] Discussion at the TraCCC trafficking conference in Moscow, May 31, 2007.

7

Trafficking in Europe

The rise of human smuggling and trafficking challenge the core of Western European identity. Few European countries had numerically significant immigration before the post – World War II period; instead they were sources of emigrants who traveled to far-distant colonies as well as to North and South America.[1] Unlike the advanced Western democracies of the United States, Canada, and Australia, most European countries have had limited experience in integrating migrants. Instead, European history has been filled with examples of persecution of minorities. Therefore, the influx of migrants from former colonies and guest workers to Europe in the post – World War II period has posed an enormous cultural, political, and social challenge to most European countries. The significant growth in the number of smuggled and trafficked people in the last two decades has only compounded the challenge.[2]

Often the migration debate within Europe has been framed within the context of maintenance of national identity and domestic and regional security.[3] Therefore, the increased numbers of illegal migrants and trafficking victims compound the challenge that already exists in Western Europe of absorbing the diverse migrants and political refugees

[1] There was immigration within Europe such as French Huguenots and British religious refugees to the Netherlands.

[2] Peter Andreas and Timothy Snyder, *The Wall Around the West State Borders and Immigration Controls in North America and Europe* (Lanham, MD: Rowman and Littlefield, 2000).

[3] Liz Kelly, "Journeys of Jeopardy: A Review of Research on Trafficking in Women and Children In Europe," www.iom.int/jahia/webdav/site/myjahiasite/shared/shared/mainsite/published_docs/ serial_publications/mrs11b.pdf (accessed January 19, 2009).

with different cultural, educational, and life experiences than Western Europeans who have grown up in prosperous democratic societies. These problems of assimilation are compounded by the fact that those who are being smuggled and trafficked often are racially different from Europeans and have different religions, as many are arriving from Africa, the Middle East, and Asia.[4] Therefore, in many countries there is a backlash against migrants that can also include victims of trafficking. Yet the backlash is greatest against visible illegal migrants, among whom trafficking victims are rare. The focus of many European countries is on removing the trafficked individuals and repatriating them rather than on assisting and admitting those often highly traumatized individuals.[5] When the Council of Europe (COE) Convention on Trafficking entered into force in early 2008, COE member states became obligated to offer assistance to trafficking victims, including a reflection period (during which the victim cannot be deported). Medical care and legal help are to be provided. Yet this is not always operational, as trafficking victims often do not cooperate with European law enforcement and are not identified as trafficking victims.[6] Bureaucratic obstacles also prevent the operation of the Convention as intended.[7]

Human smuggling and trafficking continues unabated despite the great focus on this issue in the European mass media and by policymakers, the allocation of significant resources to Europol (European police agency), and the establishment of Frontex.[8] Combating transnational crime that facilitates trade in humans has become a high priority for the member states of the European Union (EU).

[4] M. R. J. Soudijn, *Chinese Human Smuggling in Transit* (Den Haag: Boom Juridische Uitgevers, 2006); Roger Plant, "Forced Labour, Migration and Trafficking," 62, http://www.ilo.org/public/english/dialogue/actrav/publ/129/10.pdf (accessed January 17, 2009).

[5] Petra Bendel, "Immigration Policy in the European Union: Still Bringing Up the Walls for Fortress Europe," *Migration Letters* 2, no. 1 (April 2005), 20–31.

[6] C. Braspenning, "Human Trafficking in the Netherlands: The Protection of and Assistance to Victims in Light of Domestic and International Law and Policy," *Intercultural Human Rights Law Review* 1 (2006), 335.

[7] Cornelius Friesendorf, ed., *Strategies Against Human Trafficking: The Role of the Security Sector* (Vienna: National Defence Academy and Austrian Ministry of Defence and Sport, 2009).

[8] Letizia Paoli and Cyrille Fijnaut, "General Introduction," in *Organised Crime in Europe: Concepts, Patterns and Control Policies in the European Union and Beyond*, Cyrille Fijnaut and Letizia Paoli, eds. (Dordrecht: Springer, 2004), 1; Frontex is a specialized and independent body based in Warsaw to provide operational cooperation on border issues, www.frontex.europa.eu (accessed December 7, 2009).

Even though many European states would hope that their labor needs could be met within the EU labor pool, this is not possible, as there is a need for unskilled labor that is not available because of low birth rates and a generally well educated labor force. Moreover, trafficked women are in great demand in the large Western European sex markets because many women born there do not choose to engage in prostitution. The legalization of prostitution in some countries has not made this an attractive employment option for many European women despite the fact that this work may pay more than other forms of employment.[9] Also deterring supply are the European social welfare benefits, including child support and health care, that provide a social safety net. Therefore, there is not a sufficient supply to meet demand. Trafficked women are imported not only to meet the demand but also because they provide less expensive services, submit to conditions that would not be tolerated by EU nationals engaged in prostitution, and because they serve the needs of immigrant communities.[10] With demand and uncoordinated enforcement efforts, the human trade for labor and sex cannot be stopped.

Smuggled Chinese are needed in Italian sweatshops to keep their textile industry competitive, and trafficked workers harvest agricultural products at prices that keep them affordable. In 2004, Operation Marco Polo, which targeted Chinese illegal laborers, resulted in the arrests of 91 traffickers and 571 accomplices who supplied more than 600 businesses with more than 3,200 laborers.[11]

Human trafficking and smuggling into Europe has grown since the 1980s as transport links have improved and the political and economic situations in many countries in Africa and the Middle East have deteriorated. Recurrent crises and conflicts in parts of Asia have contributed to increased human flows toward Europe. At the same time, the barriers to entry into Western Europe have increased. The Balkans, a region racked by violent conflict before and after World War I, was cut off from Western

[9] Annegret Staiger, "The Economics of Sex Trafficking since the Legalization of Prostitution in 2002," *The Protection Project Journal of Human Rights and Civil Society* 2 (Fall, 2009), 103–18 indicates that incomes for women since legalization have declined.

[10] Jo Goodey, "Recognising Organized Crime's Victims: The Case of Sex Trafficking in the EU," in *Transnational Organised Crime Perspectives on Global Security*, Adam Edwards and Peter Gil, eds. (London and New York: Routledge, 2003), 161.

[11] John T. Picarelli, "Enabling Norms and Human Trafficking," in *Crime and the Global Political Economy, International Political Economy Yearbook*, vol. 16, H. Richard Friman, ed. (Boulder, CO and London: Lynne Rienner, 2009), 97; "Operation Marco Polo: An Investigation of the Illegal Trade in Asian Traditional Medicine," http://www.cites.org/common/cop/13/inf/E13i-45.pdf (accessed May 20, 2009).

Europe under Communist rule in the post – World War II period. Since the end of the Cold War, there has been a reversion to previously known violence.[12] Since the end of Communist rule, there have been constant conflicts in the Balkans that have resulted in many displaced people seeking stability in Western Europe. Furthermore, the region has reemerged as a porous, lawless region through which many migrants and trafficked people from other regions transit.[13]

In many parts of Europe, the rise of strong anti-immigrant movements has led to limited programs for refugees and strict quotas on legal admission of immigrants. In the early part of the millennium, Europe accepted approximately 680,000 legal migrants from outside the Europe Union, a small percentage of those who seek entry.[14] An additional number, estimated at half a million, entered each year illegally, primarily from North Africa, the Middle East, and before 2004 from many Eastern European countries before their membership in the EU.[15] Illegal entry continues from countries that are not part of the EU. With increasingly restrictive entry policies, the problem of human smuggling has grown relative to that of human trafficking.[16]

For the EU, 500,000 smuggled and trafficked migrants is a large number, but it represents less than one-tenth of 1 percent of the total EU population, now estimated at half a billion.[17] Illegal migrants represent a much smaller percentage of the total population than in Russia, described in the previous chapter, or the United States, discussed in the following chapter. Europeans have made great efforts to restrict illegal immigrants

[12] Robert D. Kaplan, *Balkan Ghosts: A Journey through History* (New York: Picador, 2005).

[13] Frank Laczko, Irene Stacher and Amanda Klekowski von Koppenfels, *New Challenges for Migration Policy in Central and Eastern Europe* (Cambridge: Cambridge University Press, 2002).

[14] Raimo Väryrynen, "Illegal Immigration, Human Trafficking, and Organized Crime," Conference on Poverty, International Migration and Asylum, 2003, World Institute for Development Economics Research, United Nations University, Helsinki, Finland, http://www.wider.unu.edu/publications.htm (accessed January 14, 2009); Kristiina Kangaspunta, "Mapping the Inhuman Trade: Preliminary Findings of the Human Trafficking Database," http://www.unodc.org/pdf/crime/forum/forum3_note1.pdf (accessed January 17, 2009).

[15] Väryrynen, "Illegal Immigration," 10–11.

[16] J. Salt and J. Hogarth, *Migrant Trafficking and Human Smuggling in Europe: A Review of the Evidence* (Geneva: IOM, 2000), Chapter 8.

[17] Eurostat News Release, "First Demographic Estimates Half a Billion Inhabitants in the EU27 on 1 January 2009," no. 179, December 15, 2008, http://epp.eurostat.ec.europa.eu/pls/portal/docs/page/pge_prd_cat_prerel/pge_cat_prerel_year_2008/_month_12/3–15122008-en-ap.pdf (accessed January 16, 2009).

even though this is an enormous challenge because of the large and lightly guarded Mediterranean coast and the long border that many Eastern European countries share with the former Soviet Union, along which there are many corrupt border personnel not under the control of the European Union.[18] The priority given to policing borders and the generally low levels of corruption of Western European law enforcement has reduced illegal migration in certain countries. For example, Germany, a major destination country of illegal migrants, has seen the number of illegal entrants decline since the late 1990s.[19]

Human smuggling and trafficking are not evenly distributed within Europe. According to the United Nations, five countries in Western Europe are particular destination countries for human traffickers. These same countries are also often principal destinations for human smugglers.[20] They are Belgium,[21] Germany, Greece, Italy, and the Netherlands. Austria, Denmark, France, Spain, and Switzerland fell into the next highest group as recipient countries of human traffickers.[22] Greece and Spain are not only recipient countries for irregular migrants but also "see a rise in transnational criminal organizations which want to take advantage of the position of these countries in the periphery for their easier transition of their human cargo to destinations in the north."[23] More recently, Europol has added the United Kingdom to the list.[24]

These destination countries are many of the most affluent and populous countries in Europe, which have large sex markets, either as result of large domestic demand or large tourism industries such as in the south

[18] Human Rights Watch, "Hopes Betrayed: Trafficking of Women and Girls to Post-Conflict Bosnia and Herzegovina for Forced Prostitution," *Human Rights Watch* 14, no. 9 (D) (2002), 26–34.

[19] Matthias Neske, "Human Smuggling to and through Germany," *International Migration* 44, no. 4 (2006), 125.

[20] Ibid.; Khalid Koser, "Why Migrant Smuggling Pays," *International Migration* 46, no. 2 (2008), 3–26; Gao Yun and Véronique Poisson, "Le trafic et l'exploitation des immigrants chinois en France," Organisation International du Travail, 70–72, http://www.ilo.org/wcmsp5/groups/public/–ed_norm/–declaration/documents/publication/wcms_082332.pdf (accessed January 20, 2009).

[21] See Centre pour l'égalité de la chance et la lutte contre le racisme, "La Traite et le traffic des ĕtre$ humain$: lutter avec des personnes et des ressources" Rapport annuel 2008.

[22] United Nations Office on Drugs and Crime (UNODC), "Trafficking in Persons: Global Patterns," April 2006, 92, www.unodc.org/pdf/traffickinginpersons_report-2006ver2.pdf (accessed January 19, 2009).

[23] Akis Kalaitzidis, "Human Smuggling and Trafficking in the Balkans: Is It Fortress Europe?" *Journal of the Institute of Justice and International Studies* 5 (2005).

[24] For a discussion of the situation in the United Kingdom, see "The Trade in Human Beings: Human Trafficking in the UK," *Trends in Organized Crime* 12 (2009), 379–84.

of Spain.[25] Moreover, many of the major destination countries have large immigrant populations, ports, and extensive coastlines that facilitate entry of both trafficking victims and those who pay smugglers to enable their entry into Europe.

The major source countries identified by Europol are given as Moldova, Ukraine, Bulgaria, Romania, Russian Federation, and Nigeria, whose trafficking to Europe is often facilitated by members of their own migrant communities.[26] Many of the identified source countries are the poorest countries in Europe. Yet Europol fails to mention major source countries that were once colonies of Western Europe such as Morocco and Algeria in North Africa and Brazil, the Dominican Republic, and Colombia in the Western Hemisphere, whose citizens are increasingly identified as victims of sexual but also of labor trafficking, particularly in Mediterranean countries.

No large European country has been able to curtail human trafficking and smuggling by means of effective counter-trafficking policies. Holland has legalized prostitution and the keeping of brothels. Sweden, since 1999, has criminalized the attempted or actual purchase of sexual services, and a decade later Norway made it a crime to buy sex both at home and abroad.[27] But neither of these opposing approaches has eliminated the problem, although the Dutch policies have intensified the organized crime component of the prostitution markets, which is controlled by Albanian and Turkish organized crime groups.[28] This is indicative of the fact that the choice of destination by the traffickers is more often determined by the attributes of the market of the destination country than by

[25] Alejandro Gómez-Céspedes and Per Stangeland, "Spain: The Flourishing Illegal Drug Haven in Europe," in Fijnaut and Paoli, eds., *Organised Crime in Europe*, 402–4.

[26] http://www.europol.europa.eu/publications/Serious_Crime_Overviews/Trafficking_in_human_ beings_2008.pdf (accessed November 3, 2008).

[27] "Policy Approach on Human Trafficking and Prostitution in the Netherlands," www.newr.bham.ac.uk/pdfs/Trafficking/Netherlands2.pdf (accessed January 22, 2009);G. Ekberg, "The Swedish law that prohibits the purchase of sexual services: Best practices for the prevention of prostitution and trafficking in human beings," *Violence Against Women* 10 (2004), 1187–1218; Laura Agustin, "Border Thinking on Migration and trafficking: Culture, Economy and Sex," January 9, 2009, http://www.nodo50.org/Laura_Agustin/satire-is-the-best-revenge-anti-trafficking-news-from-norway (accessed January 22, 2009).

[28] Author's conversations with Dutch specialists such as Jan van Dijk in 2007; see Laura Augustin, "What's happening in Amsterdam? An Overview of Changing Law," January 16, 2009, http://www.nodo50.org/Laura_Agustin/tag/trafficking (accessed January 22, 2009); Shared Hope International *DEMAND: A Comparative Examination of Sex Tourism and Trafficking in Jamaica, Japan, the Netherlands, and the United States*, 50, http://www.sharedhope.org/files/demand_netherlands.pdf (accessed September 3, 2009).

the deterrent policies of the state. Traffickers often operate in countries where members of their ethnic community already reside. This is also true of smugglers, but they also seek countries where there is the greater possibility for those smuggled to regularize their status.[29]

Historical Precedent

Records of human slavery within Western Europe date back as far as ancient Greece and Rome, but the practice did not end in ancient history. As the preceding chapter revealed, there are long-standing historical precedents for the exploitation of Slavs within Western Europe. Istanbul, then and now, was a destination for women trafficked from the Caucasus and parts of Eastern Europe.

Many think that slavery disappeared from Europe many centuries ago. Few know that there was also an active slave market in Palermo, Sicily, with slaves brought from Africa until the middle of the nineteenth century. The author visited the site of the slave market on her first trip to Palermo. Therefore, slavery existed in at least one Western European country as recently as in the United States. In addition to imported slaves from Africa, child slavery in Sicily was described in 1910 in the writings of a distinguished Afro-American, Booker T. Washington, who was himself born a slave. He wrote, "The cruelties to which the child slaves of Sicily have been subjected are as bad as anything reported of the cruelties of Negro slavery."[30]

But the legacy of slavery is much more important than the markets in Palermo and Istanbul at the periphery of Europe. Prestigious Europeans made their fortunes as slave traders. In The Hague, the home of the International Court of Justice, the major museum, Mauritshius, was constructed with the profits of the slave trade. A sign at the entry of this grand mansion filled with Old Masters reveals that Mr. Maurits, once the governor general of Dutch Brazil, made his fortune in the slave trade in Latin America and the Caribbean. Mr. Maurits was not unique. Much of the slave trade was run by legitimate actors and companies sanctioned by the state, some of them even receiving royal charters. An active slave trade with Africa flourished in all the large colonial powers of Europe such as England and France and even some of the smaller colonial powers

[29] Ibid., 153.

[30] Booker Taliaferro Washington, "The Man Farthest Down," http://www.annoticoreport.com/2008/01/re-child-slavery-in-sicily-1910-man.html (accessed October 14, 2008).

such as Portugal and Mr. Maurits' homeland of the Netherlands, which became the second most powerful slave trading state in the Atlantic slave trade.[31]

In addition to the Africans, indigenous American populations were also enslaved in many of the colonies of Central and South America and the Caribbean.[32] Although a few of the priests who traveled with the conquerors objected to the exploitation of the native populations, their voices were not sufficient to prevent it. Native American populations were forced to labor in mines, agriculture, and dangerous work conditions, often without any compensation.[33]

When the importation of slaves was outlawed in the colonies, as discussed in Chapter 5, bonded labor or indentured servitude, often with individuals brought from Asia, helped meet the labor shortage in agriculture. Starting in the 1830s, for example, Britain brought Indians to Mauritius and Chinese were sent in smaller numbers to British Guyana.[34] Therefore, Europeans continued to exploit unfree labor of non-Europeans long after slavery was nominally ended.

At the end of the nineteenth century, a new form of slavery, the so-called "white slavery," began.[35] The white slave trade brought women, often by means of deception, from Western and Eastern Europe into the brothels of North and South America, from which they could not escape. This slavery is also discussed in the next two chapters. This trade continued until the 1930s, when the worldwide economic depression, the military advances of the Third Reich in Germany, and the increased impediments to travel curtailed the cross-Atlantic traffic in women.

World War II saw new forms of human slavery. Jews, gypsies, and opponents of the Nazi regime were moved across Europe to slave labor and extermination camps in Germany, Poland, and elsewhere. Many women were trafficked into prostitution to serve the German troops. Although many Europeans professed to being unaware at that time of

[31] John T. Picarelli, "Historical Approaches to the Trade in Human Beings," in *Human Trafficking*, Maggy Lee, ed. (Cullompton, Devon: Willan, 2007), 35.

[32] "The Enslaved Indians of the Spanish Caribbean, Reports and Accounts 1495–1544," http://nationalhumanitiescenter.org/pds/amerbegin/settlement/text6/EnslavedIndians.pdf (accessed January 17, 2009).

[33] "Enslaved Peoples," http://nationalhumanitiescenter.org/pds/amerbegin/settlement/text6/text6read.htm (accessed January 17, 2009).

[34] Wilhelmina Kloosterboer, *Involuntary Labour Since the Abolition of Slavery: A Survey of Compulsory Labour Throughout the World* (Leiden, Netherlands: E. J. Brill, 1960).

[35] Ewa Morawska, "Trafficking into and from Eastern Europe," in *Human Trafficking*, Lee, ed., 93–94.

this exploitation, literature on the holocaust attests to broader awareness of the exploitation and murder of their fellow citizens.[36]

Well-established democracies in Western Europe and a strong commitment to the rule of law have been the hallmark of the post – World War II Europe. Yet despite this commitment to individual rights, there are some in Europe who justify the labor exploitation that goes on within their borders. For example, more than 40 percent of surveyed Italian employers felt that workers employed in their homes had no right to paid holidays, a minimum wage, or fixed work hours. Even in Sweden, with its high degree of commitment to equality and no history of colonial exploitation, 60 percent of those surveyed did not believe domestic workers were entitled to a minimum wage and 40 percent did not believe that a day off was a right.[37]

What differentiates current human trafficking in Europe from its historical precedents is that, unlike in the past, it is not controlled or sanctioned by the state, as was the African slave trade, the enslavement of native populations in the New World, or the slave labor of the Third Reich. Except for those who ran the white slave trade, the enslavers were not organized criminals or crime networks. Instead, today criminal groups and networks control much of sexual trafficking and increasingly assume an important role as facilitators of labor trafficking and human smuggling.[38] Those who obtain the services of modern-day slaves do not purchase them for life but exploit them for a limited period. Without outright purchase, they are less concerned about the long-term survival and health of their victims.[39]

[36] See, for example, Lucy S., Dawidowicz, *The War Against the Jews, 1933–1945* (New York: Holt, Rinehart and Winston, 1975) and Raul Hilberg, *The Destruction of the European Jews* (Chicago: Quadrangle, 1961).

[37] Bridget Anderson and Julie O'Connell Davidson, "Is Trafficking in Human Beings Demand Driven? A Multi-Country Pilot Study," IOM Migration Series, no. 15, 2003, http://www.compas.ox.ac.uk/about/publications/Bridget/Anderson04.pdf?event=detail&id=2932 (accessed January 17, 2009).

[38] Soudijn, *Chinese Human Smuggling*; John Salt, "Trafficking and Human Smuggling: A European Perspective," *International Migration* Special Issue (2000), 31–56; Veronika Bilger, Martin Hofmann, and Michael Jandl, "Human Trafficking as a Transnational Service Industry: Evidence from Austria," *International Migration* 44, no. 4 (2006), 59–73; K. Koser, "The Smuggling of Asylum Seekers to Western Europe: Contradictions, Conundrums, and Dilemmas," in *Global Human Smuggling: Comparative Perspectives*, D. Kyle and R. Koslowski, eds. (Baltimore: Johns Hopkins University, 2001), 58–73.

[39] For a discussion of attitude toward sex slaves and exploited domestic servants see Anna M. Agathangelou, *The Global Political Economy of Sex: Desire, Violence and Insecurity in Mediterranean Nation States* (New York: Palgrave Macmillan, 2004).

The auctions of Eastern European women at British airports announced by the United Kingdom's Crown Prosecution Service are conducted by criminal actors who often lack the right to reside in Britain.[40] In contrast with their historical predecessors, they lack official protection. Their only influence over the state can be achieved through bribery and other forms of corruption. However, the horrendous abuse of human rights exemplified by these auctions does not seem to be explained by massive corruption in the British police or airport authority. Rather, these inhumane practices endured because combating human trafficking was not a state priority. But since 2006 and the formation of the Serious Organised Crime Agency, fighting human smuggling and trafficking have been priorities.[41] Yet few countries in continental Europe, despite the establishment of dedicated anti-trafficking units, have prioritized and equipped government agencies with the resources to curtail the massive and growing international trade in human beings.

Distinctive European Conditions

Almost all forms of human trafficking exist within Western Europe. The political stability precludes the presence of child soldiers and the regulation of medical care and hospitals largely eliminates the problem of organ trafficking. Child sex tourism by Europeans generally occurs outside of Western Europe as European men travel to the Baltics, parts of Latin America, and Southeast Asia to have sex with minors.[42]

Human trafficking has distinctive features within Europe, a consequence of its history, politics and economy; its current demographic situation; its existing immigrant populations; and social welfare system. Furthermore, the proximity of Western Europe to such poor countries as Romania, with a long history of child abuse under the dictatorship of Ceausescu, and Albania, with large numbers of street children, has exacerbated the problem of child trafficking in Western Europe.[43]

[40] "Slaves Are Auctioned by Traffickers," June 4, 2006, news.bbc.co.uk/2/hi/uk_news/5046170.stm (accessed August 27, 2008); "Women for Sale in Gatwick Slave Auctions," *Evening Standard*, www.thisislondon.co.uk/news/article-23388098-details/women+for+sale+in+Gatwick+Slave+Auctions/article.do (accessed August 27, 2008).

[41] "The United Kingdom Threat Assessment of Serious Organised Crime for 2008/2009," 35–39, http://www.soca.gov.uk/assessPublications/downloads/UKTA2008–9NPM.pdf (accessed September 6, 2009).

[42] The Protection Project, *International Child Sex Tourism Scope of the Problem and Comparative Case Studies* (Washington, DC: Johns Hopkins University Paul H. Nitze School of Advanced International Studies, 2007).

[43] Vasilika Hysi, "Human Trafficking and Democratic Transition in Albania," in *Human Trafficking, Human Security and the Balkans*, H. Richard Friman and Simon Reich, eds.

Conditions unique to Europe have contributed significantly to the growth of human smuggling and trafficking. As previously mentioned, birth rates all across Europe are far below the level needed to replace the population. This decline has been occurring for several decades, thereby reducing available manpower for labor markets. Despite the need for a workforce that can engage in manual labor, the European Community has failed to develop a common immigration and refugee policy that will satisfy this demand. The desire by some countries such as Germany to maintain control over their own labor markets has meant that there has been an absence of cohesive action.[44] Therefore, just as in the United States, discussed in Chapter 8, the barriers to entry have created an enormous variety of facilitators who will assist those who seek illegal entry into the EU. The business of human smuggling and human trafficking is possibly more ethnically diversified in the EU than in North America. Furthermore, there is a full range of smugglers ranging from small groups to complex international organizations. Many different human smugglers and traffickers, operating in Africa, Asia, the Middle East, Latin America, and Eastern Europe, bring those they smuggle and traffic into the countries of the Southern Mediterranean, across the Balkans and through the English Channel and Baltic Seas.[45]

European trafficking has certain distinctive features, and its trafficking patterns are distinct from those in the United States discussed in Chapter 8. Many more minors are smuggled or trafficked into Europe on their own than to North America. Victims of sexual trafficking are more often imported foreign women than in the United States. Trafficking victims travel less than in North America but are more frequently retrafficked if they manage to return home. European television, newspapers, and radio, more than their counterparts in other industrialized countries, feature images and stories of smuggled individuals, increasing public consciousness of the severity of the problem, but also often provoking a popular outcry against these migrants.

The number of exploited children is not large, but is in the thousands, a problem exacerbated by the fact that many minors travel

(Pittsburgh: University of Pittsburgh Press, 2007), 99–105; European Network Against Child Trafficking (ENACT), "Final Report on Child Trafficking in Bulgaria, Denmark, Italy, Romania, Spain and United Kingdom," June 23, 2004, http://www.enact.it/view_news.asp?id=198 (accessed January 17, 2009).

44 "OECD Blasts German Immigration Policy," September 11, 2008, http://www.dw-world.de/dw/article/0,2144,3636129,00.html (accessed Jan. 22, 2009).

45 John Salt and Jeremy Stein, "Migration as a Business, The Case of Trafficking," *International Migration* 35, no. 4 (1997), 474–75.

unaccompanied to Europe. Leading source regions are Eastern Europe, North Africa, and Asia.[46] Their growing number is a high priority for the Spanish presidency of the EU in 2010.[47] In Belgium alone, more than 1,000 cases were recorded of minors, primarily from Asia and Eastern Europe, transiting Belgium to the United Kingdom to find work, unite with family, or escape a difficult situation.[48] Children trafficked into Europe may suffer severe abuse in contrast with native-born Western European children, who generally receive protection from the extensive social welfare systems of the region. The European situation contrasts sharply with the American, discussed in Chapter 8, where in the absence of an extensive social welfare system, native-born children are frequently victims of sexual exploitation. Children trafficked to Europe have been exploited by pedophiles and forced to become prostitutes, domestic servants, sweatshop workers or beggars or to engage in petty or violent crime.[49]

Children sent by smugglers and traffickers to Europe by parents hoping to find security for their children sometimes face a tragic fate. Some unaccompanied minors from Africa, such as Tanzanian girls in Sweden who were forced to be prostitutes on the streets,[50] become victims of international crime groups; others are enslaved by families.[51] A 9-year-old girl sent to the United Kingdom from the Ivory Coast was abused and murdered by her great-aunt and aunt's partner, and 87 refugee children went missing in Sweden in 2001.[52] In the early part of the millennium, 250 children from Somalia were sent abroad alone by smugglers, who

46 ENACT, "Final Report"; Unicef, Innocenti Research Centre, see http://www.childtrafficking.org/ (accessed January 21, 2009). "OECD Blasts German Immigration Policy," September 11, 2008, http://www.dw-world.de/dw/article/0,2144,3636129,00.html (accessed Jan. 22, 2009).

47 "Unaccompanied Minors within the European Union" Global Eye on Human Trafficking, Issue 7, October 2009, http://www.iom.int/jahia/webdav/site/myjahiasite/shared/shared/main site/proj ects /showcase_pdf/global_eye_seventh_issue.pdf (accessed December 7, 2009).

48 Ilse Derluyn and Eric Broekaert, "On the Way to a Better Future: Belgium as Transit Country for Trafficking and Smuggling of Unaccompanied Minors," *International Migration* 43, no. 4 (2005), 31.

49 ENACT, "Final Report," 74.

50 "Somalia: Chapter 2: Hambaar: The Smugglers' Network," 6 January 2003, http://www.irinnews.org/Report.aspx?ReportId=71597 (accessed January 19, 2009).

51 Melanie McFadyean, "I Tried to Kill Myself," June 15, 2007, *The Guardian*, http://www.guardian.co.uk/politics/2007/jun/15/immigrationpolicy.immigrationandpublicservices (accessed January 19, 2009).

52 "Somalia: Executive Summary," January 2003, http://www.irinnews.org/Report.aspx?ReportId=71082 (accessed January 19, 2009).

received on average $10,000 per child.[53] Many of these children were taken in by relatives in Europe, but some were abandoned to prostitution and domestic slavery.[54]

Most Europeans seeking sex with children travel overseas. But Europe has revealed trafficking rings, primarily of Asian origin, in which children were imported to be abused by pedophiles. In the mid-1990s, Italian police discovered that one of the ubiquitous Chinese restaurants was a front for human smuggling including that of young boys who transited Italy on their way to Belgium. Children have been trafficked into Spain to be used in the production of child pornography.[55]

Europol, through its investigations, has determined an increasing involvement of organized crime in the dissemination and sale of child pornography to European customers through the Internet, generating enormous profits for those organizations. Increasingly sophisticated use of the Internet by crime groups is preventing disclosure of the providers of child pornography to European viewers or the systems of payment used, preventing tracing of money flows.[56]

In 2008, analyzed computers of Islamic militants in Great Britain, Spain, and Italy were found to have significant quantities of child pornography. Although the investigators were not certain, they suspected that the pornographic images were not merely being downloaded for personal use but were being used to convey encoded messaged through steganography in which one image can be hidden with another. This is the first identified potential linkage between child pornography and terrorism within Europe.[57]

Chinese smuggled into textile workshops often arrive with their children, who are forced to work beside the parents in the underground factories. Italian analysts suggest that there has been little state response to this child trafficking because it exists within the underground economy that has kept Italian goods competitive in the face of a worsening domestic economy.[58]

53 "Somalia: Chapter 2."

54 Väryrynen, "Illegal Immigration," 6.

55 ENACT, "Final Report," 74.

56 Europol, "Child Abuse in Relation to Trafficking in Human Beings," January 2008, http://www.europol.europa.eu/publications/Serious_Crime_Overviews/Child_abuse_2008.pdf (accessed October 14, 2008).

57 Richard Kerbaj and Dominic Kennedy, "Link between Child Porn and Muslim Terrorists Discovered in Police Raids," October 17, 2008, http://www.timesonline.co.uk/tol/news/uk/crime/article4959002.ec (accessed January 20, 2009); ENACT, "Final Report," 49.

58 Ibid.

Unlike in the United States, discussed in Chapter 8, there are relatively few women in Western Europe who choose to engage in prostitution. With demand exceeding supply, the preponderance of European prostitutes are foreigners, many of whom are trafficked into prostitution. Giving some sense of the scale of the problem is the fact that in Italy alone, 11,500 foreign trafficking victims entered a state-supported assistance program between 2000 and 2006.[59] The identified victims are only a fraction of the women trafficked into Italy. An Italian trafficking specialist suggested that at least 100 different ethnic groups were engaged in prostitution in that country, "with many of those having segments of sexual slavery."[60] Many other European countries lacking extensive assistance programs are unable to identify many of their trafficked women. The percentage of foreign women engaged in prostitution varies between 50 and 90 percent in countries for which data are available. The highest national involvement is in the Netherlands, with its "lover boy" phenomenon through which pimps recruit girls through emotional dependency.[61] The highest percentage of foreign-born victims was found in Ireland, where it reached as high as 90 percent.[62] In Germany, in the late 1990s almost 90 percent of victims were from Eastern Europe or the former Soviet Union.[63] In Norway, foreign women represent 70 percent of the prostitution markets. The native-born Norwegian prostitutes are generally older, as they are able to work under better conditions than those who have been forced into prostitution.[64]

[59] Niki Katsonis, "In Greece, female sex victims become recruiters, "January 29, 2008, http://www.iht.com/articles/2008/01/29/europe/traffic.php (accessed January 19, 2009).

[60] Picarelli, "Enabling Norms and Human Trafficking," 97.

[61] Connie Rijken, "EU's Human Rights Based Approach to Trafficking in Human Beings," The Commodification of Illicit Flows: Labour Migration, Trafficking and Business, Centre for Diaspora and Transnational Studies, University of Toronto, October 9–10, 2009; Braspenning, "Human Trafficking in the Netherlands," 332.

[62] The Irish data come from a private communication from Nusha Yunkova, anti-trafficking coordinator, Immigrant Council of Ireland. September 12, 2008, discussing a report that her organization is helping to prepare on human trafficking. The Greek calculation of 40 percent was made in the late 1990s, see Gabriella Lazardis, "Trafficking and Prostitution: The Growing Exploitation of Migrant Women in Greece," *European Journal of Women's Studies* 8, no. 1 (2001), 80–81; Dutch data come from Shared Hope International *DEMAND*.

[63] Jo Goodey, "Migration, Crime and Victimhood Responses to Sex Trafficking in the EU," *Punishment and Society* 5, no. 4 (2003), 420.

[64] A. Brunovskis and G. Tyldum, "Crossing Borders: An Empirical Study of Trans-national Prostitution and Trafficking in Human Beings," Rep. no. 426, Fafo, Norway, 2004, 115, http://www.fafo.no/pub/rapp/426/index.htm (accessed January 21, 2009).

In Europe, victims can be trafficked long distances from the source country and repeatedly sold while in transit. But once they arrive in the destination country, they are not generally moved significant distances, unlike victims in the United States. In Europe, trafficked women may be moved among brothels to provide fresh faces, but they are rarely moved across national borders even though the Schengen agreement has eliminated border controls across most of Western Europe.[65] The lesser mobility of the victims at their destinations may be explained by the segmentation of national markets among different crime groups within Europe, as well as the lesser mobility among Europeans.

"Mobile prostitution," a term used to describe the organized movement of women across European borders for short periods of time to work as prostitutes, reflects a much more localized mobility than in the United States. This has occurred most frequently among Russia, Finland, and Norway.[66] This was so routinized in the Arctic region that women, controlled by pimps and traffickers, were picked up from Russia on Thursday and delivered to Norway or Finland making the return trip on Sunday.[67]

Retrafficking of victims, although not systematically studied, appears to be a much more significant problem in the EU than in the United States. In the EU, where few trafficked individuals have a path to permanent residence in the country to which they are trafficked, many are forced to return to their country of origin, where there is an absence of psychological and economic support. Many of these victims find themselves ostracized and vulnerable upon return. Data provided in the 2005 State Department Human Rights report for Albania reflect the frequency of retrafficking. "According to the Vatra Hearth Shelter ... Retrafficking was a significant problem, with 131 out of 228 victims sheltered at the Vatra Hearth Shelter during the year reporting that they had been trafficked at least twice previously and 7 of the victims were under continuous threats from the perpetrators."[68] The Czech branch of the distinguished NGO,

[65] "When Women Are Trafficked, Quantifying the Gendered Experience of Trafficking in the UK," http://www.eaves4women.co.uk/POPPY_Project/Documents/Recent_Reports/When%20Women%20are%20Trafficked,%20April%202004.pdf (accessed January 23, 2009).

[66] Liz Kelly, "Journeys of Jeopardy: A Commentary on Current Research on Trafficking of Women and Children for Sexual Exploitation Within Europe," http://www.childtrafficking.org/pdf/user/journeys_of_jeopardy.pdf (accessed December 7, 2009).

[67] Elina Penttinen, *Globalization, Prostitution and Sex Trafficking: Corporeal Politics* (London and New York: Routledge, 2008), 94.

[68] U.S. State Department Report on Human Rights Practices Albania 2005, http://www.state.gov/g/drl/rls/hrrpt/2005/61633.htm (accessed January 19, 2009).

La Strada, estimated that half its identified victims were retrafficked after repatriation, a figure consistent with the Albanian data.[69]

In many traditional societies from which girls and women are trafficked, their work as a prostitute, even though coerced, is seen as a dishonor to the family. In Albania, in many cases in which girls have returned home "families have threatened victims of trafficking, minors included, with death because of their past." With the impossibility of reintegration at home, they are extremely vulnerable to retrafficking.[70]

The Diversity of the Problem

Europeans are concerned that migrant smuggling and trafficking are growing, but there is an inadequate understanding of the scope and the dimensions of the European problem. Most researchers have focused on trafficking in a single country or one aspect of the problem and have failed to look at the problem wholistically.[71] One European researcher at the beginning of the millennium observed:

> Although public awareness of, and concern over the trafficking of women and children (and irregular migration in general) has never been greater among governments, international agencies and NGOs, the knowledge base is still relatively weak. After almost a decade of attention, research on trafficking for sexual exploitation has not moved much beyond mapping the problem, and reviews of legal frameworks and policy responses. Despite repeated calls in international documents, including from the European Union and Council of Europe, the vast majority of states are still unable to provide reliable data as to the number of cases, the victims and their characteristics and the perpetrators.[72]

[69] La Strada, "The Street Without Joy," www.childtrafficking.org/pdf/user/la_strada_the_street_ without_joy.doc (accessed January 19, 2009).

[70] U.S. State Department Report on Human Rights Practices, Albania, 2005.

[71] Some of the work on individual countries is excellent. See, for example, Judith Vocks and Jan Nijboer, "The Promised Land: A Study of Trafficking in Women from Central and Eastern Europe to the Netherlands," *European Journal on Criminal Policy and Research* 8. (2000), 379–88; Neske, "Human Smuggling to and through Germany"; Julie Kaizen and Walter Nonneman, "Irregular Migration in Belgium and Organized Crime: An Overview," *International Migration* 45, no. 2 (2007), 121–46; Sheila Burton, Liz Kelly, Linda Regan. "Stopping Traffic: Exploring the Extent of, and Responses to, Trafficking in Women for Sexual Exploitation in the UK," http://www.homeoffice.gov.uk/rds/prgpdfs/fprs125.pdf (accessed January 23, 2009); Ernesto U. Savona, Roberta Belli, Frederica Curtol, Silvia Decarli and Andrea Di Nicola, *Tratta di persone a scopo di sfruttamento e traffiico di Migranti*, November 2003, Transcrime, http://transcrime.cs.unitn.it/tc/fso/transcrime_reports/07-Tratta_e_Traffico.pdf (accessed September 7, 2009).

[72] Kelly, "Journeys of Jeopardy."

Almost a decade later much of this observation still rings true, although UN, International Labour Organization (ILO), and International Organization for Migration (IOM) studies, the Trafficking in Persons Report (TIP) report, and other international documents have forced European countries to systematize some of their data.[73] But at heart, the problem is still inadequately understood, with limited knowledge of the source, the number of victims, their forms of exploitation, the profits, and the nature of the smugglers and traffickers. The covert nature of trafficking only partially explains the absence of knowledge. There has been inadequate attention, and too limited resources have been allocated within Europe to research and analyze trafficking from a multidisciplinary and comprehensive perspective.[74] As a consequence, individual countries in Europe and the collective bodies of the European community have not crafted a response commensurate with the scale and impact of trafficking and smuggling.

Significant differences are found between those who are smuggled and those trafficked. Those who are smuggled, having paid for their transport, are often more economically privileged within their society.[75] They often have some or significant higher education but cannot find jobs commensurate with their skills in their home countries. In contrast, trafficking victims are often from the "weakest social and economic groups in their countries of origin."[76]

Most identified trafficking cases concern adult females trafficked for sexual exploitation.[77] But there are also male victims of sex trafficking. Research in Germany reveals some men from Bulgaria and Romania, often of Roma origin, are forced by traffickers to sell themselves on the streets of German cities.[78] Yet there are many other important forms of trafficking within Western Europe, including forced labor of adults and

[73] For example, see the report done by Transcrime: Andrea di Nicola, "A Study for Monitoring the International Trafficking of Human Beings for the Purpose of Sexual Exploitation in the EU Member States," Transcrime, Report no. 9, 2004, http://transcrime.cs.unitn.it/tc/421.php (accessed September 7, 2009).

[74] See work that calls for a more interdisciplinary perspective, Liz Kelly, "'You Can Find Anything You Want': A Critical Reflection on Research on Trafficking in Persons within and into Europe," *International Migration* 43, no. 1–2 (2005), 235–65.

[75] Kaizen and Nonneman, "Irregular Migration in Belgium"; Koser, "Why Migrant Smuggling Pays," 3–26.

[76] Kaizen and Nonneman, "Irregular Migration in Belgium," 138.

[77] UNODC, "Trafficking in Persons: Global Patterns."

[78] Christophe Gille, "Romanians and Bulgarians in Male Street Sex Work in German Cities," 37–59, http://www.correlation-net.org/pdf_highlight/rom_bulg_male_sex_work.pdf (accessed January 19, 2009).

juveniles, trafficking for adoptions, begging, and forced commission of petty crime.[79]

Forced labor is a serious problem in many Western European countries, with men working in construction, agriculture, and sweatshops, often in dangerous conditions with no or limited pay. Forced labor in the agricultural sector has been most often identified in Britain, Italy, Spain, and Greece.

Women more often are in forced labor in sweatshops and domestic servitude. Debt bondage is often enforced with physical coercion. Illustrative of this problem in Britain is the following:

> In 2003 a group of Eastern Europeans were brought to the United Kingdom by a gang to work illegally in a factory. They were originally informed that they would be working with permits, but en route were given false British passports. When they realized they would be in the United Kingdom illegally they attempted to leave the gang's control, but they were threatened so seriously that they were forced to continue. On arrival they were informed of their conditions: that they must work seven days a week for one year with no pay because they needed to repay their "debt" ... Their salaries were transferred into the bank account of a gang member ... Control was maintained by beatings and physical assault.[80]

In France, there are problems of exploitation not only of Eastern Europeans but also of Chinese in clandestine workshops. During the high demand season, approximately half the year, they work 15 to 18 hours daily for 310 to 450 euros monthly. Their debt to their smuggler takes three to ten years to pay off.[81]

In France since the early 1990s, the government has tried to combat the problem of women and young girls, deprived of their identity papers by their employers, who are forced to work 15 to 18 hours daily without remuneration. According to French parliamentary hearings, a quarter of them are Southeast Asian and Indian. Their wages are sent home directly to their husbands, and they are found in the most affluent communities in France. Yet the vast majority of those in domestic servitude, 65 percent, originate from Africa. Of those, one-third are minors between the ages of

79 UNODC, "Trafficking in Persons: Global Patterns."

80 Bridget Anderson and Ben Rogaly, "Forced Labour and Migration to the UK," 38, http://www.compas.ox.ac.uk/publications/papers/Forced%20Labour%20TUC%20Report.pdf (accessed January 22, 2009).

81 Gao Yun and Véronique Poisson, "Le trafic et l'exploitation des immigrants chinois en France," Organisation Internationale de Travail, 70–72, http://www.ilo.org/wcmsp5/groups/public/–ed_norm/–declaration/documents/publication/wcms_082332.pdf (accessed January 20, 2009).

8 and 15 who arrive and are exploited in the homes of their compatriots or in families of mixed couples. They are sent home or thrown out on the street between the ages of 18 and 20 and are replaced by other child domestics.[82] Once on the street, lacking papers to reside in France, they are easy prey for traffickers to exploit them for other forms of labor or sexual exploitation.

There are other forms of child trafficking within Europe. Europeans adopt babies and older children who have been obtained through coercion or deception from Latin America, Asia, Africa, and the former socialist countries. Two scandals in Albania in the 1990s raised citizen awareness of the illegal origins of the adopted children but the problem continues. In the first Albanian case, a charity designated to protect children instead ran illegal adoptions. In a more colorful case, a hospital declared children dead and prepared coffins. But the coffins were empty. The children were alive and were supplied to traffickers who sold them for adoptions.[83]

A thriving trade in babies also exists elsewhere, with citizens of Bulgaria providing babies and Greece emerging as a marketplace for Greeks and other Europeans seeking to acquire babies. Until 2004, Bulgaria did not a have a law on illegal adoptions, and subsequent enforcement of this law has been minimal.[84] With a six-year waiting list for babies in Greece, potential parents will pay as much as $33,000 to acquire a baby while the Roma mothers of Bulgarian origin may receive as little as $4,000 for the child they are sometimes forced to relinquish. Bulgarians have begun to act against the traffickers and facilitators. In 2009, Bulgarian lawyers were arrested by the state security police for running a trafficking ring that moved pregnant women to Greece so that their babies would be adopted.[85]

Women from other parts of the world can also lose their children through illegal adoptions to European parents. UNICEF estimates that 1,000 to 1,500 babies are trafficked from Guatemala for adoptions in North America and Europe.[86] In a case in Spain, a Nepalese mother

[82] Les Documents d'information de l'assemblée nationale, *L'esclavage en France, aujourd'hui*, no. 3459, 2001, Tome II, vol.1, 38–39.

[83] Vasilika Hysi, "Organised Crime in Albania: The Ugly Side of Capitalism and Democracy," in *Organised Crime in Europe* eds. Fijnaut and Paoli, 551.

[84] Niki Katsontonis and Matthew Brunwasser, "Baby Trafficking Is Thriving in Greece," *New York Times*, December 18, 2006, http://www.nytimes.com/2006/12/18/world/europe/18iht-babies.3939121.html (accessed September 11, 2009).

[85] "Bulgaria State Security Busts 2 Lawyers for Baby Trafficking," June 17, 2009, http://www.novinite.com/view_news.php?id=104772 (accessed September 11, 2009).

[86] "Child Trafficking," http://www.unicef.org/protection/index_exploitation.html (accessed January 22, 2009).

tried to recover three of her children illegally adopted in Spain through a Nepalese children's home after she was tricked into signing legal documents giving up claim to her children.[87]

Children are trafficked for begging and to commit crimes. "After prostitution, the most visible forms of exploitation in the streets are begging and peddling (selling small equipment, flowers, and cigarettes)."[88] In the 1990s, thousands of children worked in all the major cities in Greece. On average 300 children, mostly of Albanian origin, were arrested annually in Athens for begging. Child begging is also apparent in countries farther from the former USSR and Eastern Europe. "In one prominent case, a Ukrainian network sent young deaf-mute people to sell trinkets in public places in France, Spain, Portugal, and Germany, as well as throughout the rest of Europe."[89] Today young trafficked children from the Indian subcontinent are forced to sell flowers to tourists in restaurants until late at night in Sicily.[90]

Children can be forced to commit crime. Not only are they more nimble but because of their minor age, they are not liable under the laws of most European countries, and youths can commit crimes on behalf of their traffickers with impunity. Some traffickers have forced children they have brought to Western Europe primarily from Eastern Europe to engage in pickpocketing and more serious crimes such as street robbery and drugs. Often they are recruited and controlled by family members who might use significant coercion to induce compliance.[91] In one case, a trafficking organization exploited minors, some as young as 13 years of age, to shoplift in Italy. The joint Italian – Romanian investigation initiated in 2005 "revealed a total of 100 people trafficked to the Piedmont region (Italy) from the Bistrita – Nasaud District (Romania) for the purposes of shoplifting. All of the minors belonged to extremely poor families and were usually recruited in schools or discos."[92]

Child trafficking for benefit fraud occurs in the United Kingdom as in the United States, as will be discussed in Chapter 8. British officials have

87 "Nepal: Concern Rising over Illegal Adoptions," http://www.irinnews.org/Report.aspx?ReportId=80117 (accessed January 19, 2009).

88 Francesca Bosco, Vittoria Luda di Cortemiglia, Anvar Serojitdinov, "Human Trafficking Patterns," in *Strategies Against Human Trafficking*, Friesendorf, ed., 53.

89 Ibid.

90 Observed by the author in 2002 and discussions with Sicilian NGOs.

91 Rebecca Surtees, "Traffickers and Trafficking in Southern and Eastern Europe: Considering the Other Side of Human Trafficking," *European Journal of Criminology* 5, no. 1, 39–68.

92 Bosco, di Cortemiglia, and Serojitdinov, "Human Trafficking Patterns," 53.

seen an increase in this form of trafficking. In a prosecuted case in 2008, a woman housing official was convicted of acquiring a baby two years earlier in Nigeria for 150 to 200 pounds. "It is believed she bought the baby – at the time just a few months old – from a hospital and smuggled it into Britain to qualify for priority housing."[93]

Factors Precipitating Human Trafficking into Europe

Chapter 1 analyzed the factors contributing to the rise of human trafficking, but there are certain distinctive European conditions that merit mention. Although many causes have been identified by Europol,[94] the Europol analysis overlooks certain important factors. These include EU policies that create economic hardships in source countries, such as limits on agricultural imports from countries such as Moldova or the intentional misrepresentation by returning migrants of work conditions in Europe. Nor does Europol mention the increasing numbers of displaced people or refugees created by the growth of conflicts in the world that have propelled people to Europe.

For example, to support domestic agriculture in Europe, the European Union has placed numerous barriers on the import of foreign agricultural products into the European community. But an agricultural-based country such as Moldova, on the EU's border, is thus deprived of access to the half-billion-person market for its agricultural products.[95] Many delegations and projects have been financed by the European Union to combat trafficking of Moldovan women. But nothing has been done to lift the trade barriers for agricultural products that would sustain women in Moldova's rural areas and eliminate the desperate poverty that makes them vulnerable to the ploys of the traffickers.

[93] UK Baby Trafficking Case," http://www.antislavery.org/homepage/traffic%20news/index.htm (accessed January 19, 2009).

[94] Europol identifies these reasons for trafficking as the difficulties of economic survival in many parts of the world, the absence of opportunities in countries of origin commensurate with higher educational levels, large-scale human rights abuses, and the possibilities for an improved standard of living and quality of life in Europe. "Trafficking in Human Beings in the European Union: A Europol Perspective," February 2008, http://ww.europol.europa.eu/publications/Serious_Crime_Overviews/Trafficking_in_human_beings_2008.pdf (accessed January 23, 2009).

[95] Cornelius Friesendorf, "Conclusions: Improving Counter-Trafficking Efforts through Better Implementation, Networking and Evaluation," in *Strategies Against Human Trafficking*.

Smuggling and trafficking are also often fueled by irregular migrants who return home with some capital, often exaggerating their good fortune, thereby increasing the pull toward Europe and making individuals vulnerable to the ploys of traffickers. Those who will be smuggled or trafficked from Africa, therefore, often have a distorted impression of the West.

> They only see the success stories of relatives currently living in Europe or having lived there. They see their neighbour who suddenly can afford to buy a house after his daughter went to Europe.... Such success stories, backed up by the display of lavish material goods, add to the sometimes unrealistic expectations concerning job opportunities and potential earnings, social benefits, housing, or the obstacles to be overcome in order to gain a legal status among those who consider migrating to the West.[96]

Individuals also hire human smugglers because it pays. Khalid Koser, in his research on human smuggling from Pakistan to Great Britain, reveals that the costs paid to the human smugglers and their intermediaries can be recouped within a two-year period. After that relatively short period, the family member residing in Britain can send money home, which often pays for the education of younger family members.[97]

The same situation also can apply to victims of human trafficking who are able to send some money home to their families. They are resigned to their exploitation because they can see no other way to support their young children at home.[98] Therefore, human smuggling and trafficking continue because they often pay for everyone involved.

Conflicts and Political Oppression

Western Europe has represented a region of stability for those fleeing conflict and the ethnic cleansing that has accompanied many of these wars. The possibility of obtaining refugee status within Western Europe has prompted many desperate individuals to pay human smugglers to move them to countries where they could apply for asylum. Desperate individuals have sought smugglers to escape conflicts in Africa, Sri Lanka, the Middle East, and Colombia. According to Scandinavian data, "In 2001 a total of 461 and in 2002 a total of 550 unaccompanied children

[96] Bilger, Hofmann, and Jandl, "Human Trafficking as a Transnational Service Industry," 73.
[97] Koser, "Why Human Smuggling Pays."
[98] This is clearly illustrated in the documentary, *Sex Slaves*.

came to Sweden.... The entrants were mostly Kurds from Northern Iraq, but they came also from Somalia, Serbia, and Afghanistan. Swedish documentation shows that in most cases, these children are assisted both by ethnic networks and smuggling rings whose concern is money rather than a safe journey of their 'customers.'"[99] The callous attitudes of the smugglers explain why many who pay became trafficking victims. Research conducted in the Netherlands also suggests that the migration of some asylum seekers is arranged by traffickers.[100]

European Response to Human Trafficking

Smuggling and trafficking have also grown because the decline of border controls under the Schengen Agreement has not been accompanied by significantly enhanced cross-border law enforcement cooperation, legal harmonization among European states,[101] or coordinated multinational investigations. Laws have not been harmonized on prostitution, adoptions, or child exploitation, making investigations and prosecutions difficult. In some countries, the intimidation of law enforcement personnel and judges by the crime groups responsible for the trafficking has curtailed prosecutions.[102] Further complicating effective enforcement, according to a top Europol counter-trafficking official in fall 2008, insufficient numbers of European countries carry the investigations of human trafficking beyond the borders of their countries.[103] Therefore, criminals can segment

[99] Väryrynen, "Illegal immigration."

[100] Khalid Koser, "Recent Asylum Migration in Europe: Patterns and Processes of Change," *New Community* 22, no. 1 (1996), 156; Salt and Stein, "Migration as a Business," 470.

[101] There is not even harmonization on the supranational level. "The trafficking conventions of the United Nations, European Union and Council of Europe all impose an obligation to criminalise. They vary in terms of their orientation towards the victims of trafficking, and are largely silent on the actual procedures that -should be used to investigate and prosecute traffickers. All three instruments require that penalties reflect the serious nature of the crime, but only the EU Council Framework Decision on Combating Trafficking in Human Beings, adopted in July 2002, states that the maximum penalty for aggravated forms of trafficking should be not less than 8 years." Allison Jernow, "Human Trafficking, Prosecutors & Judges," in *Strategies Against Human Trafficking*, Friesendorf, ed., 345–46.

[102] Private discussions concerning the fate of a judge in a Cyprus trafficking case at OSCE-UNODC-Cyprus Regional Operational Meeting on Combating Human Trafficking and Money Laundering in the Mediterranean Rim Region, September 18–19, 2008, Larnaca, Cyprus.

[103] Steve Harvey, "A Europol Perspective on Criminal Profits and Money Laundering Linked to Trafficking in Human Beings," Paper presented at OSCE-UNODC-Cyprus Regional Operational Meeting, Larnaca, Cyprus, September 2008.

their operations among different countries and the criminal network can survive arrests in a single nation.

Law enforcement responses to trafficking across Europe continue to be understaffed and under-resourced.[104] Therefore, human smuggling and trafficking is a low-risk activity for criminal perpetrators. The prisons of Europe are filled with illegal migrants who have committed crimes. Nearly one-quarter of all those in prison in Europe (approx. 100,000 people) are incarcerated in countries where they are not citizens.[105] Many of those incarcerated have been convicted of drug-related crimes, but very few of this total have been sentenced for trafficking or smuggling human beings. As a consequence, trafficking has become more public, often unimpeded by the limited efforts of law enforcement. Auctions of women can occur in public places,[106] children beg in the streets, and foreign women can solicit customers on the streets, often without state intervention.

The number of human trafficking cases investigated is still minimal. The number of cases investigated within in the EU has risen from

> 195 in 2001, 453 in 2003, 1,060 in 2005, and 1,569 in 2006. Despite the upward trend, the number of criminal proceedings is still not high enough to reflect the presumed scale of the crime, especially given the fact that about 500,000 people might be trafficked to Europe every year according to IOM estimates. In 2006, 180 cases were recorded of this offence being committed against children. ... The conclusion has to be that, trafficking in human beings is still a low-risk crime concerning both trafficking for sexual and labour exploitation.[107]

The contribution of Italy to this total is significant. Their experience in fighting organized crime has helped them prosecute a variety of human traffickers. Their understanding of undercover work and how to combat

[104] F. Laczko, "Enhancing Data Collection and Research on Trafficking in Persons," in *Measuring Human Trafficking: Complexities and Pitfalls*, E. Savona and S. Stefanizzi, eds. (New York: Springer, 2007).

[105] This analysis comes from the EU Foreign Prisoners Project 2006, http://www.foreigners-inprison.eu/ (accessed October 14, 2008).

[106] "Slaves Are Auctioned by Traffickers," June 4, 2006, news.bbc.co.uk/2/hi/uk_news/5046170.stm (accessed August 27, 2008); "Women for Sale in Gatwick Slave Auctions," *Evening Standard*, www.thisislondon.co.uk/news/article-23388098-details/women+for+sale+in+Gatwick+Slave+Auctions/article.do (accessed August 27, 2008).

[107] Phil Williams, "Combating Human Trafficking: Improving Governance Institutions, Mechanisms and Strategies," in *Strategies Against Human Trafficking*, Friesendorf, ed., 401, data are based on the European Commission working document on monitoring and evaluating the EU Plan on combating and preventing trafficking in human beings. The figure cited here by the IOM for trafficking seems high unless it includes smuggled individuals who are vulnerable to be trafficked.

crime networks has proved invaluable. Between 1996 and 2000, Italian prosecutors opened 2,930 separate trafficking cases that targeted 7,582 traffickers who had victimized 2,741 people.[108] If the Italian cases are dropped from the total, the contribution of each other European country to prosecutions is minimal.

Further reducing the effectiveness of counter-trafficking is the failure of European law enforcement to follow the money trails of human smugglers and traffickers. They, therefore, face a small risk of asset forfeiture. The smugglers and traffickers rarely use banks but instead rely on couriers, wire transfers, money service bureaus in the United Kingdom, trade based money laundering, and underground banking to move their profits. Often the money will not even enter the European jurisdictions, making it difficult to investigate the profits of the trafficking. Consequently, following the criminals' profits is more difficult, but not impossible.[109] British investigators have traced profits from human trafficking of children to large villas being constructed in small towns of Romania.[110]

Few law enforcement bodies in Europe have diversified to hire members of the ethnic minorities, which complicates enforcement of laws against human smugglers and traffickers. Without the language skills or the cultural knowledge, it is extremely difficult to identify the human smuggling and trafficking, which often goes on within closed immigrant communities. Moreover, without the ability to converse with the victims and win their trust, the possibility of successful prosecutions is extremely limited. Cooperation of law enforcement with NGOs to ensure victim protection is not standard practice throughout Europe.

Conclusion

Human trafficking in Western Europe today encompasses many of the trafficking models identified in Chapter 4, including the Balkan, Chinese, Nigerian, and post-Soviet, but there are many other groups operating in the region, such as Turkish, Latin American, East African, and Pakistani.

108 Savona, Belli, Curtol, Decarli and Di Nicola, *Tratta di persone a scopo di sfruttamento e traffiico di Migranti*, 134–37, the Albanians and Italians were those most often convicted of human trafficking.

109 Select Committee of Experts on the Evaluation of Anti-Money Laundering Measures (Moneyval), "Proceeds from Trafficking in Human Beings and Illegal Migration/Human Smuggling," report by the Workshop 5 Project Team following the joint FATF (Financial Action Task Force) Moneyval typologies meeting held in Moscow, December 6–8, 2004.

110 Harvey, "A Europol Perspective."

Victims often originate from conflict regions to the east and south, and the sex markets are dominated by women from former socialist societies where women have been major losers in the transition. Minority groups, particularly Roma children, are also disproportionately represented as child trafficking victims. Women are not only victims of sex and labor trafficking but also serve as recruiters and managers of human trafficking.

Most victims of human trafficking originate outside of Europe. For many Europeans they are outsiders and often subject to discrimination as "others" and minorities. As non-citizens, they rarely have access to the protections of the social welfare states that characterize much of Continental Europe and Scandinavia. The fear experienced by the trafficked and absence of rights of those illegally residing in Europe are exploited by the traffickers to maintain control over their victims.

Human trafficking is not as small-scale and disorganized as some would suggest. The auctions of women and significant Balkan smuggling/trafficking operations into Europe[111] dispel the myth that this activity consists of only small-scale entrepreneurs. Many traders in humans are often sophisticated criminals who lack only the infrastructure and organization of drug traffickers operating within Europe. Some victims know what they are getting into, but many have no idea of the level of exploitation that awaits them.

Trafficking continues in Europe because, with the current demographic decline of European populations, birthrates are not at the replacement level. There is an absence of a population able or willing to do physical labor, and an ongoing demand for sexual services that is not met by the native-born population. In parts of Europe, the exploitation of foreign prostitutes is now embedded in the culture.[112] In the Netherlands, with its long-standing red light districts, the trafficked prostitutes who cannot acquire work permits exist in an underground where they are paid less, suffer greater risks, and have no security for the future.[113]

Laws are not harmonized. Traffickers exploit these differences, segmenting their operations and taking advantage of legal loopholes. But even when laws are harmonized, as has been done between Norway and

[111] See Jana Arsovska and Stef Janssens, "Policing and Human Trafficking: Good and Bad Practices," in *Strategies Against Human Trafficking*, Friesendorf, ed.

[112] Presentations by Cypriot and other speakers at the conference of OSCE-UNODC-Cyprus Regional Operational Meeting.

[113] Shared Hope International, *DEMAND*.

Sweden in the trafficking arena, there is often a dislocation effect rather than a solution to the problem.[114]

There is little effort to reduce demand in Europe for trafficked people. Even in Sweden, which was the first country to outlaw the use of prostitutes, law enforcement is reluctant to allocate the resources needed to enforce the law.[115]

Despite large European efforts to control migration and cut off smuggling and trafficking, the problem is not diminishing. Europe remains a magnet for many in the impoverished and conflict regions, especially in North Africa, the Balkans, the Middle East, and even farther countries in Asia such as Afghanistan, Iraq, India, and Pakistan. For some in those regions who are not desperate, Europe remains a land of opportunity, despite the global recession of 2008.

The dominance of the sex trade in the European discourse on trafficking may soon be overshadowed by the migrant smuggling that becomes human trafficking. As the barriers to entry increase in Europe and the pressure for migration grows in the face of increased economic hardship in the developing world, a problem compounded by the financial crisis of late 2008, individuals may not be able to repay their smugglers. Therefore, their debts will be compensated only by forced labor. Therefore, the distinction between smuggling and trafficking may be even more blurred in the future in Europe despite the established legal distinctions between these two phenomena.[116]

Assistance programs throughout Europe are inadequate and too short-term to aid the large numbers of victims. Although the COE Convention against Trafficking mandates assistance to victims, the quality of aid to victims is heavily dependent on the jurisdiction and the willingness of individual law enforcement to help. Compounding the problem is that victims often do not know where to go for help.[117] Even when they find assistance, there is an absence of coordination between state service

[114] "Policing Prostitution, 'The Oldest Conundrum,'" *The Economist*, October 30, 2008, http://www.economist.com/displaystory.cfm?story_id=12516582The Economist (accessed September 12, 2009); discussion with Ana Jonsson, a specialist on human trafficking and on leave from the Swedish National Police, on articles in the Swedish press on this topic, September 2009.

[115] Discussion with Ana Jonsson.

[116] Bridget Anderson and Julia O'Connell Davidson, "Is Trafficking in Human Beings Demand Driven?" A Multi-Country Pilot Study 9 (IOM, December 2003), http://www.compas.ox.ac.uk/about/publications/Bridget/Anderson04.pdf? event=detail&id=2932 (accessed September 14, 2008).

[117] *Trafficking in Persons Report 2009*, 40

providers and nongovernmental organizations, the police, and judicial bodies. Far too many trafficking victims are caught in a bureaucratic maze, often deported before they can obtain assistance.[118]

The failure of most European countries to address the smuggling/trafficking problem is resulting in large, increasingly marginalized populations that cannot be integrated. The large number of illegal residents arriving annually often lack education and have little knowledge of the language, culture, and values of the European societies to which they have been transported. Their illegal status denies them the rights that are the cornerstones of the system of Western European democracies achieved in the post – World War II period. As illegal workers, they exist in the "second economy" outside the welfare states that are the hallmark of contemporary European society. Therefore, the phenomenal rise of smuggling and trafficking, bringing hundreds of thousands to Europe annually, challenges not only the national and cultural identities of Western Europe but also its political and economic systems. The trade in human beings will have deep and long-term effects on Europe, as did the slave trade of previous centuries.

[118] Many articles in the collection of Friesendorf, ed., *Strategies Against Human Trafficking*, address this problem.

8

Trafficking in the United States

American trafficking is unique among affluent advanced democracies because its sex trafficking victims are younger, more often native born, and more mobile. The United States, like many developing countries, is a major source country for sex trafficking victims, has sex tourism on its territory, and its native born sex trafficking victims have Hobbesian lives that are "brutish and short." Yet many other forms of trafficking occur among the massive illegal migrant population. Despite the absence of widespread corruption and close links between traffickers and state officials, patterns of American trafficking more closely resemble those of a developing than a developed country.

The passage of the Trafficking Victims Protection Act (TVPA) in 2000 by the United States Congress, introduced with enormous bipartisan support, was signed by President Clinton and subsequently reauthorized under the Bush administrations in 2003, 2005 and 2007.[1] The TVPA raised awareness of the problem,[2] addressed prevention, facilitated prosecution, and provided resources to aid numerous victims of trafficking. The legislation combines a focus on victims' assistance with stiff sanctions for traffickers.[3]

[1] Susan W. Tiefenbrun, "The Cultural, Political, and Legal Climate Behind the Fight to Stop Trafficking in Women: William J. Clinton's Legacy to Women's Rights." *Cardozo Journal of Law and Gender* 855 (2006), 101–129; Reauthorization in 2007, www.cbo.gov/doc.cfm?index=8783, accessed December 8, 2009.

[2] Barbara Ann Stolz, "Interpreting the U.S. Human Trafficking Debate Through the Lens of Symbolic Politics," *Law & Policy* 29, no. 3 (July 2007), 311–38.

[3] Anthony M. De Stefano, *The War on Human Trafficking: U.S. Policy Assessed* (New Brunswick: Rutgers University Press, 2007).

Yet almost a decade after the passage of the legislation, human trafficking still survives on a significant scale, with large numbers of native-born citizens and foreigners subject to labor, sexual, and other forms of exploitation in the United States.[4] The impunity of the traffickers with only 77 convictions nationwide in 2008, helps explain the growth of trafficking.[5] As the Enlightenment thinker Cesare Beccaria wrote, "the certainty of punishment is more important than its severity in preventing crime."[6]

Much research has been done on American exceptionalism, explaining differences in social organization, culture, and society in the United States from those of other advanced democracies.[7] The distinctive features of the United States, cited by these scholars, help explain the unique features of trafficking in this country. According to American exceptionalism, the United States emphasizes individual achievement rather than support for an extensive social welfare system so as the one that characterizes many industrialized countries. Consequently, in contrast to Western Europe, Australia, or Japan, there is greater economic and social differentiation, and many citizens remain with only the bare minimum of a social safety net.[8] The disadvantaged population is the source of many American trafficking victims, particularly its youthful victims, estimated at between 100,000 and 300,000,[9] drawn from the million plus children who run away or are thrown out of their homes annually.[10] Trafficked

[4] Ralph F. Boyd, Jr. "Implementation of the Trafficking Victims Protection Act," in *Trafficking in Women and Children: Current Issues and Developments*, Anna M. Troubnikoff, ed. (Hauppauge, NY: Nova Science Publishers, 2003), 145–55.

[5] Attorney General's Report to Congress and Assessment of U.S. Government Activities to Combat Trafficking in Persons, U.S. Department of Justice, 2009, 38.

[6] *Modern History Sourcebook*, Beccaria: "Crimes and Punishments," http://www.fordham.edu/halsall/mod/18beccaria.html (accessed August 19, 2009).

[7] This topic was discussed by Alexis de Tocqueville, *Democracy in America, Vols. I and II* (New York: Alfred A. Knopf, 1948) and more recently by Seymour Martin Lipset, *American Exceptionalism: A Double-Edged Sword* (New York and London: W. W. Norton, 1996).

[8] Barbara Ehrenreich, *Nickled and Dimed: On (not) Getting by in America* (New York: Henry Holt, 2001).

[9] R. J. Estes and N. A. Weiner, *The Commercial Sexual Exploitation of Children in the U.S.,Canada and Mexico*, Executive Summary, University of Pennsylvania, 2002, http://www.churchwomen.org/human-trafficking/commercial-sexual-exploitation.asp (accessed June 9, 2008).

[10] Statement of Chris Swecker, Assistant Director, Criminal Investigative Division, Federal Bureau of Investigation before the Commission on Security and Cooperation in Europe, United States Helsinki Commission, June 7, 2005, citing data on NMEC (National Missing and Exploited Children), http://www.fbi.gov/congress/congress05/swecker060705.htm (accessed June 9, 2008).

into prostitution as young as 12 or 13, they live, as previously mentioned, on average 7 years after they are forced to sell their bodies.[11]

In Canada, similar trafficking problems are noted among members of the First Nations. Extensive sexual abuse of young girls makes them susceptible to trafficking. The Royal Canadian Mounted Police (RCMP) has identified the trafficking of many girls as young as 12 from this minority population.[12] Therefore, the victimization of minority members is not unique to the United States but is a North American pattern.

A disproportionate share of American-born victims of sexual trafficking are black and Hispanic, but the problem is not confined to minority group members, as victims also come from middle-class families residing in American suburbs and on farms. The state of Minnesota and other Midwest locales with low percentages of minorities have long been sources of domestic trafficking victims.[13]

Some of the trafficking victims in the United States are native born; others are foreigners purposely trafficked to the United States for exploitation, or migrants who become victims after entry. Traffickers have an enormous pool to draw on within the United States, as it is a nation of immigrants. According to the latest census data from the 2006 American Community Survey, more than 37 million Americans or 12.5 percent of the population were foreign born.[14] These numerous migrants include approximately 11.5 to 12 million individuals (80 to 85 percent of whom

[11] FBI powerpoint, "Innocence Lost Initiative," http://courts.michigan.gov/scao/services/CWS/AWOLP/FBI.pdf (accessed August 17, 2008). They die most frequently of suicides, drug overdoses, or as victims of homicide as Thomas Stack and Leland Wiley, of Montgomery County police, have learned from their experience and information obtained at law enforcement sharing conferences.

[12] Marty Van Doren, RCMP Human Trafficking Awareness Coordinator "*Human Trafficking – Canada: Law Enforcement Perspective,*" The Commodification of Illicit Flows: Labour Migration, Trafficking and Business, Centre for Diaspora and Transnational Studies, University of Toronto, October 9–10, 2009.

[13] Legislative Commission on the Economic Status of Women, Public Hearing on the International Sexual Trafficking of Women and Girls in Minnesota, November 12, 2003, http://www.commissions.leg.state.mn.us/oesw/hearings/11_12_03hearingnotes.pdf (accessed July 1, 2008); Janice Raymond, Donna Hughes, and Carol Gomez, *Sex Trafficking of Women in the United States International and Domestic Trends* (Washington, DC: National Institute of Justice, 2001); Minnesota Office of Justice Programs and Minnesota Statistical Analysis Center, "Human Trafficking in Minnesota: A Report to the Minnesota Legislature," September 2006; Shared Hope International, *Demand: A Comparative Examination of Sex Tourism and Trafficking in Jamaica, Japan, the Netherlands, and the United States* (Washington, DC: Shared Hope International, 2007).

[14] http://factfinder.census.gov/servlet/ACSSAFFFacts?_event=&geo_id=01000US&_geoContext=01000US&_street=&_county=&_cityTown=&_state=&_zip=&_lang=en&_sse=on&ActiveGeoDiv=&_useEV=&pctxt=fph&pgsl=010&_submenuId=factsheet_1&

are of Mexican origin) who entered the United States illegally or overstayed or violated the conditions of their visas.[15] Some estimate the figure of undocumented people as high as 12.5 to 15 million.[16] The toleration of this large illegal population is explained by the demand for inexpensive labor and the long-term growth rate of the U.S. economy. The American capacity to absorb both legal and illegal migrants, a defining feature of American society, stands in sharp contrast to Western Europe, where migration is often seen as destructive of national identity and security.[17]

The unprecedented size of the illegal migrant population has resulted in an anti-immigrant backlash among some Americans and a desire to control immigration among many. Moreover, since the 9/11 attacks, there has been increased emphasis on protecting U.S. borders. Billions of dollars have been spent post-2001 to heighten national security by hiring more border guards, increasing technology at the borders, and constructing a fence between the U.S. and Mexico.[18] Enhanced border security, combined with the desire to deter illegal immigrants, has decreased cross-border flows while increased corruption and barriers to entry have increased the costs of illegal entry into the United States. Illegal immigrants, still seeking a better economic life, have nonetheless entered the United States. Many now face greater hardship on arrival,[19] especially since the financial crisis that started in 2007 has reduced job availability and pay. Others have returned home, still others are deterred from entry.[20] With higher costs of illegal entry, ever larger numbers of

ds_name=null&_ci_nbr=null&qr_name=null&reg=null%3Anull&_keyword=&_industry= (accessed June 29, 2008).

15 Jeffrey S. Passel, "Unauthorized Migrants: Numbers and Characteristics," http://pewhispanic.org/files/reports/46.pdf (accessed August 16, 2008).

16 John Allen Williams and Richard E. Friedman, "Workshop Report: 'The Intersection of Immigration and National Security,'" *American Bar Association National Security Law Report* 30, no. 4 (Nov./Dec. 2008), 15–17.

17 Kitty Calavita, *Immigrants at the Margins Law, Race, and Exclusion in Southern Europe* (Cambridge: Cambridge University Press, 2005).

18 Ruth Ellen Wesem, Jennifer Lake, Liga Seghetti, James Monke and Stephen Vina, "Border Security: Inspections Practices, Policies and Issues," Congressional Reference Service, summary, http://www.fas.org/sgp/crs/RL32399.pdf (accessed June 25, 2008); Tyche Hendricks, "Study: Price for Border Fence up to $49 Billion. Study Says Fence Cost Could Reach $49 Billion," *San Francisco Chronicle*, January 8, 2007, http://www.sfgate.com/cgi-bin/article.cgi?f=/c/a/2007/01/08/BAG6RNEJJG1.DTL (accessed June 25, 2008).

19 Pew Hispanic Center, "Modes of Entry for the Unauthorized Migrant Population," May 22, 2006, http://pewhispanic.org/files/factsheets/19.pdf (accessed June 25, 2008).

20 Julia Preston, "Mexican Data Show Migration to US in Decline," http://www.nytimes.com/2009/05/15/us/15immig.html?_r=1&scp=14&sq=Illegal%20migrants%20return%20home&st=cse (accessed August 11, 2009).

illegal immigrants remain in debt bondage or in forced labor for as long as a decade to the same exploiter.[21] This long-term exploitation can often remain undetected because it occurs within closed immigrant communities not readily penetrated by law enforcement.

The Diversity of American Trafficking

Trafficking exists in every state of the United States. Victims of trafficking are exploited in rural, urban, and suburban communities and along the nation's highways. American trafficking victims originate from all regions of the world – Latin America, Asia, Africa, Europe, and Eurasia. Almost all identified forms of human trafficking, except for child soldiers, exist in the United States.

Sex trafficking of foreigners and native born,[22] labor trafficking, and debt bondage are the most widespread forms of exploitation. Forced marriages, migrants forced to beg on the streets by their criminal controllers, and adoptions of trafficked children occur less frequently. Yet recent investigations of fundamentalist Mormon communities in Texas have alleged that young girls are forced into marriages with older men, a phenomenon more commonly observed in Asia and the Middle East than in an advanced democracy.[23] The United States is also a major destination country for young children kidnapped and trafficked for adoption by childless couples unwilling to wait for a child or unable to adopt through legitimate adoption procedures and agencies.[24]

Guest farm workers who enter from Latin America, the Caribbean, Asia, and Eastern Europe on H-2 visas are routinely cheated out of wages, "held virtually captive by employers or labor brokers who seize their documents; forced to live in squalid conditions; and, denied medical benefits for on-the-job injuries."[25] They are made false promises of

[21] Kevin Bales and Stephen Lize, "Trafficking in Persons in the United States," National Institute of Justice report, November 2005, Award Number: 2001-IJ-CX-0027, 5.

[22] Janice Raymond and Donna Hughes, "Sex Trafficking in the United States," March 2001, 41–43, http://www.uri.edu/artsci/wms/hughes/sex_traff_us.pdf (accessed June 29, 2008).

[23] Peter Seven, "400 Children Removed from Sect's Texas Ranch," *Washington Post*, April 8, 2008, A1

[24] Ethan Kapstein, "The Baby Trade," *Foreign Affairs* (November/December 2003), Claire Ribando, "Trafficking in Persons: U.S. Policy and Issues for Congress," CRS Report for Congress, June 20, 2007, CRS-10.

[25] Mary Bauer, Southern Poverty Law Center, "Close to Slavery: Guestworker Programs in the United States," 2007, http://www.splcenter.org/pdf/static/SPLCguestworker.pdf, accessed December 8, 2009.

wages that exceed the possible and often incur $10,000 in debt to enter the United States.[26] Although the relationship with those that bring them to the United States starts out as contractual, the H-2 workers are all too often virtually enslaved in the United States.

Americans abroad also engage in trafficking by traveling to poorer countries to engage in sex tourism. American servicemen and peacekeepers have hired trafficked women when posted overseas.[27] In Kosovo, South Korea, Vietnam, and other countries of Southeast Asia, brothels, often run with trafficked women, have flourished, providing sexual services to American military personnel.[28] Many American peacekeepers in the Balkans hired trafficked women in the pervasive brothels. American military contractors and top-level military personnel were also implicated as suppliers and facilitators of sex trafficking in the Balkans.[29]

American trafficking occurs on American territory outside the 50 states, as a serious forced labor case in American Samoa revealed. Kil Soo Lee operated a garment factory in the U.S. protectorate of Samoa from 1998 to 2001 using trafficked workers recruited from China and Vietnam, forcing the women to work eighteen-hour days, but with only sporadic pay.[30]

Labor trafficking victims are engaged in everything from street peddling to housekeeping, from child care to construction, agricultural labor, and landscaping. All levels of prostitution have trafficked women including escort services, massage parlors, strip joints, bars, and street walkers. Indictments of human traffickers reveal that multiple forms of exploitation may occur simultaneously, with women forced to prostitute themselves at night and clean houses or engage in agricultural work during the day.[31]

[26] Kevin Bales and Ron Soodalter, *The Slave Next Door: Human Trafficking and Slavery in America Today* (Berkeley and Los Angeles: University of California Press, 2009).

[27] Protection Project, *International Child Sex Tourism: Scope of the Problem and Comparative Case Studies* (Washington, DC: Protection Project, Johns Hopkins University, 2007).

[28] Isabelle Talleyrand, Comment, "Military Prostitution: How the Authorities Worldwide Aid and Abet International Trafficking in Women," *Syracuse Journal of International Law and Commerce* 27 (2000), 151–61.

[29] John Picarelli, *Trafficking, Slavery and Peacekeeping* (Turin: UNICRI, 2002); Sarah E. Mendelson, *Barracks and Brothels Peacekeepers and Human Trafficking in the Balkans* (Washington, DC: CSIS, 2005).

[30] The owner was sentenced to forty years in prison and ordered to pay restitution to the 300 exploited workers. John Braddock, "American Samoa: Factory Owner Jailed for 40 Years over 'Human Trafficking'," July 16, 2005, www.wsws.org/articles/2005/jul2005/samo-j16.shtml (accessed June 27, 2007).

[31] "Former Wrestler Sentenced to Life on Federal Sex Trafficking and Forced Labor Charges, April 1, 2008, http://www.usdoj.gov/usao/gan/press/2008/04–01–08.pdf (accessed June 29, 2008).

Moreover, all trafficking does not require the presence of the victim. Body parts are trafficked from the organs of individuals deceased overseas to be used in American transplant operations.[32] Most Internet traffic at some point traverses American Internet service providers, thereby facilitating the transmission of child pornography internationally. Through the Internet, Americans can view images of sexually exploited children and buy videos of children sexually exploited in other regions of the world. Criminal investigations of American purchasers reveal that many of them hold positions of trust as teachers, counselors, law enforcement officers, and even legal officials.

With few prosecutions of traffickers, human trafficking is increasing because criminals can make significant profits, facing little chance of sanctions or confiscation of assets. The demand for trafficked laborers, affordable prostitutes, and babies continues unabated.

Historical Precedent

There are important historical precedents to contemporary American trafficking. Current illegal immigration strongly resembles the structure of early migration in the seventeenth, eighteenth, and early nineteenth centuries. Much contemporary immigration, as in earlier periods of American history, consists of those who arrive as slaves and indentured servants. Victims of sex trafficking in previous centuries often served members of their own immigrant community. Victims, then as now, were often recruited by means of deception. Corruption of officials overseas, at U.S. consulates, and at the border, facilitated admission in the past as well as today. Trafficking victims were moved long distances within the United States in the late nineteenth and early twentieth centuries. These enduring characteristics differentiate American trafficking from its European counterpart.

Before 1808, importation of slaves to the United States was permitted and indentured servitude was outlawed only at the close of the Civil War by the 13th amendment in 1865.[33] An estimated 645,000 slaves (5.4 percent of the transatlantic slave trade total) were brought to what

[32] Nancy Scheper-Hughes and Loïc Wacquant, eds., *Commodifying Bodies* (London: Sage, 2002); interview with Walter Broadnax, formerly chief operating officer of Health and Human Services, on problems of body parts illegally entering from China and being stopped, 2000.

[33] http://www.loc.gov/rr/program/bib/ourdocs/13thamendment.html (accessed June 26, 2008).

is now the United States, and the number of slaves had grown to four million by the 1860 Census.[34] Only immigrants from higher social classes could afford the high cost of transport to the new world.[35] Therefore, most immigrants who did not come from the elite funded their travel by coming as indentured servants. Indentured servants provided at least 50 percent of all white immigrants to the American colonies between 1633 and 1776, as well as roughly 75 percent of Virginia settlers in the 17th century, continuing on a reduced scale in subsequent centuries.[36] Today, as well, the number of indentured servants probably exceeds the number entering the United States as slaves.

The passage of the Anti-Peonage Act in 1867 extended the prohibition of involuntary servitude to all states and territories of the United States.[37] But even after the Constitutional amendment and 1867 law, debt bondage, and indentured servitude continued in covert forms as evidenced by the importation of Chinese coolies. The Chinese Exclusion Act was passed in 1882 to limit the arrival of Chinese workers but this did not curtail their entry. In fact, Chinese are still brought to the United States illegally, by human "traders" operating in the same southern regions of China, as their predecessors did in the nineteenth century.[38]

Owners and managers of farms and businesses, in the past as they do today, would use recruiters to import foreign workers to labor under incredibly harsh conditions.[39] In the nineteenth century, legitimate employers contracted with Chinese agents to provide workers for their mining operations and railroad construction. These Chinese recruiters used deception, coercion, and drugs to compel immigrants and provided false promises of a better life before shipping them off to harsh conditions in the United States.[40] Labor recruiters from the United States also traveled to Mexico and Puerto Rico acquiring low paid laborers to pick cotton in Arizona. Deception as to their conditions of employment was also part

[34] Slave Census, http://www.sonofthesouth.net/slavery/slave-maps/slave-census.htm (accessed August 13, 2009).

[35] Wesley Craven, *White, Red and Black: The Seventeenth-Century Virginian* (Charlottesville: University Press of Virginia, 1971), 6.

[36] Ibid., 5.

[37] David Northrup, *Indentured Labor in the Age of Imperialism, 1834–1922* (Cambridge: Cambridge University Press, 1995), 142.

[38] Sterling Seagrave, *Lords of the Rim: The Invisible Empire of the Overseas Chinese* (New York: G. P. Putnam's Sons, 1995).

[39] Martin Booth, *The Dragon Syndicates: The Global Phenomenon of the Triads* (New York: Carroll and Graf Publishers, 2000).

[40] Booth, *The Dragon Syndicates*, 203–4.

of the recruitment process there; workers existed in conditions of virtual peonage.[41] The problems of labor exploitation of Mexicans, identified in the 1930s in the mines in the West and in the Southwest in the cotton industry, now exist on a larger scale in the United States, with more regions with vulnerable workers and probably greater numbers exploited.

In the late nineteenth century, Chinese women brought as indentured servants were often forced to work in brothels, particularly in California.[42] Some were trafficked directly as prostitutes, forced to serve both the Chinese and white communities. Congress passed the Page Law in 1875, which required that before anyone from China, Japan, or 'any Oriental country' was given the right to enter the United States, the consul-general had to determine whether an immigrant was entering into a contract for 'lewd and immoral purposes.' The Act also barred the admission of women whom authorities believed were imported to engage in prostitution.[43] Yet this did not end the practice of sexual trafficking, as Chinese criminal organizations still trafficked girls sold by their parents into the early 1900s.[44]

For the white community, these girls were marketed as sexually exotic.[45] They also served members of the Chinese community who arrived without families, and in the racist environment of that period were cut off from sexual relations with the local population. This sexual exploitation of women by fellow migrants noted first more than a century ago is now repeated within contemporary Chinese and Hispanic migrant communities.

The sexual trafficking of Chinese women was followed by a trade in women from Western and Eastern Europe, referred to as the white slave trade. This trade had similarities to human trafficking today, as the exploiters were often either criminal syndicates or networks of human traffickers. These traffickers survived by colluding with U.S. government officials such as police, consular officials, or immigration officials.[46] In 1912, one

[41] Carey McWilliams, *Ill Fares the land Migrants and Migratory Labor in the United States* (Boston: Little, Brown, 1942), 70–90.

[42] Ko-lin Chin, *Chinatown Gangs: Extortion, Enterprise and Ethnicity* (New York and Oxford: Oxford University Press, 1996), 5–6.

[43] M. Margaret McKeown and Emily Ryo, "The Lost Sanctuary: Examining Sex Trafficking Through the Lens of United States V. Ah Sou," *Cornell International Law Journal*, no. 41, 3, 739–74.

[44] Ibid., 745–51.

[45] Ibid.

[46] Isabel Vincent, *Bodies and Souls: The Tragic Plight of Three Jewish Women Forced into Prostitution in the Americas* (New York: Harper Perennial, 2006), 126.

of the New York crime groups made the equivalent of $15 million in today's money from its trafficked women.[47] As post-TVPA investigations reveal, loose networks of individual brothel keepers and pimps still cooperate to manage vice markets throughout the United States.[48]

Government officials, then as now, are facilitators of trafficking. An early twentieth century U.S. immigration inspector was found to be selling passports identifying Japanese migrants as either Canadian or Hawaiian residents.[49] Corruption also occurred overseas. Recent investigations of consulates abroad, as discussed in Chapter 3, indicate that provision of false documents and the complicity of consular officials still facilitate sexual trafficking to the United States.[50]

Immigration data testify to the large market for prostitutes, the significant role of foreign trafficked women in prostitution markets, and the complicity of the police in the perpetuation of the trade. Brothels with women from Japan, Mexico, and the European countries of Germany, France, Belgium, and Italy were found across the United States in Los Angeles, several cities in Texas, Philadelphia, and New York.[51] Police in many urban centers often supplemented their income by protecting the brothel keepers, even tipping off the lawyers of the brothel keepers as to impending raids.[52]

Mobility was always part of American trafficking. Even in the pre-automobile era, sexual trafficking victims were moved between brothels in many cities in different regions of the United States to provide new faces for the market. In 1908, a U.S. Immigration Bureau inspector named Marcus Braun wrote in an investigative report that foreign pimps from all over Europe and Asia brought women into the United States and teamed with brothel keepers to establish a circuit for prostitutes to travel around the country.[53]

[47] Ibid., 128–29.

[48] Swecker 2005 Statement.

[49] John Picarelli, "The 'Modern Day' Trade in Human Beings: How Historical Experience Influences the Contemporary Trafficking in Persons," American University, 2007 PhD dissertation.

[50] Sheldon Zhang, *Smuggling and Trafficking in Human Beings: All Roads Lead to America* (Westport, CT: Praeger, 2007); discussions with Robert Trent, now retired INS criminal investigator who conducted investigations in India of a corrupt consular official, 1998; also an investigation was undertaken in the U.S. embassy in Prague after a trafficking victim in New York escaped her traffickers.

[51] I am grateful to the insights gained from John Picarelli's dissertation, which provide insight into the historical precedents of American trafficking.

[52] Ibid.

[53] Ibid.

Trafficking, then as now, functioned with the collaboration of legitimate businesses. Numerous reports of U.S. immigration officers in the early 1900s address prostitutes being found in hotels, saloons, and other legitimate enterprises.[54]

Distinctive Features of American Trafficking

The United States is distinctive among developed industrialized countries in its history of slavery, higher birth rates, mobility, the severity of its drug abuse problems, the presence of large-scale criminal gangs, and the role of religion in American life. These characteristics of American society, plus its reliance on technology, put a unique stamp on American trafficking.

In all Western European countries and Japan, birthrates are not even at the replacement level, even though some migrant communities in Western Europe have significantly higher birthrates than the national norm. In contrast, the American birthrate is at or above the replacement level, in part attributable to the higher fertility rates outside of marriage.[55] The United States, therefore, has more children than does Europe, and many children are unsupervised as they are born to single or unwed parents who are forced to work two or three jobs to sustain their families. It is, therefore, hardly surprising that a majority of American trafficking victims began their careers before they were 18.[56] This pattern of sexual exploitation of native-born minors of both sexes is a pattern more associated with the developing world and found in Asia, Latin America, Africa, and the Middle East.

In all other economically developed democracies, the preponderance of victims of sexual trafficking are women trafficked from abroad.[57] In

[54] Ibid.

[55] Rob Stein, "U.S Fertility Rates Hits 35 year high stabilizing the Population," *Washington Post*, December 21, 2007, A11; R. Kelly Raley, "The Role of Nonmarital Births in Sustaining Replacement Fertility in the United States," in Alan Booth and Ann C. Crouter, *The New Population Problem: Why Families in Developed Countries Are Shrinking* (Mahwah, NJ: Lawrence Erlbaum Associates, 2005), 33.

[56] Maryland Coalition Against Sexual Assault, "Prostitution, Sexual Abuse and Assault," Fact Sheet, http://www.mcasa.org/pdfs/Prostitution_%20and_SA_20070712.pdf (accessed August 13, 2009). According to the TVPA legislation, there is no possibility to consent to work as a prostitute before age 18. All are considered victims of trafficking.

[57] For discussions of this see Alexis Aronowitz, "Trafficking in Human Beings: An International Perspective," in Dina Siegel, Henk van de Bunt, and Damian Zaitch, *Global Organized Crime: Trends and Developments* (Dordrecht, Boston, London: Kluwer Academic Publishers, 2003), 85–95; Edward Kleemans, "The Social Organization

the United States, a smaller percentage of sexual trafficking victims are foreign. An estimated 14,500 to 17,500 foreign women and girls are trafficked into the United States each year for sexual exploitation.[58] Foreign-born victims of sexual trafficking are most often from Latin America and Asia, and often these victims are forced to serve members of their own immigrant groups.[59]

The United States is distinctive among developed nations in the large percentage of its population who are descendants of slaves. Sexual trafficking of American-born girls and women shares some similarities to the situations observed in Brazil, the Dominican Republic, and other Caribbean countries with long histories of slavery. There as well, minors and sex tourism are an important element of human trafficking.[60] The legacy of slavery is present not only in the racism of American society but also in the structure of black family life, where centuries of slavery emasculated the role of the father and encouraged the breeding of children without attention to their supervision.[61] American welfare policy long provided support for single mothers rather than families, further undermining the nuclear family. The absence of father figures explains the psychological hold that many pimps have over their youthful female trafficking victims who seek in the pimp the fathers they never knew.[62]

Yet the materialism of American society and the sense of personal worth based on income also contribute to female vulnerability. As an American psychologist, Melissa Farley, explains, "U.S. prostitution can be understood in the context of the cultural normalization of prostitution

of Human Trafficking," in Siegel, van de Bunt, and Zaitch, *Global Organized Crime*, 97–104;Elina Penttinen, *Globalization, Prostitution and Sex-Trafficking Corporeal Politics* (London and New York: Routledge, 2008).

58 "Attorney General's Annual Report to Congress on US Government Activities to Combat Trafficking in Persons Fiscal Year 2005," United States Department of Justice, June 2006, 3; for the difficulties of estimating this number see H. Clawson, M. Layne, and K. Small, *Estimating Human Trafficking into the United States: Development of a Methodology* (Washington, DC: ICF International, 2006).

59 "Hidden Slaves Forced Labor in the United States," Free the Slaves and Human Rights Center, Berkeley, 2004, 13, https://216.235.201.228/NETCOMMUNITY/Document.Doc?id=17 (accessed June 25, 2008).

60 Protection Project, *International Child Sex Tourism*.

61 Orlando Patterson, "Taking Culture Seriously: A Framework and an Afro-American Illustration," in *Culture Matters*, Lawrence E. Harrison and Samuel P. Huntington, eds. (New York: Basic Books, 2000), 210–18.

62 Melissa Farley, ed., *Prostitution, Trafficking and Traumatic Stress* (Binghamton: Haworth Maltreatment and Trauma Press, 2003).

as a glamorous and wealth-producing "job" for girls who lack emotional support, education, and employment opportunities.[63]

Much research on the United States highlights the mobility of its population. Americans move more often than their counterparts in Western Europe, changing cities and homes with relative frequency.[64] Patterns of trafficking in the United States also reflect this mobility, a characteristic that has its historical precedents. In the Stormy Nights case in Oklahoma, federal investigators discovered a loose network of 48 pimps who recruited more than 100 girls from Oklahoma City and moved them along trucking routes to Denver, Miami, Houston, and Dallas, thousands of miles from their homes.[65] In the previously discussed Cadena case in the Southeast United States and the Hispanic brothels, discussed in Chapters 3 and 4, there was a constant movement of victims among neighboring states to provide new faces for the customers. In Latin brothels investigated in Montgomery County, the victims traveled each week to New Jersey several hundred miles away and then were sent by van to a new locale along the East Coast for the following week.[66]

High rates of drug abuse exacerbate the American trafficking problem. "In 2006, an estimated 20.4 million Americans ages 12 or older were current (past month) illicit drug users, meaning they had used an illicit drug during the month before the survey interview. This estimate represents 8.3 percent of the population ages 12 years old or older."[67] Pimps keep many youthful and female victims of sexual trafficking dependent by introducing them to drugs as mentioned in the pimp model in Chapter 4.[68] In addition, many women addicted to drugs become prostitutes to support their habits and then fall under the control of pimps

63 Melissa Farley, "Prostitution, Trafficking, and Cultural Amnesia: What We Must *Not Know* in Order to Keep the Business of Sexual Exploitation Running Smoothly," *Yale Journal of Law and Feminism* 18 (2006), 104.

64 Larry Long, "Changing Residence: Comparative Perspectives on its Relationship to Age, Sex and Marital Status," *Population Studies* 46 (1992), 141–58.

65 Chris Swecker 2005 Statement.

66 Thomas Stack, Montgomery County Police Department, Maryland, presentation on investigating human trafficking crimes in Washington Metropolitan area, American University, Washington, D.C., November 6, 2006, subsequently excerpted in Shared Hope International, *Demand*, 88–89.

67 Department of Health and Human Services, "Results from the 2006 National Survey of Drug Use and Health: National Findings," http://oas.samhsa.gov/NSDUH/2k6NSDUH/2k6results.cfm#Ch2 (accessed June 30, 2008).

68 Tina Frundt, a former trafficking victim, contradicted this popular wisdom stating that pimps are so greedy for money that they do not allow their trafficked girls and women to use drugs, "Human Trafficking in Our Region," August 10, 2009, http://wamu.org/programs/kn/09/08/10.php (accessed August 18, 2009).

who traffic them.[69] In a case prosecuted in Oregon in 2006, a woman was trafficked from Mexico to cultivate marijuana. This forced labor in the drug industry was combined with beatings, stabbings, and sexual assault as well as coercion to witness acts of violence committed upon other children and women.[70] The same phenomenon has been observed with Vietnamese trafficked to the United Kingdom to grow marijuana.

American crime is unique in having large-scale criminal gangs who have membership across the United States. These gangs, closely tied to Central America, are now estimated to number 100,000. They have diversified their crime activities to include human smuggling.[71] Furthermore, 55 percent of the gangs are now involved in prostitution.[72] Deported members of these gangs now operate on the Mexican–Guatemalan border in the state of Chiapas, where they have established a smuggling operation for persons, drugs, and weapons. Gang members also prey on trafficking networks and their victims. In a group of Latino brothels investigated in Montgomery County, near Washington, DC, gang members used force against the prostitutes to extract their daily earnings before they were collected by their traffickers.[73]

Another distinctive feature of American society among Western developed societies is its religiosity and emphasis on volunteerism. Both these distinctive features of American society are present in the reaction to human trafficking. Much of the support offered to victims in the United States under the Bush administration was provided through volunteer organizations, particularly faith-based Christian organizations,[74] often to the detriment of secular nongovernmental organizations (NGOs).

[69] Illustrative of this in the case of Harrison Norris Jr. "Former Wrestler Sentenced to Life on Federal Sex Trafficking & Forced Labor Charges: Ring-Leader in Human Trafficking Organization Sentenced" http://www.usdoj.gov/usao/gan (accessed June 20, 2008).

[70] http://portland.fbi.gov/dojpressrel/2006/humantrafficking052406.htm### (accessed June 20, 2008).

[71] Statement of Chris Swecker, U.S. House of Representatives, Committee on Homeland Security, Subcommittee on Management, Integration, and Oversight, March 8, 2006; H. Abadinsky, *Organized Crime*, 7th ed. (Belmont, CA: Wadsworth, 2003), 4–18.

[72] Swecker 2005 Statement.

[73] Detective Thomas Stack, American University presentation.

[74] This also follows from the historical role the church – particularly the Catholic Church – has played in rescuing and restoring refugees. The U.S. Conference of Catholic Bishops, the major funded organization for human trafficking victims' assistance, began its human trafficking work in its Refugee and Migration Services, and is funded by the Office of Refugee Resettlement of the U.S. Department of Health and Human Services. Many Protestant organizations are also involved in victims' assistance as well as such groups as the Florida Alliance for Assistive Services and Technology and the Salvation Army that are not associated with a particular denomination.

Although NGOs are important in helping the victims of trafficking in many countries, the United States is distinctive in the role that has been assumed by religious groups in fighting trafficking.[75]

The Business of Human Trafficking

The FBI has identified many different types of traffickers operating within the United States. These include the international criminal syndicates that also move drugs, mom and pop family operations, and individuals such as diplomats and foreign business executives who arrive with "servants." In addition, there are the pimps who traffic the domestic victims of trafficking and are probably the most numerous of the traffickers.[76] As previously mentioned, American motorcycle gangs as well as Hispanic gangs such as MS-13 are also involved in the exploitation of people. All the business models of trafficking discussed in Chapter 4 are present except for the African model.

Research by Kevin Bales and Stephen Lize of prosecuted trafficking cases reveals:

> Human trafficking operations in the U.S. are carefully planned and orchestrated to *make* victims vulnerable and *maintain* their vulnerability and dependence. Systematic isolation and disorientation of victims occurred in every case researched for this study. Threats of violence or the use of actual violence were used to create a climate of fear. The premeditation and organization needed suggests that most instances of human trafficking and forced labor should be considered as *organized crime*, not simply the opportunistic exploitation or coincidental negligence of an employer.[77]

Many of the smaller entrepreneurs enter human trafficking because the entry costs are low, profits are high, and the probability of apprehension is infinitesimal. Furthermore, with the enormous demand for trafficked people there is not the market saturation as in the drug arena, where stabilization of drug consumption has resulted in turf wars among traffickers.

[75] Many projects are hard to evaluate. U.S. Government Accountability Office, "Human Trafficking Monitoring and Evaluation of International Projects Are Limited but Experts Express Suggestions," July 2007, GAO 7–1034 http://www.gao.gov/new.items/d071034.pdf (accessed August 17, 2008).

[76] Swecker 2005 Statement; Raymond, Hughes and Gomez, *Sex Trafficking of Women in the United States*.

[77] Bales and Lize, "Trafficking in Persons in the United States," 5.

The profits generated from human trafficking vary enormously depending on the number of individuals who are exploited, the sector of the market that is served (upscale vs. migrant workers), and whether the sexual trafficking is a primary or auxiliary activity of the traffickers.[78]

Meat or chicken processing plants can enhance their profit margins by paying trafficked workers below the minimum wage. The same can be said for construction companies and landscaping services that do not pay any form of insurance or workmen's compensation in dangerous work environments.[79]

A prosecuted adoption fraud case illustrates how American-born children can be trafficked for adoptions at great profit. The defendant, Judith Leekin, adopted eleven children in New York under four different names and then moved to Florida. She netted $1.68 million from the subsidies provided as incentives to adopt children whose age, background, or physical or mental disability makes it difficult for them to be adopted. Instead of caring for the children, she lived a luxurious lifestyle and physically and mentally abused the children and deprived them of schooling.[80]

In the sexual trafficking arena, groups that serve a diverse clientele generate greater profits. For example, a couple from Uzbekistan, one of them a researcher at a state university in Texas, trafficked two young women from their home country. Their exploitation of the girls netted them $400,000 in profits within an eighteen month period.[81] In the previously mentioned White Lace, call girls from post-Soviet states serving a high-level clientele in Los Angeles netted the traffickers $7 million annually. Pimps, exploiting young girls and women, make from $500 a night to

[78] For more discussion of the financial and criminal side of U.S. trafficking, see Zhang, *Smuggling and Trafficking in Human Beings*; Ko-Lin Chin, *Smuggled Chinese Clandestine Immigration to the United States* (Philadelphia: Temple University Press, 1999); Phil Williams, ed., *Illegal Migration and Commercial Sex: The New Slave Trade* (London: Frank Cass, 1999); Jeremy M. Wilson and Erin Dalton, *Human Trafficking in Ohio: Markets, Responses and Considerations* (Santa Monica and Arlington: Rand, 2007); Sheldon X. Zhang, Ko-Lin Chin, and Jody Miller, "Women's Participation in Chinese Transnational Human Smuggling: A Gendered Market Perspective," *Criminology* 45, no. 3 (August 2007), 699–733; Bales and Lize, "Trafficking in Persons in the United States."

[79] See Jennifer Gordon, *Suburban Sweatshops: The Fight for Immigrant Rights* (Cambridge: Belknap at Harvard University Press, 2005).

[80] Benjamin Weiser, "Judge Hints at Harsh Sentence in Adoption Fraud Case," *New York Times*, July 15, 2008, B1. 4.

[81] Beatrix Siman Zakhari, "Legal Cases Prosecuted under the Victims of Trafficking and Violence Protections Act of 2000," in Sally Stoecker and Louise Shelley, eds., *Human Traffic and Transnational Crime: Eurasian and American Perspectives*, Sally Stoecker and Louise Shelley, eds. (Lanham, MD: Rowman and Littlefield, 2004), 140–42.

several thousand dollars at times of high demand such as at sports events and conventions. Their income can exceed $500,000 annually merely by trafficking a few women, whereas the Latino brothel case in Montgomery County in which the clients were low-income Hispanic migrant workers, the traffickers earned $1 million annually from the numerous women prostitutes. Profits from trafficking may be much less where the women facilitate other illicit activities and they serve as "the loss leaders."[82]

The exposé of a prostitution ring, resulting in the resignation of Governor Eliot Spitzer of New York, revealed the large sums generated by crime groups providing high-end sexual services. Clients could pay more than $10,000 per meeting with a prostitute, a fee that was collected through an offshore account of a front company the ring established in the Caribbean. The investigation began after the governor's bankers reported multiple suspicious transactions of more than $10,000 made to an offshore bank account.[83] Although the ringleaders faced criminal charges, the governor was not charged even though he violated the Mann Act, a federal offense, for transporting women across state lines to provide sexual services.

Regional Variations and Forms of Human Trafficking

American literature and social science has described urban life as filled with vice, crime, and human exploitation. Authors such as Theodore Dreiser and Upton Sinclair and subsequently black writers such as Claude Brown and Malcolm X captured the prostitution, labor exploitation, and degradation of residents of large American cities. In tandem with these fictional representations, such eminent muckrakers as Lincoln Steffens, in *Shame of the Cities* and scholars of the Chicago school of sociology[84] described the exploitation of the migrant and the native born in the harsh slums of urban America such as New York and Chicago. Human trafficking exists in cities where migrants and poverty are concentrated. But federal and state investigations reveal trafficking

[82] In the Tarzan case, Ludwig Fainberg used trafficked women to draw Colombian drug traffickers to his strip club. For a discussion of the case see Robert I. Friedman, *How the Russian Mob Has Invaded America* (Boston: Little Brown, 2000).

[83] A senior bank official of HSBC bank informed me that colleagues made the bank report to the U.S. Treasury concerning the suspicious transactions from the governor's personal bank account.

[84] Martin Bulmer, *The Chicago School of Sociology: Institutionalization, Diversity, and the Rise of Sociological Research* (Chicago: University of Chicago Press, 1984); Lincoln Steffens, *Shame of the Cities* (New York: P. Smith, 1948).

in almost all states of the United States and every kind of community – urban, suburban, small towns, and rural areas. In all regions of the United States, there is sexual and labor exploitation, trafficked adopted children and brides,[85] and men who access child pornography from the privacy of their homes.[86]

Demographic changes in the United States help to explain the growth and diffusion of victims. Ethnic diversity is no longer confined to large cities such as New York, Philadelphia, Chicago, and Los Angeles. Rather, smaller cities such as St. Paul, Minnesota in the northern Midwest, which has welcomed waves of immigrants from conflict regions in Southeast Asia and Africa, have identified trafficking within these ethnic communities.

Human trafficking occurs in the most affluent counties in the United States, such as in Montgomery and Fairfax Counties around Washington, DC, and in states with a strong commitment to the welfare of their citizens, such as Minnesota. The problem is amplified in the border regions of the Southwest, where the sheer mass of illegal migrants strains the resources of any government to safeguard against human trafficking. It also occurs in once homogeneous states with limited minority populations, such as Iowa, Tennessee, and Arkansas, which are centers for the poultry and meat processing industry. Trafficking occurs in the communities surrounding military bases.[87]

The following geographical analyses illustrate the diversity of the phenomenon and its regional variations.

The Midwest

Trafficking in the Midwest comprises trafficking of American-born minor children, Native Americans, Asian brides, Chinese laborers, sex trafficking of foreigners, and the procurement of illegal workers by legitimate employers. Testimony in 2003 in the Minnesota State Capitol, a state known to be particularly proactive in addressing social problems, shows its efforts to combat trafficking even before the passage of the TVPA legislation. Minnesota law enforcement, in conjunction with federal investigators, had broken the Evans family trafficking ring that operated for 17 years, trafficking individuals from 24 states and 3 Canadian provinces.

[85] Hearing before the Subcommittee on East Asian and Pacific Affairs, Committee on Foreign Relations, United States Senate, "Human Trafficking: Mail Order Bride Abuses, July 13, 2004.

[86] Interviews with staff of cybersmuggling center of U.S. Customs Service, 2000.

[87] Raymond and Hughes, "Sex Trafficking in the United States."

The victims in this then largest federal trafficking case were as young as 13 years of age.[88]

Minnesota shares the sexual trafficking problems of other locales with Hispanic, Asian, and Russian women marketed to areas where these immigrant populations live. Yet there are distinctive features. "Duluth has an international harbor ... Native American girls are taken out to the ships to 'service' the sailors." The different refugee populations in Minneapolis-St. Paul are sources of human trafficking victims. Nigerian high school girls in St. Paul were addicted to drugs by their traffickers and then forced to work as prostitutes for Nigerian immigrants, and an American pimp recruited a young woman from Somalia.[89] The large Hmong population, a refugee community from Southeast Asia, creates its own trafficking problems. The Asian mail-order bride industry finds young second or third wives for members of the Hmong community, despite American laws prohibiting polygamy. Girls as young as 13 or 14 have been brought to Minnesota on forged documents showing that they are 18. They are subsequently often subjected to physical, mental, and sexual abuse in Hmong households.[90]

Trafficking in big Midwestern cities, as elsewhere, is aided by the Internet. Since January 2007, police in Chicago have conducted four stings based on Craigslist advertisements, a popular Web-based listing service, and have arrested a total of 149 people on charges including prostitution, juvenile pimping, and human trafficking.[91]

Two cases out of Detroit, Michigan, one of the poorest urban areas in the United States, reveal the broad geographical reach of the trafficking rings and the diversity of crimes that accompany child trafficking. In a late 2005 case,

[88] Matt Wente testimony, Legislative Commission on the Economic Status of Women, Public Hearing on the International Sexual Trafficking of Women and Girls in Minnesota, November 12, 2003. http://www.commissions.leg.state.mn.us/oesw/hearings/11_12_03hearingnotes.pdf (accessed July 1, 2008).

[89] Vednita Carter testimony, Legislative Commission on the Economic Status of Women, Public Hearing on the International Sexual Trafficking of Women and Girls in Minnesota, November 12, 2003, http://www.commissions.leg.state.mn.us/oesw/hearings/11_12_03hearingnotes.pdf (accessed July 1, 2008).

[90] Testimony of Xong Mouacheupau, Legislative Commission on the Economic Status of Women, Public Hearing on the International Sexual Trafficking of Women and Girls in Minnesota, November 12, 2003.

[91] Monique Garcia, "76 Arrested on Prostitution Charges in Craigslist Sting," *Chicago Tribune*, June 14, 2008 http://www.chicagotribune.com/news/local/chi-craigslist-sex-sting_both_15jun15,0,6491915.story?track=rss (accessed July 2, 2008).

The defendants were charged with 27 counts of violating federal statutes including the sex trafficking of children, sex trafficking by force, fraud or coercion, transportation of a minor for criminal sexual activity, transportation for prostitution, sexual exploitation of children, interstate distribution of child pornography, threatening interstate communications, possession with the intent to distribute marijuana, felon in possession of a firearm, money laundering, and use of an interstate facility in aid of racketeering.

The federal investigation stems from Young's prostitution enterprise that spanned from Michigan to Hawaii.[92]

In a separate case near Detroit, minors were transported from Ohio to truck stops near the college town of Ann Arbor, Michigan and subjected to violence.[93] They were then forced to have sex with truck drivers. The same problem of the recruitment of minors to provide sex to truck drivers occurred in the previously cited Stormy Nights case in Oklahoma that revealed intersecting crime networks that moved young trafficked girls long distances along the nations' highways.[94]

Chinese trafficking by snakeheads is also now a problem in the Midwest. Congressional testimony provided the following illustration of the problem there. The situation resembles that of comparable victims on the East and West coasts of the United States where there are many more illegal Chinese. A young Chinese woman felt there was no advancement in the factory where she worked near her home in China.

After being enticed by a snakehead who told her that she could make a lot of money in the United States as a waitress, Ling was persuaded to enter the United States using false documentation. Ling first started working in a restaurant in the Midwest. She was paid approximately $500 US dollars a month ... Finding herself still in debt after several years of work, Ling saw an advertisement in a local Chinese newspaper and decided to take a more lucrative job at a massage parlor. Unfortunately, the massage parlor owner forced Ling to provide sexual services and when Ling refused for the first time, he threatened to send her to the authorities for deportation. Ling was suffering psychologically and physically. Her work there only came to a halt when police raided the brothel and brought Ling back to the police station. She did not speak any English, so the police enlisted the help of a local NGO involved with trafficking victim identification. Ling declined the

[92] "Justice Department, FBI Announce Arrests Targeting Child Prostitution Rings in Pennsylvania, New Jersey and Michigan," December 16, 2005, http://www.fbi.gov/dojpressrel/pressrel05/innocencelost.htm (accessed August 13, 2009).

[93] Ibid.

[94] Federal Bureau of Investigation, "Innocence Lost Initiative," http://www.fbi.gov/innolost/case_sum.htm (accessed July 1, 2008).

offer by the NGO representative ... she was terrified that she would be deported and unable to pay off her debts, and that as a result the lives of her family in China would be threatened.[95]

The long reach of organized crime from China into the interior of the United States reveals that the protections of American law are insufficient to counter transnational crime. The crime group was able to enforce an illegal debt in the United States because they could threaten family members back in China. Without language skills and protection for family members abroad, there was no way that investigators could induce cooperation with the investigation. The same problem was observed in a federal Detroit trafficking case involving women from Ukraine forced to work as strippers.[96] The crime ring, based in Kyiv, Ukraine, was so powerful that many of the trafficked women refused to cooperate with the federal investigators, fearing reprisals against family members in Ukraine. These women had endured enormous abuse, as federal wiretaps on the traffickers revealed their total degradation and violent treatment of the women.[97]

In 2008, a large number of illegal workers at an Iowa kosher meat processing plant were detained and charged with document fraud for working with false social security cards.[98] As at the beginning of the century, managers were implicated in the recruitment of these illegal workers. Underage Guatemalan workers were found performing tasks impermissible for minors. Compounding the abuse was that they were forced to work 17 hours a day when their exhaustion made this dangerous work even more perilous. Once injured, a minor was forced back to work even before his stitches could heal.[99] This case recalls a similar investigation discussed in Chapter 4 in which the managers of a Tyson Poultry plant in

[95] Wenchi Yu Perkins, Congressional-Executive Commission on China, "Combating Human Trafficking in China: Domestic and International Efforts," March 6, 2006 http://www.cecc.gov/pages/hearings/2006/20060306/WenchiYuPerkins.php?PHPSESSID=a434a44f109dac260f724aadb19b802c (accessed July 1, 2008).

[96] "Livonia Man Pleads Guilty to Crimes Relating to Involuntary Servitude of Eastern European Women at Detroit Area Strip Clubs," March 8, 2006 press release, http://detroit.fbi.gov/dojpressrel/pressrel06/de030806906.htm (accessed July 1, 2008).

[97] Discussions with the Detroit prosecutor, 2005.

[98] Susan Saluny, "Hundreds Are Arrested in U.S. Sweep of Meat Plant," *New York Times*, May 13, 2008, http://www.nytimes.com/2008/05/13/us/13immig.html?scp=1&sq=Iowa+kosher+factory+and+immigrants&st=nyt (accessed July 1, 2008).

[99] Julie Preston, "Iowa Rally Protests Raid and Conditions at Plant," July 28, 2008, *New York Times*, http://www.nytimes.com/2008/07/28/us/28immig.html?fta=y (accessed August 17, 2008).

Tennessee were accused of contracting with human smugglers to provide illegal workers for their plant.[100]

South of the United States

Southern trafficking is affected not only by the long-term legacy of slavery and indentured servitude but also by many new realities of Southern life. The South, historically, stood in sharp contrast to the Midwest and the North. It lacked the ethnic heterogeneity of the Northern industrial cities. Its cities were divided along racial lines rather than by ethnic communities. In contrast with the North and the Midwest, much less resources were spent on education and social welfare for the community. The South has also been characterized by long-term traditions of military service, and Southern congressman and senators have secured many military bases for their communities. All of these shape trafficking. The limited educational and social resources for minorities help explain why Atlanta is the epicenter of Afro-American trafficking, particularly that of minors.[101] The service of many military men in Asia helps explain the presence of Asian women in the brothels of Southern military towns.

The South has become more heterogeneous, evolving rapidly in the post-World War II period with the influx of different waves of Cuban refugees to Florida, the migration of large numbers of Mexicans and other Latin Americans to work in Southern agriculture, and the movement of many Northerners to the South. Northern Virginia, once merely a series of suburban communities to Washington, DC, is now a major technology corridor, with nearly 20 percent of its residents born outside the United States.[102] Multiple forms of human trafficking are contained within the extremely diverse ethnic groups. Sex trafficking of Indonesians, Koreans, and Vietnamese as well as Latin Americans has been identified in Northern Virginia.[103]

100 Department of Justice, "INS Investigation of Tyson Foods, Inc. Leads to 36 Count Indictment for Conspiracy to Smuggle Illegal Aliens for Corporate Profit," December 19, 2001, http://www.usdoj.gov/opa/pr/2001/December/01_crm_654.htm (accessed January 9, 2009).

101 Alexandra Priebe and Christen Suhr, "Hidden in Plain View: Commercial Sexual Exploitation of Girls in Atlanta," *Atlanta's Women's Agenda*, 2005.

102 José Loyola-Trujillo, "Immigration and Population Change in Northern Virgina," February 2003, http://www.cra-gmu.org/alerts/NVAPopulationChange1.pdf (accessed August 18, 2009).

103 U.S. Department of Justice, "31 Korean Nationals Arrested Throughout the Northeastern United States in Federal Human Trafficking Case," August 16, 2006, http://newyork.fbi.

The Washington, DC, area is also a center of child trafficking of American-born victims. This trade is often facilitated by the Internet, as in Chicago, as the vice police in Montgomery County, outside Washington, DC, found advertisements for as many as 200 minors daily advertised on Craigslist and conducted a sting investigation netting customers specifically seeking sex with underage girls.[104] Even though several pimps were arrested in the Washington, DC, area in mid-2008 as part of a multicity law enforcement effort to target traffickers of minors, those arrested unfortunately represent only a small percentage of the total.[105]

The Washington, D.C., area, along with New York, poses specific challenges because of the presence of large numbers of diplomats at the United Nations and at embassies in Washington who enjoy diplomatic immunity. Three former Indian servants of Kuwaiti diplomats fled their employers in Northern Virginia and initiated a suit against them.[106] In another case, a Tanzanian employed in suburban Maryland for a high-ranking Tanzanian diplomat was forced to work sixteen hours a day, seven days a work for four years until she escaped.[107]

Sex trafficking in other parts of the South has distinctive features including the presence of sex tourism, numerous victims of trafficking rings, and trafficked women around military bases. Sex trafficking in Atlanta recalls that of the developing world as affluent men fly in and exploit poor local youth. Atlanta has the largest commuter airport in the world and is a site of many conventions, both of which facilitate this trade. As in the Third World, often the victim is found through a

gov/dojpressrel/pressrel06/koreantraffickingarrest 081606.htm (accessed July 2, 2008); http://www.usdoj.gov/usao/vae/Pressreleases/05-MayPDFArchive/05/5305gou w_kom alanr.pdf (accessed August 14, 2009); and information provided by Washington area law enforcement on the presence of Latino brothels throughout the area. Paul Vitello, "From Stand in Long Island Slavery Case, A Snapshot of a Hidden U.S. Problem," *New York Times*, December 3, 2007, http://www.nytimes.com/2007/12/03/nyregion/03slavery.html?scp=1&sq=From +Stand+in+Long + Island&st=nyt (accessed July 2, 2008).

104 Thomas Stack, addressing Russian law enforcement group, George Mason University, June 27, 2008; "Human Trafficking in Our Region."

105 Associated Press, "345 arrested, kids rescued in prostitution busts,"http://www.msnbc.msn.com/id/25378538/ (accessed August 17, 2008).

106 Frank Langfitt, "Servants: Diplomat Held Us as Suburban 'Slaves,'" March 1, 2007, http://www.npr.org/templates/story/story.php?storyId=7626754 (accessed July 2, 2008).

107 http://www.npr.org/templates/story/story.php?storyId=7626754 (accessed July 2, 2008)."Ex-worker Sues Envoy of Tanzania," *Washington Post*, May 2, 2007, http://www.washingtonpost.com/wp-dyn/content/article/2007/05/01/AR2007050101613.html (accessed July 2, 2008).

Web site, the appointment is set up online, and the wealthy customer flies in to have sex with a minor.[108] Yet Atlanta, named by the FBI as one of the fourteen major centers for child sex tourism, is not located in a developing country but is an economic hub of the new American South.[109]

Most prosecuted trafficking cases have few identified victims. But in an Atlanta- based case, 500 to 1,000 women from China, Thailand, Korea, Malaysia, and Vietnam were trafficked by snakeheads in their home countries to work in brothels in Atlanta.[110] This large-scale human trafficking ring continued for years unabated until one of the victims managed to escape her traffickers in the Atlanta airport.[111]

Outside of Fayetteville, North Carolina, with the largest military base in the United States, there are many massage parlors filled with Asian women,[112] recalling the brothels in close proximity to American military bases in Asia.

> Often, U.S. military personnel promise marriage or wed women formerly in sex industries around U.S. military bases in Korea, the Philippines and Okinawa. One battered women's advocate reported that over half the women seeking refuge at her shelter near a military base in Jacksonville, North Carolina, were abused wives of U.S. military personnel. From speaking with her clients at the shelter, she heard accounts of Okinawan women, married to U.S. Marines, who were pressured into the sex industry in the United States by their military husbands. Thus prostitution added another layer to the violence and control of the battering situation. Like the Korean fiancés and brides who had been in the sex industry around the military bases in Korea, many Japanese women had formerly been in

[108] Nicole Edgeworth, "Women Silenced," *The Signal*, April 1, 2008, http://media.www.gsusignal.com/media/storage/paper924/news/2008/04/01/Urbanite/Women.Silenced-3295231.shtml (accessed June 30, 2008).

[109] Verna Gates and Mickey Goodman, "Sex Tourism Thriving in U.S. Bible Belt," Reuters News Service, April 4, 2006, http://www.stopdemand.com/afawcs0112878/ID=175/newsdetails.html (accessed June 30, 2008).

[110] Regan Ralph testimony before the Senate Committee on Foreign Relations Subcommittee on Near Eastern and South Asian Affairs, February 22, 2000, http://www.hrw.org/en/news/2000/02/21/international-trafficking-women-and-children (accessed August 17, 2009); William Booth, "13 Charged in Gang Importing Prostitutes," *Washington Post*, August 21, 1999, A3.

[111] Ibid., Ralph mentions the prosecuted cases in 1999 involving more than one thousand women trafficked from different Asian countries. The case was broken up in Atlanta after one of the women escaped. The origins of the case were discussed with the author by one of the INS investigators.

[112] Rob T. Guerette and Ronald V. Clarke, "Border Enforcement, Organized Crime, and Deaths of Smuggled Migrants on the United States-Mexico Border," *European Journal on Criminal Policy and Research* 11, no. 2 (2005), 159–74.

sex industries around the military bases in Okinawa. Lacking English language and job skills and displaced in a foreign culture, many are at the mercy of their husband/abuser/pimp's demands and are recruited or coerced in massage parlors around military bases in the United States.[113]

Labor trafficking and domestic servitude, also prevalent in the South, have received less attention than sex trafficking.[114] The Ramos brothers, prosecuted in Florida, enslaved and brutalized Mexicans on farms. The victims were so numerous and the exploitation so lengthy that the Ramos brothers and a cousin were forced at sentencing to surrender an unprecedented $3 million of property purchased with the proceeds of this labor exploitation.[115] The reconstruction of New Orleans post-Katrina provides an urban Southern example of labor exploitation. Black, Native American, Asian, and poor white reconstruction workers in post-Katrina New Orleans lived "in an unprecedented level of exploitation," facing toxicity and threats of police and immigration raids, without any guarantee of a fair day's pay or any pay at all."[116] In addition, one group of Asian reconstruction workers was "held captive by contractors in a mid-city hotel."[117] There was minimal governmental response to this labor abuse and trafficking, facilitated by the presidential suspension of the Davis-Bacon Act, which requires that prevailing wages be paid on public works projects.

Human trafficking has been a hallmark of New Orleans, but extensive labor trafficking is new. New Orleans, as a major port, was one of the key locales of the white slave trade a century ago. It has remained a center of prostitution and child trafficking since then.[118] One form of human exploitation complements another.

113 Raymond, Hughes, and Gomez, *Sex Trafficking of Women in the United States*.

114 Florida State University Center for the Advancement of Human Rights, *Florida Responds to Human Trafficking*, 2003, 37–62, http://www.cahr.fsu.edu/H%20-%20Chapter%202.pdf (accessed May 25, 2008).

115 John Bowe, *Nobodies: Modern American Slave Labor and the Dark Side of the New Global Economy* (New York: Random House, 2007), 2–85. In contrast to many labor traffickers, they received lengthy prison sentences.

116 Judith Browne-Dianis, Jennifer Lai, Marielena Hincapie, Saket Soni, "And Injustice for All: Workers' Lives in the Reconstruction of New Orleans," 2008, 8, http://www.advancementproject.org/reports/workersreport.pdf (accessed August 17, 2008); David Bacon, *Illegal People How Globalization Creates Migration and Criminalizes Immigrants* (Boston: Beacon Press, 2008), 179–82.

117 Ibid.

118 Estes and Weiner did research there; Attorney General's 2009 Report to Congress and Assessment of U.S. Government Activities to Combat Trafficking in Persons.

Northeast and Midatlantic

The Northeast of the United States has been characterized for more than a century and a half by ethnically diverse populations and high urban crime rates. Competition for police resources has resulted in limited law enforcement allocated to human trafficking despite the scale of the problem.

The Northeast and Midatlantic have the greatest concentration of large cities in the United States, with Washington, DC, Baltimore, Wilmington, Philadelphia, New York, and Boston in close proximity. These cities also have traditional urban centers that are conducive to begging because significant numbers of people walk in the streets or ride public transport during the day. It is hardly surprising, then, that the Northeast was the locale of a notorious case in which several dozen deaf and mute Mexicans were trafficked and forced to beg in the New York area.[119]

Urban proximity also allows victims to be moved easily among different cities. In the Asian Cruise case, Chinese were moved from New York to Washington on the Chinatown buses that transport individuals cheaply between the Chinatowns of the Northeast. In the Montgomery County Latino sex trafficking case, women were rotated among major urban centers in the Northeast every Sunday, traveling long distances by private van to reach the brothel where they would board that week.

In this region, which has long been a mecca for immigrants, victims from all over the world are exploited in brothels, homes, and farms. A group of Korean brothels that stretched from Rhode Island to Washington, DC, was dismantled after a lengthy multistate investigation.[120] A wealthy Indian-born couple on Long Island were convicted of trafficking two women from Indonesia. The Indonesian victims were rescued after five years, but a Maryland suburban couple were convicted in federal court in 2003 after enslaving a Brazilian woman for 15 years.[121] So many women from Africa have suffered long-term enslavement in homes in the New York City area that a specialized assistance organization was established by a woman formerly enslaved in the Bronx for nine years.[122] In upstate

[119] Mirta Ojito, "For Deaf Mexicans, Freedom after Slavery and Detention," *The New York Times*, July 18, 1998.

[120] U.S. Department of Justice, "31 Korean Nationals Arrested Throughout the Northeastern United States in Federal Human Trafficking Case," August 16, 2006, http://newyork.fbi.gov/dojpressrel/pressrel06/koreantraffickingarrest081606.htm (accessed July 2, 2008).

[121] Vitello, "From Stand in Long Island Slavery Case." The author also commented on the Indonesian case on CNN.

[122] David Gonzalez, "When American Dream Leads to Servitude, Fighting Back Is No Easy Feat," *New York Times*, April 24, 2007, http://www.nytimes.com/2007/04/24/

New York, six Mexicans were charged with forced labor after enslaving forty Mexican agricultural workers, ensuring their captivity by threatening serious physical harm if they attempted escape.[123] Many illegal immigrants on Long Island suffer severe physical injuries working in jobs where violations of labor and safety codes are pervasive.[124]

Uneducated workers exploited on Long Island often find work through pickup locales where day workers assemble. More educated illegal workers are often placed in exploitative work situations through illegal unregulated employment agencies that are prevalent in the New York area. For example, educated Kyrgyz, interviewed in a research study on irregular migrants from Central Asia, endured long work hours and labor conditions that violated all labor laws because they sought to send home much needed remittances.[125] These illegal employment agencies, not part of organized crime, reveal how illicit entrepreneurship can also facilitate human trafficking.

Exploitation also occurs in rural farm areas in New York, where there is an estimated undocumented work force of 40–47,000 in the western agricultural region of the state. Only 1200 of the workers have authorized visas. Many of these workers are in slavelike conditions; their exploiters include not only the local farmers but also drug groups such as those from Tamaulipas who have diversified into human smuggling and trafficking.[126]

Southwest

Most smuggled and trafficked people enter the United States through the southern border. As discussed in the supermarket model of trafficking

nyregion/24citywide.html?_r=1&scp=1&sq=When+American+Dream+Leads+to+Servit (accessed July 2, 2008).

[123] Steven Greenhouse. "Migrant-Camp Operators Face Forced Labor Charges," *New York Times*, June 21, 2002, http://query.nytimes.com/gst/fullpage.html?res=9A0CE5D9123FF932A15755C0A9649C8B63&scp=1&sq=migrant+camp+op (accessed July 2, 2008).

[124] Gordon, Jennifer, *Suburban Sweatshops: The Fight for Immigrant Rights* (Cambridge: Belknap at Harvard University Press, 2005).

[125] Saltanat Liebert, *Irregular Migration from the Former Soviet Union to the US* (London and New York: Routledge, 2009).

[126] Renan Salgado and Elise Garvey of Farmworker Legal Services of New York, Inc. and The Human Trafficking Project, "*A Study of Natural Resources, Economics and Labor Trafficking*," The Commodification of Illicit Flows: Labour Migration, Trafficking and Business, Centre for Diaspora and Transnational Studies, University of Toronto, October 9–10, 2009. Discussion of the past prosecution of Maria Garcia-Botello for labor trafficking in upstate New York is available at http://www.farmworkerlegalservices.com/trafficking/MGCase.aspx (accessed December 8, 2009) and Bales and Soodalter, *The Slave Next Door*, 65–6.

in Chapter 4, thousands of miles of inconsistently guarded border serve as crossing points for millions of individuals from Latin America and other continents trying to enter the United States illegally. Many miles of national parks span the border. These lightly policed areas are damaged by the vehicles and the debris of the migrants whose entry is often facilitated by coyotes (professional smugglers).[127] Others enter by car, by small boats that ferry them across the rivers on the border, and through the huge underground tunnels that have been constructed to transport drugs.

This region is particularly perilous for those smuggled and trafficked. Many die each year in the deserts of the United States after being abandoned by their smugglers without food or water.[128] Increasing the dangers for these illegal immigrants are the armed American vigilantes who patrol the borders. These vigilantes have established their own organization, the Minutemen, that advocates citizen action in policing the borders.[129]

The preponderance of victimization in border areas is labor rather than sexual trafficking. Since the passage of the TVPA, assistance to the large numbers of victims of labor exploitation has been prioritized over combating the exploitation.[130]

The presence of large and affluent cities such as Dallas, Houston, and Phoenix with their many conventions and sports events increases the demand for prostitutes, much of which is supplied by pimps with victims of domestic trafficking. Dallas has been identified by the FBI as one of the high child prostitution areas in the United States.[131]

Trafficking victims are also foreign, particularly Asian and Latin American. Trafficked Thai women have been found in major cities in Texas. The FBI created the National Hispanic Sex Trafficking Initiative in December 2004 in response to the exploitation of large numbers of Mexican and Central American women. In a prosecuted sex trafficking case in Houston, resulting from this Initiative, traffickers were charged

[127] Karen E. Bravo, "Exploring the Analogy between Modern Trafficking in Humans and the Trans-Atlantic Slave Trade," *Boston International Law Journal* 25, no. 2 (Fall 2002), 277; for a larger discussion of the comparisons see 207–95.

[128] Guerette and Clarke, "Border Enforcement."

[129] http://www.minutemanproject.com/organization/about_us.asp (accessed August 18, 2008).

[130] Existing nongovernmental organizations have been provided funding by the federal government to support assistance programs. Examples of this include the International Rescue Committee in Phoenix, Arizona, Catholic Charities in San Antonio, and Refugee Services of Austin, Texas.

[131] FBI powerpoint, "Innocence Lost Initiative."

with importing and exploiting eight women from Honduras, Nicaragua, and El Salvador as bar girls between 2001 and 2005. Deceived by recruiters who told them they would work in restaurants, the 16- to 38-year-old victims were kept in peonage and paid as little as $50 a week, thereby falling deeper into debt to their traffickers, who demanded repayment of their smuggling fees. One of the traffickers also negotiated to sell a 19-year-old Salvadoran girl to another bar owner for $11,000.[132]

West

California, the most populous state in the United States, may have the greatest range of trafficking in the West, but the state of Nevada may have the greatest concentration of sexual trafficking in the United States. Four of the 13 identified centers of child trafficking in the United States are in these two states, as the cities of Los Vegas, San Francisco, Los Angeles, and San Diego attract many youthful victims from the United States and abroad. Yet all West Coast states have diverse forms of trafficking, including mail-order brides, trafficked agricultural laborers, domestic laborers, and minor and adult sex trafficking victims.[133] Foreign trafficking victims enter through both the northern and southern borders.

California alone represents more than 10 percent of the official U.S. population and is among the top states in the United States in terms of resident illegal immigrants.[134] California is a destination for many trafficking victims as well as a transit state, as traffickers run safe houses

[132] "Two More Convicted for Role in Sex Trafficking Case," http://houston.fbi.gov/dojpressrel/pressrel06/ho050806.htm (accessed May 21, 2008).

[133] Illustrative of this is a case from Washington State. The Canadian – U.S. border also contributes to trafficking of foreign victims into the state. In one case, a 15-year-old Ukrainian girl entered Washington along with three other minors and their traffickers at an unofficial border crossing where a van was waiting for them. Before reaching Washington State, the girl had been transported from her home outside Kyiv to Russia, on to Frankfurt and from there to Paris. From Paris, she was flown to Montreal and then taken by van across Canada from where she entered Washington State on foot. Office of Crime Victims Advocacy, Washington State, "New Report from Trafficking Task Force," Summer 2004, http://www.commerce.wa.gov/DesktopModules/CTEDPublications/CTEDPublicationsView .aspx?tabID=0&ItemID=30&MId=950&wversion=Staging (accessed August 19, 2009). In Idaho, a 12-year-old runaway was recruited by an escort service in Boise, Idaho and was unpaid for servicing multiple clients on weekdays and as many as ten customers nightly on weekends. Abbie Kircher, "Human Trafficking is Escalating in the United States," http://media.www.arbiteronline.com/media/storage/paper890/news/2008/05/12/Opinion/Human.Trafficking .Is.Escalating.In.The.U.s-3369825.shtml (accessed June 8, 2008). Abadinsky, *Organized Crime*, 235.

[134] Pew Historic Center, Fact Sheet, "Estimates of the Unauthorized Migrant Populations for States," http://pewhispanic.org/files/factsheets/17.pdf (accessed August 17, 2008).

there to shelter victims before moving them to further destinations.[135] The size of the state and the diversity of the trafficking provide an enormous challenge to state law enforcement, particularly as much trafficking occurs on isolated farms removed from external scrutiny and in distinct ethnic communities.[136]

California cannot match Nevada in sex trafficking, but it still draws many victims because of the attraction of Hollywood, the entertainment business, sports, and conventions. The mobility of Californians and the presence of long-distance highways have also contributed to the trafficking of minors along the state highway system.[137]

Nevada, like Thailand and other locales in Southeast Asia, has developed its economy benefiting from sex tourism and gambling. Las Vegas was at least partially built with money diverted from the Teamsters' Union treasury by the American mafia.[138]

Apart from Nevada's long-term distinction as the gambling capital of the United States, it is the only state with legalized prostitution. But in most of the state, including the city of Las Vegas, prostitution is illegal. The legalization of prostitution in parts of Nevada has not diminished the illicit trade that flourishes in Las Vegas and other parts of the state. Visiting Las Vegas, one would not know that prostitution was illegal, as advertisements for foreign-born and American women are everywhere. Moreover, 173 pages of the 2007 Las Vegas telephone book contained advertisements for escort and massage services and illegal houses of prostitution.[139]

Intense law enforcement efforts to remove organized crime from Las Vegas casinos resulted in the reduction of mob influence on gambling and its transfer to peripheral businesses such as prostitution.[140] In this respect, Nevada resembles Atlantic City, New Jersey, another urban economy

135 Bales and Lize, "Trafficking in Persons in the United States," 35.

136 California Alliance to Combat Trafficking and Slavery Task Force, "Human Trafficking in California," October 2007, http://safestate.org/documents/HT_Report_Executive_Summary.pdf (accessed August 17, 2008).

137 Adapted from Bay Fang, "Young Lives For Sale," *U.S. News & World Report* 139, no. 15 (24 October 2005), http://www.humantrafficking.org/updates/278 (accessed June 9, 2008).

138 Abadinsky, Organized Crime, 235–37.

139 Melissa Farley, *Prostitution & Trafficking in Nevada: Making the Connections* (San Francisco: Prostitution Research and Education, 2007), 148.

140 Ronald A. Farrell, *The Black Book and the Mob: The Untold Story of the Control of Nevada's Casinos* (Madison, WI: University of Wisconsin Press, 1995); interview with the former head of the Organized Crime Strike Force for Las Vegas in the late 1990s.

based on gambling. Because the Las Vegas economy is so dependent on gambling and the accompanying prostitution, there have been almost no crackdowns on the legitimate facilitators of this business (the hotels, advertising outlets, or newspapers that market the sexual services). Moreover, there have been few arrests of domestic or foreign traffickers who exploit women and young girls. As elsewhere in the world, large-scale trafficking can flourish in Nevada because of the protection of politicians and corruption.[141]

The American Response to Trafficking

The Clinton administration was the first to recognize the severity of trafficking in the United States. With the issuance of a presidential directive in 1998, the government launched a three-pronged strategy to prevent trafficking, assist victims, and prosecute traffickers that has continued despite changes in administration.[142] The orientation of the assistance providers has, however, changed with the presidents. Under the Bush administration, those assisting victims both in the United States and abroad were more often religious groups, frequently of conservative religious persuasion, whereas under President Obama, there is a less ideological approach to trafficking.

The Victims of Trafficking and Violence Protection Act, first signed by President Clinton,[143] has been reauthorized in 2003, 2005, and 2008 with significant budgets for assistance programs both in the United States and abroad to help victims and provide training for law enforcement.[144] Counter-trafficking efforts since the bill's passage have focused on victims of sex trafficking rather than the more pervasive labor trafficking.[145] Illegal migrants are more often targeted by law enforcement than the smugglers and traffickers who exploit them.[146]

141 Farley, *Prostitution & Trafficking in Nevada*, 135–43.

142 Claire Rebando, "Trafficking in Persons: U.S. Policy and Issues for Congress," Congressional Reference Service, June 20, 2007.

143 Ibid. for a discussion of the passage of this legislation.

144 http://www.polarisproject.org/content/view/198/ (accessed August 18, 2009).

145 For a discussion of the preference to prosecute sexual rather than labor trafficking see Grace Chang and Kathleen Kim, "Reconceptualizing Approaches to Human Trafficking: New Directions and Perspectives from the Field(s)," *Stanford Journal Of Civil Rights and Civil Liberties* 12, no. 2 (2007), 334–39.

146 Julia Preston, "270 Illegal Immigrants Sent to Prison in Federal Push," *New York Times*, May 24, 2008, http://www.nytimes.com/2008/05/24/us/24immig.html?_r=1&scp=7&sq=Bush%20and%20illegal%20immigrants&st=cse&oref=slogin (accessed August 17, 2008).

The TVPA requires the Secretary of State to provide an annual report evaluating foreign countries on their performance in combating trafficking, which has evolved into the Trafficking in Persons Report. This report evaluates counter-trafficking efforts, popularly referred to as "naming and shaming." Countries that fail to meet minimum standards can lose U.S. non-humanitarian assistance, a potent weapon that has goaded many countries into action against trafficking.[147]

Domestically, the efforts to protect victims of human trafficking are divided among numerous U.S. government agencies including the Departments of Labor, State, Justice, Homeland Security, and Health and Human Services as well as Defense.[148] The TVPA established the Interagency Task Force to Monitor and Combat Trafficking housed within the Department of State to improve coordination.[149] The dispersion of effort among so many different bodies has inhibited effective action despite the establishment of the interagency working group.[150]

The special T-visas established for victims of trafficking in the TVPA legislation have not lived up to their promise. These visas for victims of severe forms of trafficking who agree to cooperate with law enforcement have been awarded in limited numbers. Even though up to 5,000 can be awarded annually, in 2008, even fewer visas allowing victims to stay in the United States were awarded than in the previous year. In 2008, only 279 T-visas were approved for victims and an additional 261 for family members. Thus only 2300 T-visas have been issued since 2001 to all victims of human trafficking and their relatives, far below the annual limit.[151]

The TVPA's successes are most evident in the victims' assistance areas as victims are served by residential, medical, and psychological programs

147 Ibid.

148 Attorney General's 2009 Report to Congress and Assessment of U.S. Government Activities to Combat Trafficking in Persons, 1–29.

149 Government Accounting Office, *Human Trafficking: Better Data, Strategy, and Reporting Needed to Enhance U.S. Anti-trafficking Efforts Abroad* (Washington, DC: Government Accounting Office, 2006).

150 See analyses of law enforcement's assistance to victims, Caliber Associates, *Evaluation of Comprehensive Services for Victims of Human Trafficking: Key Findings and Lessons Learned* (Washington, DC: Caliber, and ICF International Company, 2007); H. Clawson, K. Small, E. Go, and B. Myles, *Needs Assessment for Service Providers and Trafficking Victims* (Washington, DC: ICF International, 2003); Heather Clawson, J. Nicole Dutch, Megan Cummings, "Law Enforcement Response to Human Trafficking and Implications for Victims: Current Practices and Lessons Learned," December 2006, U.S. Department of Justice award 2004-WG-BX-0088, http://www.ncjrs.gov/pdffiles1/nij/grants/216547.pdf (accessed August 1 4, 2009).

151 Attorney General's 2009 Report to Congress and Assessment of U.S. Government Activities to Combat Trafficking in Persons, 32.

as well as by hotlines. These programs, as well as others run by NGOs throughout the country, are key in assisting victims and fighting trafficking. NGOs dedicated to fighting trafficking are now functioning in several regions of the country.[152] The opening of shelters for victims in many locales in the United States has brought services and support to victims who were not known until the passage of the TVPA.[153]

Successful domestic law enforcement initiatives include the frequently cited cases of the Innocence Lost Initiative under the FBI that target traffickers of youth, the cybercrime center that combats child pornography, and the regional human trafficking working groups throughout the country that focus diverse law enforcement bodies on the trafficking within their communities. American law enforcement has worked successfully with foreign counterparts to investigate and prosecute American sex tourism and child pornography on the Internet.[154]

The U.S. military, following the passage of the TVPA and under pressure from the U.S. Congress, finally took a strong stand against trafficking, restricting American servicemen from hiring the services of trafficked women.[155] But the problem still persists absent the political will and the resources to address the problem seriously.

States have also coordinated to fight sex trafficking. Illustrative of this is that in 2008, forty state attorneys general reached an agreement with Craigslist in which the online service agreed to curb advertisements in its erotic section. But despite this agreement, the advertisements have not been eliminated, illustrating the challenge of fighting trafficking facilitated through cyberspace.[156]

Conclusion

The United States combines the problems of labor trafficking and forced and bonded labor found in advanced democracies with the problems

[152] Some of the most known are Polaris in Washington, DC, Children of the Night in Los Angeles, and Safe Horizon in Brooklyn, New York.

[153] Ibid., 22–23.

[154] Shared Hope International, *Demand*; Protection Project, *International Child Sex Tourism*.

[155] Brian Parsons, "Significant Steps or Empty Rhetoric: Current Efforts by the United States to Combat Sexual Trafficking Near US Military Bases," *Northwestern Journal of International Human Rights* 4, no. 3 (May 2006), 567–89.

[156] Brad Stone, "Craiglist agrees to curb sex ads," *New York Times*, November 6, 2008,http://www.nytimes.com/2008/11/07/technology/internet/07craiglist.html?partner=rssnyt (accessed January 5, 2009).

of sexual trafficking found in the developing and the transitional world of Eurasia. As in other advanced economies, there is significant labor trafficking in the agricultural, construction, and restaurant sectors. But American trafficking is unique among the Western developed democracies in having a significant problem of internal trafficking of its own citizens, particularly juveniles. Unlike most developed countries, where the preponderance of sexual trafficking victims are foreign, in the United States most victims of sexual trafficking are American-born minors, a fact generally unknown by American society. Sex tourism also exists within the United States as Americans travel between states to engage in sex with minors, meetings that are often arranged through the Internet.

Historical patterns of trafficking endure even though current traffickers do not appear to have links with their predecessors. Southern China still provides many of the forced laborers, just as it did in the past. Women from the Soviet successor states and Eastern Europe are still deceived into the sex trade, as were their predecessors of the "white slave trade" a century ago. Loose networks of traffickers still move their victims within the United States to satisfy market demand. The mobility of trafficking victims appears to be a distinctive American characteristic. The legacy of slavery remains in the disproportionate victimization of black minors in sexual trafficking. Today, unlike in the era of legalized slavery when race was the defining characteristic of slaves, victims can now be of any race or ethnic group. "Race and racial characteristics play a role in determining who will be a victim, the 'value' of the victim, and the type of enslavement to which the individual will be destined."[157]

The problem of trafficking appears to be growing, although the absence of reliable statistics makes it difficult to confirm trends in the problem.[158] The increasing costs of crossing the southern border since post-September 11th controls were instituted have resulted in more illegal immigrants compelled into forced servitude to pay off their debts to their smugglers. The dramatic changes in U.S. welfare policy over the past decade have resulted not only in the feminization of poverty but also in increasing numbers of children and minors in homes struggling to survive. This has expanded the number of abandoned and neglected children, making

[157] Bravo, "Exploring the Analogy between Modern Trafficking in Humans and the Trans-Atlantic Slave Trade."

[158] Clawson, Layne, and Small, *Estimating Human Trafficking*; J. Finckenauer and J. Schrock, *Human Trafficking: A Growing Criminal Market in the U.S.*, National Institute of Justice International, 2003, http://www.ncjrs.gov/pdffiles1/nij/218462.pdf (accessed August 19, 2009).

greater numbers of vulnerable youth available to traffickers. Moreover, the significant profits of the traffickers and the limited chance of punishment have increasingly made trafficking a crime of choice for many criminals.

Contributing to the growth of trafficking are the diverse sources of demand in the United States for trafficked people. Many employers, struggling to compete in a globalized economy, want cheap and compliant laborers who will work long under difficult conditions. There is also a large clientele for sexual services. Male customers exist at all social and economic levels, from the affluent who hire the trafficked women in the escort services to the legal and illegal migrants who hire the sexual services of female trafficking victims from their own cultures. In between are the truckers and many others who hire the services of trafficked minors supplied by pimps. In addition, there are childless parents who fail to scrutinize the origins of a much desired child secured for adoption.[159]

Growth is facilitated by the many ready to be smuggled and trafficked to the United States, including those who seek a better financial future, who seek to send remittances home, or who need to escape violent conflict or repression at home. Some understand the risks they face in leaving for the United States. Others are deceived, believing that they will enjoy excellent pay as domestic servants, restaurant employees, agricultural workers, or babysitters. Their subsequent labor and/or sexual exploitation is often an unexpected outcome of their long journey. Based on case analyses, a third of victims are trafficked after they enter the United States.[160]

Providing the link between the supply and the demand are the traffickers, a diverse group of individuals. Those who traffic individuals to and within the United States can range from large-scale crime groups to loose networks, to individuals or couples who compel one or more individuals into domestic servitude. The groups can be sophisticated, such as the one that supplied women to Governor Spitzer and maintained offshore accounts. Or they can be organizations such as the Latin American gangs that rely on brute force to run their trafficking operations. The trafficking is facilitated by corruption of officials overseas, on U.S. borders, and

159 E.J. Graff, "The Adoption Underworld," *Washington Post*, January 11, 2009, B2, discusses an adoption mill from Cambodia and the prosecution of an American who was part of it.

160 Bales and Lize, "Trafficking in Persons in the United States," found that this occurred in one-third of the cases they analyzed, 5.

within the United States. Moreover, much of this trafficking could not occur without the complicity of legitimate businesses – the owners of commercial real estate who rent their apartments to traffickers; the hotels that let trafficked women come to the rooms of their clients; the newspapers, yellow pages, and Web sites that advertise sex services; or the factories and farmers that employ workers with false identity documents.

9

Human Trafficking in Latin America and Africa

Latin America and Africa are the two poorest regions of the world. The regions have high birth rates, large youthful populations, and economies that are not growing at the pace needed to absorb the expanding work force. In both regions, societies are highly stratified socially and economically, with large numbers of citizens remaining permanently unemployed or underemployed with limited access to capital. They differ from Asia, discussed in Chapter 5, where there are countries with great wealth, access to capital, low birth rates, and without histories of colonial exploitation.

Much foreign aid is abused, leaving citizens with no prospects for education or a decent livelihood.[1] Many children are abandoned by desperate parents or by families displaced by conflicts or disasters, creating serious problems of street children.[2] High levels of corruption prevail in both regions, particularly in Africa, where government leaders have been especially rapacious.[3] These conditions are highly conducive to human

[1] Raymond Fisman and Edward Miguel, *Economic Gangster: Corruption, Violence and the Poverty of Nations* (Princeton: Princeton University Press, 2008); Paul Collier, *Bottom Billion: Why the Poorest Countries Are Failing and What Can Be Done About It* (Oxford: Oxford University Press, 2007); Dambisa Moyo, *Dead Aid: Why Aid Is Not Working and How There Is a Better Way for Africa* (New York: Farrar, Straus and Giroux, 2009).

[2] For discussion, Thanh-Dam Truong and Maria Belen Angeles, "Searching for Best Practices to Counter Human Trafficking in Africa: A Focus on Women and Children," Paris: UNESCO, March 2005.

[3] The report "Equatorial Guinea: Account for Oil Wealth," July 9, 2009, http://www.hrw.org/en/news/2009/07/09/equatorial-guinea-account-oil-wealth (accessed July 18, 2009) discusses the movement of the national treasury to Riggs Bank by the dictator President Obiang; "Tracking Abacha's Stolen Billions," http://www.clickafrique.com/Magazine/

trafficking. Yet, as mentioned in the introduction, the profits of human trafficking from Latin America and Africa are the least in the world. This is not explained by the absence of victims but by the low cost of human life and absence of individual rights. Gender discrimination and machismo in Latin America help explain the disproportionate female victimization, although young boys are not exempt from exploitation.

Both regions have suffered long and permanent damage from colonization. Moreover, the subjugation of people during colonial rule has been perpetuated by domestic elites after independence. Protracted civil and rebel conflicts in Central and South America as well as Africa have only compounded the number of vulnerable individuals ripe for exploitation. Armed criminal and guerilla groups have become traffickers by using their capacity to control and abuse their fellow citizens.

Colonization ended in most of Latin America and the Caribbean more than a century ago, but the legacy of this brutal rule endures in the suppression of indigenous peoples, the limited civil society, and the authoritarian traditions perpetuated in postcolonial governance in the region. The importation of large numbers of slaves and indentured servants into Brazil, the Caribbean, and other South American countries has created a permanent underclass in many countries that is ripe for exploitation by traffickers.

In most of Latin America, cycles of military rule, and violent repression have rotated with more democratic or populist governments. Serious internal conflicts have been perpetuated in Peru and Colombia in South America by funding provided by the drug trade. The Central American conflicts in Nicaragua and El Salvador often received support and training from the opposing sides in the Cold War. Some of the combatants of these conflicts are the traffickers of today and those displaced in the wars are their victims.

Most countries in Africa were freed from colonial rule only in the latter half of the twentieth century. Colonization ended much later in Africa than in Latin America, as the British, French, Belgian, and Dutch held onto their colonial empires longer than the Spanish and Portuguese. The exiting colonists, forced out by wars and protracted conflicts, never trained a postcolonial succession in governance. Rather, their successors were often rebel leaders shaped by conflict rather than by respect for individual rights, a condition conducive to the trafficking of their citizens.

ST014/CP0000000011.aspx (accessed July 18, 2009). http://www.clickafrique.com/Magazine/ST014/CP0000000011.aspx (accessed July 18, 2009).

Civil conflicts have characterized the postcolonial period in Africa, destroying traditional homelands, displacing millions, and creating vast squalid refugee camps where daily survival is an enormous challenge. African strong men have compounded the destruction and displacement. They succeeded the colonial rulers and massacred or starved their fellow citizens. These men are epitomized by such leaders as Idi Amin in Uganda, and the current president of Zimbabwe, Robert Mugabe, who has destroyed the agriculture and economy of the once fertile lands of his country. The post–Cold War period has contributed to a further wave of conflict and destruction, as Africa has become the epicenter of regional wars in the past two decades, creating ever more displaced individuals and refuges vulnerable to traffickers.[4] The more affluent seek the service of smugglers to escape this destruction but all too often they and their children also become victims of traffickers.[5]

Both regions are part of what has been coined the "global south" where large percentages of the population live in absolute poverty, often in overcrowded cities filled with recent migrants from rural areas. Frequently, the citizens have limited access to education and medical care. Also, they live with poor or nonexistent sanitation. The rise of materialism accompanying the drug trade in Nigeria and Mexico has fomented citizens' desire to migrate, and the same phenomenon exists on a lesser scale in other countries in these regions.[6] Consequently, many residents of the global south, out of desperation or unrealistic expectations, seek to move north. In Latin America their destination is most often the United States, whereas residents of North and sub-Saharan Africa seek a better life in Europe.[7] With barriers to entry in all the developed industrialized

[4] Paul Collier and Nicholas Sambanis, eds., *Understanding Civil War: Evidence and Analysis, vol.1: Africa* (Washington, DC: World Bank, 2005).

[5] An example would be Raimo Väyrynen, "Illegal Immigration, Human Trafficking and Organized Crime," Discussion Paper No. 2003/72, World Institute for Developing Economics Research, United Nations University.

[6] Jørgen Carling, "Trafficking in Women from Nigeria to Europe," *Migration Information Source*, July 1, 2005; Jørgen Carling, "Migration, Human Smuggling and Trafficking from Nigeria to Europe," produced for IOM, http://www.prio.no/sptrans/1326102309/file48438_carling_2006_migration_human_smuggling_and_traffiking_from_nigeria_to_europe.pdf (accessed July 17, 2009); also see songs on Mexican drug traffickers or narcocorridos, Howard Campbell, "Drug Trafficking Stories: Everyday Forms of Narco-Folklore on the U.S.–Mexico Border," 2005, http://www.research.utep.edu/LinkClick.aspx?link=015.pdf&tabid=24743&mid=50671 (accessed July 25, 2009).

[7] Claire Ribando Seelke, "Trafficking in Persons in Latin America and the Caribbean," Congressional Reference Service, October 9, 2009, http://policy-traccc.gmu.edu/resources/CRS-LatinAmericanTrafficking.pdf (accessed November 30, 2009).

countries to their north, human smugglers and traffickers exploit the desire of many Africans, Latin Americans, and Caribbeans to move far from their homes. Others from North and East Africa seek a better future in the oil-rich states of the Middle East. Therefore, human trafficking, although often an internal phenomenon in these regions, is increasingly becoming transnational and transcontinental.

Facilitating this movement are the ties of those once colonized to their former colonizers, the presence of diaspora communities in affluent destination countries, and the international links of the recently emergent organized crime groups. Large numbers of women from the Dominican Republic, a Spanish colony until the early nineteenth century, are trafficked to Spain.[8] Italy, home to the second largest Nigerian diaspora community in Europe, had 12,500 trafficked Nigerian women working as prostitutes in 2006, representing approximately half of the prostitutes in Italy.[9] Organized crime groups from Mexico and Central America – gangs such as MS-13–are increasingly identified with human smuggling and trafficking across the U.S.–Mexican border. Since the civil war in Nigeria in the late 1960s, major organized crime groups have developed there with tentacles throughout West Africa. Their international networks, used to facilitate the drug trade and diverse scams, have also been exploited for the international trade of Nigerian women.[10]

Almost all forms of trafficking exist in Latin America and Africa. Many of the victims are exploited in their own or neighboring countries. Trafficking for forced labor – including begging, domestic servitude, and agriculture as well as child soldiers–is more often confined to the region. In contrast, sex trafficking and tourism, the production of

[8] Migration Information Programme, "Trafficking in Women from the Dominican Republic for Sexual Exploitation," June 1996, http://www.oas.org/atip/country%20specific/TIP%20DR%20IOM%20REPORT.pdf (accessed July 15, 2009); "Dominican Republic," *Trafficking in Persons Report 2009* (Washington, DC: Department of State, 2009), 123–34.

[9] John Picarelli, "Organised Crime and Human Trafficking in the United States and Western Europe," in *Strategies Against Human Trafficking: The Role of the Security Sector*, Cornelius Friesendorf, ed. (Vienna: National Defence Academy and Austrian Ministry of Defence and Sport, 2009), 134; Carling, "Trafficking in Women from Nigeria to Europe"; Carling, "Migration, Human Smuggling and Trafficking from Nigeria to Europe."

[10] Francesca Bosco, Vittoria Luda di Cortemiglia, and Anvar Serojitdinov, "Human Trafficking Patterns," in *Strategies Against Human Trafficking*,Friesendorf, ed., 69; Kemi Asiwaju, "The Challenges of Combating Trafficking in Women and Children in Nigeria," in *Global Trafficking in Women and Children*, Obi N. I. Ebbe and Dilip K. Das, eds. (Boca Raton, FL: CRC Press, 2008), 175–94.

child pornography, trafficking for adoptions or organs, more often has international dimensions. Child victimization and forced labor are particularly pervasive in both regions and in Haiti in the Caribbean.[11]

Despite the diversity of victimization and the sheer numbers of victims, there is less systematic analysis of the scale and dimensions of trafficking in Latin America, the Caribbean, and North and sub-Saharan Africa when compared with Asia and the transitional countries of the former USSR.[12] Investigative journalism and reports from assistance agencies and the International Organization for Migration (IOM) provide information on child sex trafficking in Central America, sex trafficking from Nigeria, sexual abuse by peacekeepers, child labor in the African cocoa industry, the pervasiveness of child soldiers in Colombia and the Democratic Republic of the Congo, or the desperate attempts of impoverished Africans to reach Europe. However, much less is known about the involvement of organized crime and other nonstate actors such as insurgents and guerillas in human trafficking than in Asia. Politically motivated groups are clearly dominant actors in the business of human trafficking. Evidence of this is the large number of child soldiers in Africa and parts of Latin America.[13]

Little is being done in either region to combat trafficking. Many countries in Africa, Central America, and the Caribbean have not even achieved the first step, the passage of anti-trafficking legislation, at a time when 80 percent of the world's nations have already adopted such laws.[14] Trafficking persists in both regions because of an absence of political will, financial resources, or state capacity to act. Porous borders in both

[11] Pamela Summer Coffey, Amy Vallance Phariss and Tamar Renaud, "Literature Review of Trafficking in Persons in Latin America and the Caribbean," Development Alternatives, Inc., Bethesda, MD, 2004; UNESCO, "Human Trafficking in Nigeria: Root Causes and Recommendations," Policy Paper No. 14.2 (E), 2006, 16–17; Michale Sheckleford, "Haiti's Dirty Little Secret, the Problem of Child Slavery," September 14, 2006, Council on Hemispheric Affairs, http://www.coha.org/2006/09/haiti%E2%80%99s-dirty-little-secret-the-problem-of-child-slavery/ (accessed July 20, 2009).

[12] On paucity of research on Latin America, see Alexis A. Aronowitz, *Human Trafficking, Human Misery: The Global Trade in Human Beings* (Westport, CT: Praeger, 2009), 91–95.

[13] David M. Rosen, *Armies of the Young Child Soldiers in War and Terrorism* (New Brunswick: Rutgers University Press, 2005), 57–90; Alcinda Honwana, *Child Soldiers in Africa* (Philadelphia: University of Pennsylvania, Press, 2006); Pamela Summer Coffey, Amy Vallance Phariss, and Tamar Renaud, "Literature Review of Trafficking in Persons," 7–8.

[14] United Nations Office on Drugs and Crime, *Global Report on Trafficking in Persons*, 2009, http://www.unodc.org/documents/Global_Report_on_TIP.pdf, 23–25 (accessed July 18, 2009).

regions facilitate the trade. High levels of governmental corruption and the presence of powerful organized crime groups undermine any state capacity to counter trafficking.[15] With limited and underfunded civil societies, there is no effective counterweight to the absence of state action.

Historical Precedents

Rebel leaders in Africa traffic the women and children of their defeated enemies just as they sold their captives to slave dealers in earlier centuries.[16] Before colonial rule in the seventeenth and eighteenth centuries, millions of captured Africans were sold to slavers operating on the west coast and Horn of Africa for transport to the Americas, the Caribbean, and the Middle East. The purpose of this trade in the past was to humiliate the enemy and profit from his loss. Historical traditions are key determinants of contemporary trafficking. Today, instead of selling captured women and children to slave dealers, they are given to human traffickers.

The Librarian of Congress James Billington, in his distinguished book the *Icon and the Axe*, wrote that both Russia and Spain stayed outside the ideas of enlightenment.[17] Just as in Russia, discussed in Chapter 6, no concept of individual rights or of citizenship developed on the Iberian Peninsula. Individuals were expected to serve the state rather than enjoy inalienable rights. Therefore, when the countries of the Iberian Peninsula, Spain, and Portugal colonized Latin America and the Caribbean, their model of the state was implanted in the New World. The Spanish and Portuguese colonists enslaved many of the indigenous populations in Mexico and Central and South America who survived the conquest. Latin America colonists also imported millions of slaves from Africa and indentured servants from Africa and Asia.

Much of the transcontinental slave trade of the precolonial and colonial periods originated in West Africa, with slaves sold for shipment to the Americas originating from coastal and neighboring inland states. The legacy of the slave trade is apparent in the geography of contemporary trafficking in Africa, as mentioned in the Nigerian model of trafficking in

[15] See, for example, American Bar Association, "Human Trafficking Assessment Tool Mexico" American Bar Association, Washington, DC, 2009.

[16] Karen E. Bravo, "Exploring the Analogy Between Modern Trafficking in Humans and the Trans-Atlantic Slave Trade," *Boston International Law Journal* 25, no. 2 (Fall 2002), 207–95.

[17] James H. Billington, *Icon and the Axe: An Interpretive History of Russian Culture* (New York: Knopf, 1966).

Chapter 4. In West and Central Africa, where the slave trade was most pronounced in past centuries, trafficking is more recognized and possibly more frequent with more than 70 percent of the countries in those regions identifying trafficking as a problem, compared to one-third (33 percent) of the countries surveyed in East and southern Africa.[18]

A large-scale illicit trade in slaves persisted even after Brazil prohibited their importation in 1829, yet slavery remained legal until 1888.[19] In the 1840s, 370,000 Africans were sold into slavery in Brazil.[20] This tradition of slavery persists. Whereas most countries in Latin America and the Caribbean report only small numbers of victims, labor authorities in Brazil identify large numbers of enslaved laborers annually working in agriculture, mines, and other forms of hard physical labor. In 2007, Brazil reported that it identified almost 6,000 male slaves of Brazilian nationality toiling in rural areas and in early 2009 Brazilian authorities announced that they had rescued 4,500 slaves in remote locations.[21] Yet this problem is perpetuated not only far from the financial capital of Brazil. In the wealthiest state of Säo Paolo, slaves are imported from poorer Latin American countries such as Bolivia, Ecuador, Peru, and Paraguay.[22]

Indentured servitude in the Americas persisted for a long period on a large scale. Between 1831 and 1920, more than 300,000 Chinese, 59,000 Africans, and more than 525,000 Indians traveled to South America and the Caribbean as indentured servants.[23] As discussed in Chapter 8, many of the Chinese were recruited by deception and force. The same situation prevailed in India, where skilled and deceitful unregulated recruiters with well developed networks recruited men and women as indentured

[18] Aderanti Adepoju, "Review of Research and Data on Human-Trafficking in sub-Saharan Africa," *International Migration* 43, nos. 1/2 (2005), 76; Unicef Innocenti Research Centre, "Trafficking in Human Beings, Especially Women and Children, in Africa," Florence, Italy, September 2003, http://www.unicef-irc.org/publications/pdf/insight9e.pdf (accessed August 10, 2009).

[19] Lana Cristina, "Lula Blames Slavery for Brazil's 'Social Abyss'," July 1, 2005, http://www.brazzilmag.com/content/view/3033/1/ (accessed July 25, 2009).

[20] Picarelli, "Organised Crime and Human Trafficking," 127.

[21] Tom Phillips, "Brazilian Taskforce Frees More than 4,500 Slaves after Record Number of Raids on Remote Farms," January 3, 2009, *The Guardian*, www.guardian.co.uk/.../brazil-slavery-poverty-farm-workers (accessed July 15, 2009).

[22] United Nations Office on Drugs and Crime, *Global Report on Trafficking in Persons.*

[23] David Northrup, *Indentured Labor in the Age of Imperialism 1834–1922*, Studies in Comparative World History (New York: Cambridge University Press, 1995), 156–57; Hugh Tinker, *A New System of Slavery: The Export of Indian Labour Overseas, 1830–1920* (Oxford: Oxford University Press, 1974), 114.

servants.[24] These individuals never returned to their homelands, providing a further legacy of a significant population with recent memories of exploitation.

The Latin American countries obtained independence from Spain and Portugal in the nineteenth century. The legacies of strict class hierarchies, the subjugation of indigenous peoples, indentured servitude, and slavery combined with current limited access of many citizens in Latin America to education have resulted in many "disposable people," ripe for exploitation by traffickers.

In contrast, the colonial powers in Africa – England, France, Belgium, Germany, Italy, and the Netherlands – had all been part of the Enlightenment. The call of the French Revolution was for "fraternity and equality." The Netherlands was a haven for the victims of religious persecution in Europe, taking in the Puritans from England and the Protestant Huguenots from France.

Enlightenment concepts were not applied to rule in Africa, as those they ruled were deemed inferior. When the Western Europeans conquered Africa, they left their ideas of human rights at home. An ideology was even developed to justify this suspension of rights. The British explained their colonial rule of peoples of different races as "the White Man's Burden."

Colonial rule in Africa was as brutal if not more brutal than in Latin America. Millions were forced to work in slave-like conditions in the mines of Southern Africa and on the farms in Rhodesia and Kenya, and under the rule of King Leopold of Belgium many lost their hands and approximately ten million died as the king subjugated his colonists and forced them to labor in the Congo.[25] In addition to the virtual enslavement of local populations, large numbers of impoverished Indians were imported to British colonies in Africa such as Uganda and South Africa to build railroads, till farm land, and engage in heavy labor.[26] Often these individuals were recruited through deception and coercion by skilled recruiters.

Slavery continued in the twentieth century in Latin America and Africa despite state prohibitions. In Latin America, the problem was a white slave trade from Eastern Europe, previously mentioned in Chapters 6 and 7. Over several decades until the 1930s, Jewish women and others were

[24] Northrup, *Indentured Labor*, 62.

[25] Adam Hochschild, *King Leopold's Ghost: A Story of Greed, Terror and Heroism in Colonial Africa* (Boston: Houghton Mifflin, 1998), 225–33; Wilhelmina Klosterboer, *Involuntary Labour since the Abolition of Slavery: A Survey of Compulsory Labor Throughout the World* (Westport, CT: Greenwood, 1960), 141–53.

[26] Northrup, *Indentured Labor*, 111,146; Tinker, *A New System of Slavery*, 277–78, 290.

trafficked from Poland and other places in Eastern Europe to work in Argentina, Brazil, and Uruguay.[27] Behind some of this trade was the Zwi Migdal criminal organization that had tentacles both in the United States and in the southern cone of South America. Thousands of young women embarking from ships in Buenos Aires, Argentina, at the time the capital of one of the wealthiest countries in the world, were met by traffickers. Eventually, Jewish community members organized to meet arriving boats to warn the unsuspecting young women. But they successfully rescued only some from the devious traffickers who survived by means of high-level official protection.[28] The trade ended in the 1930s, as the conclusion discusses, as the result of an unprecedented investigation and the winds of war sweeping Western Europe.

In Africa, an illegal slave trade continued in the Red Sea region during the first third of the twentieth century after the introduction of antislavery patrols by colonial powers.[29] The slaves, obtained as tax payment or as tribute to the local Ethiopian chief, were sold to Arabian traders, who traded them for cotton or copper leaf. The traders sold them as household slaves or for other ends. This trade foreshadows the contemporary trade of domestic servants between Ethiopia, the United Arab Emirates, and Saudi Arabia. This trade includes girls from impoverished families who are placed in virtual domestic servitude.[30] Apart from these countries, an estimated 20,000 to 25,000 Ethiopian women are domestic servants in Lebanon, significant numbers are believed to have been trafficked.[31]

[27] Although much has been written about this in Argentina, I am grateful to Suzanna Sassoun for sharing her materials on this problem in Brazil.

[28] Edward Bristow, *Prostitution and Prejudice: The Jewish Fight Against White Slavery 1870–1939* (New York: Schocken Books, 1982); Isabel Vincent, *Bodies and Souls: The Tragic Plight of Three Jewish Women Forced into Prostitution in the Americas* (New York: William Morrow, 2005); Nora Glickman, *The Jewish White Slave Trade and the Untold Story of Raquel Liberman* (New York: Garland, 2000).

[29] Suzanne Miers, *Slavery in the Twentieth Century: The Evolution of a Global Problem* (Walnut Creek, CA: AltaMira, 2003), 76–78; John T. Picarelli, "Enabling Norms and Human Trafficking," in *Crime and the Global Political Economy, vol. 16: International Political Economy Yearbook*, H. Richard Friman, ed. (Boulder, CO and London: Lynne Rienner, 2009), 85–101.

[30] In UAE, servants from Ethiopia are the lowest tier of domestic servants. When the author was in Ras-al-khaimah, a young Ethiopian servant died under questionable circumstances almost immediately after her arrival. The family that had hired her would not even pay for the return of her body to her family even though this was required by law. Members of the foreign community provided for transport of the body.

[31] Elaine Pearson, "Study on Trafficking in Women in East Africa," Eschborn: GTZ, 2003, 4, www.gtz.de/de/.../en-svbf-studie-trafficking-in-women-east-africa-e.pdf (accessed August 10, 2009).

Distinctive Features of Latin American, Caribbean, and African Trafficking

The distinctive features of trafficking in these regions are explained by the extreme poverty, recent and massive rural to urban migration, the large numbers of conflicts, the low status of women, and the endurance of traditional rituals and beliefs. Sex trafficking associated with peacekeepers is particularly problematic in Africa because of the large numbers of conflicts requiring external intervention. Child victimization is endemic in both Latin America and Africa. Data compiled by the United Nations in 2009 reveal that as many as 50 percent of identified victims are children in both Latin and Central America, particularly the Andean states of South America and West and Central Africa. The only other region in the world where children are so heavily represented is in the Mekong region in Southeast Asia, discussed in Chapter 5.[32]

Child trafficking in these regions is different from that in Europe, where the exploited children are foreigners. In Europe, the children are anomalous because there is universal access to free education, combined with extensive social benefits and protections for children. In contrast, in these regions, many children lack access to education or it is required only at the primary level. When families can afford to educate only some of their children, preference is given to the education of boys in both regions, particularly in Africa. This problem is being accentuated by the financial crisis that began in 2008 as economic pressures on families force them to pull children out of school.

Numerous children live in the streets of teeming cities with limited or no parental supervision. In Brazil and elsewhere in Latin America, the children's vulnerable situation results from poverty, broken families, and drug addiction at home. In Africa, the causes apart from poverty are more often famine and violent conflict in their home regions. Because of these conditions, numerous children live in the streets in Rio de Janeiro and Sao Paolo in Brazil, in Venezuela, in Colombia, as well as in Addis Ababa in Ethiopia, Dakar in Senegal, Lagos in Nigeria, and Nairobi, Kenya. Without parental supervision, children can be forced by adults in their communities to beg or commit crimes and are sold as domestic servants. Both boys and girls from these impoverished areas are trafficked into prostitution.[33]

[32] United Nations Office on Drugs and Crime, *Global Report on Trafficking in Persons*, 49.

[33] Adepoju, "Review of Research and Data," 81; UNESCO, "Human Trafficking in Nigeria: Root Causes and Recommendations" Policy Paper No. 14.2 (E), 2006, 16;

Unique forms of child trafficking exist in Africa that are unknown in Latin America. The demand for child camel jockeys in the Middle East created a lively trade of boys from poor families in Moslem countries. This problem, previously cited in Chapter 5 with reference to boys from Bangladesh and Pakistan, also existed in Africa where 629 Sudanese[34] and 21 Mauritanian former boy camel jockeys[35] were returned in recent years from destination countries in the Gulf. Assistance programs for these boys are now run in conjunction with UNICEF and other UN agencies and financed by the Gulf States in which this abuse occurred.[36]

Rituals assume an important role in African trafficking. Rituals bind women to their traffickers as mentioned in the Nigerian model of trafficking in Chapter 4. The more deadly rituals require the use of human bones and organs for their performance. In the absence of captured enemies, traffickers become sources of supply for the human body parts needed in these rituals. Trafficking for organ removal for ritual and mystic practices has also been identified in Chad[37] and Liberia.[38] All too often the needed victims are children. In Malawi, officials have reported youthful victims being traded for their organs.[39] Albino children are traded for ritual killings from Burundi to Tanzania.[40]

Eleven traffickers who sold albinos to witch doctors in Tanzania were tried in 2009 in their native Burundi. Eight were accused of killing an 8-year-old girl and a man earlier in the year. But these cases are representative of a larger problem. At least twelve albinos were mutilated in early 2009 in Burundi and more than forty have been killed since 2007 in Tanzania. Those who kill the albinos are motivated by greed. At the trial the motives of the traffickers were disclosed. They believed they

Pamela Summer Coffey, Amy Vallance Phariss, and Tamar Renaud, "Literature Review of Trafficking in Persons," 16.

34 United Nations Office on Drugs and Crime, *Global Report on Trafficking in Persons*, 88–89.

35 Ibid, 103.

36 "UN Helps Child Camel Jockeys from UAE Reintegrate in Their Homelands," 19 December 2006, http://www.un.org/apps/news/story.asp?NewsID=21051&Cr=UNICEF&Cr1 (accessed July 15, 2009).

37 United Nations Office on Drugs and Crime, *Global Report on Trafficking in Persons*, 53.

38 Ibid., 53, 109.

39 Ibid., 124.

40 Jeffrey Gettlemen, "Albinos, Long Shunned, Face Threat in Tanzania," *New York Times*, June 8, 2008, http://www.nytimes.com/2008/06/08/world/africa/08albino.html (accessed July 15, 2009).

would receive half-a-million dollars from the sale of limbs and organs that would be used to concoct lucky charms.[41]

Organ trafficking for nonritual purposes has also been identified in both regions. Traffickers in organs for medical purposes have exploited victims in Brazil, Argentina, and Mexico.[42] The same problem has been identified in Ethiopia, where a man was repatriated from the Middle East, where he had been trafficked for an organ.[43]

In contrast with the rare practice of trade in organs for ritual killings or medical purposes, the trade in children for use in conflicts is unfortunately more common. At least 300,000 children have been recruited as child soldiers in at least thirty countries in the world. Many victims, as previously mentioned, are in Asia and the Middle East. Yet Colombia and Central America as well as Africa because of its numerous and extended conflicts are particular loci of this form of human trafficking.[44] Children in Brazil, particularly street children and those in the *favelas* (slums), are trafficked into armed groups that perpetrate the high levels of urban violence. Many similarities have been noted between these groups and child soldiers.[45]

Youth compelled into the conflicts in Central America in the 1980s and 1990s, particularly in El Salvador, founded violent international criminal gangs such as MS-13 that are now engaged in arms and narcotics trafficking.[46] Those trafficked as youth perpetuate the cycle of violence into the next generation.

Children in Chad, Sierra Leone, Liberia, the Democratic Republic of the Congo, Uganda, and Sudan have been particularly associated with the problem of child soldiers.[47] The problem of Sudanese and Ugandan children were previously cited in Chapter 2. In Northern and Eastern Uganda, large numbers of children have been trafficked into the Lord's

[41] "Albino Trials begin in Tanzania," June 9, 2009, http://news.bbc.co.uk/2/hi/africa/8089351.stm (accessed July 17, 2009).

[42] Bosco, di Cortemiglia, Serojitdinov, "Human Trafficking Patterns," 54.

[43] United Nations Office on Drugs and Crime, *Global Report on Trafficking in Persons*, 113

[44] Singer, *Children at War*.

[45] John P. Sullivan "Mars Morphing: Revisiting Third Generation Gangs," in *Criminal-States and Criminal_Soldiers*, Robert J. Bunker, ed. (London and New York: Routledge, 2008), 174.

[46] Casey Kovacic, "Creating a Monster: MS-13 and How US Immigration Policy Produced 'The World's Most Dangerous Gang'," *Gonzaga Journal of International Law* 11, no. 2 (2007–08). http://www.gonzagajil.org/content/view/183/26/ (accessed July 17, 2009).

[47] "Child Soldiers," Global Report 2008, www.childsoldiersglobalreport.org/.../FINAL_2008_Global_Report.pdf (accessed August 10, 2009).

Resistance Army and forced to work as soldiers or are enslaved as wives to the commanders. Others have been transported across the border to Sudan, where they have been forced to battle the Sudan People's Liberation Army. Other children are forced to engage in heavy work to support the combatants – hauling water long distances, carrying firewood, and working as porters. Beatings and rape are used to obtain compliance. Those who resist may be beaten to death by other trafficked children.[48]

Between 2002 and 2003, 8,400 children were abducted in Uganda, bringing to more than 20,000 the number of children trafficked into the conflict since its start in the mid-1980s. Earlier in the conflict, teenage children were trafficked. But by the later years, children 5 to 13 were targeted because of their submissiveness.[49]

Those victimized in conflict regions in Africa are not only children. Trafficked women have been forced to smuggle jewels and other commodities in their vaginas to fund the conflicts. When they are of no more utility, they are killed by being shot through the vagina.[50]

Peacekeepers brought in to police the conflicts have compounded the problem of sexual trafficking in the Caribbean and Africa. In Liberia, there were allegations of troops having sex with girls as young as 12 and in the Democratic Republic of the Congo (DRC), orphans were allegedly given two free eggs in exchange for sex. These child victims in the DRC were just one of the 150 reported cases of sexual abuse committed by the UN peacekeepers.[51] Subsequently, the sexual misconduct of UN forces in Haiti, Sierra Leone, Liberia, and the Democratic Republic of the Congo were documented in a highly critical UN study.[52]

The trafficking of children for illicit international adoption is particularly problematic in Central America and the Caribbean although cases

[48] Pearson, "Study on Trafficking in Women," 37–38.

[49] Ibid.

[50] Interview with Dr. Aleya El Bindari Hammad, co-founder and member of board of directors, Suzanne Mubarak International Peace Movement, and retired top official of World Health Organization, Geneva, June 2006.

[51] Susan A. Notar, "Peacekeepers as Perpetrators: Sexual Exploitation and Abuse ofWomen and Children in the Democratic Republic of the Congo," *American University Journal of Gender, Social Policy & the Law* 14, no. 413 (2006); Keith J. Allred, "Human Trafficking and Peacekeepers," in *Strategies Against Human Trafficking*, Friesendorf, ed., 320–21.

[52] A Comprehensive Strategy to Eliminate Future Sexual Exploitation and Abuse in United Nations Peacekeeping Operations," 2005, http://www.unicwash.org/selected/N0524790.doc (accessed July 17, 2009); Owen Bowcott, "Report Reveals Shame of UN Peacekeepers," *The Guardian*, March 25, 2005, http://www.guardian.co.uk/international/story/0,3604,1445537,00.html (accessed June 9, 2007).

have also been identified in Africa, for example, in Chad[53] and Nigeria.[54] The availability of children for adoptions in both regions is explained by the absence of birth registrations. Registration agencies are often far from the villages where babies are born. Other registration hurdles include the illiteracy, poverty, and ignorance of parents who are unaware that they need to register their children.[55] In the absence of an official record of the child's birth, he/she can easily be trafficked for adoption or other forms of exploitation.

As previously mentioned in Chapter 7, a Nigerian resident of Britain trafficked a child for adoption to exploit financially the British social welfare associated with parenthood. Guatemala is the epicenter of adoption trafficking, although cases have also been identified in Costa Rica[56] and 47 children in Haiti were given to an orphanage in the capital without their parents' permission to facilitate illegal adoptions.[57] Guatemala is known for having the highest number of international adoptions per capita of any country in the world, with approximately 1,000 to 1,500 Guatemalan babies trafficked annually.[58] Children bought in Mexico for $500 can be sold for $10,000 once they have been taken across the U.S.–El Paso border with fake papers.[59]"As Chapter 3 on criminal actors explained, illicit adoptions are facilitated by many in the legitimate economy with respectable professions. "Midwives often persuade poor mothers to sell their children, or deceive them by telling them that their babies have an illness or have died. Sometimes they even drug mothers and steal their babies in order to sell them."[60] Prospective parents in the

[53] United Nations Office on Drugs and Crime, *Global Report on Trafficking in Persons*, 95.

[54] Ijeoma Ezekwere, "Nigerian Police Crack Illicit Baby Trafficking Ring" June 12, 2008, http://www.reuters.com/article/worldNews/idUSL1280842420080612 (accessed August 10, 2009).

[55] David A. Feingold, "Think Again: Human Trafficking," *Foreign Policy* (September/ October 2005).

[56] United Nations Office on Drugs and Crime, *Global Report on Trafficking in Persons*, 138.

[57] Ibid., 146.

[58] Bosco, di Cortemiglia, Serojitdinov, "Human Trafficking Patterns," 57; "Child Protection from Violence, Exploitation and Abuse," www.unicef.org/protection/index_exploitation.html (accessed January 22, 2009).

[59] Jacqueline Bhabha, "Gendered Chattels: Imported Child Labour and the Response to Child Trafficking," http://www.hks.harvard.edu/wappp/research/bhabha_hr.pdf (accessed November 30, 2009).

[60] Bosco, di Cortemiglia, Serojitdinov, "Human Trafficking Patterns," 57.

United States and Europe are the key market for Guatemalan babies.[61] The same can be said for Mexico.[62]

The sexual exploitation of the young through prostitution, sex tourism, and child pornography is all too pervasive in both regions. As authorities in Asia crack down on child sex tourism from Europe, the problem is displaced to regions where there is less risk for the traveler. Therefore, South Africa and particularly Central America have become priority destinations. Girls are the most common victims, but boys are not excluded from exploitation. In Mexico, Central America, and the tri-border area of South America, an especially horrific practice has recently been identified – the trafficking of babies for sexual exploitation and the production of child pornography.

The infant trafficking for sexual exploitation has been identified in centers of organized crime in Mexico, South America, and the border region between Panama and Costa Rica. In these areas, life has no value to the traffickers and to the poor residents whose lives have been shaped by endemic criminality.

In testimony before the Mexican Senate on the need to adopt anti-trafficking legislation, the director of the Latin American and Caribbean branch of the Coalition against Trafficking in Women testified in late 2007 about the abuse of children as young as 6 months of age.

> In the border between Costa Rica and Panama, I saw one of the worst cases in my entire career. A number of families rent little six month old babies to perform oral sex on foreign tourists. The families don't feed them for two or three days so they suck with more force. Some of these babies die from asphyxiation. ... That was not the only case. A few weeks ago two bars were closed in Mexico City that offered oral sex with babies.[63]

After such testimony, a federal anti-trafficking law was adopted in Mexico but it is limited in scope and jurisdiction. In Mexico, because most prosecutorial authority remains with the states, individual states

[61] Discussion of this problem with Helen Mack, human rights activist from Guatemala, Washington, DC, 2008.

[62] "Madre recupera a bebé robada | AlDiaTx.com | Noticias de Dallas Fort Worth | Mexico," November 7, 2009, http://www.aldiatx.com/sharedcontent/dws/aldia/mexico/stories/DN-bebes_07dia.ART.State.Edition1.4b745c.html (accessed November 30, 2009); Ruth Rodriguez, "Recuperan a bebé robada del Hospital General – El Universal – DF," June 18, 2009, http://www.eluniversal.com.mx/notas/605609.html (accessed November 30, 2009).

[63] Chuck Goolsby, "A Focus on the Prostitution of Infants," November 27, 2008, http://www.libertadlatina.org/Crisis_Prostitution_of_Infants (accessed July 20, 2009).

must adopt their own legislation to counter trafficking. Yet only five of thirty-one Mexican states have anti-trafficking laws.[64] In Costa Rica, only in 2009 were laws against internal trafficking intensified and Panama had only a limited number of cases.[65] Therefore, in the absence of an effective response these heinous crimes persist, particularly in the most criminogenic and lawless places in Latin America. Reports of exploitation of infants continue in the drug capital of Tijuana, close to the Mexican border with California.[66] The crime also persists in the triborder area of Paraguay, Brazil, and Argentina, a smugglers' haven and an international paradise for transnational crime and terrorism. In mid-2008 during a conference to discuss human trafficking, members of Mercosur (Latin America's Southern Common Market) were informed of a recent investigation in the triborder area where twenty-nine infants had been rescued from a band of child pornographers linked to Italy who had filmed them in sex acts with adult men. The oldest victim was merely 9 months old.[67]

In contrast to this impunity is Ecuador, which has established a special unit to combat child trafficking, operating in four different regions of the country. Within two years, between 2005 and 2007, 160 cases of cases of sex tourism and child pornography and other forms of sexual exploitation were identified. All victims were younger than 18 years and all those prosecuted were local nationals and were given significant sentences.[68]

Sex tourism is less common in sub-Saharan Africa than in Latin America because there are fewer tourists from affluent countries who travel there. Many are destined for safaris, removed from the urban locales in which children are exploited. Only in South Africa, with its large cities, high standards of accommodations, and excellent transport links is there significant child sex tourism. Visitors from the Netherlands, United Kingdom, and Germany use gifts and money to lure children to nearby tourist locales to perform pornographic acts that are filmed and

64 United Nations Office on Drugs and Crime, *Global Report on Trafficking in Persons*, 134.

65 *Trafficking in Persons Report 2009*, 112–13, 234–35.

66 http://www.libertadlatina.org/Crisis_Prostitution_of_Infants.htm (accessed July 20, 2009).

67 2008 MercoSur Trafficking Conference, http://www.libertadlatina.org/Crisis_Latin_America_Argentina.htm, (accessed July 20, 2009).

68 United Nations Office on Drugs and Crime, *Global Report on Trafficking in Persons*, 161.

placed on the Internet. Some children have been brought to Europe after their parents have been given presents and convinced that their children have a better chance at a job or education abroad. Instead, the children are exploited in European pedophile networks.[69]

Forms of Human Trafficking and the Nature of Human Traffickers

The previous section discussed the distinctive features of trafficking in the two regions. Some forms of trafficking such as abuse of children for child pornography and use of their bones in religious rituals are rare whereas trafficking for child soldiers exists on a mass scale in Africa. This section examines analogous features found in Africa and Latin America. In both regions, forced labor and slavery remain the predominant form of trafficking

In sub-Saharan Africa, three main forms of trafficking have been identified: child trafficking for domestic and agricultural work; sexual trafficking of women and children within the region and overseas; and the trafficking of foreign women into the region, primarily into South Africa. The latter is the smallest of the identified phenomena but women are brought from Eurasia and Southeast Asia to South Africa for exploitation in the sex industry.[70] Many African countries responding to a United Nations survey on trafficking named forced labor as their only identified form of trafficking. This trafficking is not confined to Africa. African males are enslaved on farms in Sicily, young African girls are in domestic servitude in France, and African women have been enslaved in households by African employers in New York City for years before they were liberated from their traffickers.[71]

In North Africa, trafficking for forced labor and sexual exploitation has been identified. Large numbers are smuggled across the Mediterranean by smuggling networks from North Africa, many originating from the sub-Saharan region. Because of the exploitation of some of those smuggled, this movement of people must sometimes be classified as trafficking. The extensive tourism of North Africa has contributed to the importation of women into the region, particularly Egypt, which has an active trade in

[69] Adepoju, "Review of Research and Data," 80.

[70] Adepoju, "Review of Research and Data," 96; Bridget Anderson and Julia O'Connell Davidson, *Is Trafficking in Human Beings Demand-Driven? A Multi-Country Pilot Study* (Geneva: IOM, 2003); United Nations Office on Drugs and Crime, *Global Report on Trafficking in Persons*, 127.

[71] See discussions on this in Chapters 5 and 6.

women from the former USSR. In a case reported by the head of the IOM office in Moscow, a young Uzbek woman was taken to Egypt in 2007 by a Russian-speaking crime organization. She was raped and brutalized by the Bedouins in the desert before being handed over several months later to criminals in Israel.[72]

Analysts have documented in newspaper stories and on film the lives of African children forced to toil in the cocoa industry and fish in dangerous waters, giving some context and powerful images to this victimization. The stories of children under 11 forced to carry heavy sacks, work 100 hours weekly to grow cocoa, and constantly beaten, has mobilized consumers to demand fair trade cocoa to be used by chocolate producers.[73] Unfortunately, the fish caught by the enslaved children of Ghana have no such international market and therefore there is limited leverage over the fishermen. These children, often orphans, are forced, at the peril of their lives, to recover fish and repair nets in Lake Volta.[74] Boys are maimed or die, as they all too often get caught in the nets. Yet those who attempt to free the children often find they resist as they have bonded with their exploiters.[75]

Domestic servitude is a reality for tens if not hundreds of thousands of girls and women on the African continent. Little is done to address this all too pervasive phenomenon because of the low status of women and the absence of alternatives. Violence keeps workers submissive, and long hours, no days off, and limited or no pay are all too often the norm. A window into this exploitation has been provided by cases of African

[72] The woman was eventually rescued after an extended time in Israel when a man in a neighboring building saw too many men coming in and out of the room and reported the situation to the police.

[73] First Annual Report, Oversight of Public and Private Initiatives to Eliminate the Worst Forms of Child Labor in the Cocoa Sector in Cote d'Ivoire and Ghana, http://www.childlabor-payson.org/FirstAnnualReport.pdf (accessed July 17, 2009); Kevin Bales, *Ending Slavery: How We Free Today's Slaves* (Berkeley and Los Angeles: University of California Press, 2007), 184–96; Amos Owen Thomas, "Migrant, Trafficked and Bonded Workers: Rights Abuse of Human Resource Mis-Management," in *Repositioning African Business and Development for the 21st Century*, ed. Simon Sigúe, http://www.iaabd.org/2009_iaabd_proceedings/track10b.pdf (accessed July 18, 2009).

[74] Sharon LaFraniers, "Africa's World of Forced Labor, through the Eyes of a 6-Year-Old," *New York Times*, October 29, 2006, 8–9; Raggie Johansen, "Child Trafficking in Ghana," http://www.unodc.org/newsletter/en/perspectives/0601/page002.html (accessed August 7, 2009).

[75] Daniel Kweku Sam, "Child Trafficking for Labor Exploitation: The Case of Ghanaian Children in the Fishing Industry," presented at the conference, The Commodification of Illicit Flows: Labor Migration, Trafficking, and Business, Centre for Diaspora and Transnational Studies, University of Toronto, October 9–10, 2009.

domestic servitude disclosed in both the United States and Europe and discussed in those respective chapters.

Adult women are sexually exploited in many parts of sub-Saharan Africa. These women, along with North African women, are trafficked to Europe and the Middle East, where they are enslaved. Much has been written about the enslavement of women from Nigeria and by Nigerian crime groups, as discussed subsequently, but much less is known about the trafficking from regions other than West Africa. A tragic case from Cyprus illustrates the unique problems of women trafficked from traditional Moslem states. According to a Cypriot law enforcement official, a North African woman, engaged to be married, was offered employment as a domestic in Cyprus that would allow her to save the money needed for her marriage. Instead, the woman was trafficked into prostitution. When she was liberated from her traffickers, there was no possibility of repatriation. Her fiancé would not take her back because she had been violated. Her mother warned her not to return. Even though her mother recognized that her prostitution was not her fault, her brother, a member of the Islamic Brotherhood, would kill her for discrediting the family honor.[76]

In Latin America and the Caribbean, in contrast with Africa, many of the reported cases are of sexual exploitation, suggesting that this is the preeminent form of exploitation.[77] Very young enslaved children in Haiti empty bedpans and walk for miles to fetch water. But the pervasiveness of this phenomenon with hundreds of thousands of children has been called a "dirty little secret."[78] The absence of reporting is an artifact of the social and economic structure of Latin America rather than the existing reality of exploitation.[79] The elites in Latin America for centuries have exploited the indigenous populations, slaves and *mestizos* (mixed race individuals). It is on their lands, in the mines that they own, and in their homes where most of the labor exploitation occurs. Their properties and their elite status remain outside the scrutiny of law enforcement. Therefore, most Latin American forced labor remains unidentified, its victims unassisted, and the

[76] Talk of Rita Superman, "The Cyprus Approach to Combating Trafficking in Human Beings," OSCE-UNODC-Cyprus Regional Operational Meeting on Combating Human Trafficking and Money Laundering in the Mediterranean Rim Region," Larnaca, Cyprus, September 18–19, 2008.

[77] Bosco, di Cortemiglia, Serojitdinov, "Human Trafficking Patterns," 46

[78] Sheckleford, "Haiti's Dirty Little Secret."

[79] See the country reports on Argentina, Bolivia, Brazil, Paraguay, and Peru, on the website of antislavery.org, http://www.antislavery.org/english/resources/reports/download_antislavery_publications/latin_america_reports.aspx (accessed July 20, 2009).

perpetrators of this exploitation untouched. Only recently, since the election of President Lula, a former union activist, has Brazil begun to counter slavery with the National Commission for the Eradication of Slave Labor, explaining the impressive numbers of freed slaves cited earlier.[80]

Trafficking for domestic servitude has been identified by the governments of the Dominican Republic, the Eastern Caribbean, Nicaragua, and El Salvador.[81] Yet this is only the tip of the iceberg. The underreporting is explained by the fact that most Latin American countries do not identify such labor exploitation as a form of trafficking in their criminal codes. Labor protections, if they exist, are not observed. Therefore, tens of thousands of children, teenagers, and women continue to be exploited in homes in the Caribbean and Latin America, paid little or nothing for their hard labor. Physical and sexual abuse by their employers are all too common. Yet this practice persists as it has since early colonial rule. Employers often justify this exploitation by the fact that they are providing shelter and food for those who would otherwise be homeless.[82]

Those exploited in domestic servitude are females of all ages. Yet males are exploited in other work environments. Men are increasingly identified as victims of forced labor in Argentina, Brazil, Colombia, Paraguay, Peru, Venezuela, and episodically in Bolivia.[83] Often this forced labor is disguised. Mine owners, owners of charcoal camps, or land owners force workers into debt through overpriced stores.[84] Workers must labor lengthy hours without compensation to pay off their debt that ever compounds and can never be repaid. This same system of debt binds prostitutes to their traffickers.

Labor trafficking is an ongoing problem in the agricultural sector in Central America. In Honduras, the author met professionals whose parents had labored on Chiquita banana plantations, once extensively criticized for their exploitation of workers. Yet those Hondurans explained that they were provided education in schools provided by the multinational corporation that had served as a key to their social mobility. Ironically, they reported, labor exploitation by Chiquita's successors is worse than

[80] Kevin Bales, *Ending Slavery*, 118–26.

[81] United Nations Office on Drugs and Crime, *Global Report on Trafficking in Persons*, 54.

[82] Interview by author with elites from many Latin America, Central American, and Caribbean countries.

[83] Bosco, di Cortemiglia, Serojitdinov, "Human Trafficking Patterns," 62; see country reports of Anti-Slavery on Argentina. Bolivia, Brazil, Paraguay, and Peru.

[84] See Kevin Bales, *Disposable People: New Slavery in the Global Economy* (Berkeley and Los Angeles: University of California Press, 1999), 126–30.

four decades ago.[85] No education is available to the children of those in indebted servitude on the plantations, thereby perpetuating the cycles of exploitation and forced labor.

Much more attention is being paid to the sexual exploitation of women from Latin America, particularly that which occurs internationally. It is estimated that more than 50,000 women from Brazil, Colombia, Guatemala, Mexico, and the Dominican Republic are working abroad in the sex industry, with many being trafficked to North America, Western Europe, and Asia, particularly Japan.[86] The exploitation of Mexican and Central American women has been discussed in Chapter 8. Women from the Dominican Republic constitute a significant part of the supply of trafficked women in Spain, and women from Brazil and Colombia are increasingly identified as victims of sex trafficking in Europe.[87] The trade of women to Japan is facilitated by Japanese organized crime, whose active role in the drug markets provides ready links with Colombians.

Who Are the Traffickers?

The diversity of human trafficking in Latin America, the Caribbean, and Africa means that there is a wide range of people and groups who traffic individuals. As in other regions, there is an even more diverse range of individuals who facilitate the trafficking of individuals, including many employed in the legitimate economy such as those in the transport sector, travel agencies, and those who provide both real and forged documents.[88] For example, "Long-distance truck drivers also traffic their victims from

[85] Interviews by author during visit to Honduras in 2001.

[86] "Trafficking of Women and Children for Sexual Exploitation in the Americas, Fact Sheet, July 2001," Inter-American Commission of Women (Organization of American States), Women, Health and Development Programme (Pan American Health Organization), http://www.oas.org/CIM/english/Traffickingfactsheetfinaling.pdf (accessed July 17, 2009); International Human Rights Law Institute, DePaul University College of Law, 2002," Esclavitud Moderna: Tráfico Sexual en las Americas" http://www.law.depaul.edu/centers_institutes/ihrli/publications/ (accessed July 17, 2009); International Human Rights Law Institute, DePaul University College of Law, "In Modern Bondage: Sex Trafficking in the Americas, Central America, the Caribbean," http://www.law.depaul.edu/centers.../modern_bondage_2_edition.pdf, *(accessed July 17, 2009)*.

[87] Liz Kelly, "Journeys of Jeopardy: A Commentary of Current Research on Trafficking of Women and Children for Sexual Exploitation within Europe," 2002, 26, http://www.antislavery.org/english/resources/reports/download_antislavery_publications/latin_america_reports.aspx (accessed July 20, 2009).

[88] Adepoju, "Review of Research and Data," 79; Christopher Horwood, "In Pursuit of the Southern Dream: Victims of Necessity Assessment of the Irregular Movement of Men

Lesotho to Cape Town, Zambia, and Zimbabwe, with the help of corrupt immigration officials at the border posts."[89] The same process is at work for the smugglers/traffickers who move individuals through Central America to Mexico.

At the high status end of the spectrum are Africans who traffic the servants they take abroad with them. At the other end of the spectrum are the loose networks that often work in rural areas, locating vulnerable individuals for labor exploitation and children for diverse forms of exploitation. Yet larger criminal groups native to the regions also participate in human trafficking. Major crime groups from Mexico, Colombia, Central America, and Nigeria have diversified from the drug trade or have made their crime networks available to the traffickers and smugglers. For example, Nigerians are key facilitators in human smuggling in North Africa as the networks they use for their victims can also serve asylum seekers.[90] The increasing professionalism of human trafficking out of Africa made it one of the European Union's organized crime priorities in 2006.[91]

In addition, foreign groups such as the triads, Indian traffickers, and Russian-speaking organized crime groups also participate in human trafficking, exploiting the vacuum of enforcement in the region. As a result, large number of Thais and Chinese are trafficked to South Africa,[92] Indians are sent to Kenya,[93] and Russian-speaking women are found in North and South Africa as well as parts of Latin America. Chinese are smuggled and trafficked through Mexico and the Caribbean on their way to the United States. Groups that may refrain from cooperating in the legitimate economy cooperate in the illicit. Evidence of this is the case of the trafficking of an Uzbek girl through Egypt to Israel that involved the cooperation of diverse Russian-speaking Bedouin and Israeli criminals.

Much attention has been paid to the personnel, the logistics, and the methods of the drug traffickers of Colombia and Mexico and to a lesser extent, their Nigerian counterparts. But too little is known about the diversification of these crime groups into the trade in humans. A rare

from East Africa and the Horn to South Africa," April 2009, http://publications.iom.int/bookstore/free/In_Pursuit_of_the_Southern_Dream.pdf (accessed July 17, 2009).

[89] Adepoju, "Review of Research and Data," 79.

[90] Carling, "Trafficking in Women from Nigeria to Europe"; Carling, "Migration, Human Smuggling and Trafficking from Nigeria to Europe."

[91] Fred Schreier, "Human Trafficking, Organised Crime and Intelligence," in *Strategies Against Human Trafficking*, Friesendorf, ed., 261.

[92] Adepoju, "Review of Research and Data," 80.

[93] Adepoju, "Review of Research and Data," 79.

example of this analysis was a report by the Mexican National Human Rights Commission in early 2009 that revealed $25 million in ransoms collected by narco-traffickers and their police collaborators by torturing individuals who sought to be smuggled from Mexico and Central America.[94] Without the resources and manpower that are dedicated to dismantling drug networks, law enforcement investigations in the recipient countries have revealed and disrupted only segments of the human smuggling and trafficking organizations. Therefore, there is much still to be understood about how those organizations operate. Yet many reports reveal the increasing involvement of the drug-based organizations and gangs such as MS-13, mentioned in introduction, Chapters 4 and 8, in human trafficking.[95]

In addition to the more known groups, groups out of the Dominican Republic specialize in sexual trafficking, their victims routed more often to Spain and the Netherlands[96] than the United States. Smuggling networks out of Somalia specialize in moving children and elite Somalians who can pay their large fees to safer locales where they can apply for political asylum. Sometimes, those smuggled are able to reach their destinations and find protection as refugees from governments or multilateral organizations and be supported by family in the diaspora. But many do not make it because of the bad intention of the smugglers, their inability to secure safe passage for their customers, and the precarious ships they use to transport those being smuggled.[97] In those cases, the phenomenon more resembles trafficking than smuggling.

In Mexico as in Nigeria, the trafficking is embedded within larger migration flows with their established networks and infrastructure. Motivating the movement is the desire of many migrants to provide better lives for their families. In Mexico, remittances from migrants are the lifeblood of many communities. Likewise, in the Edo state, the source of many Nigerian migrants, grand homes have been built with remittances

[94] Dudley Althaus, "Kidnappers Make Easy Prey of Immigrants" June 18, 2009, http://www.mysanantonio.com/news/mexico/Kidnappers_make_easy_prey_of_immigrants.html (accessed July 20, 2009).

[95] Mark Wuebbels, "Demystifying Human Smuggling Operations Along the Arizona-Mexico Border," report done for Arizona State Attorney General, www.american.edu/traccc/resources/publications/wuebbe01.pdf (accessed February. 20, 2006).

[96] Barbara Limanowska and Helga Konrad, "Problems of Anti-Trafficking Cooperation," in *Strategies Against Human Trafficking*, Friesendorf, ed., 438–39.

[97] In-Depth: "Somalia: Chapter 2: Hambaar: The Smugglers' Network," http://www.irinnews.org/InDepthMain.aspx?InDepthId=44&ReportId=71597 (accessed July 16, 2009).

from women who worked in Europe.[98] Yet crime groups exploit this desire of citizens to live better. In both Mexico and Nigeria, there is a convergence between the locales of human trafficking and the bases of the mighty drug organizations.

Edo state is a center of the Nigerian drug trade but also the source of 80 percent of Nigeria's trafficking victims. The staging areas for the movement of many Mexican migrants to the United States are Tijuana and Ciudad Juarez, border cities dominated by organized crime groups, recalling the supermarket model of human trafficking discussed in Chapter 4. These two urban locales also contain many brothels with women trafficked from other parts of Mexico and are sites of child sex tourism.[99]

Ethnic networks assume a key role in South Africa, as they do in other regions of the world. Vulnerable women in South African refugee camps are recruited by ethnically based crime syndicates, often with ties to their home region. Lesotho-based crime groups recruit street children of both sexes, orphans of AIDS victims and victims of sexual abuse. They are then "trafficked by mostly South African white Afrikaans who use force and/or promise of employment in the Eastern Free State asparagus farms in the border region and Bloemfontein."[100] As in the case of the cooperation of Bedouins and Israelis mentioned previously, the cooperation of Afrikaans and native African traffickers is unexpected as there has been long-term racial prejudice. But the demand for trafficked laborers overcomes standard obstacles to trade.

Unlike in trafficking from Latin America, as mentioned in Chapter 3, women assume a key role in the human trafficking organizations in diverse parts of Africa. In South Africa, local women from Mozambique partner with their compatriots and/or South African men to transport trafficked victims from Maputo to Johannesburg or Durban, where there are large sex markets.

It is in Nigeria where women are particularly prominent, present at every stage of the process from recruitment and deception up to the ultimate point of exploitation in the countries of Western Europe. Men usually transport the women and girls on commission from the madams. "During overland journeys, men known as 'trolleys' in the trafficking network escort women individually or in small groups."[101] On arrival, Nigerian women then exploit the trafficking victims or sell them to

[98] Carling, "Migration, Human Smuggling and Trafficking from Nigeria to Europe," 30.
[99] *Trafficking in Persons Report 2009*, 206.
[100] Adepoju, "Review of Research and Data," 79.
[101] Carling, "Migration, Human Smuggling and Trafficking from Nigeria to Europe," 35.

the highest bidder as has been documented in Italy and legal cases in Belgium.[102]

Routes and Destinations

The limited profits gained from human trafficking in Latin America, the Caribbean, and Africa means that most individuals are exploited locally or in countries close to their homes. Without much to gain from most exploitation, traffickers do not invest much in the long distance transport of their victims. The exceptions are the individuals trafficked to Europe, North America, and the Arab states and those who are exploited in the sex industries of the region by foreign customers.

Diverse routes are used by traffickers in both regions. Nigerians in most cases traffick women to Western Europe by air, sea, or over land through the Sahara.[103] Violence characterizes every aspect of a "victim's journey from Nigeria to Europe, whether on foot, by road, ship or sea."[104]Yet more circuitous routes are also used. Flying via other West African and/or Eastern European countries lessens the risk of having forged documents questioned. Large numbers transit Morocco from sub-Saharan Africa on their way to Spain.[105]

In both Latin America and Africa, the most affluent and industrialized countries are destination countries for trafficking victims. Therefore, South Africa, Nigeria, Brazil, and Argentina are magnets for victims.

Nigeria and South Africa are major destinations for men from such countries as Benin, Togo, Burkino Faso, Mali, Gambia, Senegal, Sierra Leone, Lesotho, Ethiopia, and Sudan.[106] Mozambique and Swaziland are sources of child trafficking victims in South Africa.[107] Neighboring

[102] Esohe Aghatise, "Trafficking for Prostitution in Italy: Possible Effects of Government Proposals for Legalization of Brothels," *Violence Against Women* 10 (2004), 1130; Jana Arsovska and Stef Janssens, "Policing and Human Trafficking: Good and Bad Practices, in *Strategies Against Human Trafficking*, Friesendorf, ed., 177–222.

[103] United Nations Office on Drugs and Crime, *Transnational Trafficking and the Rule of Law in West Africa: A Threat Assessment*, July 2009, 41–48, http://www.unodc.org/documents/data-and analysis/Studies/West_Africa_Report_2009.pdf (accessed July 18, 2009).

[104] Esohe Aghatise, "Trafficking for Prostitution in Italy," 1136.

[105] Jørgen Carling, "Unauthorized Migration from Africa to Spain," *International Migration* 45, no. 4 (2007), 3–36.

[106] Humantrafficking.org, "Research on Trafficking of Men for Labour Exploitation in Africa,"News & Updates (December 18, 2007), http://www.humantrafficking.org/updates/786(accessed July 19, 2009). Côte d'Ivoire is also a recipient of trafficked men.

[107] "South Africa: Open Border for Child Traffickers," 24 November 2006, www.irinnres.org?Report.aspx?ReportId=61657 (accessed January 19, 2009).

countries most often supply the victims because the distances are great and transport by land is difficult, inconvenient, and can be prohibitive. Therefore, Nigeria has more victims from Benin, Togo, and Burkino Faso than does South Africa. But the relative affluence of South Africa provides a magnet for men to travel greater distances. Ethiopians were trafficked to South Africa for construction in preparation for the 2010 World Cup. Tanzanians were also trafficked to South Africa to commit petty crimes.[108]

Trafficking also occurs on a large scale between and within poorer African countries, not only to the more affluent countries discussed previously. The following illustrations do not provide every permutation of the complex patchwork that characterizes African trafficking. Ghanian women are trafficked to the Ivory Coast.[109] Trafficking of young children has been identified in West Africa on a significant scale since the 1980s. Children are taken from Mali, Benin, Burkino Faso, Togo, and Ghana to be exploited on Côte d'Ivoire's commercial farms.[110] Liberation from their traffickers is not always a solution. Retrafficking is also a serious problem.[111] Some children are sent as far as Europe and the Middle East.[112] Togolese girls are trafficked internally as well as exported for labor exploitation in Gabon, Benin, Nigeria, and Niger, and locally whereas Togolese boys are trafficked into agricultural work in Côte d'Ivoire, Nigeria, and Benin.[113]

Other countries in Africa assume an important role as transit countries to wealthier states. Their role is similar to that of Central American countries in Latin America. For example, Ghana is a transit country for Nigerian women trafficked into prostitution in Italy, Germany, and the

[108] Humantrafficking.org, "Research on Trafficking of Men."

[109] J. K. Anarfi, "Ghanaian women and prostitution in Côte d'Ivoire," in *Global Sex Workers: Rights, Resistance and Redefinition*, K. Kempadoo and J. Doezema, eds. (New York: Routledge, 1998).

[110] Adepoju, "Review of Research and Data," 77; Mike Dottridge, "Trafficking in Children in West and Central Africa," in Rachel Masika, ed., *Gender, Trafficking and Slavery* (Oxford: Oxfam, 2002), 38–41; Albertine de Lange, "Child Labor Migration and Trafficking in Rural Burkino Faso," *International Migration* 45, no. 2 (2007), 147–67.

[111] Thanh-Dam Truong, "Poverty, Gender and Human Trafficking in Sub-Saharan Africa: Rethinking Best Practices in Migration Management," UNESCO, Paris, 2006, 62–63.

[112] "Child Protection from Violence, Exploitation and Abuse, www.unicef.org/protection/index_childlabour.html (accessed July 17, 2009).

[113] Adepoju, "Review of Research and Data," 77; Kevin Sullivan, "In Togo A 10-Year-Old's Muted Cry: "I Couldn't Take Any More'," *Washington Post*, December 26, 2008, A1 and A 14.

Netherlands. "Senegal is both a source and transit country for women trafficked to Europe, South Africa, and the Gulf States for commercial sex."[114] Mali also serves as a transit country for a different type of trafficking – the movement of men from sub-Saharan Africa to North Africa and Europe. Some of these victims are stranded in Morocco for four or more years[115] as they are abandoned by their traffickers or forced to wait their turn in an endless line of those who seek to cross the Mediterranean.

In Latin America, as well as Africa, not all trafficking goes from poorer to richer countries. Movement can also occur when there is less governance. For example, the previously mentioned slave laborers toiled in rural areas of the economic powerhouse of Brazil and the earlier cited infant exploitation occurred in the virtual no man's land of the tri-border area of Argentina, Paraguay, and Brazil. Poor areas that have acquired a reputation for a particular human commodity such as babies in Guatemala or child sex tourism in Central America also become magnets for traffickers eager to market their commodity. Therefore, children are trafficked from Honduras and El Salvador to Guatemala, from Nicaragua to Costa Rica, and from Guatemala to El Salvador.[116] Just as migrants from sub-Saharan Africa are trafficked in North Africa on the way to Europe, migrants from South America attempting to reach the United States are exploited in Mexico and other Central American states while in transit. Honduran girls and adolescents seeking to migrate to the United States were trafficked in a border town in Guatemala.[117] Central American men, seeking work in the United States, have become victims of labor trafficking in Mexico, never reaching their ultimate destination.

Conclusion

Both Latin America and Africa share certain common conditions – both were dominated by colonial rulers who destroyed most of the indigenous cultures. They both have long histories of slavery and many weak and failed states, often with limited border controls.[118] Both regions

[114] Adepoju, "Review of Research and Data," 77.

[115] Adepoju, "Review of Research and Data," 78.

[116] Bosco, di Cortemiglia, Serojitdinov, "Human Trafficking Patterns," 63.

[117] "Niñas Hondureñas viven explotación sexual en Chiquimula," http://www.libertadlatina.org/LL_EN_News_11_2008.htm (accessed, July 20, 2009).

[118] Carolyn Nordstrom, *Global Outlaws: Crime, Money and Power in the Contemporary World* (Berkeley: University of California Press, 2007), 71–81.

have high birth rates and insufficient employment for their burgeoning youthful populations. Low levels of education and lack of access to education, particularly in rural areas and urban slums, further impede the competitiveness of African and Latin American populations in the global economy. High levels of corruption and regional conflicts characterize both regions. Africa, particularly, has suffered from rapacious leaders such as those of Nigeria and Chad, who have stolen much and whose economies suffer from the natural resource curse. In both Latin America and Africa, large-scale rural to urban migration into crowded and ill-equipped cities gives rise to a subculture of many individuals vulnerable to traffickers.

Human trafficking thrives in absolute poverty where there is no hope of social or economic advancement at home and many hope that life abroad will bring them greater possibilities. Yet the victims of trafficking are not always the poorest and most vulnerable. As mentioned in the first chapter, the affluent in conflict regions, particularly in Africa, pay smugglers to move them and their children to safer locales, hoping to ensure the security of their families, who all too often become trafficking victims.

The economic and social situation in these two regions differs from that of some developing countries in Asia that have lower birth rates, much investment capital, and significant investment in education. Recent decades have seen social and economic mobility and development in China, India, and South Korea. Nowhere in Africa is there a comparable situation. The recovery from the economic crisis of 2008 is occurring less rapidly than in China and other parts of Asia. It has especially hurt many Mexicans and Central Americans dependent on the U.S. economy as well as others in Africa and Latin America, increasing their vulnerability to trafficking. The global recession creates even greater desperation in those who are barely surviving and reduces investment in youth that will enhance vulnerability to trafficking in the future.

Too little has been done to address trafficking in Latin America, the Caribbean, or Africa, as evidenced by the absence of laws and limited cases. Only in Brazil have large numbers of enslaved laborers been freed since the administration of President Lula, a unique international situation representing strong political will at the top of government. In other African and Latin American and Caribbean societies, trafficking persists as a result of poor governance, absence of political will, and competing priorities such as food, health, education, and shelter.

Many Latin American and African countries have authoritarian rulers with little interest in the social welfare of citizens. Even those with more democratic governments favor domestic elites. They provide few social services to those at the lower end of the social spectrum, to indigenous peoples in the Americas, or to ethnic groups other than those of the ruling elite of African countries. Weak and poorly financed legal systems and unresponsive state bureaucracies, often rendered ineffective through corruption, provide little protection for citizens and do little to counter all forms of human trafficking. In both regions there is limited civil society and limited community involvement in helping the victims of human trafficking or running prevention programs. Much of what is provided by nongovernmental organizations is financed through foreign assistance and multilateral organizations.

The human traffickers who exploit the vulnerable include a wide range of actors. They range from elite individuals to small entrepreneurial networks to the large crime groups that operate from Colombia, Mexico, and West Africa. Most attention is given to the drug traffickers who operate in these regions, but increasingly there is a link between drug and human trafficking. This convergence is insufficiently understood and therefore does not shape the response to human trafficking internationally.

The failure to appreciate and respond to the trafficking problem in Latin America, the Caribbean, and Africa ensures that the problem will grow significantly in these countries in the future. There are no forces sufficient to curb its growth. The push factors from these regions are enormous and the numbers vulnerable to traffickers keep growing. The national and international response is pitiful when confronted with the extent of human misery and exploitation.

Conclusion

Slavery has unfortunately existed throughout history. The most recent precedent to contemporary trafficking is the white slavery that existed among Western Europe, the United States, and South America, particularly Argentina and Brazil, between the 1880s and 1930s. Most that has been written on this period addresses the role of Jewish organized crime and the bravery of one of its victims in bringing this trade to an end.[1] But the historical records of the U.S. immigration service at the beginning of the twentieth century reveal that there were many more victims of this trade than the Jewish women brought from Eastern Europe.[2]

The white slavery of the early 20th century is analogous to the current slavery and not that of forced labor camps under Stalin or Hitler, which was state controlled. The white slave trade was conducted by nonstate actors, as is 80 percent of today's human trafficking according to previously cited ILO data.[3] Like today, white slavery involved the movement of victims long distances across continents and oceans. These victims had often been deceived about their future in their destination countries. Many had hoped that their lives in the United States or the then affluent

[1] Edward Bristow, *Prostitution and Prejudice: The Jewish Fight Against White Slavery 1870–1939* (New York: Schocken Books, 1982); Isabel Vincent, *Bodies and Souls: The Tragic Plight of Three Jewish Women Forced into Prostitution in the Americas* (New York: William Morrow, 2005); Nora Glickman, *The Jewish White Slave Trade and the Untold Story of Raquel Liberman* (New York: Garland, 2000).

[2] John Picarelli, "Enabling Norms and Human Trafficking," in *Crime and the Political Economy*, H. Richard Friman, ed. (Boulder, CO and London: Lynne Rienner, 2009), 96

[3] ILO, Report of the Director General, *A Global Alliance Against Forced Labor* 2005, 10–12, http://www.ilo.org/wcmsp5/groups/public/–dgreports/–com/documents/publication/kd00012.pdf (accessed August 27, 2008).

Argentina would be better than the life they left behind. But once they had been trafficked, they could not escape because the traffickers colluded with corrupt law enforcement officials to keep the women enslaved. Even though the women had been coerced into prostitution, they were stigmatized for engaging in such work. Therefore, even if the women could leave the life to which they had been trafficked, there was no possibility of reintegration into the Jewish community to which they naturally belonged. The older women who survived created a life and society for themselves in which they provided for each other's mutual assistance, a situation that does not exist in much of the world today because of the pervasiveness of AIDS and the early mortality of many women who have been trafficked.[4]

Many confronting human trafficking today look back to this period as a precursor to the mass exploitation of women in sexual slavery today. They see the public outrage over trafficking, particularly sexual trafficking, in the 1920s and 1930s as an important component in its end. But the reality of the situation is much more complex. White slavery ended because of larger political, social, and economic conditions. The combined impact of worldwide depression that reduced demand, increased barriers to entry in the new world, and the winds of war in 1930s Europe did much to reduce the transatlantic trade. Moreover, citizen mobilization and crackdowns on traffickers in Argentina and on organized crime in the United States made the importation of women for the slave trade more difficult.

The white slave trade ended in Argentina when a zealous prosecutor was able to pursue the traffickers because a trafficking victim turned state's witness against family members and their criminal organization who had trafficked her. She helped name not only the criminals but also the high-level officials whose corruption facilitated this trade. With this information, the courageous and indefatigable prosecutor rounded up dozens of members of the criminal organization and severed their corrupt ties to state officials. However, some of the traffickers escaped to Uruguay and even traveled as far as New York to continue the trade in women.[5] Therefore, as is often the case today, the criminal investigation disrupted the network but did not lead to its demise. Parts of the criminal network were able to reconstitute elsewhere.

[4] Glickman, *Jewish White Slave Trade;* information on the culture created by the Brazilian trafficking victims comes from Suzanna Sassoun, Sao Paolo, Brazil.

[5] Bristow, *Prostitution and Prejudice*; Vincent, *Bodies and Souls*; Glickman, *Jewish White Slave Trade.*

Yet such investigators as the one who led the Buenos Aires investigation are the rarity today rather than the rule. All too infrequently, the investigation of human trafficking is assigned to low-level police or members of vice squads who lack the financing or the capacity needed to pursue transnational criminal networks. Human trafficking, unlike the drug trade, does not command the state resources or the access to intelligence needed to dismantle transnational criminal networks. This helps explain the impunity of contemporary traffickers cited repeatedly in this book.

Contemporary trafficking is much more diverse and complex than the white slave trade and cannot be stopped or appreciably slowed by the worldwide economic slowdown that began in 2008. Today's trafficking is truly global. Every country of the world is part of the problem, and the flows of people are much more difficult to chart than the unidirectional white slave trade whose victims flowed solely from Europe to North and South America. Moreover, many countries in the world today are simultaneously source, transit, and destination countries for human trafficking.

Despite the disproportionate attention to sex trafficking today, contemporary trafficking victims are more likely to be victims of labor trafficking, forced to serve as child soldiers, or trapped in domestic servitude. Although victimization is still disproportionately female, as was trafficking in the 1930s, children and minors today make up a significant share of victims in both the developing world in sex markets in the United States and are increasingly visible in streets in some Western European countries.

The Russian meltdown in the late 1980s and the Asian economic crisis that subsequently crippled Asian economies affected trafficking in diverse ways. Yet the crises were regional; many parts of the world remained largely untouched. There was still a strong demand for trafficked people in other parts of the world. Women impoverished by the crisis in Russia and desperate families in Asia sold their children into prostitution to pay debts or to ensure the survival of the rest of the family in this difficult period. Trafficked women could still easily be sold in European markets largely unaffected by the crisis. Sex tourism continued in Asia where the availability of victims merely made trafficked women and children more accessible.

The impact of the economic crisis on labor trafficking was more complex and long lasting. The crisis reduced economic output and therefore the immediate demand for labor, both trafficked and free. Only in the early twenty-first century did the human costs of the crisis of the late 1990s become more apparent. Individuals who incurred debt during this crisis and could not repay were subsequently forced into involuntary servitude or sold their children to settle these accounts. Children who were pulled out of schools by parents during the crisis often labored on family farms. Ignorant and ill prepared for the workforce, these children as teenagers and young adults became victims of labor trafficking. Therefore, the full impact of economic crises may be delayed, the consequences apparent only years later.

The same may be true for the global crisis that began in 2008. Its full human costs will be apparent only in coming decades. As this crisis is global rather than regional, there have been some notable and immediate impacts on human trafficking. Sex trafficking, the most visible and observed form of trafficking, has declined in certain markets such as the Czech Republic where customers have less disposable income.[6] In contrast, in Cambodia, with declining jobs in the textile industry, women are increasingly entering the sex trade.[7] But in the more opaque markets of labor trafficking, the trends are less discernible. Little is known on a global scale except that many trafficked workers and migrants are leaving Russia and returning to their impoverished homes in Central Asia.[8] Yet processes identified in the regional crises of the late 1990s are being replicated worldwide in the global crisis of late 2008. Children, particularly girls, have been pulled out of school and forced to work. Debts of impoverished workers mount and cannot be repaid even with an improved economy. Those offering credit are all too often criminal actors who demand repayment with human lives rather than money. Therefore, the outcome of this crisis will ultimately be more human trafficking. Its victims will be distributed worldwide as the traffickers capitalize on the global economy.

The Reemergence of Human Trafficking

Human trafficking will remain a defining problem of the twenty-first century as the Cold War was in the twentieth century and colonialism in the

[6] Dan Bilefsky, "World's Oldest Profession, Too, Feels Crisis" *New York Times*, December 8, 2008, http://www.nytimes.com/2008/12/08/world/europe/08ihtsex.4.18500177.html?_r=1&scp=1&sq=prostitution%20in%20Czech%20republic%20delcines&st=cse (accessed August 22, 2009).

[7] Siren Report, "Cambodia: Exodus to the Sex Trade? Effects of the Global Financial Crisis on Women's Working Conditions and Opportunities," July 20, 2009, http://www.no-trafficking.org/reports_docs/siren/siren_cb-04.pdf (accessed August 24, 20090.

[8] Farangis Najibullah, "As Work Dries Up, Central Asian Migrants Return Home," February 10, 2009, http://www.rferl.org/content/As_Work_Dries_Up_Central_Asian_Migrant_Workers_Return_Home/1490902.html, (accessed August 24, 2009).

nineteenth. But as shown in this book, these defining issues have shaped contemporary trafficking. A history of colonialism is an important but not the sole determinant of trafficking. Countries such as Thailand, Japan, and Turkey, which escaped colonial rule, remain major centers of trafficking. Yet the legacy of exploitation and destruction of cultures and traditional societies by brutal colonizers is manifest in diverse ways that clearly influence contemporary trafficking. Countries recently freed from colonial rule, such as those in Africa, are less capable of governance, are more authoritarian, and face endemic problems of corruption. As a consequence, these states are less able or interested in protecting their citizens.

Colonial rule tied those colonized to the colonizers. The educational systems of the colonizers and their values and cultures were imposed on their colonists. Trade and people flowed between the colonies and the European colonial powers. These forces shape not only contemporary migration but also trafficking trajectories. Trafficking often flows to the diaspora communities that now exist within the former colonial powers of France, the Netherlands, Great Britain, and Spain. The same can be said of Central Asians who work in Russia, a region first colonized by Russia in the mid-nineteenth century. This illicit trade in people often follows the same routes as the licit trade of the colonial period.

The legacy of the Cold War is seen in contemporary trafficking in many ways – diminished borders, citizens impoverished by privatizations of formerly state property to corrupt elites, and the rise of large-scale organized crime often composed of members of the displaced and criminalized security apparati. As the chapters on Asia and Eurasia have shown, the demise of the socialist system also contributed to the economic collapse of many countries. Those who have suffered most economically were women and children. These vulnerable groups have been trafficked into sexual slavery, illegal adoptions, and child pornography. Men from the most impoverished former socialist states, particularly Central Asia and economically stratified Vietnam, have become victims of labor trafficking in the more affluent Soviet successor states.

The bipolar world of the Cold War era has been replaced since 1991 by the rise of regional conflicts. More than 60 conflicts worldwide have been identified in this short period of less than twenty years. Their growth is a result of the reordering of international alliances, the decline of support for many Third World dictators financed by either side during the Cold War conflict, and the international arms bazaar that has accompanied the collapse of the Soviet Union. As diverse chapters of this book have shown, these conflicts have led to mass destruction and displacement.[9] Hundreds of thousands of children have been trafficked worldwide to fight in these conflicts and provide support and sexual services to the combatants. In Asia, Latin America, and particularly in Africa, millions of refugees and internally displaced persons have been created by these conflicts, many of whom are vulnerable to traffickers who exploit them for labor, sex, and begging as well as many other forms of trafficking. The peacekeepers brought in to control these conflicts, whether in Europe, Haiti in the Caribbean, Asia, and especially in Africa, have all too often aggravated rather than curtailed the trafficking. Peacekeepers have sexually exploited the vulnerable. Their payments to brothel keepers in the Balkans and other locales have embedded the organized crime in the fragile and transitional state.

The human trafficking of the late twentieth and twenty-first centuries, which has reemerged with such intensity, has the potential to reshape the world order in many ways that are not sufficiently appreciated. The demand in the developed world for trafficked people and the poverty and demographic growth in much of the developing world has blinded many to the long-term and very serious consequences of this large-scale and increasingly trans-border trafficking. Embedded within a mass global migration that is now estimated at 190 million living outside their country of birth[10] are an estimated 12 million trafficking victims.[11] Their numbers may seem like a drop in the bucket in this massive flow of people. But the consequences of trafficking are much greater than the composite impact of the individuals exploited.

The great English poet John Donne wrote in the immortal lines of his poem "For Whom the Bell Tolls" an apt evaluation of the impact of the deaths of trafficked people. In his verse, "No man is an island, every man is a piece of the continent, a part of the main; if a clod is washed away by the sea, Europe is the less … any man's death diminishes me, because I am

[9] Paul Collier and Anke Hoeffler, "Greed and Grievance in Civil War," 2001, http://www.worldbank.org/research/conflict/papers/greedandgrievance.htm, (accessed June 22, 2007).

[10] "Snapshot: Global Migration," *New York Times*, June 22, 2007, http://www.nytimes.com/ref/world/20070622_CAPEVERDE_GRAPHIC.html (accessed August 24, 2009).

[11] ILO, Report of the Director General, *A Global Alliance Against Forced Labor* 2005, 10–12, http://www.ilo.org/wcmsp5/groups/public/–dgreports/–com/documents/publication/kd00012.pdf (accessed August 27, 2008). Many of those in Asia are internally trafficked and not part of this global migration.

involved in mankind," he articulated the greater loss to humanity of these futile deaths. The trafficked Chinese dying before reaching British shores could not have been imagined by Donne centuries ago, but the costs of their deaths were clear. All society was less for their loss.

The same analogy applies to the broader problem of trafficking; all society loses from the exploitation and suffering of fellow human beings. The human rights violations suffered by trafficking victims contravene the basic principles of the international community and the Universal Declaration of Human Rights agreed on by the world's nations. Yet trafficking has not aroused the consistent global concern that violations of other fundamental rights such as torture, police abuse, and discrimination have had in the international arena. Rather, the egregious violations that accompany human exploitation, particularly labor trafficking, have all too often have been met by a startling indifference on the part of individual countries and multinational bodies.

As Chapter 2 explained, the effects of human trafficking are diverse and its costs to society are great. Human trafficking undermines the principles of a democratic society, the rule of law, and respect for individual rights, particularly that of women and children. Labor trafficking not only exploits those enslaved but also depresses the wages of workers in the legitimate economy.

Human trafficking undermines international security, state control of borders, and the integrity and success of international peacekeeping operations.[12] Countries that are recipients of large number of smuggled and trafficked migrants, as discussed in Chapters 6 through 8, face challenges to their governance and national identity. A rise in human smuggling and trafficking may increase nationalist sentiment and an anti-immigrant backlash.[13] Therefore, trafficking will help shape national and regional security in many parts of the world in the future.

Human trafficking undermines world health by spreading AIDS and other venereal diseases. Many other communicable diseases, including tuberculosis and scabies, are spread by those trafficked. Many are scarred for life by the psychological and physical abuse they have suffered as trafficking victims. Families and communities who have lost members to traffickers cannot heal their loss.

[12] Report of the Global Commission on International Migration, October 5, 2005, http://www.gcim.org/attachements/GCIM%20Report%20Introduction.pdf (accessed August 24, 2009), suggests that there are benefits of migration as well. But these concerns raised about legal migration are all the more real with trafficking.

[13] Ibid. This backlash is also noted in relation to migrants.

Last, but not least, human trafficking expands the wealth and affluence of organized crime. As discussed in Chapters 3 and 4, trafficking is probably the fastest growing form of transnational crime, providing an alternative for many criminals threatened by the coordinated international efforts against the narcotics trade.

Addressing Human Trafficking

The diverse consequences of human trafficking make it imperative that this problem be a higher priority to the international community. At the present, it is a far lower concern than the international narcotics trade even though its consequences may be as or even more serious.

As the following analysis shows, unfortunately there is no single strategy that will work in stemming the growth of human trafficking. The enormous variations in the problem, as shown in Chapters 4 through 9 of the book, mean that anti-trafficking successes in one region cannot easily be transferred to another.

Unfortunately, as Chapter 1 described, much of human trafficking is caused by systemic problems that transcend anti-trafficking policies. For example, the rise of globalization, the spread of AIDS, increasing economic and demographic disparity between the developing and developed world, and the growth of regional conflicts have all contributed to the rise of trafficking. These problems have been exacerbated by the increasingly international corruption that deprives citizens of many developing and transitional countries of the resources needed to provide educations, health care, and a decent wage. Hence, efforts to combat high level corruption and AIDS, to reduce conflicts, improve peacekeeping, and prevent the transfer of natural wealth and state assets from the developing to the developed are important prerequisites to an effective counter-trafficking strategy.

Cultural factors perpetuate trafficking in many regions of the world. In particular, the low status of women and children, and the expectation in many societies that family members will serve the economic needs of their family unit, even at great cost to themselves, facilitate trafficking. The lack of investment in girls' education because of their inferior status is all too pervasive in many parts of the developing world. Also all too often, families in poor countries sell their children to provide capital in a period of family crisis. These long-standing practices cannot be changed by counter-trafficking policies. Yet government programs and foreign assistance that provide financial incentives for families to educate girls and make the lives of the poor less precarious reduce the likelihood that families will sell children to provide for unanticipated medical expenses or sudden family needs.[14] Yet as Chapter 6 on the Soviet successor states indicated, providing education in poor regions is not sufficient. The trafficking of a talented musician from Kyrgyzstan to the United Arab Emirates is evidence that education, in the absence of employment and with the presence of numerous traffickers, is not a solution to trafficking.

Those seeking to limit human trafficking can do little about these larger problems themselves. But they must be engaged in the larger policy debates on the consequences of globalization, regional conflicts, and the resource drain from the developing world. They must focus on the equal treatment of girls and women. Without their integration into policy formulation in these areas, human trafficking will remain a peripheral issue. For example, in the past, before anti-trafficking activism, the trade in women and children to peacekeepers was seen as a natural consequence of war or an unintended cost of maintaining peace. Today, multilateral organizations with peacekeepers understand that this abuse undermines the integrity and objectives of the entire peacekeeping operation. Peacekeepers from some organizations and countries have been prohibited from hiring trafficked women, and counter-trafficking training is now provided to some NATO and UN troops.[15] Much more needs to be done, as discussed subsequently, but this policy change is solely a consequence of the integration of counter-trafficking into the larger peacekeeping debate.

Free trade has not been accompanied by increasingly free movement of people. This dichotomy has been conducive to trafficking as barriers to entry prevent the migration of people to locales where they can maximize their economic worth.[16] Therefore, the issue of human trafficking must be incorporated into larger trade debates. All too often, policy development

[14] See Nicholas D. Kristof and Sheryl Wu Dunn, "The Women's Crusade," http://www.nytimes.com/2009/08/23/magazine/23Women-t.html?_r=1&scp=1&sq=kristof%20women&st=cse, (accessed August 31, 2009).

[15] "NATO Policy on Combating Trafficking in Human Beings," http://www.nato.int/cps/en/SID-05DE446B-CF96DEA2/natolive/topics_50315.htm, Accessed August 31, 2009; "Human Trafficking and United Nations Peacekeeping," DPKO Policy Paper, March 2004), http://www.un.org/Depts/dpko/dpko/info/pdf/human_trafficking_032004.pdf (accessed August 31, 2009).

[16] Karen E. Bravo "Free Labor! A Labor Liberalization Solution to Modern Trafficking in Humans," *Journal of Transnational Law & Contemporary Problems* 18 (2009), 545–615.

on licit and illicit trade arena has focused on commodities rather than on people. Without integration of the human dimension, human smuggling and trafficking are perpetuated. Reducing restrictions on temporary and long-term migration to conform to opening of trade markets has been suggested as a key strategy to reduce the enormous rise in trafficking.[17] Only with deliberate policies to channel the illicit movement of people into a legitimate flow can the international community hope to stem the increase in smuggling and trafficking.

Managing the large migration flows in a rational and humane manner is also a prerequisite to countering the rise of the trade in human beings. In too many parts of the world, countering labor trafficking is left to law enforcement rather than those most in touch with the labor force. Labor inspectors, even in developed countries, have yet to be integrated into counter-trafficking efforts. Even less has been done to bring private employment agencies, which previous chapters have shown to often be facilitators of trafficking, under a broader system of governance.[18]

A large and detailed literature on countering human trafficking has already been written by scholars, specialists in think tanks, in national action plans of individual states, by the assistance agencies of different countries and multilateral institutions. Hundreds if not thousands of pages have been written on improving anti-trafficking legislation, international legal coordination, empowering victims, and improving the impact and outreach of civil society. Unfortunately, too few of these many excellent recommendations have been implemented. On the other hand, these policy prescriptions have focused too little attention on reducing demand for trafficked people and countering the business of human trafficking. The successes in combating the drug trade by identifying its money flows and its business operations have all too rarely been applied to the fight against human trafficking.[19]

A much more encompassing approach is needed if the growth in human trafficking is to be arrested. This requires that consumers of trafficked people and the businesses that facilitate this trade must become

[17] Ibid.

[18] Richard Danziger, Jonathan Martens and Mariela Guajardo, "Human Trafficking and Migration Management," in *Strategies Against Human Trafficking: The Role of the Security Sector*, Cornelius Friesendorf, ed. (Vienna: National Defence Academy and Austrian Ministry of Defence and Sport, 2009).

[19] Phil Williams, "Combating Human Trafficking: Improving Governance Institutions, Mechanisms & Strategies," in *Strategies Against Human Trafficking*, ed. Friesendorf, 417–22 for discussion of the Girasole case.

more central to counter-trafficking policies. This involves raising awareness such as CNN spots in which corporate leaders vow to fight human trafficking[20]. The International Organization for Migration (IOM) has also launched a media campaign in late 2009 urging consumers to buy responsibly. This campaign goes beyond fair trade and seeks to bring migrants in developed countries in the informal sector under the protection of labour laws and to ensure greater control of supply chain for products.[21]

Yet more is needed than words. It also requires a stick – imposing financial, reputational, and legal penalties on those who exploit others. Yet there must also be a carrot for corporations and others who counter trafficking by providing employment, jobs, and proper due diligence. Citizens must realize satisfaction from their participation in fair trade and their consumption of products made by workers guaranteed a decent wage.

The following section focuses on a six-pronged approach to anti-trafficking that includes consumers, the corporate world, researchers and universities, civil society, national governments, and multilateral institutions. More than a decade ago, Susan Strange wrote that there has been the retreat of the state in the globalized world. Nonstate actors such as multinational corporations, international organizations, transnational civil society, and even increasingly global organized crime have a larger role to play with the declining significance of borders and of nation-states.[22] Her analysis is even more relevant today. The legitimate non-state actors of the globalized world must be more effectively harnessed to counter trafficking that all too often is committed by international criminal organizations and networks.

Also essential is that an economic approach must be more central to countering human smuggling and trafficking. Smugglers and traffickers are businesses people and their commodities, human beings. Yet too little has been done to understand the business of human trafficking, as Chapter 4 has shown. There has yet to be a Judge Falcone, who died fighting the Mafia, trying cases on human trafficking. Falcone's success in

[20] Spot on CNN aired on November 8, 2009, sponsored by UN Gift.

[21] "What's Behind the Things We Buy?" *Global Eye on Human Trafficking* Issue 7, October 2009, 1–2, http://www.iom.int/jahia/webdav/site/myjahiasite/shared/shared/mainsite/projects/showcase_pdf/global_eye_seventh_issue.pdf, accessed December 8, 2009; interview with Richard Danziger, head of counter-trafficking at IOM who is behind this campaign, November 20, 2009, Dubai.

[22] Susan Strange, *The Retreat of the State: The Diffusion of Power in the World Economy* (New York: Cambridge University Press, 1996).

dismantling the Mafia, as discussed in Chapter 4, was based on his intimate understanding the inner workings of their business. No such success has been achieved in law enforcement in tackling the business of human trafficking. Moreover, too little has been done to engage businesses and consumers in the fight against trafficking.

The Consumers

The demand for trafficked people starts with consumers – those who seek low paid or free domestic servants, cheap goods, babies for adoption, organs for transplant that cannot be obtained legitimately, and sexual services. Not all human trafficking is, however, demand driven. Child beggars are created by traffickers, as are children trafficked into the commission of petty crime. Yet the vast majority of trafficked people provide goods and services that meet a consumer demand.

Not enough attention is being focused in counter-trafficking policies worldwide on reducing demand for goods produced by trafficked peoples, diminishing the clients for victims of sex trafficking, or penalizing those who exploit workers in their homes. Unfortunately, diminishing this demand is difficult in an increasingly globalized economy where there is enormous pressure on producers to reduce costs and where consumers in many regions of the world are often more concerned about the accessibility and affordability of goods than the conditions of the workers who produced the commodities. Yet a disproportionate amount of the world's consumption is in the developed world where much can be done to educate consumers and to get them to buy products that are not produced by forced labor.

As the head of anti-trafficking programs at the International Organization forMigration explained:

> And yet if one were to look at other examples of information campaigns that have focused on consumers (e.g., anti-fur, anti-smoking, energy conservation, recycling, etc.) to suppress demand, many appear to have proved their worth, particularly when buttressed with supporting measures such as strict implementation of specific legislation and policies. Indeed, studies increasingly show that consumers, and those in destination countries in particular, want their choices to match their human values, and are willing … to change their habits of consumption to better reflect their values if this requires paying more for a particular product or service.[23]

[23] Danziger, Martens and Guajardo, "Human Trafficking and Migration Management," 275, 424; See, for example, Michael Rock, "Public Disclosure of the Sweatshop Practices

Yet responsible consumerism has not been adequately incorporated into anti-trafficking messages. There are, however, some hopeful signs that the expansion of anti-trafficking messages to consumers might work. As the following section discusses, communities working with commercial producers in areas prone to labor trafficking have had some success in creating effective certification programs and rewarding good business behavior.

Reducing the demand for sexual trafficking has not been sufficiently tried. Some suggest that outlawing prostitution and criminalizing the hiring of prostitutes as has been done in Sweden are the most effective approaches.[24] Yet as Chapter 7 on Europe made clear, the jury is still out on the success of the Swedish policy, as it may have driven trafficking underground in Sweden or merely displaced trafficking to neighboring countries. Moreover, the inability to replicate this approach is already apparent within Europe. The Netherlands has taken the opposite perspective of legalizing brothels staffed by prostitutes with work permits for the Netherlands and enhancing prosecutions of traffickers.[25]

Reducing demand among peacekeepers can possibly be achieved with greater facility as military personnel follow orders. If their commanders ban the use of prostitutes and follow up with meaningful sanctions against violators such as court-martials, steep financial penalties, and deportation from the operations, a high degree of compliance can be obtained.[26]

Curbing consumption among the civilian population is more difficult. Much more needs to be done on educational campaigns for potential customers of prostitutes, explaining the exploitation of the women and the nature of the criminals who control them. This might reduce the purchase of some trafficked women by men who believe that the

of American Multinational Garment/Shoe Makers/Retails: Impacts on their Stock Prices," *Competition & Change* 71, no. 1 (2003): 24.

[24] Leslie Holmes, "Corruption & Trafficking: Triple Victimisation?" in *Strategies Against Human Trafficking*, Friesendorf, ed., 113.

[25] Rudolf E. H. Hilgers, Dutch National Public Prosecution Office, "The Programmatic Approach of Trafficking in Human Beings in the Netherlands," The Commodification of Illicit Flows: Labour Migration, Trafficking and Business, Centre for Diaspora and Transnational Studies, University of Toronto, October 9–10, 2009; see also discussion of the Sneep Case, Rutger van Santen, "Violent People Traffickers on Trial," October 7, 2008, http://static.rnw.nl/migratie/www.radionetherlands.nl/currentaffairs/region/netherlands/080710-people-traffickers-trial-redirected (accessed December 8, 2009).

[26] Keith J. Allred, "Human Trafficking and Peacekeepers," in *Strategies Against Human Trafficking*, Friesendorf, ed., 311–41.

women engage in this activity voluntarily. Beyond this, different societies must find culturally appropriate measures to stem consumers. In the Philippines, the Coalition Against Trafficking in Women organized an educational program, taught in part by former trafficking victims, to educated 17- to 18-year-old males in communities where there was extensive use of prostitutes.[27] This program such as those in the United States to educate customers have encouraged cultural change among customers. For example, in the United States, so-called "John's Schools" have been established in several major cities where arrested customers of prostitutes are forced to attend.[28] Just as in programs for drunken drivers, the vivid consequences of their actions are explained. Curriculum shows the risk to men of hiring prostitutes, the health consequences, the suffering of the women, the effects on the community, and the system of control over the prostitute by the pimps. Recidivism has been reduced and sustained among some of those who have gone through these programs.[29]

Business World

The business community must engage more in counter-trafficking efforts. This is particularly important in sectors where exploitation is most likely to occur, such as agriculture, meat and poultry processing, tourism, and construction, as well as among care providers. The hospitality industry has many trafficked workers cleaning rooms and toiling in its restaurant kitchens, and in many hotels customers bring trafficked women to their rooms, view pornography on pay channels, or receive referrals from hotel staff to brothels where trafficked women are enslaved. Newspapers, website owners, limousine and other transport services, and owners of apartment complexes are often important facilitators of human trafficking, particularly sexual.

As counter-trafficking specialists have stated, businesses in these enumerated economic sectors "have an opportunity and a responsibility to prevent the problem, and to protect those migrants who suffer

[27] Iris Yen, "Of Vice and Men: A New Approach to Eradicating Sex Trafficking by Reducing Male Demand through Educational Programs and Abolitionist Legislation," *Journal of Criminal Law and Criminology* 98, no. 2 (2008), 675–6.

[28] An analysis of the first John School in San Francisco called SAGE, Michael Shively et al. "Final Report on the Evaluation of the First Offender Prostitution Program," March 2008, ABT Assoc. http://www.ncjrs.gov/pdffiles1/nij/grants/221894.pdf (accessed August 29, 2009).

[29] Ibid., iii; see also http://www.pbs.org/now/shows/422/prostitution.html (accessed August 26, 2009).

exploitation. In some cases, private companies have partnered with international organizations to distribute information materials to migrants considered vulnerable to exploitation; others have helped rehabilitate trafficked persons by providing skills development and job opportunities, or support to income-generating projects."[30]

There is increasingly involvement of the corporate sector in this area but this is not well known. Rather, information on this activity is hidden within corporate responsibility reports of corporations, evaluations of funded programs, or corporate magazines. Although many believe good works are best done anonymously, this is most probably not the case in human trafficking. Corporate leadership that is visible in the anti-trafficking movement would probably be of much greater value in changing the culture of the business world. As one senior corporate executive who has taken a lead has said, "Many CEOs still do not understand the magnitude of human trafficking and the dire need for a coordinated global business response."[31]

Manpower, a British human resources firm, has taken a lead in promoting anti-trafficking. Its 2007 corporate responsibility report explains that they were the first signatory of the Athens Ethical Principles, which "declares a 'zero tolerance' policy for working with any entity benefiting in any way from human trafficking, and is working to get 1,000 of the world's leading corporations to join in signing the Principles.[32] The following year they reported additional efforts,

> we introduced a new global procurement procedure designed to ensure all of our vendors adhere to Manpower's strict guidelines to eliminate forced labor, human trafficking and corrupt business practices ... not only by being vigilant about ensuring that our own supply chains are free from human trafficking, but also by lobbying, generating awareness and leaning on our peers to commit to the best practices of prevention.[33]

Unfortunately, not much is generally known about the Athens Ethical Principles and efforts of corporations to change modes of conduct.

[30] Danziger, Martens, and Guajardo, "Human Trafficking and Migration Management," 275.
[31] http://files.shareholder.com/downloads/MAN/713473184x0x267311/84ed6503-da74–4e56–8752-e88cad074522/CSR%20Release.pdf (accessed August 29, 2009).
[32] http://www.manpower.com/investors/releasedetail.cfm?releaseid=276447 (accessed August 29, 2009).
[33] 2008 Social Corporate responsibility Report, http://files.shareholder.com/downloads/MAN/713473184x0x267311/84ed6503-da74–4e56–8752-e88cad074522/CSR%20 Release.pdf (accessed August 29, 2009).

Major international corporations have worked with the International Labour Organisation since 2003 to help employers identify problems of forced labor in their supply chain. In early 2008, Coca-Cola hosted a meeting in Atlanta, Georgia along with the U.S. Council for International Business and the U.S. Chamber of Commerce, introduced by the CEO, attended by 80 representatives from employers' organization, individual companies, U.S. government officials, civil society, and the ILO to explain how abusers can infiltrate the supply chains of international companies. It focused on organizations and companies that are working to eliminate forced labor and to eliminate goods in their supply chain produced by exploited workers.[34] This event in the United States is part of a larger international initiative and the publication the *Costs of Coercion* addresses the problem of labor abuse in the supply chain.[35] As a result of such actions, companies are paying more attention to labor concerns in their codes of conduct.[36]

Major international food companies in the United States have responded to the Campaign for Fair Food, initiated by the CIW (Coalition of Immokalee Workers), a worker-based organization founded in the early 1990s. "Consumers have played a vital role in bringing the problem of modern-day slavery to corporate buyers' attention, through informational actions, boycotts, letters to management, petitions. They have made it clear, as end-users, that they want buyers to be able to guarantee to their customers that no slavery exists in their supply chains."[37] As a result of these activities, buyers of corporations such as McDonald's and Taco Bell have entered into agreements with the CIW to have a zero-tolerance policy for slavery as well as third party monitoring.[38]

[34] "Engaging Business: Addressing Forced Labour," http://www.ilo.org/sapfl/Events/ILOevents/lang–en/WCMS_092170/index.htm (accessed December 8, 2009); also interview with Roger Plant of ILO who was responsible for this initiative, October 9–10, 2009.

[35] Eradicating Forced Labour: The International Business Challenge by Roger Plant, London, 1 May 2008, http://www.ilo.org/sapfl/Informationresources/Speeches/lang–en/WCMS_097000/index.htm (accessed December 8, 2009); Beate Andrees and Patrick Belser, *Forced Labor: Coercion and Exploitation in the Private Economy*, Boulder, CO: Lynne Rienner, 2009; ILO, *The Cost of Coercion* – Global Report under the follow-up to the ILO Declaration on Fundamental Principles and Rights at Work 2009, International Labour Office, Geneva, 2009.

[36] Interview with Roger Plant for the Illicit Trade Council of the World Economic Forum, November 2009.

[37] Interview with Greg Asbed for Illicit Trade Council of the World Economic Forum, November 2009.

[38] Sean Sellers and Greg Asbed (Institute for Agriculture and Trade Policy/Coalition of Immokalee Workers [CIW]]) "*Beyond Investigations: Workers and Consumers Join in*

Corporate involvement with the public sector and law enforcement has helped stem the dissemination and sale of commercial child pornography. The Financial Coalition Against Child Pornography (FCACP) founded in 2006 is managed by the International Centre for Missing & Exploited Children and has grown rapidly since its initiation. The coalition is composed of leading banks, credit card companies, electronic payment networks, third-party payments companies, and Internet services companies that represent nearly 90 percent of the U.S. payments industry. Through their coordination with the Centre and officials responsible for combating money laundering they have been able to stop the sale of much child pornography. Evidence of this is that in the three years since the launch of the coalition, "there has been a 50% drop in the number of unique commercial child pornography websites reported into the U.S. CyberTipline."[39] Also "There has been a significant increase in the price of child pornography ... disruptive efforts of the FCACP are making the cost of doing business much higher for child pornography websites."[40] As a result of these successes, the European Financial Coalition was launched in early 2009 and an Asian Pacific Coalition is laying out its strategy and priorities.[41]

In the tourism sector, since 2004 the number of tour operators, travel agencies, and tourism associations has grown from fifty to more than six hundred who have agreed to voluntarily abide by the International Code of Conduct for the Protection of Children from Sexual Exploitation in Travel and Tourism. Yet more needs to be done to expand and publicize this program outside the tourism industry. Its protections should apply not only to children but also to trafficked adults.[42]

a Market-Based Approach to Prevention of Slavery Operations in the U.S. Agricultural Industry"; The Commodification of Illicit Flows: Labour Migration, Trafficking and Business, Centre for Diaspora and Transnational Studies, University of Toronto, October 9–10, 2009; see also Kevin Bales and Ron Soodalter, *The Slave Next Door: Human Trafficking and Slavery in America Today* (Berkeley and Los Angeles: University of California Press, 2009), 54–65 which includes discussion of other corporations such as KFC, Long John Silver and Pizza Hut in this effort to prevent slavery and pay higher wages to farm workers.

[39] It is also managed by the sister organization, the National Center for Missing & Exploited Children. Background Paper, Financial Coalition Against Child Pornography, December 2009; meeting with Christina Portz, Program Manager, International Centre for Missing & Exploited Children, December 9, 2009.

[40] Background Paper, Financial Coalition against Child Pornography, December 2009.

[41] Ibid.

[42] USAID, *Combating Trafficking in Persons in the 21st Century* (Washington, DC: USAID, 2008), 29.

Another example of good corporate anti-trafficking behavior has been shown by Microsoft, which has provided $1.5 in funding and software for prominent nongovernmental organizations (NGOs) in the Philippines, Cambodia, Thailand, Indonesia, and India to fund computer training programs for women who are at risk of trafficking. Approximately 10 percent of the 28,000 individuals who were trained in an eighteen-month period were considered as surviving victims of trafficking. In India, where the program was most successful, 70 percent of the highly vulnerable trainees were placed on jobs and 75 percent of survivors found work. Many fewer successes were identified in the Philippines.[43] Yet many smaller and worthy NGOs never obtain corporate funding.

Corporate involvement appears most successful where there is a strong entrepreneurial culture and an active civil society. A careful evaluation of these programs revealed that this training prevented the return of some women to sexual exploitation and prevented the subsequent exploitation of their children.[44] Although improvements could be made in the programs, they are an important first step by a major corporation to provide large-scale job training for potential trafficking victims and survivors.

Yet too many companies do not incorporate statements on human trafficking in corporate policies or codes of conduct. Changing this is imperative, especially for companies that work internationally. One success occurred at Lockheed Martin, a global security firm with 146,000 employees worldwide, which reported that until one of their employees who works on human trafficking issues brought the problem to their attention, it was not incorporated into the company's code of conduct statement that employees pledge to uphold each year. Now there has been a major policy shift and all employees at Lockheed Martin have to agree not to engage in trafficking behaviors.[45] Yet such a change should not be dependent on the voice of an employee. Such policies should be incorporated into standards of behavior of large international corporations as well as smaller ones. Perhaps this might be a subject for stockholder initiatives at corporate Annual Meetings.

Businesses that buy products in the Third World can do much to prevent labor trafficking and exploitation. For example, the Cocoa Sustainability Alliance, working in West Africa with farmers and the international

43 http://cis.washington.edu/employability/2008/09/25/antitrafficking/, 24 (accessed August 29, 2009); interview with the report writer, Judith Gilmore, in April 2009.

44 Ibid.

45 "Professionals Providing Solutions Employee Profile: Ruth Pojman," GAIN. Insight, Lockheed Martin employee newsletter (July/August 2009).

cocoa industry, has helped ensure that cocoa harvesting of beans is not performed by trafficked children. Support for the Alliance from international assistance programs such as United States Agency for International Development (USAID) have helped sustain the monitoring mechanisms, revealing how a tripartite alliance of business, community members, and foreign assistance programs may be necessary to prevent trafficking.[46]

Specialized organizations such as Rugmark address the problem of trafficking of children into the carpet industry, a problem mentioned in Chapter 5 on Asia.[47] Rugmark certifies new rug production, assuring consumers that rugs and carpets produced are not made by exploited children. In some ways, this certification process is similar to the Kimberley process that ensures that diamonds sold are not "blood diamonds," which help fund and sustain regional conflict.

Advocacy and consumer groups have made companies attach greater importance to the working conditions of their employees. Yet, unfortunately, many consumers appear to be unwilling to pay the additional costs associated with goods produced by workers paid a living wage under decent conditions.[48]

Yet other means have and must be used to ensure that businesses and property owners do not facilitate human trafficking. For example, the police in France have sealed apartments used by Brazilian prostitutes, often trafficked women, in expensive neighborhoods in Paris. The financial costs to apartment owners who have lost subsequent revenue for extended periods because they facilitated prostitution and trafficking have served as important object lessons to French investors in real estate. French planning to rent their apartments are now much more diligent in assessing their potential renters.[49] The lessons of the French experience could be replicated elsewhere, reducing income for those who facilitate trafficking.

Commercial facilitators of trafficking need to be shamed more frequently. Hotels and other parts of the tourism industry are key actors in sexual trafficking. In Turkey, and in other parts of the Middle East,

[46] USAID, *Combating Trafficking in Persons in the 21st Century*, 26.

[47] See Kevin Bales, *Ending Slavery: How We Free Today's Slaves* (Berkeley: University of California Press, 2007), 205; see the website of Rugmark, www.rugmark.org.

[48] David Vogel, *The Market for Virtue and the Potential and Limits of Corporate Social Responsibility* (Washington, DC: Brookings Institution Press, 2005), 75–109; "Fighting Against Sweatshop Abuses," *America*, May 27, 2000, http://americamagazine.org/content/article.cfm?article_id=772 (accessed August 26, 2009).

[49] Interview with French real estate investor in June 2009.

concierges and staff of top-end hotels collude with the limousine services that operate at top hotels to take clients to brothels often staffed with women trafficked from other regions. This problem also exists in many Soviet successor states, in Asia, and even in high-end hotels in Beverly Hills, California. These hotels have failed to have adequate or ongoing due diligence. Much more could be done to expose the bad and inadequate practices of these hotels. The parliamentary forum of the Nordic Council adopted a zero-tolerance measure on prostitution and hotels in 2006 and urged the parliamentarians of the EU to follow suit.[50] The possibility of reputational loss would provide an incentive to many hotel chains that pride themselves on their good names to cease facilitating trafficking and marketing pornography to their clients through pay programming in hotel rooms.

Newspapers, telephone books, tourist publications, and websites continue in many countries to market trafficked people through advertisements for massage and escort services. Numerous criminal investigations against sexual traffickers in the United States, the United Kingdom, and elsewhere, initiated on the basis of newspaper and telephone book advertisements, point to the need to combat these facilitators of trafficking. Too little has been done in almost all developed countries to force these media outlets to perform due diligence over their advertisers. State and local prosecutors, as mentioned in Chapter 8, have initiated numerous trafficking cases, particularly of minors, as a result of advertisements on the popular website Craigslist. The difficulties of states' attorneys general in curbing advertising promoting sexual trafficking is illustrative of the problems of engaging the business world where their financial interests conflict with good corporate behavior.[51] Clearly, the cost – benefit ratio must be changed, just as with the French apartment owners, to make the owners of Craigslist change their behavior.

Not all news media owners are as irresponsible as Craigslist. For more than a decade, there has been excellent cooperation between the owners of Internet Service Providers (ISP) and investigators of child pornography disseminated through the internet. Because of this cooperation, the

[50] Vanessa Mock, "Kick Out Prostitutes from Our Hotels, demand Nordic MEPs, October 24, 2008, *The Independent*, http://www.independent.co.uk/news/world/europe/kick-out-prostitutes-from-our-hotels-demand-nordic-meps-971494.html (accessed December 8, 2009).

[51] Kelly Wallace, "Attorneys General Want Craigslist Clean-Up," May 5, 2009, http://www.cbsnews.com/stories/2009/05/05/eveningnews/main4993632.shtml (accessed August 29, 2009).

cybercrime unit of the U.S. Customs Service has been able to trace messages through the Internet dealing with the distribution and purchase of child pornography. Many important cases of child exploitation, with links in diverse countries, have been prosecuted with the cooperation of this element of the corporate world.[52]

The World Economic Forum, a powerful NGO that brings together top business leaders, government officials, and NGOs, has taken on the issue of illicit trade including human trafficking. If members of the international business elite can be made to understand the larger costs of trafficking and develop responsible global strategies, important progress may be made in countering the rise of trafficking.

Yet a significant response to trafficking is still needed from the global business community. Just as companies such as banks, real estate companies, and car dealerships have become much more diligent in ensuring that they are not facilitators of the narcotics trade, the same must occur with the corporate response to human trafficking. The efforts of the corporate world against drug traffickers were not the result of voluntary compliance. Banks, real estate companies, and car dealerships that were complicit in laundering drug money have suffered significant financial and reputational costs. Nothing similar has occurred to businesses that have facilitated human trafficking.

The freezing of assets and the seizure of homes and car dealerships from businessmen who aided drug traffickers have done much to improve the due diligence and accountability of businesses. Although human traffickers, as Chapters 3 and 4 have shown, most often launder their money outside of the banking system, other business sectors are deeply implicated in the perpetuation of trafficking. Businesses that facilitate human trafficking by moving people or money or renting hotel rooms and apartments to traffickers must incur costs similar to those born by facilitators of the drug trade. Only then will there be a more proactive response by members of the business community.

Research and Education

Human trafficking needs much more basic research. Numerous reports have been written on the subject and field assessments but too little scholarly research has been produced. Many topics in need of study remain

[52] Louise Shelley, "Crime and Corruption in the Digital Era," *Journal of International Affairs* 52, no. 2 (Spring 1998), 179–94.

inadequately researched. For example, trafficking in Latin America, the Middle East, and Africa; comparative analyses of trafficking in different regions of the world; and the business of labor trafficking remain inadequately researched, particularly by scholars outside of Western Europe and the United States.

The traffickers, as earlier chapters have shown, often have higher education. Therefore, to oppose trafficking we need to harness the best minds not only as researchers and activists but also as counter-traffickers capable of outsmarting the traffickers. Fundamental research on human trafficking and incorporation of its study into university programs worldwide remain important priorities for counter-trafficking. Centers of excellence, courses of study, and integrated research programs must be initiated. Without the knowledge base, those who oppose human trafficking will be a poor match for the intelligent, well-educated and wily traffickers Moreover, they will be unable to address the diverse policy challenges caused by human trafficking in the coming decades of the twenty-first century.

Civil Society

Civil society has a key role to play in countering human trafficking. Its members can raise public awareness, force engagement on this issue by pressuring governments and multilateral institutions to develop laws, enforce legislation, and implement national counter-trafficking strategies. Civil society members run broad-based prevention programs through the media and schools, in cities as well as in rural communities. They often staff hotlines to receive complaints and assist families or advise potential trafficking victims. NGOs are key providers of services to victims, including medical and psychological help and job training. Illustrative of this was the Microsoft-funded example discussed earlier. NGOs, often assisted by members of diaspora communities, deliver services to trafficking victims outside their home countries with cultural sensitivity and in the language of the victim.[53] Civil society groups help with the repatriation of victims and provide shelters for domestic as well as returning victims of human trafficking. In many societies, they work with law enforcement to train police, prosecutors, and judges. They also work with victims, empowering them to pursue cases against their traffickers.

53 Danziger, Martens, and Guajardo, "Human Trafficking and Migration Management," 276.

The founders of programs initiated by activists, such as La Strada in Eastern Europe and the Ukraine and Somaly Mam in Cambodia, can rarely find support among local philanthropists or governments and need to obtain funding from abroad.[54] Even in the wealthy United States, service providers to trafficking victims such as the well-established Children of the Night in the Los Angeles, California area are constantly struggling to maintain their operations.[55] Supporting victims of trafficking is not a priority in most societies, and its victims all too often receive less assistance than that accorded victims of domestic or gender violence, although as this book explains, the needs of trafficking victims are great and diverse.[56] If sustained results against trafficking are to be achieved, reliable and continuous funding for counter-trafficking efforts must be ensured.

The media, through investigative journalists and documentary filmmakers, has an important role to play in countering trafficking. Reports in newspapers, on the nightly news, and on documentary specials have gone a long way in raising awareness of the problem. Many of the cases discussed in this book, such as that of the fifty-eight Chinese who died in a van crossing the English channel, the torture of girls in the subterranean chambers of Cambodian brothels, or the numerous girls murdered by their traffickers in the Russian Urals in Nizhnyi Tagil, received broad media attention. Many documentaries on trafficking, including such prize-winning ones as *Born into Brothels* and *Selling of Innocents*, and films such as *Lilya 4-Ever*, have been widely shown in movie houses, on television and at universities, raising awareness of the human tragedy of trafficking and the venality of the traffickers.

Many celebrities have used their visibility in the media to raise awareness of the human trafficking issue. Examples of this include Oprah Winfrey on child exploitation in the cocoa industry, Ricky Martin to fight child trafficking, Julia Ormond and Ashley Judd to fight sex trafficking, as well as many others. Some of them have worked with multilateral

[54] Somaly Mam Foundation in Cambodia, http://www.somaly.org/ (accessed August 31, 2009); La Strada International Network Against Trafficking in Human Beings, which unites 9 NGOs, primarily in Eastern Europe, http://lastradainternational.org/?main=home (accessed August 31, 2009).

[55] http://www.childrenofthenight.org/ (accessed August 31, 2009).

[56] William Finnegan, "The Countertraffickers," *New Yorker*, May 5, 2008, http://www.newyorker.com/reporting/2008/05/05/080505fa_fact_finnegan (accessed September 1, 2009).

organizations such as the UN and IOM to use their recognition to publicize the problem of human trafficking.

Reportage by the media and civil society activism exposed the exploitation of young boys from Pakistan, Bangladesh, and several African countries as camel jockeys in the Gulf States. Public outrage over this activity resulted in high-level government commitment by Gulf State governments to use robots instead of young boys as camel jockeys. Hundreds of trafficked boys have been identified, and they and their families have been assisted in community-run programs in their home countries administered by the United Nations with support from the Gulf States.[57] This example illustrates how activism can lead to policy change and victims' assistance.

In Asia, as was indicated in Chapter 5, civil society activism against trafficking is particularly strong. *Ending Slavery* reported on a village in India that mobilized against those that kept them in indentured servitude.[58] In the highly authoritarian state of Cambodia, the activists of Somaly Man empower girls who have been trafficked to recover and develop new lives.[59] But such actions take courage and often place trafficking victims at risk. Civil society is key in empowering trafficked individuals and groups to take control of their lives and throw off their exploiters.[60]

A more active role for religious organizations might also help counter trafficking. Many religious groups have been at the forefront of providing services to victims. Yet there is considerable scope for the world's major religious organizations and institutions to play a more dominant role in counter-trafficking, particularly in source countries in the developing world where their influence is often greatest and in rural areas where their capacity for social organization often exceeds that of the state. In working to combat the stigmatization of persons who have been trafficked for sexual exploitation, in particular, or in countering xenophobia, for example, religious leaders have occasionally played a pivotal role in shaping the view of the communities they serve. If religious organizations were to decide to take on the challenge of human trafficking more comprehensively, at an institutional level,

57 www.uae-embassy.org/uae/human-rights/human-trafficking (accessed August 31, 2009).

58 Kevin Bales, *Ending Slavery*, 62–68.

59 The activism has been written about by Nicholas Kristof for the *New York Times*. The author met with one of the activists of the program on her visit to Washington in Spring 2009.

60 Bales, *Ending Slavery*.

and leverage their religious authority against this crime, the impact could be dramatic.[61]

Religious groups are not alone in failing to commit at a more global level. Civil society, working against human trafficking, is more often local than transnational. Transnational anti-trafficking organizations such as Free the Slaves, CATW (Coalition Against Trafficking in Women), and ECPAT (End Child Prostitution Child Pornography and Trafficking of Children for Sexual Purposes) exist, but none of these groups enjoys the wide recognition or the political clout of Amnesty International or Transparency International. There is no global constituency to combat any form of illicit trade. In this regard civil society anti-trafficking activism does not differ from that seeking to counter the trade in small arms, blood diamonds, or counterfeit goods.[62]

Activism by civil society is also weakened because there is no comprehensive movement to protect victims of all forms of human trafficking. Instead, there are separate advocacy groups to address child soldiers, victims of sexual trafficking, and labor exploitation. This splintering of counter-trafficking by forms of exploitation weakens the potency and efficacy of activism.

Therefore, a large coordinated international advocacy movement to counter all forms of trafficking is an important prerequisite to progress in this area.

Role of Government

What is the purpose of government if not to protect the lives of its citizens? The role of government in counter-trafficking is fundamental. Yet far too many countries have done little, as many analysts have shown. Even though most countries are signatories of the UN protocol on human trafficking, few have shown the political will or allocated the resources necessary to combat trafficking effectively. Human trafficking remains a crime of choice for criminals because the law enforcement response of most states is strikingly inadequate. That which exists is undermined

[61] Danziger, Martens and Guajardo, "Human Trafficking and Migration Management," 276.

[62] There are organizations that focus on this trade such as Global Witness, business organizations such as the U.S. Chamber of Commerce and the International Chamber of Commerce that focus on counterfeiting and the International Action Network that focuses on small arms, http://www.iansa.org/about.htm (accessed September 1, 2009) but these do not have a large global constituency.

by the absence of harmonized laws and state sovereignty that impedes international cooperation.

Yet the role of the state in counter-trafficking is much broader than investigating crimes after their commission. States have an important role in preventing trafficking, in regulating migration to prevent smuggling and trafficking, and in identifying and helping those who have been victimized. More affluent countries with foreign assistance programs must provide and coordinate assistance with other donor countries to counter trafficking.

This is the ideal. Many countries still lack the fundamentals such as adequate anti-trafficking legislation and national strategies to address the problem. As Chapter 9 explained, the legislative prerequisite to counter-trafficking is still absent in Mexico and many countries in Africa and Central America.

Migration policies in the world facilitate the entry of only high skilled workers. But many countries that need manual and low-skilled workers have strict migration policies that keep out this needed component of the work force. This dichotomy between manpower needs and their national stance on migration has fueled human smuggling and trafficking. This was shown in Chapters 7 and 8 on Europe and the United States. Russia provides short-term work permits for workers from Soviet successor states as a means of stemming human trafficking. Yet much more needs to be done to make international migration policies consistent with the needs of a globalized economy.[63]

Many countries immediately deport illegal residents before they can be identified as trafficking victims. According to the UN protocol on trafficking, victims are to be provided a period of reflection in which to recover from the trauma of trafficking and decide whether they will cooperate with law enforcement. In many countries in Europe, victims of trafficking are given very short periods of reflection.[64] This compounds victimization. Without the cooperation and testimony of victims, governments often have great difficulty in dismantling criminal organizations.

An effective governmental counter-trafficking response requires many components that have been discussed at length in many other publications and elsewhere in this book.[65] This response includes

[63] See, for example, Bravo, "Free Labor!"

[64] Jana Arsovska and Stef Janssens, "Policing & Human Trafficking: Good and Bad Practices," in *Strategies Against Human Trafficking*, Friesendorf, ed., 197.

[65] See, for example, E. Benjamin Skinner, *A Crime so Monstrous Face-to-Face with Modern-Day Slavery* (New York: Free Press, 2008); Kevin Bales, *Ending Slavery*; Anthony

government-sponsored public education campaigns and awareness raising to prevent trafficking and identify victims, victims' assistance, training programs for law enforcement officials, enhanced coordination between NGOs and diverse government agencies, and intragovernmental and international cooperation.[66] Governments must be also vigilant to combat the corruption that facilitates trafficking and sanction government and nongovernmental facilitators.

Development of a more effective law enforcement response to trafficking should be a higher priority throughout the world. As the book has shown, no region of the world has many prosecuted cases. Human trafficking is the only common form of transnational crime where the perpetrators enjoy near total impunity. The few who are sanctioned face light penalties that rarely serve as deterrents. Investigation and conviction of traffickers needs to be prioritized. Just as in narcotics cases, criminal cases must target the whole criminal network or organization, witness protection programs must be established, and investigators must follow the money trails. The profits of human trafficking must be confiscated and used for victim assistance and reparations. But human trafficking cases are not often given the priority assigned to drug trafficking. Therefore, little that was enumerated as necessary has been done. Instead, most human trafficking investigations target only the lowest level of criminal participants, leaving human trafficking networks in place.

Governmental foreign assistance programs to counter trafficking must not only pay for shelters, training, and prevention programs. Their focus must be broader if they are to counter the conditions that lead to trafficking. They must focus on gender issues and greater opportunities for children and women if they are to prevent human trafficking. Programs such as microcredit with low interest rates can be powerful in creating viable family businesses, thereby decreasing the vulnerability of family members to trafficking. Foreign assistance must involve several years funding commitment so that results can be sustained and program managers do not become fundraisers rather than service providers.

M. De Stefano, *The War on Human Trafficking: U.S. Policy Assessed* (New Brunswick, NJ: Rutgers University Press, 2007); Conny *Rijken*, *Trafficking in Persons: Prosecution from a European Perspective* (The Hague: Asser Press, 2003).

[66] *Strategies Against Human Trafficking*, Friesendorf, ed.; USAID, *Combating Trafficking in Persons in the 21st Century*.

Multilateral Efforts

This book has been filled with positive examples of multinational and multilateral organizations' efforts against human trafficking. The International Organization for Migration (IOM), as previously discussed, has taken a lead role in counter-trafficking as it has expanded its mission beyond migration and refugee concerns. The International Labour Organization (ILO) has done much to combat labor exploitation and trafficking. Much has been done on counter-trafficking by the United Nations Office on Drugs and Crime (UNODC) as well as such other UN-affiliated bodies as UNICEF, United Nations Interregional Crime and Justice Research Institute (UNICRI), and UN Office of the High Commissioner for Human Rights. International financial institutions, such as the Asian Development Bank, have analyzed strategies to contribute to more effective counter-trafficking policies. Multilateral bodies with member states such as the Organization for Security and Co-operation in Europe (OSCE) and Organization of American States (OAS)[67] have ongoing counter-trafficking programs, as does the European Union (EU), providing law enforcement training and assistance programs for victims. Multinational regional efforts also exist on a smaller scale within Europe than the level of the EU. For example, the Southeast Europe Cooperative Initiative Regional Center for Combating Trans-Border Crime (SECI) Center, a regional law enforcement coordinating center for the Balkans has made counter trafficking and smuggling institutional priorities. One of the results of this concern was the Tara case discussed in Chapter 3.

This partial shopping list of multilateral efforts reveals the diversity of actors trying to address trafficking. But multilateral assistance delivery is often undermined by duplication of effort and competition for financial resources. Training programs for the same law enforcement groups, hardly separated in time, may be funded by both the OSCE and the European Union without coordination. Different UN agencies may compete for funds and authority to run a similar counter-trafficking program. Cooperation between UNICEF and UNODC such as occurred in the Mekong Region project discussed in Chapter 5 is all too rare.

However, more fundamental concerns exist than the absence of cooperation and competition among multilateral bodies. Although part of the

[67] http://www.osce.org/activities/13029.html (accessed September 1, 2009); Anti-trafficking in Persons Section, http://www.oas.org/atip/atip_AbouUs.asp (accessed September 1, 2009).

EU may run good trafficking programs, larger EU trade and investment policies may create the preconditions for trafficking. For example, the ban on the import of agricultural products from Moldova, as mentioned in Chapter 7, to maintain support for European agriculture deprives Moldova, a primarily agricultural country, of a key market.[68] Structural adjustment loans to Nigeria, as shown in Chapter 9, were closely correlated with the initial rise of human trafficking. Therefore, many policies implemented for larger economic goals aggravate human trafficking.

Those policies merely compound the likelihood of trafficking in a globalized world that is highly conducive to trafficking. Nothing has yet been done to reverse the fundamental problems that led to the reemergence of human slavery worldwide. Population growth is continuing unabated in the developing world where there are neither jobs nor capital to absorb ever greater numbers of young people into the legitimate economy. According to the United Nations Population Report, the world's population is expected to grow from 5.4 billion in 2007 to 7.9 billion in 2050, with most of the growth in the developing world enhancing the already existing imbalance in the world.[69] Women and girls still have an inferior status in many regions of the world. Illicit trade is growing unabated, often hidden within the much larger global legal trade. Human trafficking continues to grow because state bureaucracies are no match for the flexible criminals. Migrants worldwide are now estimated at 740 million people. But most of these are internal migrants, as those who cross borders are estimated at one-quarter the total. [70]Yet more than 150 million cross-border migrants is an enormous number. Many of these migrants are residing in locales where there are neither the basic necessities of life nor the mechanisms for legalization of their status.

As if these already existing conditions were not enough, the coming decades should add even more conditions conducive to the further growth of human trafficking. As global warming worsens, even more people will be displaced from island states and coastal lowlands, particularly in highly populous states of South Asia and the Indian subcontinent, where

[68] Cornelius Friesendorf, "Conclusions: Improving Counter-Trafficking Efforts Through Better Implementation, Networking and Evaluation," in *Strategies Against Human Trafficking: The Role of the Security Sector*, Friesendorf, ed., 505.

[69] Thomas L. Friedman, "What They Really Believe," *New York Times*, November 18, 2009, A 35.

[70] Human Development Report 2009, *Overcoming Barriers: Human Mobility and Development* http://hdr.undp.org/en/reports/global/hdr2009/ (accessed December 8, 2009).

human trafficking is already endemic. Increasing droughts in Africa will compound the number of refugees, a population that already yields many human trafficking victims. Therefore, the prognosis for human trafficking is one of enormous growth in the twenty-first century.

Written human history since Hammurabi's Code in 1790 B.C. has identified the practice of slavery. Mankind has never eliminated slavery. But what has changed over time is humanity's recognition that this exploitation of man by man is wrong. In 1948, through the UN Declaration of Human Rights, governments concurred that human slavery was unacceptable. In the early 2000s, through the Protocol on Human Trafficking, the international community outlawed this form of exploitation. Yet the national laws adopted in response to this protocol are not sufficiently harmonized to facilitate cooperate. Even worse, far too many countries have failed to show the political will to honor these agreements. The current counter-trafficking response is not commensurate with the scale, diversity, or the social harm of the problem.

Unless governments perform their true function, which is to protect the lives of their inhabitants, trafficking will be a defining issue of the twenty-first century. All humanity will be diminished by its prevalence.

The bell is tolling.

Index